Ride The Devil Wind

Ride The Devil Wind

A History of the Los Angeles County Forester & Fire Warden Department and Fire Protection Districts

David Boucher
Captain, Los Angeles County Fire Department

Rugged terrain, rugged times and rugged men typify the origination and development of what is today known as the Los Angeles County Fire Department. Diversity of personalities, problems and circumstances even today permeate the organization and the 2,200 square miles under its protection. Literally from a seedling to a sophisticated organization of 2800 employees; from gunny sacks to helicopters for wildland fire suppression; from ranch shacks to hi-rise buildings; from farmlands to commercial complexes; the Los Angeles County Fire Department represents perhaps the most complex and diversified fire service organization in the world. RIDE THE DEVIL WIND tells that story.

ABOUT THE AUTHOR

Captain Boucher began his fire service in 1953 as an auxiliary fireman with the Altadena branch of the Crescenta-Canada Civil Defense Corps, serving for two years out of fire station 12. He graduated from Pasadena City College with an Associate of Arts degree in 1955, and during that summer continued his career by joining the United States Forest Service as a tanker crewman at the now-defunct Newhall Ranger Station. Upon being drafted into the U.S. Army in February 1956, he served for two years in Germany, returning to the U.S.F.S. as an assistant crew leader for helispot construction out of the Glendora Ranger Station, and later as a tanker operator at Mt. Baldy Village.

Wishing to follow a full time service fire service career, he took the examination for fireman for the City of Pasadena in 1958, and was hired as a hoseman. After serving at each of Pasadena's nine stations and on Truck Co. 1 as a relief operator and tillerman, he served as the unit's photographer and assistant arson investigator in addition to his regular duties. He was the first inspector to inspect homes in connection with the hillside "brush clearance" ordinance passed by the city board of directors in 1962.

Captain Boucher departed the City of Pasadena in March of 1964 to join the L.A. County Fire Department as a fireman. After assignments at various stations in the San Gabriel Valley (Bn's 4 and 10) and a concurrent stint as assistant weather officer, he simultaneously passed the Engineer's and Captain's examinations, receiving his Captain's appointment to the Fire Prevention Bureau in the City of Commerce in April 1971. Shortly thereafter, he qualified for a second A.A. degree, in fire science, attending various colleges throughout the San Gabriel Valley.

Preferring the fire fighting and prevention challenges found in the Urban-Wildland interface areas, he has spent the bulk of his time as a Captain in various foothill stations of Battalion 4. He also served from 1975 to 1978 as a dispatcher supervisor at the "Valley" dispatching center in El Monte.

A native of Green Bay, Wisconsin, Captain Boucher currently resides in Glendale, California with Shirley, his wife of 23 years, and daughters Annette and Jacqueline, who attend the University of California at Santa Barbara and San Diego, respectively. He plans to retire from active fire service duty sometime during 1992 to pursue various avocations, including beginning work on his second book, "A History of L.A. County Fire Department Apparatus."

Dedication

During the writing of a book with the scope of this one, many opportunities arise to choose someone to whom to dedicate it. But to the author, one person seemed to best epitomize the heart, mind and spirit of the Los Angeles County Fire Department. That person is Captain John Whelan, who became a Forester & Fire Warden fireman in 1945. He spent the bulk of his early career at the Malibu Division (currently Battalion 5). He had been the patrolman working out of the Topanga Station (69), assistant warden and lieutenant in Mountain Battalion 5 and a captain when the districts and F&FW combined.

In later years, Whelan gravitated naturally toward becoming a resident training captain at the Cecil R. Gehr Training Center, where he instructed hundreds of recruit firemen, as well as the entire department many times over during the annual "trek" to the training center for in-service training. He also composed many special department training manuals. Always in demand as a representative to present the department's programs to outside agencies, he also taught Fire Science classes through East Los Angeles Junior College for several years.

John's demeanor was always impeccable, his smile broad and his voice commanding, yet he always maintained a friendly tone. You knew you were in his favor when he tossed you the greeting, "How are you, you old snake?"

John was an avid historian in general, and of the Los Angeles County Fire Department in particular. As such, he collected many pieces of information concerning it, and contemplated writing the department's history upon his retirement in 1976. He was well into the project when he passed away suddenly in August of 1981. His widow, Jeanne, was kind enough to give me all his research material upon our discovering it in her garage in January of 1988. Contained in the material was the last remaining copy of the Forestry Department *Annals*, carefully preserved, which covers all the activities of that department up until 1934. This is, without doubt, the most valuable document extant concerning the department.

Chief Keith Klinger recalled John Whelan as being "a very loyal type," an understatement, to be sure. John's love of the department, and the fire service in general, is legendary. We are all fortunate to have had Captain John Whelan as one of our members.

David Boucher

All rights reserved. No part of this book may be reproduced in any form without permission of the publisher.

Director: John A. Ackerman

Editors: R. Dale Magee
Carol Carlsen Brooks
Winifred R. Marshall
Assistant – Cynthia Strickler

Design: Technical Advertising & Marketing
Art Director, Wayne Hulsey

Typography by Publishers Typesetting, Inc., Anaheim, California

Camera work by Color Ad Corp., Boise, Idaho

Dust Jacket separations by Graphic Depot, Inc., Santa Fe Springs, California

Printing by John M. McCoy Printers, Inc., Los Angeles, California

Ride The Devil Wind

A History of the Los Angeles County Forester & Fire Warden Department and Fire Protection Districts

David Boucher
Captain, Los Angeles County Fire Department

Best Wishes to Mitch Lee

David Boucher

Fire Publications, Inc.

Introduction

To the average citizen, the fire department is often thought of as being a community service that is taken very much for granted. Being employed by the fire department is considered merely another occupation, albeit a governmental function. "Somebody has to do it!" is a common attitude.

To others of us, the fire service has always been an area of deep avocational interest. Although remaining on the sidelines, we are nonetheless steeped in its unique ways, traditions, and services to the community.

For those who are members of a fire department, it is a commitment unlike any other. The fire department's prime function, that of the protection of life and property from the ravages of fire, makes it singular unto itself. It brings together a distinctive coterie of men and machines.

RIDE THE DEVIL WIND tells the story of the formation and development of the Los Angeles County Fire Department. It is a history of a fire service organization unlike any other on the American scene. Captain David Boucher carefully records its complex evolution, its leadership, its men and machines, its traditions, and its services. Beginning with the first stages of a mere concept and continuing up to its present-day multifarious functions, it is chronicled here as an important facet of local history.

– R. Dale Magee, M.S.
Assoc. Prof. (Ret.)
Pasadena City College

Special Acknowledgements

Beginning in late 1987, one or more interviews were held with the following retired, or close to retirement, department personnel. Enormous gratitude is extended to each of them for supplying any pieces of information from their personal experiences during their careers for verifying obscure information, and for donating anywhere from a few minutes to as much as two days of their time in assisting the author. The time spent with each was a rewarding and pleasurable experience.

Harvey T. Anderson
Grant D. Brown
Dale R. Cauble
John Englund
Herman H. Fischer
Richard Friend
Bronelle Greer
Richard H. Houts
Charles Johnson
Toni King
Keith E. Klinger
Kenneth Knowles
Ben E. Matthews
Ezra Miller
George Murray
Roland W. Percey
Franklin G. Reavis
Paul H. Rippens
Hiram H. Swallow
Ralph Van Wagner
George Workman
William G. Zeason

Special thanks are also extended to the following people for their offering special help, procuring special documents, photos, news articles and the like, and for arranging meetings and/or introductions with people important to the writing of this book.

John A. Ackerman
Michael Andrade
Robert P. Blackburn
Charles A. Blakeslee
Grant D. Brown
Dan Coffman
Stan Cohen
Mike Conti
John C. Cummings
Max Davis
Phil Dupre
Tracy Ertel
Scott Franklin
Bronelle Greer
Justin Griott
Kathy A. Hale
Daryl Higuchi
Joe Hinson
Wayne Hulsey
John Ireland
Owen Jacobs
Carol Jorgensen
Daryl Lockhart
Allan Mac Leod
Dale Magee
Winifred R. Marshall
Mike Mc Intyre
Jerry Meehan
Dale Miller
Eugene Noller
James O. Page
Dennis Pearson
Gordon Pearson
Mican A. Priest
Martin Rippens
Paul H. Rippens
Floyd Stubbs
John R. Todd
Ralph Van Wagner
Frank G. Zalaha

Table Of Contents

Foreword		VIII
I	The Beginning	1
II	the Greening	9
III	The Cornerstone Years	15
IV	The Transition Years	29
V	A Decade with the Districts	53
VI	The Pre-War Years	69
VII	The War Years and Beyond	101
VIII	The Klinger Era, Part 1	131
IX	The Klinger Era, Part 2	155
X	The Klinger Era, Part 3	175
XI	Adding to the Mission	197
XII	Near Disaster, Recovery and a Bright Future	215
	Bibliography	240
	Appendix	241
	Index	251

Foreword

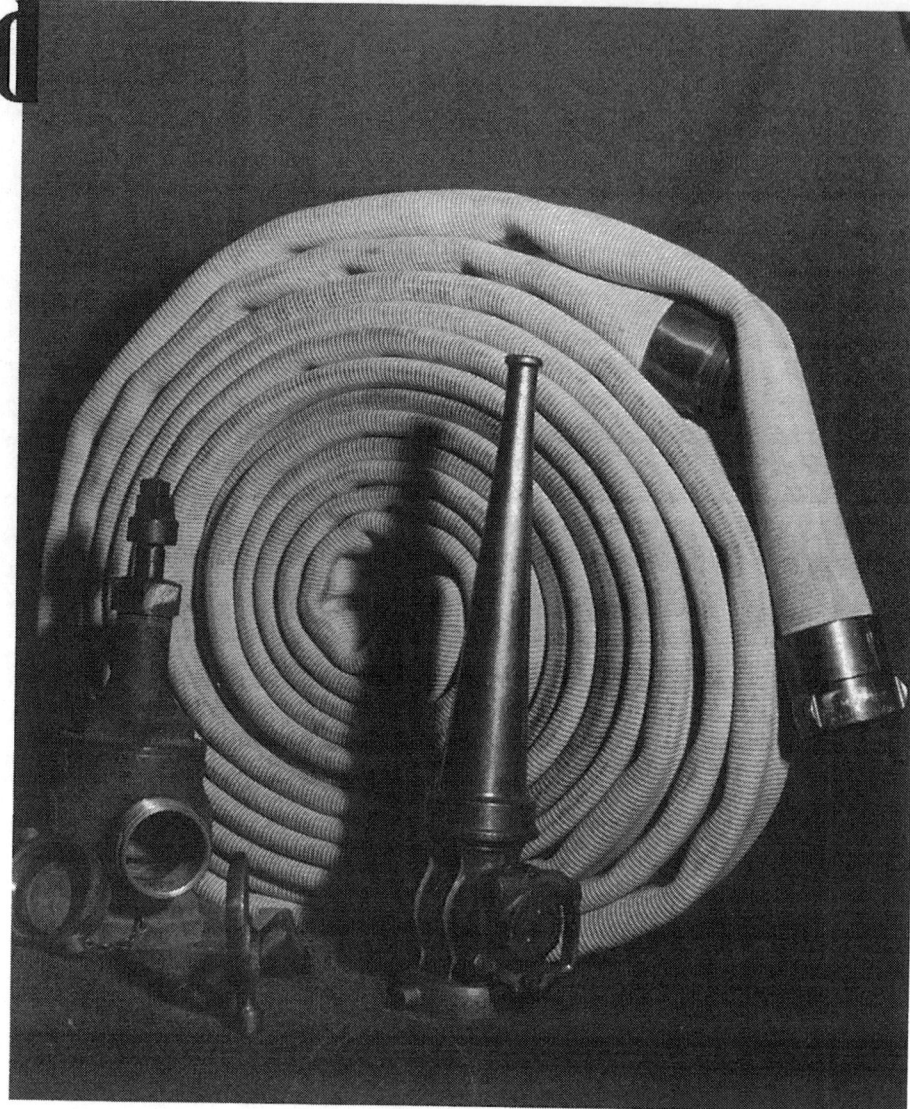

A collection of typical Dept. paraphernalia: 1" straight-bore tip with Metropolitan shutoff, a sold brass coat spanner, 2½" "Wharf" hydrant head and a section of 2½" double cotton-jacketed fire hose, circa 1950. LACoFD photo.

In the course of the history of institutions, there appear from time to time circumstances that produce the need for a very special organization. The response to such a rising need can be found today in the County of Los Angeles, California. It is known as the Los Angeles County Fire Department. This institution's inception and the tasks it was originally called upon to perform yield a rich and colorful story that over the years has been a constant source of fascination to the historian, the firefighter and the friends of the fire service.

It has been well established that, in order to survive and remain a viable force in society, an organization must remain flexible. This includes adaptability to changing conditions and demands from without, and ingenuity to satisfy evolving internal requirements.

This book is about the Los Angeles County Fire Department, beginning with its formative years. It is about many of the leaders of all ranks – who guided and inspired the organization throughout the over eighty years it has served the county, surrounding cities and the state of California.

The book will also take a look at many of the major emergency incidents that have tested the department's readiness to react and respond. How these impacted its prevention efforts will also be explored.

Although there are additional areas of interest which could be expanded upon for the benefit of the hard-core historian, a sincere attempt has been made to include a cross section of information interesting to all.

Every effort has been made to make this compendium as thorough and complete as possible; we hope you will find it to be so.

For those unfamiliar with the mechanics of the Santana Wind, a brief explanation will probably suffice, for as awful as the effects of one of these winds can be, its source and movement present a prime example of the beauty of the science of weather.

The Santana – "Devil Wind" – also named the "Santa Ana" after the large river drainage northeast of Los Angeles and Orange Counties, is nothing more than the result of two areas of greatly differing air pressure attempting to equalize. In Southern California, the source of air of higher pressure is generally located in Nevada and Utah, with the area of lower pressure located in Baja California. As this air flows over the San Gabriel/San Bernardino Mountains, it is compressed into the narrow passes and canyons as it travels, which increases the wind velocity. At the same time, the air descends from a higher elevation to a lower one, causing two important things to happen: The temperature rises at a rate of about five degrees F. per 1,000 feet of elevation drop; the result of this temperature rise is the lowering of the relative humidity by one-half (50 percent) for every 20 degree rise in temperature.

All of these features have a marked effect on the behavior of people, animals and living in general. Especially profound is the effect produced on an uncontrolled fire of any kind, with the open free-running wildland fire being especially susceptible, for, along with the warming and drying effect on the ground cover, the doubling of the wind velocity will increase the oxygen supply to the fire and spread rate by a factor of four. Join us as we experience the first 10 minutes of one of these fires in an actual location within Los Angeles County.

That year, October brought an unusual number of days of cooler air settling in to the Great Basin area. On the 15th, at about dawn, air pressure to the east increased. As a particularly strong current of air spilled down the coastal slopes of Los Angeles County's San Gabriel Mountains, seasoned firefighters felt a little extra adrenalin begin to pump into their systems in response to the infamous Santana – "Devil Wind" – that had appeared once again, as it did several times every fall and winter.

As the families living along Alzada and Jaxine roads in northwest Altadena arose to begin their daily activities, they were well aware of the unusually strong northeasterly wind gusts, which had by now reached 60 to 70 miles per hour. Temperature was 60 degrees F.; humidity 15 percent.

But, what residents didn't know was that an electrical transmission line had just snapped and set a fire in the grass- and brush-covered hills one mile northeast of their homes. This ignorance didn't last long, however, as, within minutes, the odor of smoke began to permeate their neighborhood, and the rising sun appeared to grow a little dimmer. Stepping outside, the residents could now see an ominous dark-brown layer of smoke, held aloft by 50-foot flames, speeding down the mountain slopes south of Chiquita Canyon. It was heading directly for their neighborhood.

The first call on the emergency 911 number had come in seconds earlier at the Altadena Sheriff's Station and the L.A. County Fire Department's Valley Communication Center. It came from the Zorthian Ranch at 0725 hours. At 0727, Engines 12, 11, 66, 82, 282, two patrols and the battalion chief mounted their response to a "possible brush fire . . . many calls of smoke near the north end of Fair Oaks Avenue."

Engine 12's captain was uanble to see any smoke as he departed the fire station, for it was obscured by a number of large trees. As his pumper and four-man crew sped north on Lincoln Avenue, the captain was acutely aware that the 80-foot-tall Washingtonian Palm trees lining the road were being bent by the wind to a 60-degree angle, and that small branches were breaking off other trees. If there was indeed a fire, it would mean big trouble.

Rounding the corner to the east on Loma Alta Drive, his worst fears materialized as he sighted the ever-expanding smoke mass ahead. Reaching for his Frequency 2 "white" radio, he outlined the situation to Valley Communications:

"Valley, Engine 12, we have heavy smoke showing . . . at least 25 homes threatened . . . requesting a command frequency on "blue" radio . . . Engine 12 will be "Fair Oaks" IC (incident commander) . . . have all units proceed to Cheney Trail and then east on Alzada Road for structure protection. After a one-minute pause, he continued, ". . . Valley, Engine 12 requesting a second alarm plus two strike teams (five engines per team) . . . staging to be at Loma Alta Park at Lincoln and Loma Alta."

In the meantime, the balance of the first-alarm assignment of one bulldozer and a helicopter out of Pacoima Warehouse had been dispatched by Valley Communications. It also mustered four ground crews of hand firefighters, along with their camp superintendents, from Camp 2 in Oakgrove Park and Camp 15 in Big Tujunga Canyon. A second alarm would bring equipment equal to the first-alarm assignment. In addition, the Battalion 10 chief and Assistant Chief Harold McCann of Division 5 would respond. The three chiefs would organize the fireline into divisions in an attempt to cope with what would prove to be terrible firefighting conditions. The thought was that perhaps they could save some homes, perhaps not. If the gusting Devil Winds persisted, they might be fortunate in stopping the fire's southerly progress at Loma Alta Drive and its westerly progress at Lincoln Avenue.

What you have just read is a fictional, albeit wholly plausible account of the first five minutes of a typical wildland urban interface fire, the like of which occurs several times in the course of a fire season in Southern California.

In fact, this very fire did occur in October, 1935, with disastrous results.

Since 1935, the quantity of equipment and manpower available to handle these incidents has increased enormously through the offices of the L.A. County Fire Department and other fire agencies in Southern California. Quality of service and overall effectiveness has also greatly improved, but in spite of all efforts, fires in the grass and brush still occur, and they still have a devastating effect on the surrounding urban areas when driven by the Santana wind.

The primary organization charged with the responsibility to provide fire protection in the unincorporated areas of Los Angeles County, as well as assist other neighboring jurisdictions with their efforts as needed, is the Los Angeles County Department of Forester and Fire Warden and Fire Protection Districts, aka the Los Angeles County Fire Department.

The following pages will hopefully provide the reader with an in-depth history of this department's formation, and a clear picture of how it developed into the fire protection machine it is today.

The Beginning

Dec. 6, 1906 fire burning up Sister Elsie Peak (Mt. Lukens) above La Crescenta. USFS Ranger Tom Sloan was in charge of the fireline on the mountaintop. Don McLain and his gang of "Green Mtn. Boys" from Pasadena-Altadena worked the lower line. Photo, Tom Sloan, USFS.

The Big Picture

The County of Los Angeles: 4,085 square miles of phenomenal diversification! Blessed with as agreeable a climate as can be found anywhere in the world, it is attracting hundreds of new residents each day.

This influx of people has brought with it a boom in housing, schools, shopping centers industrial and commercial facilities and high-rises, all crisscrossed by 21 major freeways.

The resulting encroachment into the hills and outlying valleys of the county has also brought with it fire protection problems unparalleled in the relatively short history of the Los Angeles County Fire Department.

This urban sprawl is a modern development. Picture a 60-mile stretch of Pacific shoreline, the land gently sloping upward to the north and east. Its grasslands are dissected by rocky, brush-lined creeks that flow only after winter rains. The land progresses through occasional ranges of east-west oriented hills, then to intermediate valleys and foothills. The rugged northwest, south-east, trending ranges of the San Gabriel Mountains lend a majestic background to the scene. North and east of these blue ranges lie the vast Antelope Valley and arid Mojave Desert. To complete the picture, add to Los Angeles County San Clemente and

Santa Catalina Islands, situated 25 miles offshore.

This presents a benign and tranquil scene when viewed without the presence of modern man and his civilization. In times past, it would not matter if the brush-covered hillsides and mountains occasionally blossomed into acres of flame, ignited, perhaps, by a passing lightning storm during the dry summer or fall months. Or, the sparks from a Gabrieleno Indian's or Spanish explorer's unattended campfire could have been the culprit. No matter, for the chaparral ground cover would grow back soon enough. Wild grasses, barley, and oats would temporarily fill the voids left by the absent laurel, sumac, sagebrush, oak and pine. In due time it would grow back.

Nor did it matter if the mountain slopes, denuded by the fire, would wash away when pelted by heavy winter rains. Topsoil, rocks, broken trees, debris from previous fires – all would form a rushing cascade, roaring down the steep hillsides and flowing into tributary canyons, then main canyons. It would gradually spread out over the land of the intermediate valleys, finally wending its way to the sea. No lasting harm would result; merely another layer of alluvium would be added to the already rich topsoil of the San Gabriel, San Fernando and Santa Clarita Valleys.

Then, as now, one of the enormous earthquake faults that network the area would slip a bit, causing the earth to tremble and crack. Terrified animals and astonished Indians would startle, of course, at the rumbling, rolling temblor. Then the earth would be still again for a time – perhaps even for several years.

But, add modern man and his present-day accouterments to this scenario, and massive problems can be anticipated. When such incidents occur, usually without warning as they do, the results can be disastrous.

This is where the Los Angeles County Fire Department comes in. Dedicated to protecting the lives and property of a population estimated at 2,700,000, it serves all of the citizens of the unincorporated areas as well as 45 incorporated, contract cities. Its 2,800 men and women operate emergency services through the vast Southland. How the Los Angeles County Fire Department has been tested in the past and how it has been shaped and guided during its continuous and rapid growth is an ongoing, exciting saga of community history.

In the Beginning . . .

In 1987, the Los Angeles County Fire Department, or at least the Fire Warden's office, reached 80 years of age . . . probably. Determining the exact year of its formal founding is largely a matter of researching the available historical documents – and then making an educated guess. The calculations are clouded by the fact the department was, at various times, a conglomeration of two, three or four different organizations under one department head.

The chief of the Department, wearing as many as four different hats, led an organization that, among other things, operated a sea-going patrol boat with an armed crew, built and maintained a number of lookout towers in the mountains, developed the first fog nozzles, helped pioneer water-dropping helicopters, experimented with pack mules carrying portable pumps on their backs to relay-pump water on mountain fires and operated fire engines painted two different colors – green rigs for the mountain areas and red rigs for the fire districts in the valley.

Obviously, the Los Angeles County Fire Department has undergone constant change over the decades. To fully understand and appreciate where it is today with respect to its original organization and mission, we must go back to its beginning. In fact, we must go back just a bit further than that.

Surprisingly, the department was at first an outgrowth of attempts to solve very early problems in the forestry domain, both at the state and the national level. Some years would pass before attendant structural activities would be added. Only later did many of the features of the "standard fire department of today" appear.

Linked tightly with early forestry work in Los Angeles County was the urban growth pattern that had begun to spread across the vast area. The county's political relationship with the state of California and the efforts of several prominent local citizens who dealt with the state in an influential manner also were of prime importance in the development of the department. All of these factors evolved almost simultaneously.

Red Cars and Green Trees

With the gradual influx of settlers from the East and Midwest into Southern California in the late 1800s, the Los Angeles area began to grow in every respect. Near the turn of the century, and well into the mid-1900s, a marvelous system of electric trains serving the coastal basin was developed by Henry E. Huntington. From this system, the Pacific Electric Railway Company was formed. Such distant towns as Redondo Beach, San Fernando, Glendora, San Dimas, Redlands, Newport Beach, Long Beach and Pasadena were connected to both one another and the hub city of Los Angeles. Large, fast – and very red – interurban cars ran on wide-gauge tracks, along whose routes additional towns sprang up, thanks to efforts of aggressive land developers. These towns and the "Big Red Cars" became dependent upon one another for survival and continued expansion, largely throughout the unincorporated county areas. (Yes, Southern California had a "rapid transit" system in its formative years.)

With the advent of the horseless carriage, the existing random network of wagon roads crisscrossing the coastal basin was upgraded to meet the needs of the automobile. Main highways were constructed across entire counties, connecting Southern California with the rest of the state and nation. These highways traversed many miles of open land that was still in its original, semi-barren condition.

Since the countryside had a paucity of native trees and other greenery, the vista was often not the most pleasing of scenes to the eyes of incoming tourists –

View from the Hotel Green in downtown Pasadena in July, 1897, shows a fire burning in the upper Arroyo Seco drainage of Bear and Grand canyons. Thomas Banbury and a large group of citizens finally hiked in and extinguished it. The larger peak to the right of the smoke column is Mt. Lowe. Below and to the left, a sharp eye can pick out the various road cuts of the Mt. Lowe railway incline and Echo Mtn. Chalet. From the collection of the L.A. County Museum.

nor to the local residents as they traveled from town to town. Grass and brush fires burned largely unchecked, often for days at a time, adding further to the barrenness of the summer and fall months. Then rainfall during the following winter would wash out the roads and bury the farms and ranches in mud and silt.

Los Angeles and its surrounding neighbors had problems, but help would come in due time from both governmental and outside entities. A groundwork for legislative help was already being established at the state level, since Los Angeles County was not alone in its needs.

Fire and Politics

In the late 1800s, the state of California was concerned about forest and watershed destruction brought about by the random harvesting of large areas of virgin forests by loggers. No thought was being given to replacing the cut acreage. Fires in brush and timberland were being caused by hunters and ranchers. In the southern areas such as Los Angeles County, hunters considered brush to be an impediment to travel. Ranchers thought brush to be a cause of the loss of open grazing land, and sheepherders set rings of fire around their flocks at night to keep predatory animals at bay. Often these fires were simply allowed to burn out – perhaps many days and hundreds of acres later. Homes, ranches, wooden bridges and railroad trestles would be lost to these fires. Flooding that followed the fires also began to affect villages and towns statewide, especially those adjacent to steep slopes and canyons.

Because of these problems, the State Penal Code was amended on March 12, 1872. The new portion read:

"Every person who willfully and maliciously burns any bridge exceeding $50 in value, or any building, snowshed or vessel, not the subject of arson, or any stack of grain of any kind, or hay, or of any standing grain, grass, tree or fence not the property of such person, is punishable by imprisonment in the state prison for not less than one nor more than 10 years."

At the same time, to the State Political Code was

added Section 3345, which read:

"Whenever the woods are on fire, any justice of the peace, constable or road-overseer of the township or district where the fire exists may order as many of the inhabitants liable to the road poll tax, residing in the vicinity, as may be deemed necessary, to repair to the place of the fire and assist in the extinguishing or stopping of it."

The law was modified in 1905 to read:

". . . any able-bodied citizen between the ages of 16 and 20." Presumably, this included women. The words, "inhabitants liable to the road poll tax" were eliminated.

Further legislative help was on the way with the writing of Chapter 36 of the State Health and Safety Code in 1881. It was titled,

"An act to allow unincorporated towns and villages to equip and maintain a fire department, to assess and collect taxes, from time to time, for such purpose, and to create a Board of Fire Commissioners." It was later amended to read, ". . . within one-and-one-half miles of populated areas."

An extremely-significant act was passed by the California State Legislature in 1885. On March 3 of that year, Governor Stoneman signed into law Senate Bill #6, which created the California Board of Forestry. The stated purpose of this board was to "manage the mountain lands." The board was required to issue biennial reports.

In 1887, a most fortuitous appointment was made to the State Board of Forestry in the person of Abbot Kinney. Kinney was a successful rancher from the Kinneloa Mesa area, just north of the city of Pasadena. His governmental service was at once meritorious and articulate. Together with with James Bettner, Jr., of Riverside, and Walter S. Moore, fire chief of the City of Los Anneles, Kinney was to profoundly affect the thinking of the state government of California with respect to forest management. Many of his writings appeared in the press. His efforts netted California, and Los Angeles County in particular, excellent treatment in later years in matters pertaining to funding for forest and watershed protection.

Starting in 1887, the influence of the Board of Forestry began to be felt. Four state nurseries were established for the purpose of growing reforestation stock. One of them was located in Los Angeles County in Santa Monica Canyon. The board petitioned for the California Redwood Park at Big Basin. All members of the board were made peace officers with powers to arrest anyone violating forest regulations.

The cause of forestry began to be taken up by the national government, as well as state and local agencies. In 1890, President Theodore Roosevelt substituted action for rhetoric in setting aside the Yosemite area as a National Forest Reserve. In 1892, Roosevelt created the San Gabriel Forest Reserve, located in the San Gabriel Mountains of Los Angeles County. This area covered over 550,000 acres of brush and timberland, extending from Pacoima Canyon on the west to the Cajon Pass on the east. It is now known as the Angeles National Forest, extended now to cover some 693,000 acres, with extensive boundary modifications.

The recognition of the need for wildland fire control in Los Angeles County had finally begun, even though the means to accomplish the task had yet to be developed. Actual organized firefighting forces did not exist as yet. Each fire season brought with it varying amounts of devastation.

In its 1892 biennial report, the Board of Forestry wrote:

"The state should either employ a sufficient force to patrol and efficiently protect the forests, or adopt some other method of protection. A solution to this problem may be found in the bill prepared by this board and presented in this report, which provides for the appointment of fire wardens in every county, who shall be paid for by the counties for actual services rendered."

However, the bill was never passed in that exact form.

In addition, in time the Board of Forestry was legislated out of existence, due to political pressures exerted in large measure by private interests. Steps backward, indeed! It was again the efforts of Abbot Kinney that effected forward progress.

On March 8, 1899, a meeting at the Los Angeles Chamber of Commerce headquarters, Kinney, along with several others, formed a private organization called the Forest and Water Society of Southern California. Promoting the cause of forest protection, it published a magazine called Water & Forest. The society soon had some 5,000 members statewide. It influenced legislation at state and national levels for several years. Unfortunately, all of the records of this endeavor were lost in the San Francisco earthquake and fire of April 1906.

The fire seasons of 1896 and 1897 were especially severe in California. In 1897 alone, 350,000 acres burned. The annals of the L.A. County Forestry Department indicate a special expenditure by the Board

Abbott T. Kinney, a leading forestry-oriented environmentalist of the 1920s. His leadership helped pour the sound foundation upon which forest preservation efforts were built. LACo Forestry Dept. photo.

of Supervisors on October 8 for the sum of $1,180.84 for a Thomas Banbury to hire 25 men to help extinguish a brush fire "behind Pasadena." The crew worked on the fire until October 20, at which time it was disbanded.

The fire season of 1904 in California was particularly catastrophic. Fully 800,000 acres burned. As a result, the state legislature at last acted to organize itself to protect its forests. It passed what is known as the Forest Protection Act of 1905, signed into law by Governor George Pardee on March 18 of that year. The Act reestablished the Board of Forestry and also empowered it with many regulatory functions.

Sections #6 and #21 were of special interest to Los Angeles County. The salient portions of these sections read:

". . . any county, or combination of less than four counties, shall be made a separate fire district upon request of the County Board of Supervisors, in which case such special fire district shall pay the cost of maintaining its district fire warden (#6)" and "County boards of supervisors may appropriate money for the purposes of forest protection, improvement and management (#21)."

In 1906, the Los Angeles County Board of Supervisors took at least cursory action after the passage of the Forest Protection Act of 1905, by appointing then-current Fish and Game warden, W.B. Morgan, to the additional position of fire warden. His salary was accordingly increased $300 per year.

The fire warden could appoint as many assistant wardens as he deemed necessary, but could not spend more than $20,000 for fire prevention or control activities. The warden's first record of expenditures for fire control was made in 1908. During this fiscal year, $710 was spent to extinguish 21 fires of all kinds in the unincorporated areas of Los Angeles County.

T.P. Lukens and Henninger Flats

A member of the Forest and Water Society who had a strong influence on the development of watershed protection in Los Angeles County was T.P. Lukens. Lukens was an avid supporter of forestry in general, a member of the Angeles Forest Reserve and a person willing to experiment. At the urging of several civic groups, he planted thousands of various pine and cedar tree seeds at both the Mary Street nursery that he developed with the USFS in Pasadena, and at the present site of the main nursery facility of the Los Angeles County Fire Department, at Henninger Flats.

The Henninger site is located in Fire Station 66's district, on state interest land at the 2,500-foot level in the San Gabriel Mountains, northeast of Altadena. The access road is the old Mt. Wilson Toll Road, which begins at the mouth of Eaton Canyon. The road traversed three-and-one-half miles to a beautiful tree-covered meadow. Lukens initially found the meadow to be quite bare, but with the support of the Forest and Water Society, leased the land from the Mt. Wilson Hotel Company and built a small water reservoir.

He made extensive plantings in the fall of 1903, using 600 pounds of seed donated by the Pasadena Board of Trade.

After the plantings were completed, Lukens recognized the need to protect the areas from wildfire. He set out to clear all flammable grass and brush around the planted areas. These cleared strips of land became the first known "firebreaks" in Southern California.

As the plantings at Henninger Flats became more extensive, a small cabin was constructed on the site to house Lukens. Materials for this structure and nursery supplies were hauled up on mule back. The project gained security and an increased chance for success as more and more seeds were planted in the years that followed. Few of the first year's seeds germinated, however. This was due to winter drought conditions, as well as the fact that the seeds provided meals for the numerous birds, squirrels and rabbits who were also on-site residents.

In 1908, George Peavy of the Forest and Water Society assumed the supervision of the Henninger Flats Project. T.P. Lukens continued to work there and at the Pasadena Mary Street nursery until 1910, when forestry support for the Henninger project dwindled. The Pasadena nursery continued, however, and underwent further transition.

In honor of this pioneer in watershed preservation and afforestation, the largest peak in the front range of the San Gabriel Mountains, due north of Fire Station 63's district of La Crescenta, formerly called Sister Elsie, was renamed Mount Lukens.

T.P. Lukens, circa 1895. He had a caring and steadfast personality, traits that evidenced themselves in his life's goals of afforestation, reforestation and general environmentalism. Photographer unknown, photo courtesy of Shirley Sargent and the Henninger Flats Museum.

Transition Years

Up until 1911, the County of Los Angeles dealt with its forest and watershed problems without an organization in place designed to take aggressive action. Private groups and individuals had shown what needed to be done, but the resources were not available to fully accomplish the task.

The entire area continued to grow rapidly in terms of population and land use. The 1910 U.S. Census placed the population of Los Angeles County at 504,131, of which 319,198 lived within city limits. The remainder of the population was scattered throughout the county on farms, ranches, villages and townships.

Rare photo shows a group of picnickers at Henninger Flats about the turn of the century. The nursery was established in the large field seen left center. Photographer unknown.

Horses and pack mules haul lumber up the Mt. Wilson Toll Road for construction of the county Forestry nursery at Henninger Flats, circa 1904. From the collection of John Whelan.

One of the few surviving glass plate photos shows a spike camp that was set up to plant seed on the slopes above Altadena about 1906. Photographer unknown, from the collection of John Whelan.

Some population centers chose incorporation as a way of obtaining needed services and maintaining identities. Along the routes served by the inter-urban Red Cars, cities formed: Pasadena and Santa Monica in 1886; Monrovia in 1887; Pomona, South Pasadena and Compton in 1888; Redondo Beach in 1892; Long Beach in 1897; Whittier and Azusa in 1898; Covina in 1901; Arcadia, Alhambra and Hollywood in 1903; Venice in 1904; Vernon and Wilmington in 1905; Glendale, Huntington Park, La Verne, San Pedro, Sawtelle and Hermosa Beach in 1906; Sierra Madre, Watts and Claremont in 1907; and Inglewood in 1908.

Even with the creation of these towns and the early annexation of Wilmington, San Pedro, Watts, Sawtelle and Hollywood to the City of Los Angeles, a huge area of Los Angeles County still remained as unincorporated territory.

The responsibility for fire suppression in the unincorporated areas still rested on the shoulders of Fire Warden W.B. Morgan, assisted by the temporary wardens he needed to appoint and laborers conscripted at times of fire emergencies. The challenge facing Morgan during the summer of 1910 was evidently most severe. His report for that year shows 37,000 acres of grass and brush burned. There were 23 reportable fires of all kinds, with a dollar loss of $125,320. This included three homes, hay and grain fields and numerous beehives.

Whether or not it was from the strain of his position is unknown, but Fire Warden W.B. Morgan passed away near the end of that fire season. W.J. Duram was temporarily appointed as his replacement on September 12, 1912, but held the post only four months. Major changes were in the offing.

One township anticipated the direction of change. An item appearing in the San Dimas Press, dated March 12, 1910, described the town's purchase of a 60-pound, two-wheeled, soda-acid fire extinguisher, equipped with 200 feet of one-inch hose, to be placed in a garage near the center of town. This may well have been the first piece of publicly-owned and operated fire apparatus to serve in an unincorporated area of Los Angeles County.

T.P. Lukens (r., with beard) directing the planting of seeds on the south slopes of the San Gabriel Mountains above Altadena. The failure of this method led to the development of the Mary St. Nursery in Pasadena. T.P. Lukens photo, courtesy of the Huntington Library and Henninger Flats Museum.

Advocated by Gifford Pinchot (USFS) and directed by T.P. Lukens, the Mary St. Nursery, seen here in 1903, was established to develop seedlings for the afforestation of the San Gabriel Mountains. The site is now under the 134-210 freeway interchange. T.P. Lukens photo, courtesy Huntington Library and the Henninger Flats Museum.

The Greening

Stuart J. Flintham, County Forester from 1912 until his death in 1925. His brilliant mind conceived and developed the Forester & Fire Warden organization, and later, the system of Fire Districts for the unincorporated townships in the valleys. A. Muench photo, LACo Forestry Dept.

Patterned after the State Board of Forestry, the Los Angeles County Board of Forestry was established by the County Board of Supervisors on May 8, 1911. That action was to be a key factor in the eventual organization of the Los Angeles County Department of Forester and Fire Warden.

Forestry Board appointees were Mrs. C.L. Lumis, Prof. A.B. Ulrey, Mrs. E.P. Rhoades, E.A. Sweetzer and Ernest Braunton. Braunton was also appointed to the new position of county forester, only to resign a short time later due to a "conflict of interest."

On January 30, 1912, Stuart J. Flintham was appointed as county forester at a salary of $150 a month. Flintham was a graduate of both Cornell and Yale universities with degrees in Forestry. He had served seven years with the United States Forest Service. With a small staff composed of a secretary and two assistant foresters, Flintham occupied office space at 237 Franklin Street in downtown Los Angeles. (Franklin Street, which ran diagonally between Spring and Broadway, was earlier known as Jail Street, then Court Street. It was eventually eliminated during the 1930s.)

Forester Flintham was assigned a well-used Premier automobile to use for departmental business. The Premier was said to have an "individuality all of its own," requiring "special training" by its users in order to master its many operational peculiarities.

From the very beginning of his term in office, Flintham took up the causes of afforestation and reforestation. His many duties included care of the park surrounding the County Court House at Second and Spring Streets in downtown Los Angeles. The Forestry budget for 1911-1912 showed an expenditure of $1,052 for the courthouse gardens. In later months and years, the Exposition Park grounds in south-central Los Angeles, the County Hospital grounds in East Los Angeles and the Olive View Sanitarium grounds in the Sylmar area were also developed and cared for by the Forestry Department.

The workload increased over the months, as did the need for more office space. On December 4, 1911, Flintham and his staff moved into larger quarters in the Trust and Savings Building, Room 1101. Rent was $20 per month.

The "Good Roads" System

Concurrent with the appointment of Stuart Flintham as county forester, public sentiment influenced the Board of Supervisors to approve the placing of a bond issue before the voters. The issue was for $3.5 million, to be used to improve 160 miles of county roads. This included the afforestation of roadsides with shade trees, thus providing protection for the road surfaces from the elements, as well as furnishing shade for the population using the roads. Some of the bond funds were to be used for advertising. The county government wanted it known that their road system was a "good system."

Flintham began the roadside plantings, as directed by the Board of Forestry. The first project completed was a four-mile stretch of Foothill Boulevard between the town of Monrovia and Azusa, through the township of Duarte. (This is the present district of Fire Station 44.) The plantings were alternate, using Jerusalem pine and live oak. Initial plantings were completed on March 5, 1912.

Later planting in 1912 included 12 miles of Long Beach Boulevard south from the Los Angeles city line; six-and-one-half miles of Wilshire Boulevard west from the city line; and San Fernando Road between Tropico (now South Glendale) and Burbank. Later, an extension of Foothill Boulevard from East Pasadena to Monrovia was planted. Plantings continued for 20 years, eventually encompassing virtually all major county roadsides.

During 1915, in order to beautify the county roads for the San Francisco Exposition, iron pipe trellises and climbing roses were added to the tree rows. Fraught with maintenance problems, most of these iron structures were removed for scrap during World War I.

The Domain Progresses

During the period from 1912 to 1919, the budget for the Forestry Department climbed steadily from $23,000 to $41,000 annually, due entirely to an increased workload and the addition of more laborers. As a typical example, during 1914, five foremen (at $2.50 per day) and eight laborers (at $2.25 per day) were added. By 1919, total Forestry Department personnel had risen to 65 employees.

Transportation costs also were increasing steadily. These were the last years of the $5-per-day rental of horse-drawn water wagons used to irrigate the road plantings. Dual-purpose irrigation and firefighting tank trucks were soon to appear.

Much to everyone's relief, by 1914 the cantankerous Forestry Department's Premier car had been replaced by an EMF. EMF – Everett-Metzger-Flanders, of Detroit, Michigan – built automobiles from 1908 until being absorbed by the Studebaker Corporation in 1910. The EMF, like the Premier, was also previously owned, but was reportedly a much-better-behaved vehicle.

The department also acquired two 1914 Indian motorcycles, which were used primarily for trips to inspect the condition of roadside tree plantings.

During the 1914-1915 fiscal year, several events accelerated marked changes in the Forestry Department. On October 5, 1915 the entire San Fernando Valley, excepting the city of San Fernando, was annexed to the City of Los Angeles, no longer requiring the services of the Forestry Department. On November 9, 1915, T. P. Lukens recommended to the Board of Forestry that the Henninger Flats Nursery be abandoned due to a 98 percent failure of bare root plantings. A search was begun for a new nursery.

After a brief survey, a site was located in the township of Altadena. Now known as Farnsworth Park, this eight acre plot at the intersection of Lake Avenue and Mount Curve Drive provided ground suitable for the construction of a large lathhouse and related seed-germination projects. (Currently, it is in Fire Station 11's district.) On February 8, 1916, Forester Flintham and the Board of Supervisors executed a lease of the property with the owner C. M. Gordon. Charles A. Hess was engaged as head gardener, with Lukens being retained as a consultant for a short time.

The first seeds were planted on March 30, 1916. During the first year of operation, $6,200 was spent on site development. This did not include the monthly land rent of $40. Over the years that followed, literally millions of seeds were germinated at the Altadena facility.

It was at about this time that the need became apparent for a roadside park on the long stretch of Foothill Boulevard (then named Michigan Avenue) between Pasadena and the San Fernando area. Through social and business contacts with the Percey family of Sunland, Forester Flintham found several acres of land covered with oak trees at what is presently the intersection of Foothill and Sunland boulevards. L. S. Percey was hired, at 75 cents per hour, to grade the land, and over the next three years the site was gradually improved and picnic tables installed. It became known as Monte Vista Park. The Forestry Department engaged itself in a major tree surgery and trimming project to ensure the health of the native oak trees at the new park.

Significantly, the development of Monte Vista Park (now known as Sunland Park) and the subsequent development of other parks throughout the county, gave Forester Flintham his second of four hats. He was now the head of both the County Forestry Department and what would eventually become the Department of Parks.

It was during this period that the Forestry Department's transportation section added two Ford Model T touring cars to its fleet, in order to help service the ever-growing system of plantings throughout the county. The cars, which were hand-me-downs from other county departments, were assigned a value of $85 each in the 1916-1917 annual report. They hauled laborers, towed trailers on work projects and ran stock from the ornamental nursery at Griffin and State streets to the several sites having formal gardens. However, the car and trailer combination was soon to have a modified configuration and an entirely different purpose – that of firefighting.

Answering the Challenges

From a political standpoint, 1917 and 1918 were critical years for the Forestry Department. Some members of the Board of Supervisors began to feel that the Forestry Department was expanding too rapidly. They believed it possible that the newly-formed Road Department could plant and maintain the roadside trees and roses in conjunction with road maintenance operations. Additionally, pressure was building from another quarter within the Board to eliminate the Forestry Department entirely, disseminating its functions among several other county departments.

Answering the first challenge, Forester Flintham defended his department in a vigorous and articulate manner during a lengthy hearing before the Board of Supervisors. He was successful in convincing the Board that Road Department personnel lacked the scientific expertise to plant and maintain the various specialized plant specimens.

In the latter case, Flintham called upon several influential people from diverse and sundry backgrounds to testify before the Board. Mrs. Hibbins of the Pasadena Shakespeare Club, Mrs. Elliott of the California Federations of Women's Clubs, the Pasadena Independent's Editor Parish, W. G. Fields of the San Dimas Water Company and Mr. Gilman Bowring of the Monrovia Chamber of Commerce – all appeared on Flintham's behalf. The testimony of these carefully-chosen witnesses in combination with Flintham's adroit handling of the situation caused the Board of Supervisors to drop the matter entirely.

Later, Forester Flintham was able to convince the Board that his department was understaffed and its personnel underpaid. Larger and more permanent office space for the headquarters staff was also requested. As a result, Suite 914, Hall of Records Building, located at Temple and Broadway was procured.

As it turned out, these defensive actions by Flintham would be major contributing factors in the formation of the Los Angeles Department of Forester and Fire Warden.

A Definition of Duties

As part of the Annual Reports for 1918-1919, a formal definition of duties for each county department was entered into the record. The Forestry Department duties were described as follows:

"It is the duty of the County Forester to protect the forest interests of the County; to establish forest planting in the mountains for reforestation and protection; planting along the stream channels for control of the stream channels; to grant permits for trimming, planting and removal of roadside trees; to establish and maintain ornamental and shade trees along county roads and highways; to develop and maintain County Parks and the grounds of County institutions, and to operate and maintain nurseries for the growing of plants and trees needed for various planting and development work; and to perform other work as may be required by the Board of Supervisors."

Only now formally described after eight years of operation, the duties of the Forestry Department were to be radically changed in the following year.

The Fish & Game responsibilities of the County Forestry Dept. included raising young deer somehow separated from their mothers. LACo Forestry Dept. photo.

A Warden in Decline

According to the 1914-1915 Annual Report as described in the annals of the Forestry Department, Fire Warden B. N. Powers' office apparently shifted to an ever-decreasing level of efficiency. Each succeeding yearly report indicated that lethargy seemed to be the norm.

The 1915-16 report stated:

"There is no record of an annual report or any other report being submitted by the Fire Warden this year. In fact, there is every indication as evidenced by the meager expenditures that this official was not particularly energetic in prosecuting the important work."

In 1916-1917, a similar report was submitted – with the sole exception of a $135.85 expenditure for a fire in Coldwater Canyon.

The 1917-1918 report states:

"No reports were rendered by the Fire Warden to the Board of Supervisors, and records indicate no particular activity on the part of that individual."

In 1919-1920, it was:

"... it must be very apparent the Fire Warden/Fish and Game Warden did very little in the interests of his work, while in every year except this one he expanded his salary appropriations, he never used up any great percentage of his expense appropriations. This point alone will indicate that this official was not active."

In each of the years mentioned, only two or three damaging fires are listed as having occurred, although dozens of fires are listed as having been "investigated."

Apparently the Board of Supervisors appreciated the close connection between watershed conservation, afforestation, reforestation and watershed fire prevention and control. There are indications that the Board intended to place the Fish and Game and Fire Warden's office under the control of the County Forester as early as 1919.

Fire Warden Powers had complained of a lack of funds in 1919-1920, so the Board increased his budget by $8,000. Still, he failed to use the increase, even though there were two very large brush and forest fires during the summer of 1919. In the opinion of Joe Davis, the Forestry Annals author, this infusion of money was a final effort to revive the office of Fire Warden, and possibly the fire warden himself. But even with the extra funding, actual expenditures showed the office to be vacant during part of the period.

The official tendency to treat the Fire Warden's office as a "stepchild" of the Department of Fish and Game was about to end. As occurs in many historic instances, a disaster had to occur before any decisive, remedial action was taken to correct a longstanding deficiency.

Two Big Fires and New Leadership

Beginning in 1908, a standard item of the Fire Warden's annual budget was a gift of several thousand dollars to the United States Forest Service. This money was spent for firebreak and trail construction in the Angeles National Forest. In 1908, the amount given was $4,937. By 1920, the amount had risen to $10,000. Approximately 95 percent of each year's allocation was actually expended, with the balance being carried over into the next year. The Board of Supervisors firmly believed that the money spent for forest protection in the mountain regions above the valleys would have a direct benefit for all of the citizens of the county.

Prior to 1919, the Angeles National Forest had experienced an average of about 100 fires per year. The area involved amounted to an average of approximately 20,000 acres annually. But all past precedents were shattered late in the summer of 1919. Many of the road and firebreak projects were soon put to their first major test, for this was the onset of two fires that would severely tax all available firefighting forces.

On September 12, 1919 John Robb, a local miner in the San Gabriel Canyon north of Azusa, set a small fire in order to clear brush for a garden near his claim. The fire almost immediately became out of control and began burning up the dry ravines to the east. Control of this fire was not effected for two weeks, and only then after it burned some 40,000 acres of brush and timber. Most of the San Gabriel River east fork drainage was consumed, as well as most of Glendora Ridge, Big and Little Dalton Canyons and the upper San Dimas Canyon area. (These are now initial-action areas for Fire Stations 97, 86, 151, 64, and 102, with the USFS.)

Three days after the start of the San Gabriel Canyon fire, a second major blaze was ignited near the Southern Pacific Railroad's Ravenna siding in Soledad Canyon, between the towns of Acton and Solemint Junction (now Fire Stations 107 and 81's territory). This fire burned to the east and south, heading up Mt. Gleason, Aliso Canyon, Mill Creek, Pacoima Canyon and Upper Big Tujunga Canyon (presently Fire Stations 80, 81, 74, and 63's initial-action area). This fire overlapped the burning period of the San Gabriel fire and consumed some 75,000 acres of prime watershed.

The sheer logistics of conscripting hundreds of unskilled and ill-equipped men to fight fires of such magnitude proved extraordinarily difficult. Problems of organization and tactics needed to fight simultaneous large fires in rugged and partially-inaccessible terrain proved too difficult for the combined efforts of Angeles Forest Supervisor Rush H. Charleton and the County Fire Warden's organzation. A Board of Fire review held in later years concluded that "... had the 'breaks' of the fires in 1919 been carefully analyzed, it would have disclosed that the disasters resulted from mistakes in fire suppression techniques rather than from deficiencies in the protection forces."

If there was ever a "straw that broke the camel's back," the fires of 1919 were it, as far as the organization for fire protection in Los Angeles County was concerned.

Forester Flintham was reasonably certain that he would soon be appointed County Fish and Game and Fire Warden. He consequently included in his upcoming year's budget additional funds for "... assistants to aid him in the fire work."

The United States Forest Service supported the county's transfer of departments. A quotation from the diary of an early County forestry assistant, James Emslie, clearly sums up the situation. Emsile writes:

"This year brought to a head the much-debated question of merging the Fire Warden's office with that of the County Forester, and steps were taken to force the change. The publicity necessary to put this over was one of the finest pieces of work done by the late County Forester Flintham, and regardless of statements to the contrary, born of professional jealousy, the late Mr. Charleton, then Supervisor of the Angeles Forest, was one of the strongest supporters of this change. I personally heard him make a plea before the (County) Board of Supervisors which bore much weight when it came to making the

Mountain cabins and resorts, such as this one in the Arroyo Seco north of Pasadena, were common throughout the mountains until fire or subsequent flooding removed them. From the collection of John Whelan.

Horse and mule pack train on the trail to Mt. Gleason construction camp, circa 1922. Photographer unknown, from the collection of John Whelan.

These two stages were never the same after severe flooding in the Arroyo Seco in January of 1927. From the collection of John Whelan.

Magnificent aerial view of the greater Los Angeles basin, taken in 1941, shows many salient topographical features such as the San Gabriel Mtns. (A), Verdugo Mtns. north of Glendale (B), and Chatsworth Hills (C). Oat Mtn. is to the right of the latter; the Malibu Mtns. to the left. The river in the lower foreground is the Rio Hondo Channel, that in the left center is the L.A. River. Aerial service photo from the collection of John Whelan.

final decision."

An entry in the Forestry Department Annals underlines the significance of the event. It reads:

"On July 1, 1920, Forester Stuart J. Flintham was appointed to the position of Fish and Game warden and ex-officio fire warden. The consolidation of the two departments, that is, Forestry and Fire, Fish and Game office, was a turning point in the history of conservation in this county. From that day on, guided by the determination and tenacity of Forester Flintham, the department grew steadily under an impetus which would not be denied. The Forester's vision and executive ability, together with his uncanny manipulation of protective organizations, built the foundation of the great structure that was to be. Those fortunate enough to have worked with him during this year, and in subsequent years before his untimely death, know that this association was in itself an education of a finer quality than could have been acquired in any university."

And so it was that the Los Angeles County Fire Department drew one step closer into being.

The Cornerstone Years

Over the years, the Los Angeles County Department of Forester and Fire Warden has passed through several periods of inordinate growth, reorganization and general constructive progress due to various pressures and demands. The time span between 1921 and 1925 was a prime example. It culminated with one of the most difficult of firefighting challenges – and, ultimately, the death of Chief Flintham.

The hub of the LA Co. Forestry Dept., circa 1922. Asst. Forester Spence Turner (l). Harry Merrill (c.) and secretary Arlene Somers (r.). Photographer unknown, from the collection of John Whelan.

Men to Match Mountains

In the person of Stuart J. Flintham, the County of Los Angeles was endowed with the services of an extremely dedicated and talented man. Flintham's bearing and interest in every aspect of the Forestry Department were an inspiration to all who worked with him. The new part of the Forestry Department called "Fish and Game and Fire Warden" immediately received much of his constructive attention.

It was at once apparent to Flintham that the fire protection organization he envisioned needed additional staffing to accomplish its mission. He appealed to the Board of Supervisors, who approved his request to increase his top staff to four men.

During the spring of 1921, personnel hired included Spence D. Turner, H.R. Merrill, L.S. Percey and O.M. Thurston. These men would hold key positions in the Forester and Fire Warden organization for many years. In addition, 11 "daily men" were hired to perform fire prevention and construction duties. Depending on the level of skill, these positions paid $2 to $2.50 per day.

Further support was shown by the Board's approval of 40 additional laborer positions for the Forestry Department. Also, 130 volunteer Fish and Game and Fire wardens were appointed throughout the county, to be compensated at the daily rate only when called upon to actually fight fire.

The county also took on the protection of 100,000 acres in the Santa Monica Mountains that were within the Los Angeles City limits, on a contract basis. In addition, a cooperative arrangement with the city existed whereby some county personnel were issued city badges on a reciprocal basis. Twenty-five U.S. Forest Service "agents" in the Angeles National Forest were also deputized in order to assist.

The Forester and Fire Warden's 1921-1922 budget showed other substantial increases in fire prevention appropriations. The annual allocation to the Angeles National Forest from L.A. County for firebreaks and trails was increased to $20,000. For the first time, three *new* vehicles were purchased, adding to the fleet two Ford Model T touring cars and a Dodge Brothers touring sedan. With the addition of a used Ford touring sedan, the complement now consisted of six automobiles and two motorcycles.

Vehicles purchased during the following fiscal years showed a new direction. Heavier-duty and more specialized vehicles were deemed necessary as more and more emphasis was placed on firefighting.

Within the Forestry Department, the existing reforestation nursery in Altadena had become a success over the years. A move was made to purchase the property for the county. On February 15, 1921, what had by now become a 10-acre plot was purchased for $13,005 from the private owner. The nursery continued to function until 1928, at which time the entire operation, including buildings, was moved back to Henninger Flats, again on mule back. The Altadena site would eventually become what is known today as Farnsworth Park.

Fuel Breaks as Fire Breaks

It was in 1921 that the Forester and Fire Warden office tested a theory of firefighting wherein a fire was accessed, and possibly controlled, by separating it from its fuel supply. First applied around the Henninger Flats nursery, the T.P. Lukens idea of a "firebreak," or more properly, a "fuel break," was put into operation many times throughout the early and mid-'20s. Eventually, all agencies with extensive flammable ground cover in their jurisdictions would adopt this method of fire control.

An excerpt from an address given in 1931 to the Conservation Society of Southern California by its executive secretary, George H. Cecil, describes the firebreak as constructed in the Southern California mountains:

"Fire lines, or breaks, built before the need develops, are of paramount importance. The breaks are constructed with due reference to the groundcover, the values at stake, steepness of slopes and similar factors. They are, as a rule, located along the summit of the ridges and vary in width from 20 to 100 feet, being wider along moderate slopes and in areas of high hazard and values. The name 'fire break' is almost a misnomer when applied to these preconstructed fire lines, in that they are not built with the idea that they will stop a fire. Rather, their purpose is to furnish a vantage point by which a fire may be reached and fought and, more particularly, for backfiring."

In the spring of 1921, the county began to construct this fire access and control feature in its forest and brushland areas. Assistant O.M. Thurston was placed in charge of a program to collect funds from local property owners for fire breaks under a special formula devised by Chief Flintham and the county, as described below.

The first of several breaks in the Malibu Hills was completed on June 15, 1921. Under the direction of Assistant Forester H.R. Merrill, a break was constructed over 19 miles of the main dividing ridge of the Santa Monica Mountains between Topanga Canyon and Laurel Canyon. Cost for this was $11,404.06, 75 percent of which was paid by the protected landowners. The break was constructed *entirely by hand*, by temporary, unskilled labor, as were all of the early firebreaks in the county. The tractor-turned-bulldozer was still a few years away.

Temporary Trailers

O.M. Thurston had been hired under a special contract by Chief Flintham to act as assistant forester under Spence Turner's command. He was to be in charge of fire control. But Thurston must have possessed special talents in salesmanship as well: not only did he collect funds from landowners for firebreaks, he was also in charge of collecting donations from interested neighborhoods for the first attempt at providing mobile fire apparatus for the rapidly-growing townships in the valleys.

The Forester and Fire Warden ordered the construction of 12 two-wheeled trailers made of steel and oak and outfitted with the following equipment:

- 6 Shovels
- 1 Axe
- 1 Funnel
- 8 Five-gallon Water Cans
- 6 Extinguisher Slings
- 2 Mattocks
- 4 Canteens
- 10 Gunny Sacks
- 10 Extinguisher Recharges

Each trailer was designed to be towed behind any automobile equipped with a towing hook. Local volunteers were trained to use the equipment by a volunteer fire warden.

It was also the field responsibility of these local volunteer fire wardens, as commanded by O.M. Thurston, to canvass their neighborhoods and local businesses for donations to help pay for the fire trailers. Each trailer cost $600 to build and equip, but the total county outlay for the project was $2,500.

Typical of a well-constructed fire break (fuel break), this 1933 example adjacent to the Henninger Flats Nursery in the San Gabriel Mtns. also provided fire protection for the telephone line poles running through the middle of the break. LACo Forestry Dept. photo.

Contents of one of the 12 fire trailers placed throughout L.A. County during 1920. A. Muench photo, LACo Forestry Dept.

Fire Dist. Trailer #4 being towed by one of the original Forestry Dept. Ford Model T's, circa 1920. A. Muench photo, LACo Forestry Dept.

Local assignment and sponsorship of the new trailers was as follows:

#1. **Flintridge** – Paid for by Senator Flint.
#2. **Covina** – Money raised by Golden Groves Packing House.
#3. **Azusa** – Money raised by Eastside Water Committee.
#4. **Topanga Canyon** – Money raised by house-to-house canvass.
#5. **La Crescenta** – Money raised by Thurston, Mr. S. Bissel and deputies Young and Waste via house-to-house canvass.
#6. **Brandt Rancho** – Moved to that location after being placed at the Oaks Garage, Calabasas, by Deputy W. Lotridge.
#7 & 11. Unable to place due to lack of funds. Eventually assigned to the county road department after being temporarily assigned to Bouquet Canyon, Beverly Glen, Laurel Canyon and North Whittier Heights.
#8. **Newhall** – Money raised by Thurston and Deputy Hitchcock via canvass.
#9. **Eagle Rock** – Paid for by Edison Company substation, Scholl Canyon.
#10. **Tujunga** – Money raised by Thurston and Deputy W. Lang.
#12. **Walnut** – Money raised by Thurston and deputies Slack and Palmer.

While these trailers, in the hands of volunteers, were not effective against a structure fire of any magnitude, they were useful for support at grass and brush fires as well as other small incidents. Of equal importance was the fact that they prepared the general population to accept the idea of volunteer fire districts with motorized apparatus and, eventually, districts with paid personnel. And these benchmarks were not long in coming. The momentum toward adequate fire protection in the unincorporated areas of the county was now well underway.

Chief Flintham had performed his duties well, and state legislation toward his goals was about to be set in motion.

The Clarke-McNary Bill

In 1920, the California Board of Forestry held a meeting with William B. Greely, chief forester of the United States. The outcome was U.S. Senate hearings pertaining to the major problems facing forestry concerns throughout the country, with emphasis on taxes, public ownership of public lands, harvesting regulations and *fire*.

During the meetings, Senator Charles McNary of Oregon asked Forester Greely, "What's to be done first?"

"Stop the forest fires," replied Greely.

Senator McNary acted, and secured the creation of the Senate Select Committee on Reforestation, with McNary as chairman. Over the next three years, the committee heard testimony from many sources concerning problems facing forestry in the United States.

Early in 1924, after much revealing testimony, Senator McNary authored a bill that provided a system of grading the relative value of forested land. It assigned funds accordingly to provide firefighting equipment, buildings and general support for fire protection throughout the country.

Simultaneously, a similar bill was written by another avid forester, Congressman John W. Clarke of New York, to be presented in the House of Representatives. Combining both bills seemed to be a prudent step for all concerned. Once approved, the bill was passed and signed into law by President Calvin Coolidge on June 7, 1924.

Interestingly enough, a reference to "brush-covered land" did not appear in the Clarke-McNary Bill in its initial form. Thus, much of the watershed in Southern California would not have been covered by the provisions of the bill. An amendment was added to correct this oversight during the 1925 Congressional Session, but only after concerted lobbying by Southern California interests such as the Los Angeles County Forester and Fire Warden.

The initial formula for disbursement of federal funds for watershed protection was 50 percent to federal land, 25 percent to state lands and 25 percent to county lands.

By 1925, the cost of protecting the watershed lands in the County of Los Angeles amounted to 8 cents per acre. This included reforestation, fire break construction, lookout towers, equipment, fire prevention and firefighting. Clarke-McNary expenditures in California totaled $67,825 by 1925, of which a major portion went to Los Angeles County.

A Measure of Service

Until the coming of the Clarke-McNary funding and paid fire districts in 1923, the volunteers in the valleys and paid foresters in the hills endeavored to serve in the most efficient manner possible. Still, the amount of men, their training and available equipment often did not match the task assigned. The following account is from the diary of H.R. Merrill.

"About October 21, 1921, we fought a rather serious fire in the vicinity of Charles Decker Ranch in the Santa Monica Mountains, and at about 2 a.m. on the 21st, a heavily-armed party consisting of Mr. Flintham, Mr. Turner, the county chauffeur and myself surrounded a cabin occupied by a one-armed sheepherder by the name of Shouey, and the criminal who confessed to starting the fire, one Charlie Decker, was escorted to the 'County Bastille' and locked up.

"I cannot remember how many fires Mr. Turner, Mr. Thurston and myself (sic) attended during this year, but there were plenty of them. On December 2, Mr. Flintham told us that the fire season was over, there having been a rain of about two inches the day before. He decided that we should go to Baldwin Lake on a duck-hunting expedition. The party consisted of Messers. (sic) Flintham, Turner, Thurston, Harrison and myself. We left here about noon, and, after an enjoyable trip to the Arctic (sic) regions,

returned Sunday night. During our absence, a north wind had sprung up, and a fire started in the Malibu Mountains, which, as near as we could ever figure out, burned about 8,000 acres in three hours' time. Due to the County Fire Warden's Department being out of commission at this time, with the exception of one young chap named Hannason, the Board of Supervisors turned the fire over to the Mechanical Division and the Sheriff's Office. On Monday morning, we started a very interesting week mopping up the fire and locating and rescuing 'fire fighters' who had been sent out with plenty of shovels to fight fire, but with very few canteens and no food with which to stoke their own boilers."

From the diary of L.S. Percey there is this account:

"Malibu Fire, December 5 to 7, 1921. Left home December 5. Went to the Los Angeles Office, then to the Malibu Fire, meeting Mr. Turner near Corral Canyon. Later that night, with Mr. Hannason and about 30 men, arrived at Solstice Canyon, together with provisions, and we made camp near the watering trough, but did not attempt to work the line at night. I would like to point out the kind and amount of equipment furnished for a fire fighting camp. The kitchen equipment consisted of one large dripping pan, which was used as a fry pan. No coffee boiler was provided, so a five-gallon round water can was used for that purpose. Mr. Hannason pointed out that the round water can was firefighting equipment, and questioned the wisdom of using it over a fire, but I decided that coffee had to be made for the men, and used the round water can. For a cook, one of the fire fighters was assigned to that duty, and breakfast was served consisting of bacon, eggs, coffee and bread and butter. No blankets were provided for the men. All slept around the fire. No cutting tools were provided for this crew, and we broke up a number of shovels trying to cut the thick brush."

Lookout!

Throughout the history of the fire service, an ongoing problem has always been the amount of time required to identify a hostile fire, report it to the proper dispatcher and keep to the minimum travel time by fire apparatus to reach the scene to begin initial attack. The rapidity of response has always been of prime importance to the success of the operation. What occurs during the first five minutes of a developing fire most often determines the ultimate size of the fire, the amount of damage it will cause and, in grass, brush or forest, the acreage the fire will consume.

During the early 1920s, the Department of Forester and Fire Warden had no rapid system by which the public could report a fire. Public and private telephones were scarce in the rural areas. Volunteer fire protection districts were free to devise their own methods of alerting personnel in the townships. Those who finally managed to reach the Forestry Department headquarters in downtown Los Angeles to report a wildland brush or forest fire were often told something to the effect that "We'll get someone out on that right away." Often that "someone" came from the downtown office in the form of whomever was available. Whatever Forestry agents might be in the field and any pickup labor they were able to conscript rounded out the response. Delays of an hour or more were common for responses to Palos Verdes, San Dimas and the Verdugo-San Rafael or Malibu Hills areas. In the even-more-distant Antelope Valley, Leona Valley, Palmdale or Little Rock, one could expect additional hours of delay.

One of the several solutions to the early detection problem was the construction of a series of steel-framed glass lookout towers. Those towers were placed at strategic locations throughout the more remote, moutainous areas of the county, eventually including the Angeles National Forest as well. A county-owned-and operated private telephone line was constructed between the tower and other county facilities to provide around-the-clock communicaton. Some of these facilities would eventually be fire stations, although not necessarily county fire stations.

Warden Joe Davis wrote about the construction of the first lookout tower in unincorporated county territory. His description, in the *Forestry Department Annals*, reads:

"On February 9, 1923, while on fire investigation, I met Ralph Carr of the Pacific Telephone and Telegraph Co., also a Deputy Warden, at a little restaurant in Castaic. In the conversation, Mr. Carr suggested that we should get contributions from the various telephone, oil and railroad companies who had interests in the general area around Newhall for the construction of a (fire) station at Newhall, and a lookout tower on Oat Mountain. On my return to the Los Angeles office, I informed Forester Flintham of this conversation, and he liked the idea. He immediately appointed me to go out and 'bring home the bacon.'

"On March 9 (after a series of town meetings had been held), I started negotiations for contributors for the Oat Mountain Lookout Tower and scouted Oat Mountain for an appropriate lookout tower site.

". . . On April 3, we received posts and #12 copper wire sufficient enough for one-and-one-half miles of completed line from the U.S. Long Distance Co. Other equipment and monetary contributions had been received from telephone companies, oil companies and railroad companies, etc., so that the construction of the telephone line and tower was an assured thing. On April 7, I, in conference with Supervisor Jordan of the Santa Barbara National Forest (now in the Angeles National Forest) made final arrangements regarding the U.S. Forest Service participating in the lookout tower's maintenance. The Forest Service was to furnish the man and

rangefinder, and also would pay for the observer. Mr. Jordan advocated the wooden type of structure as (now) used by the U.S. Forest Service, but Flintham advocated and adopted the steel type, which is still our standard specification tower.

"On April 17, Assistant Turner and I met Assistant Supervisor Mendenhall and Ranger Peterson of the Saugus (USFS) District, and looked over the site which we had chosen for the tower. The site was approved by these gentlemen. On April 27, I commenced survey for the Oat Mountain Telephone Line, and in the month of May I secured a right of way to the tower site from the owner, Mr. Wigdol, and for the telephone right of way from the Standard Oil Co. The latter granted us permission to install a circuit on the Standard Oil Company's pole lines up Wiley Canyon after the construction of the new line from the terminus of said line. The bulk of the construction material for the Oat Mountan tower was hauled up by mule from Newhall.

"On June 9, I started to set out the tower footings, and erect same, but was taken off this job and replaced by Ass't. Johnson."

The tower was completed in August, 1923 at a cost of $650, and assigned county number FD 44. Its general dimensions measured 30 feet, 4 inches to the top of the tower roof from the concrete foundation. It basically consisted of a steel and glass "penthouse," 8 feet by 8 feet square, positioned on four steel legs that were cross-braced and strengthened against Santana wind gusts by several steel guy wires anchored in the ground. Subsequent towers varied only in height. (Several years later, replacement towers would have a new design.)

The Oat Mountain Tower and those that followed all had the same equipment and manning procedures during fire season. Each tower was manned 24 hours a day for five or six days. On the sixth or seventh day, a relief observer filled in. The observers were required to make a complete survey of all areas in view every 15 minutes, from sunrise to sunset. At night, the observer lived in a hut built near the base of the tower. A water tank/cistern was located near the site to supply the facility, and for firefighting operations, if required.

A fire control motorway was constructed to each site and maintained for use in local firefighting – or possible evacuation by observation personnel if conditions warranted.

The towers were equipped with an Osborn Range Finder, binoculars, maps of the area being observed and a telephone. Later, weather observation equipment was added.

All towers were connected by telephone lines to fire stations or switchboards that could connect them to the proper dispatcher. The terminus of the Oat Mountain tower was the USFS Station at Newhall, located at San Fernando Road and Hart Street. Eventually, the phone lines became a part of a countywide system of interconnecting lines built and maintained by the Communications Division of the Forester and Fire Warden Department.

Observation from on High

As a result of World War I, the United States government had begun to understand the type of services that the "aeroplane" could provide. It was willing to experiment further. Local governmental agencies benefited as a result of this experimentation – especially the fire service.

During the years of 1921 and 1922, Chief Flintham availed himself of two new services, both of which became vital parts of his department's operations. The first was quite unique for its day. It came about through a close working relationship with the Santa Monica Land and Water Company. The Santa Monica Mountains, including the Malibu Hills portion, had never been accurately mapped. Both of these agencies needed highly-detailed maps for day-to-day planning and construction. Topographical maps proved to be invaluable tools for planning firefighting strategies.

Contracted from the Marshall Neilan Motion Picture Company, a helium-filled "pony" blimp with a two-man gondola suspended beneath was flown over the Malibu Hills, crisscrossing them as many times as necessary to provide information more readily discernible from the air than from the ground. The entire range was mapped by February, 1921. Throughout the late '20s, blimps were also utilized in fire-spotting patrols and fire progress checks during large fires.

The blimp's partner in the air was the DeHaviland DH-4 biplane, a two-place observation aircraft used extensively in the latter part of World War I. Flying experienced pilots from that time, these workhorse biplanes took to the air over Southern California to watch for incipient wildland fires in the more-remote mountain regions.

This operation was the result of a social meeting between State Forester Coert DuBois, who was an Army lieutenant colonel, and H.H. "Hap" Arnold, who was at that time an Army major. Army Air Corps personnel had little to do at that time, and the operation of air patrols would help not only the Forestry Service, but also the Air Corps. In 1920, a federal appropriation for $60,000 was made, and the air patrols began.

This was not without mishap, for in July 1920, an Army flyer and two Forest Service men were killed while taking off on patrol from Alturas, California.

In early 1920, the Army Air Patrol network included only California. By the close of that year and during 1921, the entire Pacific coast was included. Permanent bases were established at Spokane and Vancouver, Washington; Eugene, Oregon; and Mount Lassen and Sacramento, California. The Southern California base was at Griffith Park, but was later moved to the Grand Central Air Terminal in Glendale. Other locations in Southern California included Riverside and San Diego. Dozens of small, temporary fields with dirt runways and few facilities were scratched out in the rural areas.

Peter M. Bowers, in an article for *Western Flyer*, wrote:

"During the 1920 operation, the Army (aircraft) discovered 1,632 fires, of which 818 were discovered before 'regular' sources could report in. All of the 37 planes involved were modified versions of the DH-4 observation plane, powered with the 400 hp water-cooled Liberty engine. 2,779 flying hours were put in with only 13 forced landings occurring."

Bowers continued: "With federal purse-strings tightening in 1922, no funds were appropriated for the aerial patrol program. The Army, however, chose to keep up its pilots' training and morale by continuing to operate under the camouflage of 'training missions,' and other subterfuges. From 1923 on, the activity was scaled to what could be accomplished on an annual budget of $50,000."

During 1927 and 1928, the United States Forest Service took over the operation from the army. After that, the project was managed by private concerns under contract.

The *County Forestry Annals* mention that the patrolling aircraft had two-way radios by the late '20s. However, no details are given.

The lookout's cabin was adjacent to the tower. Cabins such as these accommodated only the most meager of sleeping and sanitary facilities. LACo Forestry Dept. photo.

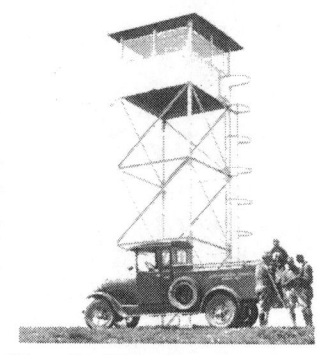

The F&FW's first lookout tower on Oat Mtn., south of Newhall, shortly after completion. Also shown is the department's second truck, a 1924 REO. LACo Forestry Dept. photo.

Trucks and Transportation

All during 1922 and 1923, it became ever more apparent to Chief Flintham that his department's transportation fleet was lacking in ability to move men

A historic moment: President Louis Evans of the Santa Monica Land and Water Co. hands the completed maps of the Santa Monica-Malibu Mtns. to Chief Engineer Wilkie Woodard of that company. Pilot M. Beck looks on. The Forestry Dept. now had its first complete aerial survey of those ranges accomplished using a leased "pony" blimp. LACo Forestry Dept. photo.

and material around the county in an efficient manner. The hand-me-down automobiles were rapidly wearing out, not only from age, but from being used for tasks for which they were never designed. Assistant Davis described the state of affairs and the corrective action taken by Flintham:

> "Two of the original Fords 'gave up the sponge' during 1922. Later, Chevrolet touring car #155 'gave its last gasp' in Hollywood after a response from Los Angeles to the Leona Valley (in the extreme northwest corner of L.A. county). The car was condemned and called in for auction by the Mechanical Department."

Chief Flintham requested the Board of Supervisors to replace the retired vehicles with "additional auto service," including at least one truck ". . . that we can equip as a fire truck through the summer to get fire equipment out to a fire in a hurry."

In July and August, 1922, three new vehicles were received: one Ford touring car, one Dodge Brothers touring car and one Dodge "screen truck" on a ¾-ton chassis. The truck had a screen similar to chain-link fencing along a portion of its sides, in order to better secure cargo, mules or men. This vehicle was the first real *truck* ever received by the Forester and Fire Warden. A supplementary request made in December by Chief Flintham produced a similar second truck, this time a REO Speed Wagon. The Dodge was given county number 261; the REO, number 290.

Early in 1924, another style of truck was purchased. This was a stakeside truck on a one-ton chassis, manufactured by the White Motor Company. Assistant Davis described the process used to switch to the White:

> "The purchase of the first White truck was done after a heavy conference during which all of the top assistants met with Chief Flintham in the office one evening. After the smoke had cleared away, it was found that assistants Turner, Davis and Merrill had vanquished the opponents of the White truck, and Flintham declared that by their valiant stand the new purchase would be a White. This choice has never been regretted, as the mileage shown on the speedometers (odometers) of these faithful

A DeHaviland DH-4 idles prior to takeoff on a field division inspection trip. This plane was used by staff personnel for familiarization of back country territory and fire patrol/reconnaissance during the fire season. LACo Forestry Dept. photo.

Army General H. "Hap" Arnold, the man credited with establishing the air patrol system over the western states, using idle aircraft and pilots from WW I. U.S. Army photo.

A DeHaviland DH-4 is refueled at March AFB prior to a patrol mission over forested areas. USFS photo, courtesy of Stan Cohen.

iron mules has proved conclusively their stability and efficiency."

The truck was given the county number 329, and was a departmental workhorse for a number of years.

In March, another Dodge screen truck, Number 398, was delivered, and in June the department placed Number 405, its first Buick touring car, in service. This was followed by the purchase of a heavy and powerful motorcycle, chosen to handle the longer, more-demanding trips often required. It was a Harley-Davidson two-cylinder model, given county number 37.

Early Modes and Methods

Generally, the supervisory personnel in charge of operations at the early fires fought by the F&FW were regular paid men or volunteer wardens. However, many of the firefighters had no such affiliation. The larger the fire, the more men that had to be conscripted off the streets. Los Angeles County had passed an ordinance supporting this state-approved procedure of recruiting that was utilized on a regular basis.

What would happen was that, upon receiving an order for a given number of firefighters, an assistant warden or two would drive the most-suitable vehicle available, usually one of the screen trucks or a rented truck, to the Midnight Mission or one or two local taverns. Soon thereafter, a load of newly-"hired" men would be delivered to the fireline. this process might have to be repeated a number of times, in several locations, depending on the number of men required. Additonal conscription efforts were directed toward smaller towns nearer the fire. Since the U.S. Forest Service rangers were agents empowered to conscript, they, too, visited the local streets or taverns nearest the fire to conscript on an "as-needed" basis.

Interviews with several of the men who actually participated in the conscription process indicate varying degrees of success. Some have said that the conscripted men worked well for as long as they were needed. Others indicate that some men would work for a day, earn a day's pay, then slip away to town and resume their previous positions in the local drinking establishments.

As the months during the fire season wore on, many of the regular tavern inhabitants would recognize the wardens as they came in the front door. The men quickly fled out the back door to avoid conscription. To counteract this, the experienced warden first backed the truck up to the tavern's back door, left one man stationed there and proceeded to enter through the front door. Fleeing bar patrons found themselves inside the truck immediately upon exiting the building!

Once they were inducted, conscriptees were trained in the use of hand firefighting tools just prior to being dispatched to the fireline. It was then up to the assistant warden to watch the inexperienced crew carefully.

The Horse Patrols

In spite of the increase in numbers and types of vehicles being used by the Forester and Fire Warden, the fact remained that many areas of Los Angeles County were not accessible by motor vehicle, and would not be for some years to come. In the foothills of the San Gabriel Mountains, Whittier Hills, Palos Verdes Peninsula and Malibu Hills, large ranches covered sometimes hundreds – or even thousands – of acres. The only practical access to these areas by the Fish and Game wardens was by horseback.

The very first mounted patrolman, G.W. Frownfelter, wrote this description of his work:

'In May of 1923, I was assigned a job through the department to ride on the Malibu Ranch as a Deputy Fire and Game Warden. My salary (was) to be paid by the ranch. Mr. Turner and Mr. Thurston assured me, at a conference in the corridor, that it was a dangerous assignment, as 'the Hillbillies of Malibu would shoot a Warden as quick as a snake.' After a few days on the ranch, I was detailed to ride beach patrol

Two 1924 White 600-gal. water tankers were converted during the fire season to firefighting use. Note the portable pumps on the top of the tanks for supplying water pressure to monitors at their rear. Pacoima Peak, site of a later lookout tower, is at center right. LACo Forestry Dept. photo, from the collection of Dale Magee.

and chase away any picnic and bathing parties. This I continued to do, more or less efficiently, for almost a month, but my efficiency must have been questionable, because I was finally discharged. After some idleness, I was again assigned through the Department to ride through deer season on the Bell Estate with Deputy Malden. We covered the upper Santa Monica Canyon; also Sepulveda, Mandeville and Rustic Canyons. While on this job, Malden and I arrested a Japanese with a 35-pound fawn, and got a fine of $750."

On the Air

The Los Angeles County Fire Department has always had to surmount the problems of moving large amounts of equipment and personnel over long distances during major emergencies. From 1920 to 1922, adequate and rapid communication with units in the field did not exist. This presented an equally serious concern in emergency logistics.

Chief Flintham became interested in the possible use of two-way radio as a way of improving communications with field commanders. He discussed the idea at length with Assistant Warden Joe Davis, who described the project in the *Annals:*

"The early part of September, 1922, Forester Flintham and I discussed the needs and possibilities of a radio communication system for the Department. Mr. Flintham and I went over each member of the Department as to their suitability as radio operator. He discarded some as they were too busy with other work; others because they were too lazy, etc., etc., and in a nice pleasing manner chose me as the goat. Therefore, on September 23, 1922, I devoted my first day to the study of the radio situation as applicable to the work of the Department. After various conferences with Mr. Dean Farren, Forester Flintham decided to purchase a portable radio transmitter and receiver. On November 1, 1922, a 50-watt radiophone set, to cost $1,485, was ordered. On February 2, 1923, Roy Chase and I picked up the Kennedy receiving set and brought same into the L.A Office. To experiment fully with these receiving sets, I secured aerial, masts, wire and other appurtenances, and assigned one set, together with those necessary things, at the homes of Assistant Turner, Assistant Johnson and myself. On April 13, 1923, I enrolled in the YMCA Radio School, from which I eventually graduated and was assigned a second-grade commission operator's license by the Federal Radio Commission."

Early White transport truck at the L.A. warehouse, circa 1926. LACo Forestry Dept. photo.

A 1924 White freight truck prepares to leave the Pacoima Warehouse for parts unknown with a load of pack horses/mules, circa 1926. LACo Forestry Dept. photo.

Although no specific date can be pinpointed for the completion of the installations, the 50-watt transmitter was built into a specially-designed panel truck. The historical significance of the construction and use of this set was most surely underemphasized, with only the following statement being noted in the *Annals:*

"A portable transmitting and receiving set with its own power plant mounted on a truck, which can proceed to every fire, has been especially designed and built. License for the operations of a portable station of this nature was secured from the government only after extended negotiations, since this is probably the first use of radio communication for fire control. It is the first portable radio set that has been built and operated for such purpose."

A true firefighting landmark indeed!

In order to communicate with the field portable unit, a 100-watt transmitter/receiver with antenna was purchased and installed. At great personal risk to the Forestry staff, the antenna was strung from the Hall of Records flagpole to the 12th-floor office of the F&FW. Assistant Davis noted:

"A merry time was had by said assistant, together with four or five men, when the 400-

foot antenna was swung between the flag mast on top of the Hall of Records Building and the roof of the Bank of Italy Building. One man was almost dumped overboard from the gutter to ground 12 stories below, and Assistant Davis received a break in his little finger which still mars the beauty of the nail thereof."

Further F&FW Expansion

During 1922 and 1923, the Forester and Fire Warden began several important new programs. Due to both the legal requirements and early successes, many programs were expanded. Among these was an inspection operation developed as a result of the passing of the Fire Hazard Abatement Act, #1355. This act required the removal of flammable vegetation and debris from vacant property upon receipt of a complaint. The first inspection under this act was made in the Township of Tujunga, Lot 89, Tract 3980. Countless inspections countywide followed in due course.

In later years, this early abatement program led to the formation of the Fire Prevention Bureau. Within the bureau's structure was a "Weed Abatement Section." During the spring months, the Weed Abatement Section sent personnel into the field to post vacant lots with a "Notice to Destroy Weeds" sign. This notice required the owner to remove the potential fire hazard in a specified time. Otherwise, the Weed Abatement crew would do the work and add the expense to the owner's property tax bill.

About this time, a program was begun to alleviate the personnel conscription difficulties faced by the volunteer fire wardens. Men conscripted in the field to fight fires, as well as volunteer firefighters, often lacked the proper hand tools. The department built a series of tool caches, each equipped to supply a specified number of men with the needed hand tools. This equipment was placed in large boxes or small sheds strategically located throughout the "back

Very rare photo, circa 1925, shows a horse patrolman ready to march in a local parade. No doubt the sign and bow tie remained at home while he was actually on patrol. Unknown photographer.

country." Ranch hands were given training in firefighting by the local wardens.

A famous road intersection at the Mount Wilson turnoff from Angeles Crest Highway in the San Gabriel Mountains is called "Red Box," after the color of the tool cache container that was located there.

Improvements in Pacoima

Due to space limitations at both the ornamental nursery and the central warehouse, a decision to move both facilities was made. A large parcel of land on Osborne Street, located in the northern San Fernando Valley area known as Pacoima was chosen for the new accommodations. Deputy John Nieto made a fortuitous purchase of a large amount of used lumber from the defunct Beverly Hills Race Track, and the Pacoima warehouse was constructed from this used, clear redwood. The building measured 50 feet by 50 feet, and was 20 feet high. It had a corrugated iron roof. The warehouse, which cost $2,572 to build, was given the county number FD #23.

Known as the Pacoima Warehouse, the site was to have many additions and several additional uses over the years. It remains today as the hub of the service and distribution system for the Los Angeles County Fire Department, and is the center for Air Operations activities out of nearby Barton Heliport.

Ongoing Activities

In addition to new projects, ongoing programs were meeting with success. During 1923, an additional 100 miles of fire breaks were constructed. "Spike" camps were built in various ranches in the vicinity of the new construction to house the dozens of men involved. Completed breaks included those in Malibu, Calabasas, Saddleback, North and South Tuna, the Verdugo Peak and several in the La Crescenta-Glendale area.

On November 19, 1923, Roland W. Percey joined the Forester and Fire Warden Department. He began as a screen truck driver, delivering supplies to the various construction camps located throughout the mountainous areas. Percey was later placed in charge of the construction and maintenance of the hand tool caches being spotted throughout the county. These caches were considered critical to the program, and Percey's efficient handling of this program was an indication of his capabilities as an organizer and supervisor. Roland W. Percey would be heard from often over the next four decades.

During May of 1923, in response to distance and logistical considerations, Chief Flintham established the first field division of the Forester and Fire Warden Department. Called the Soledad Division, it covered all of the county lying north of the San Gabriel Mountains. Deputy wardens J.A. Graves and Pierre Daries were assigned to the Soledad office during fire season. Daries acted as the dispatcher, with both men returning to firebreak construction during the winter months. On July 1, 1924, Assistant Warden

Leslie W. Percey was placed in charge of the Soledad Division, with Daries remaining as year-around warden-dispatcher.

Once again, cooperation between the U.S. Forestry Service and Los Angeles County had come into play. Warden Daries' office was located at the USFS Newhall ranger station on San Fernando Road near Hart Street. This was also the terminus of the county phone line from the Oat Mountain Lookout Tower – Dispatcher Daries' "eye in the sky."

Early Federal, State and County Mutual Aid Agreements

The Los Angeles County Forestry Department had come into being due to comprehension of a need at the state and federal level. It followed that fighting fires crossing county lines and involving State Interest Lands needed to be dealt with from a legal standpoint. Action by the state legislature in 1923 created a state fire district out of many counties, including Los Angeles County. The county fire warden was then appointed state fire warden. All of his top assistants received appointments as state fire wardens.

In order to obtain reimbursement from the state for protecting its lands, the Forestry Department was required to write a complete set of specifications pertaining to facilities, equipment of all kinds, manpower and projects planned for the coming year. Then, to the extent that these expenses applied to State Interest Lands, money was given to the county for them. This document was called the "fire plan," and was produced in handbook or pamphlet form each year for distribution to each administrative site. At a later date, the state reimbursed the county for providing fire protection to state lands within the county as a budgeted item.

These actions materially improved cross-jurisdictional fire protection agreements, especially where State Interest Lands were involved. A similar agreement between Los Angeles County and the Angeles National Forest was signed, going into effect on July 5, 1924. It provided a formula for initiating attack on a wildfire, regardless of jurisdictional boundaries, a method of establishing a common command structure in firefighting operations and, once the smoke had cleared, a method of compensation for the various expenses incurred.

This agreement was to receive its first test only a few weeks after being signed into law. Two great losses, one material, one human, were about to be felt by all concerned with watershed fire protection in California.

The San Gabriel Fire

Southern California is classified as a semi-arid zone. Rainfall, wind velocity, temperature and relative humidity will often vary widely from year to year. The Forest Service report on the 1924 San Gabriel Fire shows that the intensity and timing of winter storms and rainfall have had little or no influence on the severity of the following summer's fire season. It seems that the weather and the condition of the fuel during the summer itself is the primary influence. Records show the meteorological data for 1924 to be average in most respects. However, the San Gabriel Fire *did* occur during a warm, dry period in the month of September at a time of low humidity and inherently low moisture content in the vegetational fuel.

On August 31, 1924, Andy Gunsalus and his family were picnicking in the San Gabriel Mountains on private property near the O'Melveny Ranch. The ranch was on the west side of the river in the main fork of San Gabriel Canyon, several miles north of the town of Azusa (currently, Engine 97's response area). As the Gunsalus family prepared to leave the area, Mr. Gunsalus lit a cigarette, discarding the match in a grassy area adjacent to the edge of the hillside. He thought the match had been extinguished, and, as he later stated, was startled to see the dry grass erupt into flames. He failed in his attempts to beat out the rapidly-spreading fire with a blanket. He and his family left the scene, driving quickly southward on San Gabriel Canyon Road toward their home in South Los Angeles. The time was 12:15 p.m.

A U.S. Forest Service guard named Newman was patrolling on San Gabriel Canyon Road when he spotted a smoke column arising upcanyon. A U.S. Army patrol in a canyon to the north of Yucca Flats also spotted the smoke, as did the U.S. Forest Service San Dimas Lookout to the east. District Ranger Froelich received the telephone alarm from the San Dimas Lookout in his Glendora Ranger Station office at 12:20 p.m. Crews were rounded up to respond to the fire.

By 1:10 p.m., Patrolman Newman and six men began cutting a control line along the south flank of the fire. Reinforcements arrived soon and helped in this sector. They were successful in halting the southerly spread of the fire out of O'Melveny Canyon. However, the fire burned unchecked to the west and north, toward Pine Mountain and Camp Rincon, where the east and west forks of the canyon

Chief Forestry Asst. Joe Davis in action with the Forestry Dept.'s communication radio set, circa 1926. The set was built onto a screen truck. The F&FW used radio continuously from that time on. LACo Forestry Dept. photo.

join with the main fork. Flames swept into Camp Rincon by the next morning.

On the evening of the 31st, Fire Warden Flintham offered the services of the county to the U.S. Forest Service under the terms of the newly-signed Mutual Assistance Agreement. The offer was refused by Forest Supervisor Charleton.

However, on September 2, the U.S. Forest Service requested six crew leaders, specialized equipment and mules from the county. All were supplied by noon the following day.

By September 4, the fire was partially contained on the south flank near Fish Canyon, and on the north flank along the west fork of the San Gabriel River. Plans were being made to backfire along a break running from Pine Mountain north to the West Fork River in order to halt the fire's westerly progress.

On September 7, a frustrated Chief Flintham sensed that Fish Canyon could be saved from firing out after the Forest Service had completed its firebreak. He again offered the services of the county to Supervisor Charleton. This communication never reached the supervisor. On the 8th, Flintham decided that the services of the county were truly needed, and, on the morning of the 9th on his own sent 250 county men into Fish Canyon in an attempt to make a direct attack on the fire. The attempt failed. The fire burned out Fish Canyon and proceeded to burn westward, taking out Van Tassel and Monrovia canyons. After three days, the fire was finally halted along a secondary firebreak that was cut north to Monrovia Peak and then down into the West Fork Canyon.

Communications were reestablished with the Forest Service, and what was described as "a well-coordinated effort by the Forest Service and the County Fire Warden" concentrated on control measures along the upper west fork of the San Gabriel River. However, in spite of their efforts, the fire jumped the West Fork River on September 12, and began to burn north into the Devil's Canyon wild area. Desultory attempts by now-exhausted crews working in poor visibility from heavy smoke to build a control line to halt this slopover failed. It became obvious that the fire was going to consume all of Devil's Canyon and possibly Bear Canyon to the northeast.

On September 14, Chief Flintham and his county crews worked to contain the fire within the Devil's Canyon area by constructing a firebreak out of the West Fork up to the ridge leading north to the Charleton Flats area and then to the east toward Mount Waterman. This effort proved successful, and the county crews were taken off the lines on September 24. Some crews were then moved to assist the Forest Service in the Bear Canyon area to the northeast, where control was finally obtained two days later.

However, on September 26, inadequate cold trail-

The San Gabriel Mtn. Fire of 1924, photographed from Mt. Wilson. Here, the main fire is burning toward the west behind Mt. Mooney and Charleton Flats, toward Chilao Flats. The Devil's Canyon-Bear Canyon wild area is right foreground. The large peak right center is Mt. Waterman. The large peak to the extreme left is Mt. Pacifico. Photo source unknown, possibly USFS.

ing allowed the fire to jump the lines once again. This time, the fire burned to the highest ridge in the San Gabriel range, taking out the Devil's Canyon/Bear Canyon areas and the south face of Mount Waterman. It then hooked around to the northwest to burn into Chilao Flats, Mount Mooney, Horse Flats and general vicinities.

The fire was finally controlled along this line after burning for a total of 27 days. It consumed over 50,000 acres of prime watershed and timber and was fought by 5,000 men.

Chief Flintham's health began to deteriorate steadily after this monumental effort. He had been suffering from an "ulcer condition" from time to time. Now the flareups became more frequent and severe. The firefighting operation had not gone well, in spite of his best efforts. The Forest Service launched a formal inquiry into the handling of the fire at the *national* level.

The chief of the U.S. Forest Service, Colonel W.B. Greely, appointed eight prominent persons connected with watershed management and fire control to sit on the board of inquiry. They heard testimony from 80 witnesses over a 26-day period beginning on November 17, 1924. Strengths and weaknesses of the campaign were duly noted. Many recommendations were put forth for sweeping changes in the fire protection program for the Southern California mountain regions. Supervisor Charleton no longer retained his position with the Angeles Forest. Although Chief Flintham remained in office, his health continued to deteriorate.

Forestry Assistant Joe Davis's description of what next transpired is probably as succinct an entry in the *Annals* as can be found:

"At 10:50 a.m. on June 10, 1925, the Forester passed away after having been bedridden for several weeks. The cause of his death was of long standing, although he had not given up until around the first of June. Funeral services were held on June 14. With his passing, the Forestry Service lost one of its most brilliant minds, and the personnel of the Department (lost) a real friend. It was the irony of Fate that prevented Forester Flintham from living to see the Department grow into the organization whose structure he had so well planned."

Taken from a glass plate negative, this 1925 photo shows the completely unscarred brush-covered slopes of the San Gabriel Mtn. foothills north and east of La Canada in the vicinity of Devil's Gate Dam. NASA's Jet Propulsion Laboratory now covers the entire center area of this photo.
Photo courtesy of Dale Magee.

The Transition Years

LA Co. Forester & Fire Warden Spence D. Turner. He was named to the post following the sudden death of Stuart J. Flintham in 1925, and held the post for 27 years.
LACo Forestry Dept. photo.

During the two years following his appointment as county fire warden, Chief Flintham continued to encourage expansion and improvement of the system of volunteer fire companies scattered throughout the unincorporated areas. But in spite of his best efforts, the effectiveness of the volunteer system began to wane. This was largely due to a lack of monetary support by the communities involved, in addition to an overwhelming growth factor.

Many of the communities had provided themselves with Ford Model T trucks equipped with small hose, a chemical system, ladders and various other firefighting tools. Some towns retained only the original fire trailers that had been distributed in 1920, while others had an assortment of miscellaneous rolling stock.

Various public groups, like Chief Flintham, realized that new legislation was needed in order to hire fulltime, paid firefighters and purchase fire apparatus equal to the ever-growing task. The currently-existing laws affecting the unincorporated areas were far too restrictive to meet the burgeoning need for fire protection.

Early in 1923, Edward T. Bishop of the Los Angeles County Counsel's office was instrumental in submitting a bill to the state legislature that would dissolve the volunteer districts and replace them with districts paid for by the citizens within each district. If the citizens wished to form such districts, funds would be collected by additions to existing district property tax bills. The bill, as proposed by Bishop, was passed (Act #2583), and welcomed by all concerned. The forester and fire warden immediately set about to form a system of fire protection districts. Fire protection was about to take a monumental step forward.

Establishment of Fire Protection Districts

With the passage of state legislation sanctioning the formation of separate fire protection districts within the counties, Chief Flintham embarked on a vigorous public relations program, urging the districts' establishment by means of special elections. Assistant Fire Warden Norman Johnson was placed in charge of this effort and met with immediate success.

However, it seemed that all of the newly-formed districts desired instantaneous, paid, fulltime fire protection, not fully realizing that it would take several months to organize and collect the required funds through property taxes. After several hearings, the County Board of Supervisors concurred with various citizens' groups that an immediate appropriation of $50,000 be made to cover the expenses for "handling Fire Protection District equipment," and to pay at once for the soon-to-be-trained personnel. Repayment would be made through the use of a "deferred payment scheme worked out between the county counsel and the county auditor."

The Board of Supervisors, having been assured of the legality of such an action, also entered into a contract with the districts – after having been given a verbal promise of repayment on an installment plan after the necessary property taxes could be collected. Under this agreement, 28 pieces of fire apparatus were purchased at a cost of $280,000. Added to this was $60,000 for 56,000 feet of 2½ inch hose, along with "competent men . . . employed to operate such equipment."

Special elections were held in each township or area desiring to form a fire protection district. The first two districts were formed on September 4, 1923. These were the Santa Monica Canyon District and the Signal Hill District. On December 17, 1923, Palmdale, San Dimas, Norwalk, Maywood, Lomita, Lawndale, La Crescenta, Clearwater-Hynes, Belvedere, Downey and Bellflower districts were formed. Santa Fe Springs formed on December 24, and Moneta Gardens on December 31. The balance were formed in 1924 or thereafter. This was followed by an irregular pattern of district formation, dissolution and combination.

The Disparity of Funding Sources

The newly-formed fire protection districts were funded by entirely different sources than was the Forester and Fire Warden Department. The districts received their money from property taxes within each district. The money could be spent only in that district. The Forester and Fire Warden received money from the county general fund, which was supplemented by a cooperative fund that included Federal Clarke-McNary funds and substantial funding from the state of California for protection of State Interest Lands within the county. In addition, each incorporated city within Los Angeles County paid a small amount into the general fund to assist with forest land protection. In exchange, the Forester and Fire Warden was obligated to send one F&FW engine into any incorporated city upon request. (These are the basic funding procedures that are followed today, although a few other funding sources have been added.)

Organization Changes

Within a nine-month period, a complete supervisory structure was created within the Forester and Fire Warden Department to handle the newly-created fire protection districts. On July 1, 1924, C. Tillotson of Los Angeles was hired to be a field battalion chief for the districts. On December 1, 1924, J.R. Baker, from the city of Monrovia, was appointed as a district battalion chief, followed on January 1, 1925, by A. Heinzman.

A few weeks before his death on June 10, 1925, Chief Flintham had been presented with his fire chief's badge at a well-attended ceremony at Graham Fire District Station Number 16 on April 16. He did not live to see the completion of the district's organization. It was left to his successor, Spence D. Turner, to finish the task.

After Turner's appointment as Forester and Fire Warden on June 8, 1925, two additional appointments were made. On June 18, 1925, R.L. Dunlap was chosen to head the newly-created Fire Prevention Bureau, and Joe Davis was assigned as chief assistant forester and fire warden within two weeks.

The relationship of the fire districts as a subsection of the Forester and Fire Warden is discernible in the wage disparity between them. Battalion chiefs in the districts received an annual wage of $2,160. Chief Turner's annual salary was $5,000, and, of that amount, $4,700 was compensation for heading the Forestry Department. Only $300 was earned as the head of the Fire Warden and Fish and Game Department. Adjustments in this imbalance were made during the years that followed.

FPD and F&FW Differences

At this point in the evolution of the Los Angeles County Fire Department, differences between the Forestry Department and the fire protection districts, with respect to equipment, uniforms and procedures, were most marked. These differences were to remain for over 20 years.

The forestry stations were grouped geographically into "field divisions," with an assistant warden in charge of the headquarters station of each division. The district stations were grouped into battalions, with a battalion chief in charge of each one. The boundaries of each field division or battalion were determined by major geographic features, e.g., the ridge of the Whittier Hills or the Los Angeles Riverbed. This custom is somewhat applicable even today.

Both organizations purchased their own uniforms. The forestry uniform consisted of a dark-green coat and whipcord pants, optional tall riding boots and a broad-brimmed stetson forest service-type hat.

The district uniform was similar to that of the Los Angeles City Fire Department, consisting of dark-blue wool pants with suspenders, dress coat, black work boots or shoes, a blue uniform cap for firemen and engineers and a white cap for the rank of captain and above. Work uniforms were blue wool pants and jacket, and grey chambray work shirts. Standard turnout coats, pants and boots, along with Cairns, Pettybone or Forker fire helmets completed the outfit.

Most significant were the differences in fire apparatus. Forestry fire apparatus were pumper/tanker models, painted two-tone green. The smaller cargo trucks and pickups were painted similarly, but with black fenders. The district rigs were standard triple combination pumpers made by American LaFrance, Stutz or REO-Oberchain-Boyer. They were painted the standard red of the particular manufacturer and trimmed with gold leaf. Later, a standard color called L.A. County Red, or "Swift Red" was developed and utilized. The district's name, such as "Lomita," usually adorned the hood.

From the 1928-29 Fiscal Year Report:

FIRE REPORT

FOR TERRITORY INSIDE FIRE PROTECTION DISTRICTS

Los Angeles County Fire Districts Apparatus and personnel responded to calls as follows:

Name of Fire Protection District	Eng. Co. No.	Loss to Improvements	Insurance on Improvements	Loss to Contents	Insur. on Contents	Total Loss	Total Insurance
Altadena	11	2,893	88,500	1,977	34,500	4,870	123,000
	12	2,457	14,900	1,200	1,740	3,657	16,640
Artesia	30	1,020		805		1,825	
Baldwin Park	29	13,602	16,690	5,781	4,500	19,383	21,190
Bellflower	23	863	6,810	900	2,125	1,763	8,935
Belvedere	1	16,798	163,400	16,552	55,850	33,350	219,250
City Terrace	32	2,715	20,000	1,220	35,500	3,935	55,500
Belv. Gardens	3	9,630	2,649,310	13,000	37,450	22,630	2,686,760
Clrwtr-Hynes	31	10,100	13,700	35,570	29,200	45,670	42,900
Downey	10	5,215	47,200	715	100,600	5,930	147,800
Flintridge	28	2,510	25,000	2,000	17,000	4,510	42,000
Hollywood	8	6,065	159,250	7,845	114,750	13,910	274,000
Sherman	7	8,382	106,370	2,040	32,600	10,422	138,970
Howard	14	1,485	24,100	180	6,400	1,665	30,500
La Crescenta	19	2,885	32,960	805	6,100	3,690	39,060
Laguna	2	7,518	123,120	7,065	45,948	14,583	169,068
Lancaster	33	2,060	1,600	600		2,660	1,600
Lawndale	21	5,540	19,050	1,864	6,200	7,404	25,250
Lennox	18	2,450	2,300	657	2,600	3,107	4,900
Lomita	6	1,820	8,700	5,255	800	7,075	9,500
Mira-Florence	9	11,972	124,050	7,673	96,647	19,645	220,697
Graham	16	5,678	54,700	1,960	10,600	7,638	65,300
Moneta-Gard.	22	2,447	25,025	600	6,950	3,047	31,975
Norwalk	20	1,736	131,500	3,025	13,600	4,761	145,100
Palmdale	37						
Puente	26	1,885	57,250	1,860	32,800	3,745	90,050
San Dimas	25	1,531	1,300	630	60	2,161	1,360
Santa Fe Spgs.	17	188,935	3,500	158,610	1,900	347,545	5,400
Walnut Park	24	4,705	63,375	869	28,400	5,574	91,775
Total		324,897	3,983,660	281,258	724,820	606,155	4,708,480
Outside		26,635	617,500	25,950	101,626	52,585	719,126

Outside of County Fire Protection Districts 78 fires were responded to by the personnel in the various County Fire Protection Districts to territory in close proximity to the Fire Districts.

FIRE REPORT

LOS ANGELES COUNTY FIRE PROTECTION DISTRICTS

Name of Fire Protection District	Engine Co. No.	Phone Alarms	Still Alarms	Box Alarms	Total Alarms	False Alarms	Incendiary Fires	Miles Run to Fires	Hours Motor Pumped at Fires (Hrs.Min.)	Feet 2½ in. Hose Laid at Fires	Feet 1½ in. Hose Laid at Fires	Hydrants Inspected
Altadena	11	95	3		98	2		331.9	13-36	9750	1900	704
"	12	41	3		44			107.4	12-23	14300	6100	359
Artesia	30	9			9			11.0	6-20			
Baldwin Pk.	29	25	11		36	3	3	59.3	6-25	3700	800	1000
Bellflower	23	12	9		21		1	58.4	5-25	2600	600	428
Belvedere	1	94	13		107	13	2	89.9	17-18	28150	2600	1750
Belv(CityTer)	32	63	13		76	3	1	196.4	12-27	19100	3400	724
Belv.Gardens	3	44	12	52	108	18	1	156.7	38-34	5700	950	1048
Clrwtr-Hynes	31	27	18		45	1		114.2	12-07	6750	1900	506
Downey	10	20	2		22			31.5	17-30	13250	2600	390
Flintridge	28	8			8			32.4	1-50	3300	700	387
Hollywood	8	62	2		64	2		104.9	10-00	9600	1600	166
Sherman	7	53	9		62	1	1	99.0	12-46	42980	4000	406
Howard	14	71	11		82	2	1	139.9	22-10	7500	400	832
La Crescenta	19	45	2		47	2	1	118.5	10-05	10150	1500	288
Laguna	2	63	12		75	6	3	113.1	8-17	7800	1850	1848
Lancaster	33	14		1	15	1		7.5		350		
Lawndale	21	44	23		67	2	1	128.9	11-10	5350	600	650
Lennox	18	57	8		65	3	3	139.6	7-59	12350	3700	333
Lomita	6	34	2		36			54.7	35-45	6000	1700	346
Mira-Flor.	9	85	6		91	2	4	171.8	27-53	14550	2000	1170
Graham	16	83	8		91	1	3	113.9	8-05	5400	300	386
Moneta-Gar.	22	41	12		53			61.8	6-50	4000	500	1170
Norwalk	20	23	19		42			87.2	6-59	2150	250	1011
Palmdale	37											
Puente	26	18	15		33	3		62.0	14-21	18500	6200	468
San Dimas	25	7	5		12			36.0	4-00	7000	5000	216
Santa Fe Spr.	17	48	10	1	59	5	1	173.8	285-25	16200	1450	506
Walnut Park	24	23	2		25			38.4	11-52	8700	3950	1032
TOTALS		1209	230	54	1493	70	26	2845.1	621-32	285180	56550	18124

The Henninger Flats nursery in preliminary developmental stages in January 1929. Sites for tree planting and seedling development have been staked out, and trenches are being cut with a plow. Carson photo, LACo Forestry Dept., courtesy Henninger Flats Museum.

The intermediate county nursery in Altadena, circa 1927. The following year it was moved back to Henninger Flats. A. Muench photo. LACo Forestry Dept.

Three steps in potting seedling trees at the Henninger Flats nursery were forming a tarpaper pot on a jig (l.), placing the seedlings in the pot after it was filled with dirt (c.) and arranging the pots prior to their being placed in open-air storage for watering and maturation (r.). LACo Forestry Dept. photo, courtesy of Henninger Flats Museum.

1929 view of Henninger's cabin. It was later torn down and replaced with a seed house. The garage on the right was moved approximately 200 feet further right. Photo by Carson.

Forestry rigs worked in rural areas where water mains were scarce and hydrants were rare. They carried water tanks ranging from 350- to 600-gallon capacity and were equipped with only 1½" and 1" cotton jacketed hose.

District rigs usually served in established communities. They had smaller water tanks, ranging from 80 to 120 gallons. Some had 40-gallon soda-acid tanks. (These were later converted to water tanks.) They carried varying amounts of 2½" and 1½" hose, and often carried hard rubber "chemical" or ¾" hose on reels above the hosebed.

Normally, neither organization responded to fires in the other's jurisdiction on the first alarm. Mutual response patterns were a thing of the future, and even proximity was not considered.

The F&FW Expands Further

With the passage of the years between 1924 and 1934, the Forester and Fire Warden continued its rapid growth commensurate with increased demands. On November 1, 1924, assistant Graves resigned from the department. He had served in the capacity of field supervisor for the nine winter construction camps scattered throughout the mountainous areas. These served as bases for firebreak and motorway construction. L.S. Percey, who had been in charge of the Soledad Field Division, replaced Graves.

At the time of this personnel change, the department decided that all field construction activity should be coordinated through one office. Percey was given an examination for assistant fire warden, passed "satisfactorily" and was thus qualified to retain his position as head of the first Construction Division.

R.L. Dunlap had been hired from the city of Los Angeles Fire Department to work in the area of fire prevention because of his knowledge of building construction as it related to firefighting. He was placed in charge of Fire Prevention Engineering, and in 1924, along with Chief Assistant Forester Joe Davis, began to write the first fire code for Los Angeles County. On February 20, 1925, the first "plan check" for new construction was put into effect by the new Fire Prevention Bureau.

In July, 1925, the first coordinated inspection program of the hundreds of wooden derricks of the Santa Fe Springs oil fields was carried out by Dunlap and his men, and, according to Joe Davis' notes in the Forestry Annals, ". . . a real cleanup was accomplished."

The fire protection districts had no county repair facilities available to them because they were funded separately. (The Forestry Department retained the services of the county Mechanical Department to perform its automotive repairs.) Therefore, on November 1, 1924, a small shop located at 4921 E. Whittier Boulevard in East Los Angeles was hurriedly opened to take care of repair and service to district apparatus. S.W. Dobson was retained as the first district mechanic, taking the title of "mechanical engineer."

The Los Angeles County Forestry Department, 1924-1933

While in the valleys fire protection districts were constantly forming, dissolving and combining, in the hills the Forestry Department was modernizing and expanding as rapidly as funding would allow.

Roadside trees were still being planted (99,000 by 1933) and cared for. The Henninger Flats and Ornamental nurseries were in full operation. The Parks Division developed several new regional facilities.

Although fires were being better prevented and more-skillfully fought, construction growth and increased public usage within mountainous areas escalated the number of fires.

New equipment of all kinds was purchased and manned during this period in an effort to meet the proliferating demands. An important item on the agenda was the Forestry Department's Lookout Towers.

Los Angeles County Forestry Department Lookout Towers

(All-inclusive except for one very late entry; see Chapter 10)

OAT MOUNTAIN, SOUTH OF NEWHALL: August 1, 1923. Cost: $650.
CASTRO PEAK, CENTRAL MALIBU HILLS: June 1, 1925. Cost: $757.
SAN JOSE, SOUTH OF SAN DIMAS: August 1, 1925. cost: $700.
MT. ISLIP, E. OF MT. WATERMAN: Summer 1926 (USFS)
MT. GLEASON, S. OF ACTON: October 29, 1926. Cost: $2,046.
BLUE RIDGE, S.W. OF WRIGHTWOOD: Summer 1928. Unknown cost.
SAWMILL MOUNTAIN, S. OF LEONA: March 1, 1929. Unknown cost.
PACOIMA, N.W. OF PACOIMA WHSE: Spring 1930. Unknown cost.
BODEL PEAK, MALIBU HILLS: Spring 1930. Moved from Blue Ridge.
PARKER MTN., S. OF ACTON: Spring of 1934. Unknown cost.
VERDUGO PEAK, N. OF GLENDALE: (contract) July 9, 1934.
TOPANGA, E. MALIBU HILLS: Fall 1934. Cost unknown.
SAN RAFAEL, S. OF FLINTRIDGE: Spring of 1935. Unknown cost.
TRIUMFO, W. OF DECKER, MALIBU: Spring of 1935. US. Govt. donated.
GILMAN, N. OF CARBON CYN., E. OF OLINDA: Sept. 1, 1935. Cost unknown.
TEJON, NEAR GORMAN: September 1, 1935. Moved from Sawmill Mountain.
TEMPLE, PECK ROAD, SO. OF MONROVIA: October 13, 1936. Cost unknown.
ZUMA, JUST NORTH OF ZUMA FORESTRY STATION, MALIBU: Spring of 1940. Cost unknown.

Several other towers such as Mt. Lukens, Los Penitos and Grass Mountain, all in mountainous regions, were built by the USFS and the county as cooperative towers. The two entities worked together closely in locating these towers to provide uniform coverage. The county also worked with the city of Los Angeles in constructing the San Vincente tower in the Santa Monica Mountains. (The towers varied in height above the ground, the shortest being Castro, at 22 feet, the tallest was Verdugo, at 60 feet.)

Rolling Stock

Between 1925 and 1931, the following equipment was purchased by the Forestry Department:
Screen Truck, Dodge, #407, ¾-ton.
Patrol Cars: Dodge, #408 & 409; Buick, #455, 484, 687 through 690 (#484 to Chief Turner).
Squad Trucks: White, #708 through 710, ¾ ton.
Freight Trucks: White, #711, 712, 727, 732, ¾- to 2-ton; REO, #415, 1-ton.
Squad Trucks: Moreland, #927, 928, 983, 1½-ton.
Patrol Trucks: Ford, #922 through 925, ½-ton.
Pumper Trucks: White, #742, 745, 746, 2-ton (Pumpers C, E and F).
Pumper Trucks: Moreland, #913, 914, 2-ton (Pumpers J and K).
Pumper Trucks: Moreland, #877, 878, 7½-ton (Pumpers G and H).
Pumper Trucks: Moreland, #935, 936, 988, 7½ ton (Pumpers L, M and P).
Patrol Motorcycles: Harley-Davidson, #210 through 213, 2-cyl.
Bus: Pierce-Arrow, 27 passenger.
Motorcycle Ambulance: Harley-Davidson, 2-cyl.

Also purchased were a winch truck, various compressors, a Bearcat power shovel and a Killifer "Scarifier." Ten mules and a horse were also acquired.

Division Boundary Adjustments

During the years following 1924, the incorporation of townships into independent cities and the annexation of unincorporated areas into adjacent cities brought about a number of Department of Forestry boundary adjustments. The Sunland-Tujunga area incorporated on May 1, 1925 (and was annexed by the city of Los Angeles in 1932). This move initiated changes in several divisions. The Fernando Division, the area around the Pacoima warehouse and mountains north of the San Fernando Valley, was dissolved. The La Crescenta Division, the area around the Verdugo Hills and mountains north of the Crescenta-Canada Valley was dissolved. The Pasadena Division, composed of Altadena, Sierra Madre and the mountains directly north, was dissolved. The Arroyo Seco division was created to replace these three divisions. Its boundaries ran all along the San

Up she goes! A series of four photos show the construction stages of the Dept.'s second lookout, the 60-ft. Mt. Gleason tower, in 1926. A. Muench photo, from LACo Forestry Dept.

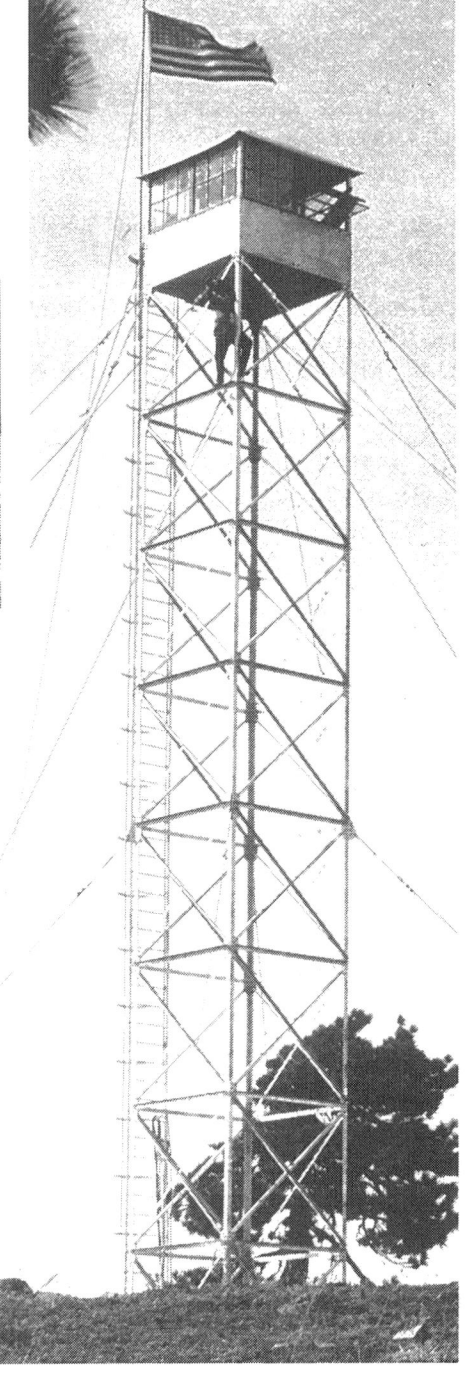

The nearly-completed 60-ft F&FW lookout on Mt. Gleason, south of Acton, in 1926. Lumber can be seen protruding from the window, probably awaiting construction of interior cabinetry. LACo Forestry Dept. photo.

The 60-ft. Verdugo Peak lookout tower, upon completion in 1934. This design featured a poured-in-place concrete base for added stability. The City of Glendale contracted for this tower and an observer until it was closed in the middle 50s. Photo courtesy Clifford Riggs.

Seven foresters pose beside the newly-completed lookout tower on Castro Peak. LACo Forestry Dept. photo.

The LA City San Vicente tower, in the Santa Monica Mtns., built with the assistance of the County Forestry Dept. in the early 1930s. This tower spotted and reported the Trippet Fire of 1938. Photographer unknown, from the collection of John Whelan.

A direction sign points to the Sawmill Mtn. lookout several miles east of Gorman, south of Highway 138. Its location indicates it was a cooperative tower with the USFS. LACo Forestry Dept. photo.

A worker uses a gasoline-powered shovel to construct a fire control motorway, location unknown, about 1928.

From the collection of John Whelan.

37

These two photos show early construction of the USFS cooperative lookout tower dwelling cabin on Mt. Islip in Sept. 1926. Arthur Aiken, laying rock in poured concrete, later became the construction supervisor for the F&FW's famous rock stations such as those at Vincent, Big Rock, Mint Cyn, and Eaton Cyn. A. Muench photo. LACo Forestry Dept.

Gabriel Mountains from Newhall Pass to Fish Canyon, north of Duarte. It skipped the Sunland-Tujunga area.

Temporary headquarters for this new division were located at Altadena (Farnsworth) Park, the North Lake Avenue site of the county nursery. They remained there until 1929, when the new and permanent headquarters constructed at the corner of Michigan Avenue and Georgian Road in La Canada were completed in March of that year. (This is the present location of Battalion 4 headquarters and Fire Station 82.)

In June of 1930, a two-room frame dwelling originally built at the Pacoima warehouse at a cost of $450, was trucked north to Dexter Canyon Park. Known as the Kagel Canyon Patrol Station, it was at the present location of Fire Station 74.

In the spring of 1934, an additional patrol station was built on the east bank of Eaton Canyon, replacing a temporary cabin near the entrance of the Henninger Flats-Mt. Wilson Toll Road. This was the eastern-most station in the Arroyo Seco Division. It was known as the Eaton Canyon Patrol Station, and is the present Fire Station 66.

The dispatching office, which had been located in the main Pasadena Office building, was moved to the Arroyo Seco Division Headquarters in La Canada.

Soledad Division (originally called the Newhall Division) boundaries remained the same. This comprised all of the county north of Newhall Pass in the San Gabriel Mountains, including the desert.

The Los Angeles Division encompassed the territory around the city of Los Angeles, the Palos Verdes Peninsula, Catalina island and the San Clemente Islands.

The Forestry Dept.'s first tractor, a Caterpillar #30, in action during the summer of 1925, clearing brush on Sawmill Mtn. The dozer blade had not been invented yet. This tractor dragged the brush with a large rake mounted at the rear. Photographer unknown, from the collection of John Whelan.

Forestry Dept.'s communication truck and crew pose in knee-deep snow en-route to a repair job. Personnel and location unknown. From the collection of John Whelan.

Wardens Dan Barnes, on the motorcycle, and Jesse Graves, in the Buick, pose as if responding from the first Arroyo Seco Div. HQ at Lake and Mt. Curve in Altadena. This was also a nursery site for several years. A. Muench photo, LACoFD.

Newly-appointed Forester & Fire Warden Spence Turner, in his 1926 Buick, Machine #484, a roadster pickup. Photographer unknown.

Deputy Warden L. Lang strikes a "Popeye" pose in front of La Crescenta (Verdugo) Div. HQ in La Crescenta, in the spring of 1928. Note that badge being worn on his belt is a very early version; it merely states "Deputy Warden." Walter Noller photo, from the collection of Eugene Noller.

Eight motorcycles and patrolmen of the Forestry Dept. pose in front of La Crescenta (Verdugo) Div. HQ during the fall of 1927. Walter Noller photo, from the collection of Eugene Noller.

La Crescenta Div. HQ was next to the La Crescenta Hardware store on Michigan Ave. (Foothill Blvd.) in 1927. This REO apparatus is probably the rig turned back to the Forestry Dept. when the Temple District dissolved. The La Crescenta Fire District rig was a 1924 Stutz. Walter Noller photo, from the collection of Eugene Noller.

The Malibu Division included all of the Malibu Mountains and Chatsworth Hills; the San Jose Division (originally called the San Dimas Division) included the eastern section of the county from Fish Canyon on the west to San Antonio Canyon on the east. It also included the South Hills-Whittier Hills area.

Further Growth

By June, 1926, the Forestry Department had again outgrown its offices. When the county acquired a building at 202 N. Broadway, Los Angeles, space was found on the second floor for the Forestry headquarters. Each division head had a desk and a secretary. Although the general condition of the facilities was described as "unsanitary," the roominess was most appreciated.

During 1932, fire department headquarters moved to 524 N. Spring Street, Los Angeles, where it remained for the next 20 years.

Until 1926, the county of Los Angeles was lacking a policy concerning the issuance of badges to sworn personnel. Problems arose when unauthorized persons displayed county badges at inappropriate times. To prevent such misuse, a general ordinance was passed describing to whom, and by which branches of county government, badges could be issued. Oddly enough, Ordinance #1389 failed to mention the Forestry Department! This oversight was corrected the following year.

Prior to 1926, various organizational changes had been made in the structure of the Fire Warden branch of the Forestry Department. At that time, a stabilization occurred that would last through the Great Depression of the 1930s. The Fire Warden branch contained five divisions. The function and duties of each were outlined in the Annals:

Construction Division – Construction and maintenance of fire breaks, trails, roads, telephone lines, lookout towers, division headquarters and patrol station buildings.

Fire Prevention Bureau – Structural and vegetable growth hazard inspections and enforcement of fire prevention measures.

Fish and Game Warden – Protection of fish and game in cooperation with Law Enforcement Division.

Law Enforcement Division – Investigation and enforcement of Forestry, Fire and Game Laws.

Service of Supplies – Ordering and distribution of equipment and supplies, together with supervision of warehouse and fire tool caches.

Transportation Division – Supervision of mechanical transportation equipment and departmental trucking.

The five field divisions: Arroyo Seco, Soledad, Los Angeles, Malibu and San Jose, were evidently most appreciated by the County Board of Supervisors. In its 1927 report to the public, the following description was made:

"Each division is under the supervision of an assistant county fire warden, and the personnel is made up of junior assistant fire wardens, dispatchers, patrolmen and observers. (Lookout tower personnel.) The division organizations have been built up this year to a maximum of size consistent with available funds; as a result of the three-day intensive training schedule held at the commencement of the fire season, this department's mountainous fire fighting equipment is, no doubt, the most powerful of its kind in the country."

The touted "three-day intensive training schedule" was inaugurated on May 12, 13 and 14, 1927, at Camp Brewster, a private camp in the Malibu Mountains at the terminus of the Castro Peak telephone line. The training session consisted of the dissemination of information gleaned from years of experience by the existing wardens to the newly-hired men, and included a review and practice of all standard operational procedures. Also covered were firefighting tactics, operation and use of fire equipment of all kinds, fire prevention codes and their application and installation and repair of departmental communications equipment. This camp became a required part of the preparation for each fire season for many years, and was held at various camps and parks countywide.

It was during this time that another permanent organizational change was made. All warehousing operations on Lehigh Street were moved to the Pacoima Facility on Osborne Street in Pacoima and were placed under the supervision of Cecil R. Gehr.

Many new buildings were constructed at the facility, including an addition to the original warehouse, corrals for livestock, a blacksmith shop, oil house and carpenter shop. The well-established nursery at the Pacoima location continued to operate there for another 15 years, when it was moved to the town of La Puente.

From the Pacoima Warehouse carpenter shop, the first portable patrol station was fabricated. (Since year-round fire protection was not yet justifiable in some of the more remote areas of the county, portable patrol stations were established each spring that operated through the hunting and the fire seasons, and were then dismantled in the fall.) The facility was known as the Bulldog Canyon Patrol Station. Its patrolman, R.E. Christie, had a reasonably trustworthy Ford Model T, as well as a horse, to transport him over the roads and trails throughout the season.

Permanent Patrol Stations

Once locations were determined for substations in each forestry field division, permanent structures were built as quickly as funds became available. The patrol stations were not only of value as local fire stations, but served as offices where fish and game licenses could be issued and fire permits obtained. Seedling trees for flood control and erosion prevention were grown at each station, or brought from county nurseries for no-cost distribution to the public. This practice, although reduced in scale, still exists.

An often-overlooked feature of these stations was their enormous public relations value. They became a focal point where the citizens could find aid for almost any problem, a friendly gathering place and, most likely, the location of the only telephone for several miles around.

Although a few of the patrol stations were either designed to be temporary, or eventually phased out or moved, a number became permanent landmarks that remain in their original locations today. These include:

Soledad Headquarters – Located in Newhall. Presently Station 73, erected in May 1923 at San Fernando Road and Hart Street and shared with the USFS.

San Dimas District Headquarters – (Later renamed San Jose Division), located in San Dimas. Presently Station 64, originally a four-room frame building erected in May, 1926 at a cost of $878.

Malibu Division Headquarters – Located in the Malibu Hills in Topanga Canyon, presently Station 69, originally a three-room frame building erected in May, 1926.

Arroyo Seco Division Headquarters – Temporary location was at Altadena Park in 1927. It then moved to its permanent location in La Canada in 1929. Presently Station 82.

Pine Canyon Patrol Station – Originally placed in service in 1927 at the home of Harry Eshelman, near Munz Lake, who also had a field office in Kniep Hardware Store in Lancaster, where, he stated, ". . . The citizens were generally uncooperative." Presently Station 78.

Vincent Patrol Station – Originally a rock station with a shingle roof, constructed in May, 1927 for $940. Soledad Division. Presently Station 80.

Kagel Canyon Patrol Station – Originally a frame building moved from the Pacoima warehouse in May 1929. Located on Dexter Park Road. Presently Station 74.

Quail Lake Patrol Station – Built east of Gorman in June 1930 for $1,300, Soledad Division. Presently old Station 77, due to be abandoned.

Chatsworth Patrol Station – Built east of Santa Susana Pass in 1931, in the Malibu Division. Presently Station 75, on a new site.

Las Flores Patrol Station – Built in Las Flores Canyon in February, 1930, Malibu Division. Presently Station 70.

The entire F&FW staff gathers on May 19, 1928 in the auditorium adjacent to HQ during the first annual "School of Instruction" administered to all hands. Carson photo, from the collection of John Whelan.

All of the men of the LA Co. Dept. of Forestry were photographed in front of the newly-constructed federal building in downtown Los Angeles around 1933. A. Muench photo, LACo Forestry Dept.

Mint Canyon Patrol Station – Opened in October, 1932, at a cost of $1,139. Soledad Division. Presently Station 81, although moved into a new house east of the original site.

Padua Hills Patrol Station – Opened in October, 1932, San Jose Division. Presently Station 62.

La Cheusa Patrol Station – Opened in 1932 (temporary in 1931), Malibu Division. Presently Station 72.

Other permanent patrol stations that were built in the years that followed were: Castaic, Zuma, Monte Nido, Cornell Corners, Calabasas, Palmdale, Eaton Canyon, Escondido, San Gabriel Canyon, Big Rock, South Hills, Paramount, and Temple. Some locations still contain Los Angeles County Fire Department fire stations, although, perhaps, on a different building site.

The Fire Warden and Sheriff

For several years, a loose interpretation of the law had been followed by the field division personnel and the outlying patrolmen in that they could be used to "police" the areas within their jurisdiction. This was occasionally done in the absence of a deputy sheriff. One occurrence that helped develop a short-term remedy for law enforcement occurred on private property where a "no smoking" policy was in effect. From the Annals of the Forestry Department comes this description:

"On May 29, 1927, a very unfortunate happening occurred when Patrolman R.E. Christie and his brother, Harry, who was accompanying him on patrol, were attacked and severely beaten on Bulldog Canyon Road, Malibu Lake Club, when attempting an arrest of smoking violators. Harry Christie was the most severely injured, having a fractured skull, and lay for many days in General Hospital at the point of death, but eventually recovered. Three men implicated were arrested . . . the second trial sent the offenders to the penitentiary convicted of attempted manslaughter."

In response, the Forestry Deprtment was swift to institute what it felt was a justifiable change in policy. Again quoting from the Annals:

"This occurrence has occasioned a change in policy toward the carrying of firearms by deputy wardens and patrolmen . . . It (the department) has always felt that the public would not feel too kindly toward being approached by an armed man and ticketed in a fire or game case. However, since there is apparently a class of people who do not hesitate to convert a misdemeanor into a high felony, (and) rather than permit any further jeopardizing of the lives of the patrolmen of this department who have been thoroughly schooled in the proper approach and contact with the public, it was felt advisable to change the firearm policy, and the public can now observe our patrolmen equipped with a sidearm. It is believed that all law-abiding citizens will bear with the department in the arming of its personnel . . ."

This firearms policy did not *require* personnel to arm themselves, and with the increased number of deputy sheriffs in the field by the 1950s, the need for carrying firearms waned.

The ornamental nursery at Pacoima, constructed in 1925 and supervised by Ezra Miller. Photo was taken in October 1930. A. Muench photo, LACo Forestry Dept.

The Henninger Flats Forestry Dept. main nursery, circa 1933. Seedling trees from this facility were (and are) distributed throughout the county for flood control and reforestation. A. Muench photo, LACo Forestry Dept.

First field patrolman, R.E. Christie, with his Ford Model T at the Bull Dog patrol station in the Malibu Mtns., circa 1922. From the collection of John Whelan.

Firefighting and communication equipment carried in the back of the standard F&FW patrol truck circa 1930 and beyond. This is probably one of the 1928 through 1930 Buick trucks custom built by the mechanical shops. Jas. Foote photo, LACo Forestry Dept.

Foresters of the Malibu Div. in front of the newly-opened Paramount patrol station on the Paramount Ranch, circa 1928. The Ford Model T chemical engine belonged to Paramount Studios. LACo Forestry Dept. photo.

A better view of the Paramount Ranch's Ford Model T apparatus. This equipment appears to be entirely homemade. LACo Forestry Dept. photo.

Patrolman Al Jackson at the first Las Flores patrol station in Malibu, around 1927. This was one of the early portable stations. From the collection of John Whelan.

The Topanga Station of the Malibu Div. and its available fire equipment for local fire wardens and/or volunteers. Rack at left holds a dozen shovels. Rack at right holds 24 canteens and fire extinguishers. The warden's Ford Model T, and his assistant's Harley Davidson motorcycle complete the roster. Unknown photographer, from the collection of John Whelan.

A rare photo shows the "new" Calabasas patrol station in the Malibu Div., exact year unknown, but probably the late 1920s. Patrolmen Jack Albright and Joe Wernett are ready to roll. From the collection of John Whelan.

The Topanga patrolman, probably Bill Frownfelter, checks in at the Las Virgenes Cyn. call box on routine patrol, circa 1930. Such call boxes provided the only connection between the field patrolman and his headquarters. A. Muench photo, LACo Forestry Dept.

The long-forgotten Temple patrol station and Temple lookout tower on California St. near Peck Rd., east of Temple City. This was a two-man facility. It had a commanding view of the San Gabriel Mtns. before the advent of smog. LACo Forestry Dept. photo.

The Eaton Canyon station's apparatus barn. Except for different doors, the structure is unchanged today. The original 1934 White 250 gpm pumper/tanker is shown. LACo Forestry Dept. photo.

The Eaton Canyon Patrol Station in 1937, shortly before the front porch was enclosed for the captain's office. The bulk of east Altadena/Pasadena was still vacant. St. Luke's Hospital, left, center. LACo Forestry Dept. photo.

F&FW Patrolman Harry Merrill takes target practice while on Fish & Game patrol near Fairmont Reservoir in 1925. From the collection of John Whelan.

A reinactment of the assault on Patrolman Harry Christie, who was nearly killed by two uncooperative men whom he had told to stop smoking in the dry brush near Paramount Ranch. As a result of this attack, Forestry patrolmen were allowed to carry revolvers if they so desired. LACo Forestry Dept. photo.

F&FW Patrolman George Frownfelter lounges against his Ford Model T while on Fish & Game patrol near Fairmont Reservoir, circa 1925. From the collection of John Whelan.

The San Francisquito Dam Disaster

On March 13, 1928, the Los Angeles County Forestry Department was confronted with a type of disaster within its jurisdiction that it had never before experienced. From this one event alone, it could be clearly seen that the fire service in general – and L.A. County forces in particular, would be relied upon for help in any sort of emergency.

At 11:58 p.m. on March 12, a key dam in William Mulholland's Owens Valley-L.A. City aqueduct in San Francisquito Canyon gave way only two years after being filled with water for the first time. The 200-foot-high terraced concrete-and-rock structure gave way near the west end, not far from where it adjoined the steep canyon walls. A 100-foot wall of water thundered down San Francisquito Canyon, west of Bouquet Canyon near present Fire Station 111, and proceeded west through Station 76's district at Saugus. After it roared into the Santa Clarita Riverbed, then Ventura County, it eventually found its way to the Pacific Ocean south of the City of Ventura.

Four hundred and twenty people perished. Property damage was described as "in the millions." All three river drainages were scoured clean of structures, citrus groves, automobiles and livestock. While all public agencies responded to the emergency, the Los Angeles County Forestry Department played a key role in the disaster operations.

The reports of the collapse were received shortly before 4 a.m. by the Soledad Division dispatcher in Newhall. By 7 a.m., Chief Turner and Assistant Taylor were at the scene beginning an on-foot walk down the canyon to survey the problems and tag bodies as they chanced upon them. Assistant Davis had started up the canyon from the Harry Carey Ranch near Saugus, meeting Turner and Taylor halfway.

Chief Turner, responding to County Supervisor McClelland's directive, threw the full weight of the Forester and Fire Warden's office into action. Since all roads were washed away, temporary roads were built out of flood sand. In order to locate victims, pockets of flood water were pumped out with the department's portable Pacific pumps. Piles of debris were torn apart and later stacked and burned using the department's tractor in conjunction with available manpower.

L.A. County construction camps were temporarily erected using tents. One was located south of the Del Valle station and north of the Santa Clarita Riverbed, and another behind the former dam. Assistant R.L. Dunlap, in conjunction with the county coroner, coordinated the morgue activities in the town of Newhall.

Patrolman Heine Wertz was assigned to photograph the remains of the dam and remove for later analysis samples of the concrete that was supposed to bind the dam to the canyon walls.

All available Forester and Fire Warden vehicles were utilized at the height of activity to remove debris, reconstruct roads and transport food and medical supplies into the area.

Debris in San Francisquito Canyon being salvaged or piled and burned. A. Muench photo, LACo Forestry Dept.

A large center section of St. Francis dam following the failure of Mar. 13, 1928. The initial break was near a previous seepage location, left (west) side. Turbulence and vibration also allowed the right (east) side to give way. LACo Forestry Dept. photo.

An inspection crew examining the fracture in the St. Francis dam following its failing. The 200 ft. dam's breaking translated to an 80' high wall of water in the canyon below for many miles, scouring out everything in its path. LACo Forestry Dept. photo.

The Forestry Dept.'s #30 gasoline tractor clearing debris after the St. Francis dam collapse. The woman in the photo could be Forester Turner's secretary recording the events. LACo Forestry Dept. photo.

At one of the "spike" camps set up for disaster work following the St. Francis dam collapse. L. to r., foresters Hoag, Thrapp, Hosfeld, Gehr, Percey (L), Muench, Bodine, Cesena, Taylor, Jones, Carter, and Medaris. LACo Forestry Dept. photo.

Assistant Forester Clarence Thrapp shows that nothing was spared in the Santa Clarita Valley. A. Muench photo, LACo Forestry Dept.

The Santa Clarita Valley along HWY 126 was scoured clean of everything. A. Muench photo, LACo Forestry Dept.

While the state and county road departments, health department, sheriff's office, and others certainly assisted, the Forestry Annals state:

"During the rehabilitation work, it was brought out very forcibly in the minds of the personnel of the (Forestry) Department that, as usual, they did most of the hard and useful work while other departments received the glory."

The Great Cigarette-Cigar Experiment

On September 6, 1929, the Los Angeles County Forester and Fire Warden elicited the cooperation of the Rio Grande Oil Company, currently known as ARCO, to assist in an experiment relating to a fire cause peculiar to that time.

The "Air Age" was well underway, as was the then-fashionable (albeit deadly) habit of smoking cigarettes and cigars. Smoking while traveling in an airplane was quite acceptable. In fact, commercial airliners placed ashtrays at each seat. However, these

Asst. Chief Thrapp (Districts), Chief Assistant Forester Joe Davis and Asst. Chief Dunlap (Districts) prepare streamers for attachment to cigar butts in the "Great Cigar & Cigarette butt experiment" of Sept. 1929. A. Muench photo, LACo Forestry Dept.

A major portion of the top staff pose next to the California Flying Service's Lockheed "Vega" to commemorate the "Great Cigar and Cigarette Butt Experiment" conducted near the Pacoima warehouse. The photo was taken at Lockheed Airport, now Hollywood-Burbank Airport. Crown Aerial Photo Service photos, from the collection of John Whelan.

receptacles were not always utilized by the smoking public. Windows in early airliners could be readily opened, and, in smaller aircraft, an open cockpit was still common. With this in mind, the fire service wanted to know if a danger existed from a still-glowing cigar or cigarette stub thrown out of the aircraft into the open brushlands below.

A large field of grass and brush was located for the test in the vicinity of the department's Pacoima warehouse, located north of San Fernando Road and west of Osborne Street. (This site is presently the location of Whiteman Airpark.) Fire wardens stationed themselves every few hundred feet in the field, and, at 10 a.m. the Rio Grande Oil Company's Fokker Tri-motor aircraft took off from the Grand Central Air Terminal in the nearby city of Glendale. It circled the field location at various altitudes. At pre-arranged times, 30 lighted cigarette and cigar butts were dropped. They had brightly-colored streamers attached to indicate the height from which released.

Although it was quite a challenge to observe the fall of so small an object as a cigarette or cigar butt from 5,000 feet, no less than 21 of the 30 dropped pieces were located. A few small fires and one "good-sized fire" were started by some of the cigarettes and cigars. They were extinguished by the firefighters guarding the area.

It was noted that, the greater the height from which these objects fell, the greater the chance they had of igniting a fire.

The primary message the fire warden wanted to pass along to the public was that it was dangerous to discard smoking material from an aircraft.

The public received this advice through a feature article in the Los Angeles Times newspaper shortly after the experiment. However, there is no ordinance of record prohibiting such a practice.

Early F&FW Fatalities

When performing labor as inherently dangerous as firefighting and its attendant activities, injuries and, occasionally, death are perhaps inevitable. An assistant foreman, Clyde Radenmacher, age 18, was the first fatality in the field history of the Los Angeles County Forester and Fire Warden. On October 2, 1929, while working on the Shake Canyon fire road construction project (Saugus District) he was struck and killed by a falling tree being cleared for the road right-of-way.

On October 26, 1929, a fire broke out in a eucalyptus tree plantation in Downey. During the overhaul operations, Ray Metz was killed by a tractor. No details of this event found their way into the Annals, however.

On November 4, 1930, a wind-driven brush fire occurred in the Malibu Division on the Paramount Ranch, consuming 400 acres. it was named the "Picture City Fire," and was described in the Annals as being especially difficult to control due to erratic winds and rugged topography. Fire suppression man Ray Taylor was trapped by the flames and was severely burned. He died the following day.

These three men were the first fatalities, but they would not be the last, even in the early years of the department.

Special Events, People, Places and Things

A project, some three years in its development, came to fruition on June 18, 1927. The Forester and Fire Warden, along with a number of civic groups, gathered in upper San Dimas Canyon to dedicate a memorial to the late Forester Stuart Flintham. A small stone mound holding a plaque and a flagpole was dedicated in Flintham's honor, within a grove of pines he had planted seven years earlier.

On June 8, 1927, Harvey T. Anderson joined the forces of the Forester and Fire Warden. Anderson had just received his Master's Degree in botany from UCLA, and was hired as a patrolman and truckdriver at the L.A. Headquarters Division.

By late 1927, the first county line telephone link between the desert and the San Gabriel Valley was completed. It ran from the Acton Store in the Soledad Division to the Mount Gleason Lookout and the Colby Ranch behind Strawberry Peak to the USFS Arroyo Station, and finally connected with the Pasadena Division headquarters in the Pasadena main post office.

On October 30, 1930, Number 30 tractor, equipped with a bulldozer blade, helped fight a brush fire near Tapia Park in Malibu Canyon. This was the first such use of a bulldozer in Los Angeles County.

On May 3, 1929, the Forestry Department's first patrol boat, the "Ethel," was commissioned. Its duty was to patrol the Catalina Channel for fish and game violations. On its first patrol, the captain of the purse seiner Cleveland was arrested and fined $100 for illegal fishing. The Ethel had but a short career, however.

Personnel Matters, the Depression Years

Although the full effects of the Great Depression following the stock market crash of 1929 were not immediately felt in Los Angeles County, they did appear in due time. Several key decisions concerning personnel procedures and staffing occurred during this period.

Beginning in 1929, hiring for fire protection district personnel was subjected to the county civil service system for the first time. Forestry Department personnel did not fall under its jurisdiction until July 1, 1931. The system apparently did not quite compare with the plan in use today, as is revealed by careful examination of the following letter:

COUNTY OF LOS ANGELES

E. G. DAUPHINE
OFFICE MANAGER

DEPARTMENT OF FORESTRY
FIRE AND GAME WARDEN
SPENCE D. TURNER, FORESTER
11 BROADWAY ANNEX, 202 N. BROADWAY
TELEPHONE MUTUAL 9211

JOSEPH J. DAVIS
CHIEF ASSISTANT

LOS ANGELES, CALIFORNIA

Feb. 3, 1932.

Mr. Charles L. Johnson,
700 Ladera St.,
Pasadena, Calif.

Dear Sir:

There are thirty vacancies to be filled in this Department for position of Suppression Man, guaranteeing permanent appointment at $125 to start, provided satisfactory service is given. The Los Angeles County Civil Service Commission have certified your name to me as having passed the necessary examination, and therefore eligible for appointment.

In order that you may have no mistaken interpretation of the duties and nature of the work involved in this position, the following information is given to you.

At the close of this year's fire season and until the opening of next year's fire season, June 1st, 1932, there will be only nine Suppression Men assigned to station duty. The locations of these nine assignments are as follows:

Malibu Divn. Headquarters	2
Las Flores Patrol Station	1
Soledad Division Headquarters	2
Arroyo Seco Divn. Headquarters	2
San Jose Division Headquarters	2

During the winter months, the other 21 appointees will be assigned to any other duties that this office may see fit.

Plans at present contemplate the establishment of one or more camps in the field, working on such undertakings as telephone line construction, motorway construction, firebreak and trail maintenance and construction. While working in these camps, $1 per day meal deduction will be made. At the commencement of next year's fire season, sufficient assignments will be made from these camps to round out the necessary summer personnel in the Field Divisions, and the remaining number of Suppression Men will be assigned to some close-in camp job where they can act as an emergency crew available on short notice for fire control.

These appointments are the first rung in the ladder of forestry work in this County, and appointments can be made without further examination for position of Junior Assistant. However, it should be borne in mind that these positions are for emergency work, and no guarantee can be given that any appointee will be permanently located for any considerable length of time in any one locality or station.

If after taking into consideration the above conditions, you would be willing to accept appointment if offered it, I would be glad to have you advise me immediately in the affirmative. If, however, you decide to refuse appointment, I would also request that you send me immediate written notification of this fact in duplicate.

Yours truly,

County Forester and Fire Warden.

SDT-JP

The first Construction Camp #2 near the Arroyo Seco east of La Canada, circa 1931. Note that most of the buildings are portable. LACo Forestry Dept. photo.

Several foresters working to develop the Saddle Peak reforestation project in the Malibu Hills. Projects like this abounded during the late 1920s and 1930s. A. Muench photo.

An early Fire & Game Warden badge from the late 1920s and early 1930s. Obviously an active member did not have the word "retired" on his badge. A. Muench photo, LACo Forestry Dept.

When in 1926, all of the construction efforts of the Forester and Fire Warden were consolidated under the direction of L.S. Percey, a number of camps, usually temporary, were scattered throughout the mountains of the county to accomplish specific projects. By 1931-32, Camp #10 in the San Dimas Division was made permanent on an experimental basis and was manned with 18-year-old "juvenile delinquents." Its success led to the building of a series of similar camps that would house both paid and incarcerated men to work as firefighters.

The men who supervised juvenile construction camp #10 were enthusiastic about the potential of the system. This is revealed in the diary entry of straw boss L.L. Lang, whose crew was working on the Sunset Motorway, located south and west of Mount Baldy.

"This year, the work was new to me, as I had never had experience handling juvenile delinquents. Many real problems were encountered, and, in most cases, solved. During the early history of Camp 10, the Forestry Officers received little assistance from the Probation Officer in charge working out ways and means of getting production. For this reason, the task seemed hopeless, but, after trying various methods, a plan was evolved by the inauguration of a competitive system, charted daily, which credited each boy with the work actually done. The idea worked right from the start, and at the end of the year, production was almost doubled, and morale much improved. Owing to the fact that Camp #10 was experimental, much satisfaction was enjoyed by the forestry men in the knowledge that it had emerged into a useful adjunct to the Department's set-up. All the work was done on the Sunset Peak motorway during this year. Owing to a legal restriction, no fire suppression work was allowed. We are still hoping some way can be found to have a selected group detailed as 'firemen.'"

Twenty years hence, the first major public note of the work of this camp would be made, albeit in a tragic manner. By then, its number would have been changed to No. 5, and all the other camps would have undergone renumbering as well.

A chronological history of the various camp numbers, dates of openings and closings, relocations and alterations of funding sources will not be attempted here. Only partial information is available, and while a complete history might be interesting, to submit only a partial listing might prove frustrating to the true historian.

Suffice it to say that numerous temporary and permanent construction camps have been utilized by the Los Angeles Co. Fire Department over the years. As well, selected "strike teams" of crews and their supervising captains and/or battalion chiefs from these camps have been utilized on large fires all over the western United States. Crews numbering from one, to occasionally four or five, are special called on a contract basis by the Los Angeles City, Glendale and Burbank fire departments each summer for brush fires in their jurisdictions as these entities cannot support or justify the year-round maintenance of such camp crews.

Since the 1930s, the work of these camp crews has formed an integral part of the departmental battle with the "Devil Wind." As long as the ground cover in the Southern California hills continues to be subjected to periodic wildland fires, their work will continue to be highly valued.

A close-up of the dedication plaque on the Flintham memorial in upper San Dimas Canyon. A. Muench photo, LACo Forestry Dept.

The faces of Dorothy and Elinor Flintham, the late forester's daughters, say it all, at the dedication of the 20-acre Flintham Forest in upper San Dimas Canyon in June

1927. Judge Cuzan, of the San Dimas Township Court, delivers the dedicatory address. LACo Forestry Dept. photo.

A Decade With The Districts

In reviewing the gestational history of urban fire departments, it may be noted that the first fire station was usually located near the center of town. Additional stations were built as the town gradually expanded outward. In 1923, Los Angeles County had no "center"; rather, it consisted of numerous small townships scattered throughout the unincorporated areas. When the California State Legislature passed Act 2583 (which went into effect August 17, 1923), a great rush ensued to form fire protection districts in the territory surrounding and including most of the unincorporated towns. Thus, the third-largest fire department on the West Coast was about to be created – all in a matter of a few months.

The County Board of Supervisors delegated the task of coordinating the districts' formation to the County Forestry Department. Assistant Warden Norman C. Johnson was put in charge of the process. He called for elections and presented the requests for district formation to the board whenever election results in a given town were in the affirmative. After each district was formed, arrangements had to be made for temporarily housing fire apparatus until permanent stations could be constructed. Men needed to be hired to operate the apparatus and contracts drawn up with the myriad of local water districts for installing adequate water mains and fire hydrants. Warden Johnson was given the title of assistant chief engineer, and was placed in command of all fire district operations under the direction of Forester Spence D. Turner.

The table on page 54 shows Los Angeles County fire districts for the years of 1923 and 1924, the period during which almost all of the districts were formed.

Most district companies were formed from already-existing volunteer fire companies. Correspondingly, the first men hired tended to live within the districts hiring them. The now-paid firemen earned $100 per month. Engineers were paid $125, and captains made $150. These salaries served as compensation for being on duty what amounted to all the time. However, as it was not uncommon to have a fire telephone extension installed in the captain's or a fireman's home, some allowances could be made for the phone-owner to have a day, or at least a few hours, off once in a while.

Apparatus for the new companies was housed in rented garages. The Ford fire equipment was left over from the volunteer days. The American LaFrance and Seagrave units were loaned to the districts by

An asst. chief's badge of a Forestry Dept. member assigned to the Fire Protection Districts Div. LACo Forestry Dept. photo.

American LaFrance pending the arrival of the first shipment of 15 of that company's Type 75 triple combination pumpers. Several REO-Obenchain-Boyer rigs were also purchased, along with five Model K-3 450 gpm triple combinations built by the Stutz Fire Engine Company of Indianapolis, Indiana.

Within a year or so of the districts' formation, a permanent fire station was built in most districts and assigned a number. Most of these first permanent stations are no longer in fire department use. Some have been torn down, others converted to commercial buildings, churches and – in at least two instances – private homes. (Station 28, in Flintridge, has been completely remodeled, and is now an award-winning residence.)

Throughout the years 1924 and 1925, as the fire districts became more firmly established and stabilized, a number of changes materialized. American LaFrance sales records for this period show its 750-gallon-per-minute, rotary-gear, triple-combination pumpers to be in service in the fire districts of Altadena, Belvedere, Belevedere Gardens, Downey, Green Meadows, Home Gardens, Howard, Laguna, Lennox, Lomita, Maywood, Mira Monte-Florence-Graham, Signal Hill and West Hollywood-Sherman (two).

Stutz apparatus was in service in Bellflower, La Crescenta, Lawndale, Norwalk, Santa Fe Springs and Tujunga-Sunland.

REO-Obenchain-Boyer equipment served in Artesia, Baldwin Park, Clearwater-Hynes, Flintridge, Puente, Temple and Walnut Park.

The Walnut Park District was formed in December 1924, and the Temple District was dissolved in 1925. Signal Hill became an incorporated city in July 1925, and left the fire district.

Personnel were added. The Belvedere Gardens District employed eight men; the Hollywood-Sherman District had two stations and 11 men. The Howard District moved out of its leased garage into a new station in March, 1925.

It was soon discovered that the 350 gpm REO-Obenchain-Boyer apparatus were too small for the task assigned. Those districts that could afford to do so sold their REOs, or traded them in on heavier equipment. The Forestry Department absorbed some of the REOs – a process later judged to be illegal because of fire district tax base regulations that did not allow F&FW and district funds to be comingled. Nevertheless, at least two of these little fire engines remained in first-line service for over 20 years.

FIRE PROTECTION DISTRICTS FORMED 1923-24

District	Date Formed	Person in Charge	Station Location	First Apparatus
Santa Monica Canyon	9/4/23	None	None	Unknown chemical
Signal Hill	9/4/23	Lester Krepps	Cherry Ave. N. of P.E. crossing	American LaFrance 750 triple
Bellflower	12/17/23	A.C. Conrad	Unknown	REO, 2 Fords
Belvedere	12/17/23	Harvey Reynolds	Brooklyn & Gage	Ford Model T 1-ton
Clearwater-Hynes	12/17/23	None	None	None
Downey	12/17/23	H.W. Lewis	Unknown	Hand-drawn chemical
Green Meadows	12/17/23	Harry J. Nord	108th & Main	Unknown hose wagon
La Crescenta	12/17/23	C.J. Young	130 Hermosa	None
Laguna	12/17/23	C.D. Jones	Whittier & Record	Kissel car chemical hose
Lawndale	12/17/23	Herbie Smith	5th, N. of Market	Seagrave chemical
Lomita	12/17/23	Charles Smith	Narbonne Ave. (Cent. gar.)	Ford Model T chemical
Maywood	12/17/23		Slauson & King St.	None
Miramonte-Florence-Graham	12/17/23	H.F. Wood	1508 E. Florence	Seagrave chemical
Norwalk	12/17/23	J.R. Hunt	1405 N. 1st	Ford Model T chemical
San Dimas	12/17/23	J.S. McIntyre	Various garages	Hand-drawn chemical
Palmdale	12/17/23		Water dist. garages	Hand-drawn hose cart
Santa Fe Springs	12/24/23	A.J. Marty	Four Corners	Graham chemical
Bell	12/31/23	J. Carroll	Chamber of Commerce Building	American LaFrance pumper
Moneta-Gardena	12/31/23	Homer Sprague	None	No activity
Tujunga-Sunland	12/31/23	Harry Rice	Privage garage	American LaFrance pumper
Lennox	1/28/24	No activity		
Puente	1/28/24	Harry C. Apgar	None	None
Artesia		No activity		
Belvedere Gardens	2/4/24	R.K. Dere	Whittier & McBride	Ford chemical
Baldwin Park	2/18/24	J.E. Kennedy	140 E. El Monte	American LaFrance pumper
Hollywood-Sherman	2/18/24		7518 Santa Monica Bl.	Seagrave chemical
Howard	2/18/24	T.F. Schneider	No activity	
Flintridge	2/25/24	No activity		
Temple	2/25/24	No activity		
Altadena	2/28/24	J.R. Bittle	Lake Ave. & Marchetta	Dodge Bros. Touring auto
Home Gardens	5/12/24	No activity		

CHANGES IN FIRE PROTECTION DISTRICTS 1924-1925

Santa Monica Canyon	–	George Lewis in charge.
Signal Hill	–	No change
Bellflower	–	George C. Elsey appointed captain. Stutz 450 gpm Model K-3 pumper placed in service on April 23, 1924 (Cost: $7,500). One man employed.
Belvedere	–	750 gpm American LaFrance rotary-gear pumper placed in service at 4503 Brooklyn Ave. in a rented garage. Ford placed at 5198 Eugene, also in a rented garage. Ten men employed.
Clearwater-Hynes	–	REO-Obenchain-Boyer 350 gpm pumper placed in service on September 25, 1924. Two men employed.
Downey	–	E. Metz, new captain. Chemical moved to 117 E. First St. American LaFrance 750 gpm rotary pump triple combination placed in service on September 25, 1924. Two men employed.
Green Meadows	–	Fire station constructed at 108th and Main St. at a cost of $5,500.
La Crescenta	–	A.R. Duncan appointed captain. Stutz 450 gpm Model K-3 pumper placed in service on December 5, 1924. Call men used. One man employed.
Laguna	–	H. Warrick appointed captain. Kissel automobile turned in on an American LaFrance 750 gpm pumper, August 9, 1924. Four men employed.
Lawndale	–	R. Franklin appointed captain. Stutz 450 gpm Model K-3 pumper delivered December 22, 1925 and housed at 5412 Market St. One man employed.
Lomita	–	American LaFrance 750 gpm rotary pumper delivered on September 3, 1924. (Cost: $10,450.) Housed in Myers' Garage. Lot purchased at 2934 Weston. Three men employed.
Maywood	–	S.O. Meyers appointed captain. Four men employed.
Miramonte-Florence-Graham	–	Building leased at 1553 E. Florence. Graham District leased at 8500 Graham Ave. American LaFrance 750 gpm pumper placed in service on October 10, 1924. Twelve men employed. Capt. E.W. Jordan.
Norwalk	–	Roy Yeager appointed captain. Stutz 450 gpm Model K-3 placed in service on December 17, 1924. (Cost: $7,500). Two men employed.
San Dimas	–	No change.
Palmdale	–	No change, but collected $264 in district taxes, of which $11.10 was spent. This was, by far, the smallest district budget in the county!
Santa Fe Springs	–	G.G. Griswold appointed captain. Used a Shell Oil Company shed to house a 450 gpm Stutz K-3 pumper that was delivered on December 22, 1924. The Graham chemical rig was then retired. Three men employed.
Bell	–	No change.
Moneta-Gardena	–	No change.
Tujunga-Sunland	–	Stutz 450 gpm K-3 pumper delivered on August 18, 1924, and placed in a rented garage, location unknown. One man employed.
Lennox	–	No change.
Puente	–	On January 21, 1925, a 350 gpm REO-Obenchain-Boyer pumper was placed in service at a cost of $5,285. Two men employed.
Artesia	–	Lewis Boers appointed captain. A 350 gpm REO-Oberchain-Boyer purchased for $5,285 and placed in Boers' garage at 17th and Main St. One man employed.
Belvedere Gardens	–	A 750 gpm American LaFrance rotary pumper placed in service, housed at the rear of the Red Mill Theatre. Ford chemical rig retained and moved to 742 Williamson St. with one man. Eight men employed.
Baldwin Park	–	A 350 gpm REO-Obenchain-Boyer installed on January 28, 1925, and moved to new quarters at 118 E. El Monte St. (leased). One man employed.

Hollywood-Sherman	– A 750 gpm American LaFrance rotary pumper installed at 7808 E. Santa Monica Blvd. on October 1, 1924. On April 1, 1924, a similar engine was placed in service at 875 Westbourne, Sherman. Captain George Plympton was in charge of both stations and 11 men were employed.
Howard	– An American LaFrance 750 gpm pumper was delivered on September 15, 1924, and housed in a leased garage at 10518 S. Normandie. A new station was built at 1348 W. 99th Place and occupied March 19, 1925. Six men were employed.
Flintridge	– On January 24, 1925, a REO-Obenchain-Boyer 350 gpm pumper was delivered to Inverness and Glen Eagles, the equipment yard for the Flintridge company. John L. Cates was appointed captain on June 24, 1924, and two men were employed.
Temple	– Captain K.L. Grogan was placed in charge of a 350 gpm REO-Obenchain-Boyer pumper that was housed in a private garage (leased) on Agnes St. This district was dissolved on June 23, 1925.
Walnut Park	– District was formed December 23, 1924. A 350 gpm REO-Obenchain-Boyer pumper was placed in service at 2705 E. Hill St. A.J. Kelly was placed in charge, with one man plus four call men.
Altadena	– On October 1, 1924, a 750 gpm American LaFrance pumper was placed in service at the Piedmont Garage, Lake Ave. and Marcheta St. J.R. Bittle was captain, L.V. Merrill, enginer and Marion Smith, fireman. A lot for a permanent station was donated by L.G. Collison at 910 E. Foothill.
Home Gardens	– A.W. Swanson was appointed captain July 1, 1924. A 750 gpm American LaFrance pumper was delivered to 9844 San Gabriel (a leased garage and quarters) on October 30, 1924. The crew consisted of two men plus a call man.
Las Flores Canyon	– Formed February 24, 1925. No activity.

The following alphabetical listing of the districts summarizes activity up to 1933-34, prior to any move toward eventual consolidation.

FIRE PROTECTION DISTRICT CHANGES 1926-1933

Altadena, E-11	– Station 11 constructed at 910 E. Foothill, October 25, 1925. Rescue No. 1, a 1927 Lincoln, donated by Archie Andrews, body built by F.D. shops, placed in service March 7, 1928.
Altadena, E-12	– Station 12 constructed in 1928 at 2760 Lincoln Ave. Cost: $12,368. A 1928 Seagrave 750 gpm centrifugal triple placed in service at a cost of $12,150. W.H. Franklin and Marion Smith were the captains in charge. The district personnel numbered 14. In March 1932, a 15 hp Caterpillar tractor was purchased for maintaining firebreaks near the hills and clearing vacant lots in the district.
Artesia, E-30	– On January 1, 1925, a REO-Obenchain-Boyer apparatus placed in service. Captain L. Boers in charge; two call men.
Baldwin Park, E-29	– Captain J.L. Morin, two firemen and five call men.
Bell	– Incorporated on August 27, 1928 and left the district organization.
Bellflower, E-23	– Brick building rented at 464 Somerset damaged by earthquake, March 10, 1933; later reconditioned and reoccupied.
Belvedere, E-1	– On February 15, 1926, lot purchased for a new station at 154 N. Gage. Captain A.L. Lowrie in charge with 10 men in 1933.
Belvedere, E-32	– On May 20, 1926, station opened at 1407 Eastern Ave. Cost: $12,650. A 1926 American LaFrance (cost: $12,750) in service. Six men were assigned to each station. Captain V.T. Keyes was in charge of Station 32. (Note: Belvedere is commonly known as "City Terrace.")
Belvedere Gardens, E-3	– Building at 4921 Whittier Blvd. sold March 11, 1932. A new building at 760 Ferris St. was occupied and a lot purchased for a second station.
Belvedere Gardens, E-22	– Building at 922 S. Gerhart opened with a 1931 American LaFrance 750 gpm rotary pumper. Captain W.F. May was in charge at Station 3; Captain L.W. Costello at Station 32.

Central Manufacturing	–	This district formed on October 21, 1930, for the purpose of installing fire hydrants. Belvedere Gardens FPD handled the calls.
Clifton Heights	–	Formed on September 20, 1926 for the purpose of installing hydrants. Response was from the cities of Redondo Beach and Manhattan Beach at $25 a call; Lomita's Engine 6 responded to large fires.
Casa Verdugo	–	Formed on February 1, 1926. Dissolved April 17, 1926; annexed to the city of Glendale.
Clearwater-Hynes, E-31	–	On February 20, 1929, the station moved to 415 N. Paramount Blvd., rented quarters. Captain S.D. Hogan was in charge. This district suffered heavy damage in the March 10, 1933 earthquake.
Downey, E-10	–	No changes through this period. Four men employed.
East Montebello	–	No fire station. Formed June 27, 1927 for the purpose of installing hydrants. City of Montebello responded.
El Porto	–	No station. Formed to install hydrants. Lennox or Lawndale covered the area at no cost.
Flintridge, E-28	–	On December 3, 1928, a lot was purchased on Inverness Dr. west of Chevy Chase Dr., and a station constructed there for $18,986. On December 15, 1930, a 750 gpm Seagrave centrifugal triple-combination pumper was placed in service. The original REO was sold to Lancaster. By 1933, seven men were employed.
Green Meadows	–	Annexed to the City of Los Angeles February 18, 1926. Became LAFD Engine Co. 64.
Hollywood-Sherman, E-7	–	Station constructed on previously-purchased lot for $18,980. Ten men employed there.
Hollywood-Sherman, E-8	–	No change except for increase to 10 men employed.
Home Gardens	–	Annexed to City of South Gate August 20, 1928. Became South Gate Engine Co. 2.
Howard, E-14	–	No changes. Capt. T. Schneider in charge; eight men employed.
La Crescenta, E-19	–	Concrete-and-stone fire station at 2537 W. Foothill Blvd. built. Occupied April 23, 1930. Cost: $8,719. Capt. F.J. Lee in command of two firemen and four call men. Capt. W.E. DeLamere in command in 1933.
Laguna, E-2	–	No changes. Unable to construct a permanent station due to shortage of funds in 1933.
Lancaster, E-33	–	No changes. Capt. E.A. Kneip in charge with eight call men.
Las Flores	–	Dissolved October 22, 1928; Canyon annexed to Los Angeles.
Lawndale, E-21	–	Capt. L.W. Costello replaced by Capt. Jack Gregory in 1933. Three firemen and four call men.
Lennox, E-18	–	Lot purchased and building constructed at 4518 W. Lennox Blvd. for $5,100. Capt. John Hunt in charge with three firemen and three call men.
Lomita, E-6	–	Capt. Frank Laski in charge with two firemen and two call men.
Maywood, E-5	–	Dissolved on February 13, 1926; reformed on August 30, 1926 as Maywood District #2, covering an area between Maywood and Vernon. Walnut Park Engine 24 also covered this district.
Miramonte-Florence-E-9	–	Two-story brick station, occupied August 5, 1928, at 7313 S. Compton, cost $20,558. Capts. B.W. Jordan, H. Eastridge and W.L. Horne succeeded one another in quick succession.
Graham E-16	–	One story brick station constructed at 8614 S. Cedar (Holmes), opened July 27, 1929. 1924 American La France pumper in service as Engine 16. Capt. E.W. Jordan in command of 7 men.
Moneta-Gardena, E-22	–	On April 3, 1926, a 750 gpm American LaFrance pumper was installed at 1328 Palm St. On August 1, 1931, the area incorporated as the City of Gardena. The company number of 22 was later reassigned to Belvedere Gardens.
Norwalk, E-20	–	On November 1, 1924, Roy Yeager was appointed as district captain. On December 17, 1924, a 450 gpm Stutz Model K-3 was placed in service. On August 22, 1932, R.C. Jones was appointed captain in

Palmdale, E-37	–	charge of three firemen and four call men. On October 30, 1930, an REO chemical and hose wagon was purchased from the Lancaster District. Deputy Fire Warden Frank Ikeler was in charge of one fireman and eight call men.
San Dimas, E-25	–	On August 1, 1926, J.S. McIntyre was appointed captain, and an American LaFrance 750 gpm pumper was placed in service at the San Dimas Garage, 18 W. Bonita Ave. Two firemen were employed.
Santa Fe Springs, E-17	–	On February 1, 1926, the company moved to a location north of Four Corners on Norwalk-Mills Rd. In May 1929, a 1,000 gpm Seagrave pumper was placed into service at a cost of $13,080.
Santa Fe Springs, E-15	–	On November 17, 1930, land was purchased next to the temporary quarters where a new, two-story, reinforced-concrete station was built at a cost of $30,080. In June 1931, a 750 gpm Seagrave costing $12,150 was placed in service as Engine 15. Fourteen men, under the command of Captains Thomas Cullen and E.T. Petersen, were working on a two-platoon system by 1932. A Stutz fire engine that had been in service was taken over by the Fire Warden as relief equipment.
Santa Monica Canyon	–	Dissolved on August 1, 1925.
Signal Hill	–	Incorporated on October 24, 1925. The company number 12 was reassigned to the Altadena FPD in 1928.
Tujunga-Sunland	–	Incorporated on December 13, 1926, and later annexed to the City of Los Angeles.
Walnut Park, E-24	–	Capts. Kelly and Lounsberry were in charge, with a two-platoon system and four call men. By 1932, six men were employed (three per shift). Heavy damage was experienced throughout this district as a result of the March 10, 1933 earthquake.
Walteria	–	Formed on March 12, 1926, this district was dissolved on March 7, 1927, due to its annexation to the City of Torrance.

Instant Supervision

Since the county territory now had what amounted to an "instant fire department," it followed that supervision of the dozens of fire stations would also have to be immediate. The districts were divided into three general areas, designated as battalions. Three men, each with a background in fire department supervision, were hired to be battalion chiefs. A. Heinzman came from the Monrovia Fire Department, Clarence Tillotson from the Los Angeles Fire Department and Assistant Fire Warden J.T. Baker from the Forestry Department. All received their appointments as battalion chiefs from Chief Spence Turner.

Chief Heinzman took the North Battalion, which consisted of all the territory north of the City of Los Angeles. Chief Tillotson had the East Battalion; Chief Baker had the West Battalion. The Los Angeles River was the dividing line. These battalion chiefs oversaw all business, public relations and firefighting activ-

Sparkling in their new dress uniforms and 1924 American LaFrance pumpers, the members of Sherman District Engine 7 and Hollywood District Engine 8 pose in front of Engine 7's garage. From the collection of Martin Rippens.

Belvedere District Engine 1 personnel, in full turnouts, appear proud of their REO Obenchain-Boyer pumper. The two men in white helmets are Chief Reynolds and Asst. Chief Henze. George Popovich and Richard Henze are two "jr. firemen" (runners). Others (l. to r.) are firemen Epp, Burtola, Windover, McLure, McLure and Burrett. These quarters, at 4503 E. Brooklyn St., were typical of the very austere dwellings first rented by the fire districts. Richard Henze photo, from the collection of John Whelan.

An interior photo of Belvedere District Station 1, circa 1924. A hot game of checkers may be in progress here. Richard Henze photo, from the collection of John Whelan.

Altadena District receives its new 1924 American LaFrance 750 gpm pumper at the temporary Marcheta St. garage station. L. to r.: Eng. Lance V. Merrill, fm. Marion Smith, unknown, Capt. Ira Bittle. Capt. Bittle's Dodge Bros. touring vehicle had been the only fire rig until this moment. Photographer unknown, from the collection of John Whelan.

Firemen Reynolds and Henze pose at Station 1 beside their new REO. Note chemical tank recharges on running board. Richard Henze photo, from the collection of John Whelan.

Three early badges as utilized in the East LA area. The asst. chief's badge is the only one of its kind ever made and is of great historical value, dating from 1920 to 1923. The lower badge indicates it is the first retired captain's badge. From the collection of Jackie Deere.

Engine 11's 1924 ALF parked in front of its new quarters at 910 E. Foothill, Altadena. Note salvage covers on top of fender. Dale Magee photo.

Fire protection at Olive View Hospital in Sylmar, circa 1926. The Cadillac ambulance and the 1926 ALF pumper were property of the hospital, and never left the grounds.

This was the only rig ordered by the LACFD with solid rubber tires. LACo Forestry Dept. photo, courtesy Floyd Stubbs.

Puente Fire District's 1924 REO-Obenchain-Boyer 350 gpm pumper, seen in front of its quarters about 1930. Water bucket full of wet gunny sacks on running board is for fighting small grass fires. From the collection of Dale Magee.

Capt. James S. McIntyre with Engine 25, in San Dimas. It's a 350 gpm American LaFrance that McIntyre kept at his house or shop. As a one-man station, he was ready to roll from either. Carson photo, LACo Forestry Dept.

Engine Co. 8 (l. to r.): Capt. E.J. Burkhart, engs. K.S. Williamson, D.C. Curry, firemen J.J. McHugh, N.C. Carson, E. Heyser, Roy Emmons, E. Reed and D.W. Woods. Carson photo, LACo Forestry Dept.

Home Gardens FPD was included in the incorporation of the City of South Gate, and its fire station became South Gate Station 2. Here, its unidentified crew poses with the original 1924 County American LaFrance. Photo by Glen Alton, from the collection of Dale Magee.

The Signal Hill Fire Dept., after forming its own city purchased the existing L.A. County 1924 American LaFrance. Note additional tank wagon, extreme left. Mascot, looking over the shoulder of the fifth man from the right, strikes a simian pose. Photographer unknown.

The department's first rescue squad, a 1927 Lincoln phaeton with special body built by the mechanical shops. This unit was donated to the Altadena district by Archie Andrews of that town. Its arrival eliminated the need for a fireman to respond in his private car on an inhalator call. Photographer unknown.

ities in their respective areas, and were responsible for the district captains' performance. Their offices were located at Los Angeles headquarters.

Hiring under county civil service procedures did not begin in the fire protection districts until 1929. The first district captains were usually whomever had been in charge of the volunteer department that the newly-formed district replaced. Whether or not a man was retained in his position of fireman, engineer or captain was largely determined by his on-the-job performance. This was judged in large part by the battalion chiefs, subject to a final review by Chief Turner.

Relatively speaking, the district captains had considerable power in their positions, and were expected to act in an independent, yet competent, manner, taking aggressive action in all situations. After all, help from the next district might well be 15 minutes or more away—much more, in some cases. If the battalion chief was not in his Los Angeles office or near a phone, he might not be notified of an incident demanding his attention for some period of time. Initiative on the part of the district captains was, indeed, a necessity.

District Training

On December 15, 1926, the first attempt by the fire districts to train their captains began. Several classes taught by assistants Davis and Thrapp were presented. The classes were held at Howard District Station #14. Whether these classes were repeated, or with what frequency they convened, is not known.

It was felt that captains should assist in the overall training in their districts by attending additional special classes. The City of Los Angeles had established an intradepartmental "fire college" that dealt with most aspects of performing as a fire department supervisor. On May 17 and 18, 1928, several key captains from the county fire protection districts attended this school at the request of Chief Turner. However, most of the training was of an "on-the-job" sort, for it would be many years before fire science classes would be offered to the entire fire service by local colleges.

From the time of their formation, some districts purchased resuscitators to aid firemen in combating smoke inhalation during and after fire operations. Occasionally, a member of the public would request the resuscitator during a breathing emergency.

Some districts allowed the public to receive "inhalator" service, and some did not. Controversy on this subject remained strong for several years, as some districts felt that the public might take "undue advantage" of the service. Whenever it was, in fact, used on a member of the public in a private dwelling, the resuscitator was transported to the scene by one of the on-duty firemen in a private auto.

Evidently, the policy of public use prevailed in the Altadena Fire Protection District, and that policy was given reinforcement by Archie Andrews, a wealthy resident of that township, who donated a 1927 Lincoln Phaeton to be used as Rescue Co. #1. The utility body for this car was constructed by the mechanical shops. Carried on board were extensive first aid supplies, a Stokes Litter (rescue basket) and, of course, the resuscitator.

Too Close a Call!

July of 1928 marked barely three years since Chief Flintham had died while still heading the Forester and Fire Warden Department. On the 7th of that month, Chief Spence Turner, along with several other members of his staff, almost met their demise in a spectacular fashion.

Engines 7 and 8 of the Hollywood-Sherman District had responded to a fire at the Russian Eagle Cafe, located at 6840 W. Sunset Boulevard. The 75-foot-by-100-foot, two-story frame restaurant was engulfed by a fire that was believed to be of incendiary origin. Soon after initial knockdown, Chief Spence Turner and Assistant Reinmuller, along with district captains Grogan and W.B. Klinger, began an immediate investigation into the cause of the fire.

Suddenly, a pocket of natural gas that had accumulated under the structure found a source of ignition. An explosion ensued, causing additional damage to the structure and injuring the investigating team to varying degrees. Most seriously injured was Chief Turner. He had been standing in front of a window on the first floor when the explosion occurred. The force of the blast blew out the window and knocked him onto the pavement outside. He remained in the hospital with serious injuries for 16 days. Turner was, however, able to return to full duty, but only after an extended recuperation.

The investigation of the fire was nonetheless a success. The individual who set the fire was arrested, convicted, and, due to the injuries to the firemen, sentenced to life imprisonment in the state penitentiary.

The Russian Eagle Cafe on West Sunset in Hollywood the day after the fire and explosion there that nearly cost Chief Turner and several others their lives in 1928.
A. Muench photo, LACo Forestry Dept.

Capt. W.B. Klinger works on the fire investigation at the Russian Eagle fire. A. Muench photo.

Fire Protection Districts and Forestry Field Divisions

While the county fire protection districts were going through their growth and adjustment periods, the frequency of structural fires in the mountain areas continued to increase. Forestry Department engines were committed to structural protection outside any district boundaries. The *Forestry Annals* notes two significant changes that occurred in the late '20s that helped this situation, and incidentally aided in the ultimate unification of the two agencies:

"Outside of County Fire Protection Districts, response by (Forestry) Field Divisions to structural fire was growing with each passing year. The acquisition of tank truck equipment was assisting materially in combating this class of fire. It was very apparent, because of the increased cabin construction in mountainous areas, as well as in the lowland outside of the

Fire Districts, that more and more structural protection would be necessary. With this in mind, on November 30, 1926, Assistant Taylor was instructed to draw up a schedule which would place various (Forestry) Assistants to receive fire apparatus drilling under (District) Battalion Chief Tillotson. Drills were held in various Fire Protection Districts, and proved to be an extremely worthwhile detail.

"During this year, a permanent Central Dispatcher was placed in the Los Angeles Office during the daylight hours, and this proved so successful in not only dispatching of apparatus to structural fires, but also mountain fires, that on January 1, 1927, a second man was installed, the two dispatchers working on a 24-hour two-platoon system. The first log entry was dated July 9, 1926. Not only did these dispatchers increase fire control effectiveness, but also that of routine business."

It was during the late '20s that the fire protection districts received a new name – *the Los Angeles County Fire Department.* As nearly as can be determined, the name had no formal christening. Rather, it simply grew into favor by usage over a period of time. The green Forestry rigs in the hills were differentiated by using the term "Forester and Fire Warden" to identify them. Their common name became just F&FW rigs, and they are still referred to in that manner today. In modern times, it is the *funding* that determines the name.

During this period, subtle forces came into play that would eventually point the two department sections toward unification. During the 1924 San Gabriel Mountain Fire, some district engines were utilized for pumping to large supply hoses as well as in direct structural protection. In the 1928 and 1929 fire seasons, a rash of serious fires, two of them structural, occurred in the Angeles Forest and Malibu Mountains. The Malibu Colony, located near Malibu Canyon Road and Pacific Coast Highway (presently Engine 88's district) experienced a major fire in which 11 homes in a row were destroyed. In 1929, the Munz Lake post office and market burned. (This is now Engine 78's district.) A multiple response of district apparatus with larger pumps and more manpower would certainly have assisted with these incidents. But none was available near these fires – no districts existed in the Malibu region. This meant, also, that no public funds for fire hydrants were available. What few hydrants did exist were installed voluntarily – often as a result of friendly persuasion from the local fire warden.

Unification and common jurisdictions were the ultimate answer to the problem. But more than a score of years was to pass before this could occur.

The Santa Fe Springs Getty Oil Fire

The town of Whittier, California lies at the north end of the coast plain, immediately south of the Whittier Hills. An earthquake fault, named for the town, long ago trapped a rich deposit of oil in the sand beneath the immediate area. After the turn of

A monitor (stream, lower left behind shed) keeps a "gusher" that's under tremendous gas pressure cooled down in Santa Fe Springs in the late 1930s. LACoFD photo.

The newly-delivered 1931 Seagrave 750 gpm pumper purchased for Santa Fe Springs Engine 15. Note the 2½" suction hose on a Chicksan swivel and the preconnected bypass hose used in conjunction with the Blake 4-way hydrant valve. Photographer unknown.

the century, a small town was established on the Santa Fe Railway line near a sulfurous artesian spring just south of Whittier. Ranchers began to plant orange groves, the town grew and the populace named the new town Santa Fe Springs.

Suspecting that the sulfur content of the ground water might indicate other deposits, exploratory drilling was initiated. At a depth of only 2,000 feet, oil was struck. The oil flowed to the surface under tremendous natural gas pressure, a feature that was to spell real trouble for the Los Angeles County Fire Department and the Getty Oil Company.

On September 15, 1928, a well being drilled in the "Buckbee Sand" struck oil under immense gas pressure, throwing rocks, mud and oil high into the

63

A giant tower of flame rises from ignited subterranean natural gas over a Santa Fe Springs oil field in 1925. This was thereafter referred to as the "Getty Oil Fire."
From the collection of John Whelan.

air. The gas ignited, creating a gigantic torch with flames 100 feet high. The gas pressure and radiant heat rendered the resulting roaring inferno totally unapproachable. Wooden oil derricks located hundreds of feet away burst into flame.

Five engines from the closest districts were dispatched to protect the exposures surrounding the fire. They had only limited success. Oil workers and firemen worked together, pushing over burning derricks toward the fire in an effort to prevent the fire from spreading further outward. Extinguishing the flames proved to be impossible by ordinary means. Nothing like this had ever been experienced by county firefighters before.

Petroleum and mechanical engineers were called on to assist. On their advice, an angular tunnel was constructed toward the well casing, 50 feet below its opening at ground level. An opening was next made in the side of the casing itself, and the gas was directed to an absorption plant. The gas was flowing at a rate of 30 million cubic feet per day, and not enough could be redirected. The fire continued to burn.

Finally, a large plate of steel weighing three tons, with a 20-foot chimney and valve attached at the top, was lowered over the casing by a huge crane. The ground near the chimney base was packed with mud to absorb the excess oil, while valves and lines were attached to direct the oil flow. With the success of these procedures, the valve at the top of the chimney was closed. The gas fire went out.

The crews involved in this incident had tried something new, under conditions of extreme hardship and danger. They somehow managed to succeed, stemming the flow of some 7,000 barrels of oil per day. Teamwork, innovative methods and Herculean efforts by the Getty Oil Company workers and the Los Angeles County Fire Department won the 49-day battle. This lengthy struggle was the first of many to follow, as the petroleum industry continued its expansion as a major enterprise in Los Angeles County.

Onset of the Great Depression Years

Almost from the very beginning of the fire protection districts, ongoing community growth constantly threatened to outstrip the resources available. Support services were no exception. In fact, with the coming of the Great Depression in 1929 and extending to the onset of World War II, adequate fire equipment and manpower were a constant concern of the entire Forester and Fire Warden Department. Adjustments were made as required.

Just prior to the Depression, two key changes were made in the districts' organization. These changes were to last for over a decade. Battalion Chief J. Baker left the districts and returned to the Forester and Fire Warden Department. Chief Turner then reorganized the district into two battalions. Battalion 1 (South) was placed under the command of Chief Tillotson. Battalion 2 (North) was under the command of Chief Heinzman.

Battalion 1	Battalion 2
Artesia	Altadena
Bellflower	Baldwin Park
Clearwater-Hynes	Belvedere Gardens
Clifton	East Montebello
Downey	Flintridge
Howard	West Hollywood
Lawndale	Sherman
Lennox	La Crescenta
Lomita	Laguna
Miramonte-Florence-Graham	Lancaster
	Palmdale
Moneta Gardens	Puente
Norwalk	San Dimas
Santa Fe Springs	
Walnut Park	

A special clerk's position was newly created to coordinate the districts' contracts and supervise the inventories.

As a result of the information uncovered by the clerk, A.J. Parks, it was decided that the fire protection district shops needed to become considerably more efficient. S.W. Dobson was replaced by a new master mechanic, Wallace E. Powellson. Powellson determined that the amount of work for the existing shops had seriously outgrown the space available. The *Forestry Annals* describe what followed:

"Detailed by the Chief Assistant (Davis), Powellson located a very suitable structure at 1406 Mission Road, Los Angeles, which was leased by order of the Board of Supervisors, and on April 1, 1928, Powellson and his personnel were moved thereto. This location was centrally located, and also adjacent to the County Mechanical Shops, making it possible for Powellson, by proper arrangement with the Mechanical Department, to use the latter Department's machinery facilities."

In October 1928, the Mechanical Department took over the fire protection district shops. As a result of this move, the shops' personnel became members of the Mechanical Department. This was done because the machinery and facilities of the Mechanical Shop would make it unnecessary to purchase heavy repair equipment, which was becoming needed as district apparatus deteriorated.

One of the projects of the mechanical shops was to convert the pumpers that had been delivered with soda-acid chemical tanks to pumpers with water tanks. (Water tanks could be easily resupplied from a fire hydrant, whereas chemical tanks were difficult to recharge in the field. This was important when operating in a rural environment.) Tank capacities on the units ranged from 80 to 120 gallons, depending on the space available.

By the end of 1928, the first general order governing fire protection district work was developed. Others were to follow, applying to various aspects of fire department activities. The first of these was Order No. 1, concerning flow testing of district fire hydrants. No. 20 was the district's "drill manual," a small pamphlet describing standard hoselays.

A district aid to supplementing manpower was the "call man." This personnel system was functioning well, and was of special significance during the Depression years, when district funds were scarce, and during World War II, when manpower was scarce. The call firefighter is still used to generate additional manpower in Battalion 5 (Malibu Mountains) and Battalion 11 (Antelope Valley).

Under Law 2583, the Board of Supervisors was empowered to "fix the wage or pay of employees," and the wage could be fixed in terms of "board, room, lodging, meals or other things of value." The County Counsel therefore had no legal objection to the Board of Supervisors fixing the wage of call firemen at a "cash figure ($25 per month plus $2 per drill) and a paid-up accident policy plus a sum sufficient to pay the premiums of such policy; such additional sum to be paid, of course, out of the funds of the district." This practice went into full effect on March 19, 1929.

Several of the districts, La Crescenta for example, had only one or two men on duty per shift. Where these areas were far removed from other districts, and yet near an F&FW station, a forestry engine was sent to help whenever a fire threatened to overwhelm the district forces. This custom helped the financially strapped districts immeasurably.

In June of 1929, a dinner dance was held at the Mayflower Hotel in Los Angeles for purposes of raising funds to found the Benefit and Welfare Association for members of the districts and their families. Captain Burkhart of the West Hollywood District coordinated the affair, which raised a whopping $9,000 from ticket sales and advertising donations for the program. (Amazingly, several copies of that program still exist and occasionally surface to be read with wonder by those unfamiliar with them.) The Los Angeles County Fire Department Band and Orchestra played at the gala, and a fine time was reported by all.

While an annual benefit dance was held thereafter, the system of payroll deductions in later years and outright donations from individuals and groups carried the Association. It remains a vital and active organization today.

During these early days of the department, it was a common practice for the captain on any engine to carry several nickels on his person. Field radio communications for the districts were a thing of the future, and additional help could only be summoned by telephone, with the exception of East Los Angeles, where a signal could be sent through the box alarm circuit.

The Los Angeles County Fire Department experienced an increase in fires of an incendiary origin during the Depression years. This was not uncommon throughout the United States during this financially-troubled era. The task of arson investigation for the county had been assigned to the Fire Prevention

The second station in Belvedere Gardens, Station 22, at 922 N. Gerhart St., with both shifts present. The 1931 American LaFrance was the only one of its kind purchased by the districts. At the end of the Great Depression, a department-wide switch to Seagrave apparatus was made. Carson photo, LACo Forestry Dept.

Both shifts line up in front of Flintridge District's 1930 Seagrave 750 gpm pumper at their station at 1028 Iverness Dr., circa 1932. The Ford Model A roadster pickup patrolled out of this station during the day. L. to r.: Capt. J.R. Bittle, Eng. S.C. Hancock, Eng. E.L. McClure, firemen W.A. Lee and H. Davis and Capt. W.L. Correll. Carson photo, LACo Forestry Dept.

Bureau in 1928. Until 1930, the bureau had sufficient manpower to conduct investigations, but, by the middle of 1931, the surge in criminally-originated fires prompted county officials to acknowledge that a change was needed.

On June 16, 1931, the Los Angeles County Sheriff's Office assumed the responsibility for all cases of arson. Certain Deputies received special training in arson investigation techniques. They were armed and had the backing of the entire sheriff's department whenever it was needed in dealing with the criminal aspects of arson.

Until 1931, the only firefighters lost during active duty had been three Forestry members. However, the districts' luck ran out during this year. While fighting a transformer fire located at the top of a power pole, Captain George C. Elsey of Bellflower District Engine Company 23 was electrocuted by a falling power line. This, the fire protection districts' first fatality, occurred on April 26, 1931.

Further Adjustments

By 1929, the following stations had sufficient manpower to allow them to operate on the two-platoon system: Stations 1, 2, 3, 6, 7, 8, 9, 11, 12, 14, 16, 17 and 28. The pattern was 24 hours on, 24 hours off, rather than the 10-hour, 14-hour system used by some other fire departments, such as the Los Angeles City Fire Department.

Gradually, as greater assessed property valuation provided more funds, sufficient manpower was added to allow all of the fire protection districts to operate on the two-platoon system.

With the establishment of permanent fire stations in each district, reliance on station personnel for public service assistance of all kinds increased. Public reports of hazardous conditions, fire code violations, need for first aid and all manner of other major and minor services were answered. The judgment call, determining what action needed to be taken, was (and often still is) in the hands of the on-duty district captain.

After only four years of service with county, Battalion Chief Tillotson resigned in the summer of 1932. Promotional examinations were given to fill his position. As a result, Captain W.B. Klinger was appointed to the rank of battalion chief, the first such appointment from within the ranks of the fire protection districts. Klinger, a name that was to become familiar to all within the realm of firefighting, was placed in charge of the South Battalion on August 1, 1932.

Norwalk FPD's 1924 Stutz 500 gpm pumper in front of the station in 1937. Photographer unknown.

La Crescenta District's Station 19 at 2537 W. Foothill, an example of the F&FW's construction technique of poured concrete with rock facing that was used throughout the 1930s. Capt. Lee, r., stands next to the 1924 Stutz 500 gpm pumper. Other personnel are not identified. Mt. Lukens can be seen just right of top center. Carson photo, LACo Forestry Dept.

The great changeover: a new 1924 American LaFrance 750 gpm pumper arrives for Belvedere District Station 1 in the summer of 1924. Much volunteer equipment, such as the Ford Model T chemical rig on the right, disappeared from the face of the earth shortly after the new equipment arrived at the paid department. R. Henze photo.

Fire Station 7 of the Sherman District in 1932. L. to r.: Eng. E. Artley; firemen M.E. Files, C. Fahrforth, R.A. Williams and J. McKelvey; Eng. B.S. Keufer; firemen C.E. Burkhart and E.E. Quietzsch and Capt. W.E. Delamere. The 1924 ALF, with original equipment, can be seen in the doorway. Carson photo. LACo Forestry Dept.

The Pre-war Years

Personnel of Altadena District Station 11 repair toys for underprivileged children of the district, circa 1934. Franklin (l.), Carl Burkhart (r.). Others are unidentified. A.A. Blakeslee photo, from the collection of Charles Blakeslee.

Although the stock market crash that initiated the Great Depression occurred in October of 1929, the ripple effect did not reach the Forester and Fire Warden Department with any measurable force until 1931. Its influence lasted through the '30s; however, it gradually eased as the effects of the Depression lessened in 1938 and 1939, and, later, as the nation began to gear up for World War II.

The net effect of the Depression on the department was a marked decrease in public funds available from taxes and from state and federal allocations. This, coupled with the previously discussed upswing in incendiary fires, curtailed the department's ability to function at its previous level.

In order to save funds, the annual week-long Fire School was held in the assembly room at L.A. headquarters rather than at Camp Brewster, Henninger Flats or some other distant outdoor campsite. In addition, the number of paid men in the Forestry Department, especially in the Construction Division, was reduced. Yet the need for funds increased to provide for additional paid supervisory positions. This need was created primarily because hundreds of homeless and unemployed men were being placed under the direction of the county to act as construction and conservation crews. In order to reduce layoffs of paid personnel, employees were asked to donate two percent of their salary back to the county in order to compensate men who would otherwise lose their positions.

The purchase of new and replacement equipment of all kinds was reduced to a minimum during the Depression. Nothing of any possible value was discarded, and what existed was carefully maintained. A typical example of this is found in the following memo from Spence Turner to L.S. Percey, the head of the Construction Division at Pacoima warehouse.

April 12, 1932

Asst. L.S. Percey:

At Vincent Station you have stored some old redwood poles salvaged from part of the Mint Canyon phone line. Soledad Division has made the request that if any of these are unserviceable for further use that they be permitted to retain them at Vincent to furnish floor for the hay barn.

As the Depression deepened, the County of Los Angeles had under its supervision 9,500 men of all ages. About 1,000 of them were utilized by the Forester and Fire Warden. Of the remainder, about half were involved in the Civilian Conservation Corps, commonly referred to as the CCC. The men in these camps were supervised by U.S. Army personnel when not in the field on work projects. The CCC was a subsection of the Works Progress Administration, the WPA, which was developed by Congress when it passed into law President Roosevelt's requested National Recovery Act.

The men in these camps did an enormous amount of work in the form of road construction, bridge building, firebreak maintenance and general building construction. All of the forester and fire warden patrol stations built during the early '30s were built by WPA crews under foreman Arthur Aikens.

This was accomplished in spite of the fact that the Forestry field supervisory staff was stretched to the limit. Assistant Warden L.S. Percey, in charge of the Construction Division, explained the situation confronting the department as follows:

"The bark of the Construction Division has many times sailed through troubled waters and stormy seas, which has all but caused the ship to sink. With the extending financial depression

Winter sets in at the construction camp on Mt. Gleason. Three feet of snow in one day trapped many workers here in December 1930. Photographer unknown, from the collection of John Whelan.

The line forms on the left in the barber shop at Mt. Gleason construction camp in 1926. Perhaps the cots behind the barbers were for the customers' recovery period. Photographer unknown, from the collection of John Whelan.

A temporary relief camp, location unknown, circa 1936. Note small ranches, orchards, palm and eucalyptus trees across valley, upper right. LACo Forestry Dept. photo.

Chow call at an unknown CCC camp, circa 1936. Note army-style mess kits. A. Muench photo, LACo Forestry Dept.

of the nation, the need has from time to time been stressed for the necessity of employing more men. This plan is greatly depreciated by the fact that the taxpaying group has demanded drastic cuts in operating budgets.

"The unemployment situation brought about by the general depression indicated a particular need for the alleviation of suffering among the unemployed without dependents. At one time, over 200 paid men were employed by the Construction Division, together with 225 Welfare men. Projects upon which the men were actively engaged were spread out over the four large Field Divisions, making the supervision of each crew extremely difficult."

Of the 11 paid camps in the field, four were closed down due to shortage of funds. However, additional welfare and CCC camps were gradually opened through the '30s, as described in the *Annals*:

". . . it was necessary for the welfare agencies to consider the establishment of additional camps for the homeless men, with the result that four camps of approximately 200 men each were established. The Haines Canyon Camp remained in operation. Three additional camps (were) located at Cobal Canyon, San Jose

CCC crews build a fire control motorway by hand near Gleason Camp. A. Muench photo, LACo Forestry Dept.

Off-loading CCC recruits at unknown station about 1936. Chief Asst. Forester Joe Davis (l.), Forester Spence Turner, unidentified army officer and Warden Roland W. Percey (r.). A. Muench photo, LACo Forestry Dept.

Division; Brewster Ranch, Malibu Division; and Mitchell Ranch, Mint Canyon, Soledad Division."

Assistant Percey's description continues:

"Through the efforts of the department, and particularly the Forester himself, four CCC camps were allotted to Los Angeles County for operation on fire protection projects located for the most part on privately-owned lands where cost of improvements would not enhance the value of the property. These camps . . . included Malibu Mountain, P-221, established at Earl Canyon, Arroyo Seco Division; Cobal Canyon P-225, three miles north of Claremont in the San Jose Division; and Salt Creek, P-227, situated 15 miles east of Saugus on the Newhall Ranch, Soledad Division.

"Despite the difficulties of management and the handicaps encountered, splendid progress was made on the various projects which will add to the much-needed fire protection facilities within the county. At Mint Canyon Camp, a number of artisans assisted in the construction of the new Mint Canyon Patrol Station, and (it) is a monument to their best efforts."

(The Mint Canyon Patrol Station became Fire Station 81.)

Many State Relief Camps (SRA) were scattered throughout the county as well, and the hundreds of men working in those facilities were utilized on an "as-needed" basis by the County Forester.

As the Depression waned and the military began to prepare for World War II, the men in these programs gradually were absorbed into the armed forces and defense industry.

Today, in battalions 2, 4, 5, 6 and 11, many examples can be found of the construction accomplished by the men in all three programs.

An asst. warden and juvenile crew conduct roadside weed removal, circa 1939, location unknown. LACo Forestry Dept. photo.

A new arrival at Forestry-operated Construction Camp #10 in San Dimas is shown where to report for work by the warden in charge, circa 1936. This scene was repeated hundreds of times throughout the Great Depression. LACo Forestry Dept. photo.

A probation dept. construction crew cuts a fire trail, circa 1933, location unknown. Working or safety gear was nonexistent. A. Muench photo, LACo Forestry Dept.

Driver Reinmuller and his marvelous 1927 Pierce-Arrow bus used by the Forestry Dept. to transport juvenile probation crews from Camp #10 near San Dimas to various construction projects. A. Muench photo, LACo Forestry Dept.

Patrolman "Bill" Williams sits astride his mid 1930s Harley Davidson patrol vehicle somewhere in the Soledad Div., revolver at the ready. These bikes were utilized by the Forestry Dept. extensively until after WW II. Jas. Foote photo, LACo Forestry Dept.

Grass Canyon horse patrol station about 1930. This was located near the head of Little Tujunga Canyon north of Pacoima and southwest of Mt. Gleason. Only rugged individualists needed apply for this position. Photo by A. Muench, LACo Forestry Dept.

An unidentified starlet is designated an honorary fire warden in front of the Topanga Station (presently Station 69). This was one of the many benefits of being a county forester in 1928. Unknown studio photo.

The Role of the Patrolman

All through the Depression years, the Forestry Field Division continued to maintain its motorcycle patrol force. Several people who were involved at the time have stated that Forester Spence Turner believed also in using horse patrols whenever possible. Motorcycle Patrolmen C.L. "Chuck" Johnson of the Pine Canyon Patrol Station and Ward Kleinsmith of the Paramount Patrol station had their equestrian counterpart in H. "Heine" Wertz of the Arroyo Seco Division, who patrolled daily on horseback. His La Crescenta patrol route was along the foothills of the San Gabriel Mountains from the Arroyo Seco to Tujunga and back, a distance of some 12 miles. Horses could travel anyplace a motorcycle could, and many places where a motorcycle couldn't. This was particularly valuable in reaching backcountry regions and isolated farms and ranches.

These patrolmen were the department's closest and best contact with residents in the wildland/urban interface areas, just as they are today. In addition to issuing fire permits, posting signs, enforcing fish and game laws, spotting incipient fires and enforcing fire prevention codes, patrolmen also performed the all-important function of first-level public relations with the citizens. Everyone in these areas knew that the patrolman's intent was to serve and protect his jurisdiction. In general, this feeling still prevails. Today's one-man patrol vehicle, with its 100 gallon water tank, 300 feet of 1-inch hose, medical aid equipment and miscellaneous firefighting tools, plays a vital role in the overall fire protection efforts of the Los Angeles County Fire Department.

All of the personnel of the San Jose Div. (N.E. County area) pose in front of the San Dimas office in 1932. Front row (l. to r.): Joe Trout, Clint Bowman, Monty Shorey, unk., Al White. Second row: Ralph Pleasant, Bob Lawrence, unk., Art Boyles. Third row: George Reichart, Sam Trout, Al Schwartzkopf, John Weisbrod, Sid Wheeler, Bill Frownfelter. Fourth row: Al Cordes, Ken Carter (div. head), Russ Ireland. Carson photo, LACo Forestry Dept.

Forestry Dept. field personnel learn how to string telephone communication lines in the field. Hundreds of miles of such line was strung and maintained by the F&FW for over 40 years. A Muench photo, LACo Forestry Dept.

A display of telephone communications equipment used by the F&FW, circa 1933. Photo was taken at Arroyo Seco Div. HQ in La Canada. Warden Roland W. Percey is on the right. A Muench photo, LACo Forestry Dept.

A leased early Curtiss biplane operated out of Monrovia Airport during the early 1930s in service of the Forestry Dept. A. Muench photo, LACo Forestry Dept.

The crew of Pumper E, a 1924 White 600-gallon tanker, practice 1" hose evolutions and operate the monitor on the rear of the tank, location unknown, circa 1930. LACo Forestry Dept. photo.

An unidentified 1931 Moreland pumper and crew assist in controlling a weed-abatement fire. The first 10 ft. alongside each road was generally burned out each spring as a fire prevention measure. Photo by A. Muench, LACo Forestry Dept.

Early-style "no smoking" sign ready to be erected in the brush-covered hills of the county, circa 1932. Box at lower left holds firefighting hand tools for volunteers and conscriptees. Arnold Muench photo, LACo Forestry Dept.

Intelligence Div. Head Barney Paul shares information after a flight with Asst. Forester Claire "Spider" Meridith. Location unknown, about 1934. Dick Whittington photo, from the collection of John Whelan.

Newly-appointed Asst. Warden Harvey Anderson with his 1930 Ford Model A in front of the Kagel Cyn. patrol station in 1932. This was a live-in station, with families allowed. Current Station 74 was constructed on this site. LACo Forestry Dept. photo.

Asst. Warden L.S. Percey's mobile lighting plant, circa 1937. It was used for providing electrical power to the main fire camp during extended brush fires. A. Muench photo, LACo Forestry Dept.

Personnel of the Soledad Div. (Newhall) pose in the warden's 1929 Buick circa 1932. Carson photo, LACo Forestry Dept.

Fire Wardens Dan Barnes and Cliff Machin pose in 1932 with their 1929 and 1931 Ford Model A's in front of the first Eaton Cyn. patrol station, located about 500 ft. south of the present bridge on Mt. Wilson Toll Rd. in Eaton Cyn. Note the little house on the hill, center. Carson photo, LACo Forestry Dept.

The South Hills Patrol station with its first permanent building and a 1926 White 400-gal tanker/pumper. Personnel assigned to these units have stated that they were very low geared and slow on the road. These were the last Whites purchased. Carson photo, LACo Forestry Dept.

Looking very much like a roadside vegetable stand, the portable patrol station at South Hills (current location of Station 61), stands ready to protect the F&FW territory from the Covina Hills to the Whittier Hills, and from the Puente Fire Dist. to the San Bernardino-Orange Co. line, circa 1932. Its 1924 White "squad" had its 100-gal. water tank removed during the winter so it could be used to haul freight and men. The station building was folded up and stored at the Pacoima Warehouse. Carson photo. LACo Forestry Dept.

District Asst. Dunlap (l.), talks over plans with Chief Forester Asst. Joe Davis, F&FW Warden Spence Turner, HQ Staff Chief Tillotson and Staff Chief Meridith in front of their new 1929 Buick pickup, one of several custom built by the mechanical shops. LACo Forestry Dept. photo.

District and Field Division Growth

In the mid and late '30s, additional growth took place in both the Forester and Fire Warden field divisions and in the fire protection districts. Some districts annexed adjacent land, but did not add additional engine companies. This enabled these districts to increase their respective tax base income and, thus, add to existing company manpower. Eventually, the four-man, paid-engine-company, two-platoon system became the norm throughout the districts. A few districts never were able to afford this addition, however, and several engine companies continued to utilize call men well into the '40s.

In May, 1933, one new district was created in county territory adjacent to West Los Angeles. This was known as the Angeles Mesa District. It was served by adjacent districts until 1939, when a station was contructed and a Seagrave 750 gpm triple combination purchased. (This is presently Fire Station 38.)

The F&FW field divisions also expanded during this period, primarily in the form of new patrol stations and some new apparatus. Since the Clarke-McNary funds were not sent to the county treasury before being utilized by the Forester Department, the funds could be expended on whatever the forester felt was needed at the time, with the stipulation that they could not be used for anything other than Forestry purposes. The following improvements took place:

1932 – Padua Hills Patrol Station constructed northeast of San Dimas, on donated land, for $5,026. (Presently Fire Station 62.)
1934 – Eaton Canyon Patrol Station constructed in East Altadena, on donated land, for $5,700. (Presently Fire Station 66.)
1936 – A new Malibu headquarters completed at Cornell Corners, and a new Moreland pumper tanker installed. (Presently Fire Station 65.)
1937 – Monte Nido Patrol Station in Malibu constructed. (Presently Fire Station 67.)
Several new lookout towers were also constructed.

Throughout the 1930s, as fire-control motorways were constructed, 5,000-gallon tanks were installed along the routes. These tanks were filled either by rainfall or tankers. Dozens of them were installed over the years. Many during WW II were made of wood; the later ones were constructed of concrete. A 300,000-gallon cistern constructed in 1937 in the Topanga Canyon area of the Malibu mountains was called the Owen Catchment Basin. This fed local water mains by gravity.

Reorganization and Expansion

In order to better fulfill its multiple missions within the county, the Department of Forester and Fire Warden underwent both expansion and reorganization. A new division, called the Intelligence Division, had been added in 1930, its function being that of drafting, mapping and surveying – all of which had up to now been woefully neglected. By 1937, this division had been absorbed into the Construction

County-style hose drying tower in use at Arroyo Seco Div. HQ (currently Station 82), circa 1938. All of the structures and trees in sight are now gone, and the tower has been relocated. LACo Forestry Dept. photo.

A 1931 Moreland Pumper M was assigned to the San Jose Div. in San Dimas (currently Station 64). Here, it demonstrates the straight stream generated by a 1½" hoseline, circa 1932. Note Pacific pump mounted on top behind driver. A. Muench photo. LACo Forestry Dept.

Division, and the entire organization had been restructured. The following table reflects these changes.

Additional tables show an increase in fire protection. It will be noted that several districts were still without assigned apparatus, even though they

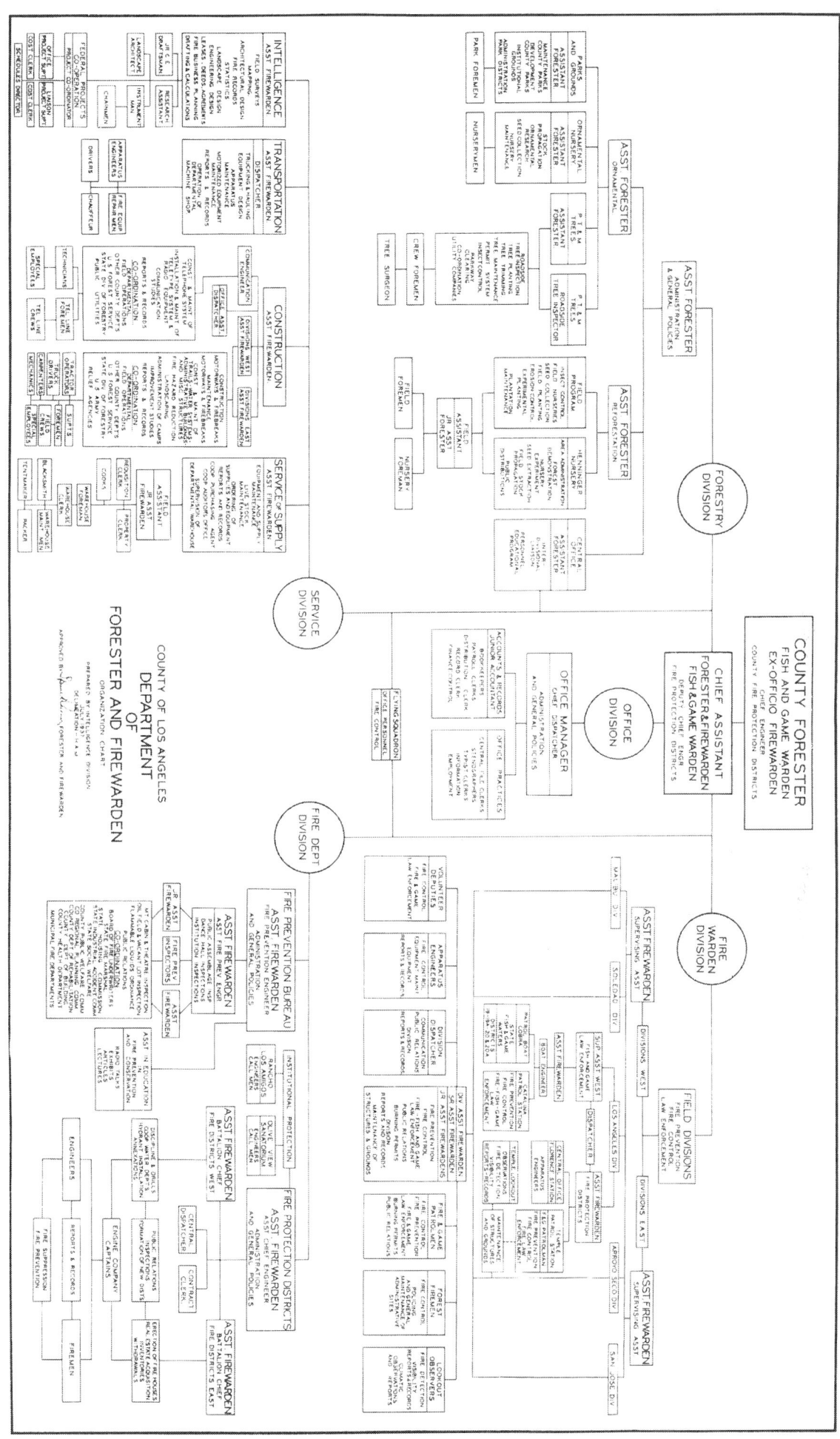

FIRE REPORT
LOS ANGELES COUNTY FIRE PROTECTION DISTRICTS

Name of Fire Protection District	Engine Co. Number	Phone Alarms	Still Alarms	Box Alarms	Total Alarms	False Alarms	Miles Run to Fires	Hours Motor Pumped at Fires Hrs.	Min.	Hours Worked at Fires Hrs.	Min.	Feet of Hose Laid at Fires 2½"	1½"	Chem.
Altadena	11	89	3		92	1	170.4	14	30	49	16	9100	1400	4550
	12	41	2		43	3	63.3	5	06	13	20	1700	200	3150
Angeles Mesa	38													
Artesia	30	28	24		52		59.4	8	30	21		1400	500	6800
Baldwin Park	29	25	16		41	1	70.5	9	40	25	57	1050	250	6300
Bellflower	23	51	21		72	1	102.5	10	47	31	36	2000	600	13800
Belvedere	1	139	11		150	4	309.2	20	47	77	41	8300	2900	9650
	32	157	15		172	3	470.7	11	39	93	16	3500	800	14500
Belvedere Gardens	3	84	8	52	144	10	246.0	9	09	45	51	3950	1200	7600
	22	121	9	51	181	8	549.0	25	54	108	26	6450	2600	15050
Central Manufacturing	13													
Clearwater-Hynes	31	53	18		71	1	183.0	21	42	47	58	4850	1600	10900
Clifton Heights	35													
Downey	10	29	11		40		85.5	5	29	17	08	2050	400	4800
East Montebello	34													
El Porto	27													
Flintridge	28	8			8		22.7		39	3	15			700
Hollywood-	8	72	2	1	75	3	70.1	4	30	24	28	3850	1150	4700
Sherman	7	91	3		94	1	75.2	4	54	26	34	4250	800	6200
Howard	14	78	6		84	1	123.6	7		30	34	3550	1500	4550
La Crescenta Valley	19	66	9		75		161.0	8	29	25	44	4250	100	5865
Laguna	2	61	13		74	5	98.4	10	43	38	2	5950	1450	7400
Lancaster	33	15			15		13.1	1	25	8	19	2550	100	1050
Lawndale	21	19	9		28		45.7	2	15	12	33	2250	650	1750
Lennox	18	59	9		68	4	93.5	7	50	27	08	5900	1400	6500
Lomita	6	29			29	2	41.2	2	42	11	03	1950	450	1750
Maywood	36													
Miramonte-Florence-	9	100	5		105	4	162.9	17	23	54	55	11350	1900	4275
Graham	16	95	2		97	4	79.2	12	11	35	56	6400	1500	3000
Norwalk	20	35	10		45		108.8	16	04	41	02	1450	600	4300
Palmdale	37	3			3		3.2			1	35			100
Puente	26	10	1		11		8.2		53	4	38	550	200	1000
San Dimas	25	13	2		15		17.4	3	17	5	44	1800	200	1950
Santa Fe Springs	15	79	7		86		513.5	23	32	62	57	8550	3650	10650
	17	22	2	1	25	1	78.4	2	23	41	07	3800	1100	1250
Walnut Park	24	37	4		41	2	22.5		39	8	37	550		600
Total		1709	222	105	2036	59	4048.1	270	02	995	40	113300	29200	164640

FIRE REPORT
LOS ANGELES COUNTY FIRE PROTECTION DISTRICTS

NAME OF FIRE PROTECTION DISTRICT	Eng. Co. No.	Loss to Improvements	Insurance on Improvements	Loss to Contents	Insurance on Contents	Total Loss	Total Insurance
Altadena	11, 12	$ 7,653	$ 101,775	$ 2,120	$ 102,121	$ 9,773	$ 203,896
Angeles Mesa	38	11,530	28,650	4,144	21,335	15,674	49,985
Artesia	30	1,372	14,000	300	1,000	1,672	15,000
Baldwin Park	29	2,619	26,150	707	5,200	3,326	31,350
Bellflower	23	2,481	95,000	1,569	33,450	4,050	128,450
Belvedere	1, 32	12,715	205,650	9,134	118,840	21,849	324,490
Belvedere Gardens	3, 22	9,337	138,920	4,121	28,829	13,458	167,749
Central Manufacturing	13	1,300	40,800	1,350	23,500	2,650	64,300
Clearwater-Hynes	31	2,612	239,365	1,487	98,850	4,099	338,215
Clifton Heights	35	75		10	1,000	85	1,000
Downey	10	1,566	32,650	575	7,500	2,141	40,150
East Montebello	34	687	1,182	978	350	1,665	1,532
El Porto	27	0	0	0	0	0	0
Flintridge	28	1				1	
Hollywood-Sherman	8, 7	7,065	2,161,580	7,338	1,730,435	14,403	3,892,015
Howard	14	3,637	25,440	1,117	3,080	4,754	28,520
La Crescenta Valley	19	1,692	33,690	1,575	12,500	3,267	46,190
Laguna	2	7,120	98,010	4,430	16,700	11,550	114,710
Lancaster	33	3,055	7,650	1,415	3,775	4,470	11,425
Lawndale	21	1,512	3,575	440	100	1,952	3,675
Lennox	18	2,425	16,300	1,155	2,800	3,580	19,100
Lomita	6	1,050	19,200	645	600	1,695	19,800
Maywood	36	2,094	4,500	650		2,744	4,500
Miramonte-Florence-Graham	9, 16	15,981	157,814	16,607	34,650	32,588	192,464
Norwalk	20	3,205	41,123	1,659	25,500	4,864	66,623
Palmdale	37	0	0	0	0	0	0
Puente	26	645	9,375	1,100	36,220	1,745	45,595
San Dimas	25	139	4,400	6	1,400	145	5,800
Santa Fe Springs	15, 17	6,991	100,195	5,530	31,020	12,521	131,215
Walnut Park	24	1,961	91,355	1,000	19,950	2,961	111,305
Total		$112,520	$3,698,349	$71,162	$2,360,705	$183,682	$6,059,054

FIRES RESPONDED TO OUTSIDE OF DISTRICTS

In unincorporated area	50
In the City of Beverly Hills	2
" " " Huntington Park	2
" " " Long Beach	1
" " " Los Angeles	7
" " " Maywood	1
" " " Montebello	3
" " " South Gate	4
" " " Whittier	1
Total	71

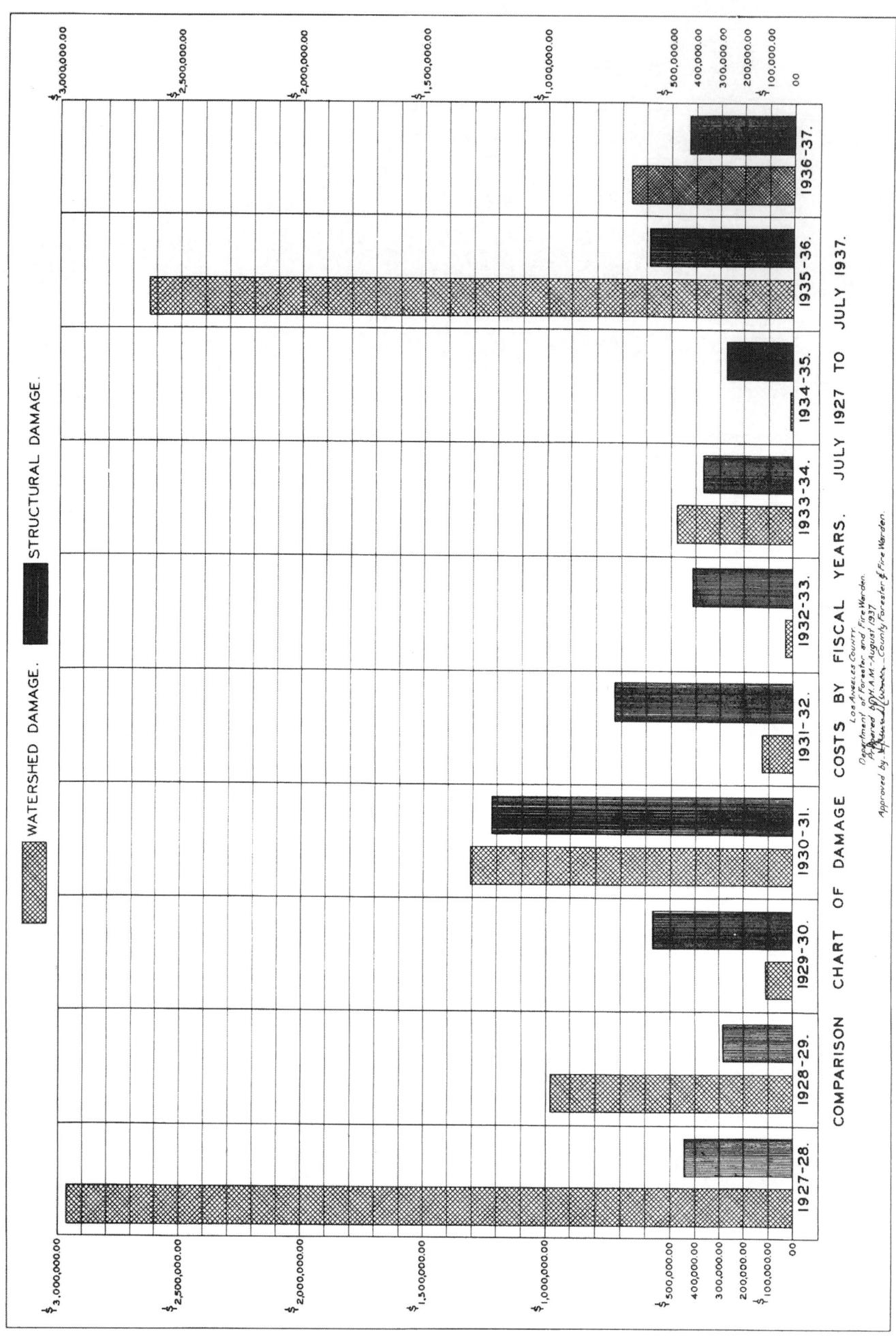

were given an engine company number. In every such case, a neighboring district handled the calls.

Forester and Fire Warden engines responded to areas between districts. This led to some very long response times in some areas of the county. This point alone encouraged more and more areas to annex to fire protection districts or form districts of their own.

In the years just prior to World War II, four districts were formed, and all but one had at least one assigned engine company, as can be seen below:

Bell Gardens, Engine Co. 39, formed January 27, 1940

Willowbrook, Engine Co. 41, formed April 9, 1940

Arnaz, (no engine)

San Gabriel Valley District, formed January 21, 1941 consisting of the following engine companies:

Engine Co. 4, South San Gabriel
Engine Co. 5, North San Gabriel
Engine Co. 42, Rosemead
Engine Co. 43, Five Points
Engine Co. 44, Duarte

Lakewood, Engine Co. 45, formed September 10, 1941.

Stations for these new engine companies, with the exception of Station 42, were constructed during 1942, shortly before building materials became scarce due to WW II's onset.

Stations 4, 5 and 44 used the new "Type I" floor plan configuration: an apparatus room having one door, but room for two engines in tandem, all living quarters along one side of the station and a built-in and enclosed hose-drying tower. As of this writing, only Station 5 remains extant.

The table on page 80 is an extension of the previous one. Of particular significance is the small section at the bottom that shows the number of fires outside the districts that were responded to by district companies. The large number of entries indicating "incorporated area" are indicative of a tendency by the fire protection districts to protect county territory, knowing that the Forester and Fire Warden apparatus would take much longer to arrive on the scene.

Post-Fire Critiques

While the L.A. County Forester and Fire Warden had a reputation for being progressive and innovative in its fire-control efforts, it was also eager to appraise itself of the actions and programs of other organizations to see what might be of material benefit. Such an application was made in the winter of 1933 when the "post-fire critique" was established.

The first critique focused on the 1932 fire season in L.A. County. Two verbatim entries from this critique's report serve to illustrate the process, which continues today to be a valuable tool for improving the efficiency of the department.

Chief Turner's cover letter to his men follows:

February 1, 1933

To Field Division Personnel,
Los Angeles County Forestry Department:

For the past nine years, Region Five of the United States Forest Service has annually employed the Board of Review method of studying their fire control problems, and careful investigation shows that their meetings have been an unqualified success. This success is undoubtedly due to the frank and impersonal way in which errors have been disclosed and analyzed, and to the fact that their personnel realized fully that the purpose of these meetings is not to "get" some unfortunate individual who has made a mistake but rather to bring out all commendable action as well as errors of judgment, so that the organization as a whole may accrue benefit from both.

In the past, to this Department, the term "Board of Review" has usually meant something unpleasant, inasmuch as it has been applied to hearings where it was already pretty well established that disciplinary action was necessary. Therefore, to get away from the odium attached to this term, it has been decided to use the term "Fire Control Conference."

This year sees our first attempt along this line, and doubtless our methods of approaching various problems will be improved as the years go by, it already having been decided that such a discussion should be held annually as part of the routine work of this department. The cooperation of all concerned will materially aid in the success of this plan.

Yours very truly,

Spence D. Turner
County Forester and Fire Warden

Of the six critiques in the first year's reports, there is one in particular that is notable. It covers every aspect of Fire #107, and is both brief and to the point. The fire occurred in the San Jose Division on August 11, 1932. Its location and acreage are not discussed, but the critique appears to be an excellent example of constructive criticism. It is followed by a brief critique from the Arroyo Seco Division.

San Jose Division
Fire 107
Carpenter Fire
August 11, 1932

We find that the report from San Jose Division concerning this fire was well prepared and presented.

The action record, consisting of the chain of elapsed time periods, was satisfactory. We further find that the organization was well directed and functioned properly.

The fact that the Patrolmen, scattered over the various Patrol Districts, were on the job and knew what to do is of importance. The action of the Suppression force, under the leadership of the Assistant personnel, functioned properly, as shown by the short Control Time.

It is apparent that the Division Assistant had the situation well in hand, as indicated by his contacts with Central headquarters and Patrol

The marvelous Pacific pump, shown here drafting from a canvas cistern, was used extensively by the F&FW from 1930 through WW II. Weighing 75 pounds, it could be carried by one man to any remote location to obtain water from a creek. It pumped a maximum of 38 gpm. LACo Forestry Dept. photo.

A Pacific pump en route to the scene of a fire, location unknown. During longer hikes, the two men probably traded cargo from time to time. Jas. Foote photo, LACo Forestry Dept.

Portable hand-powered "Indian" water pump/tank was used mostly for final overhaul work. Jas. Foote photo, LACo Forestry Dept.

and Suppression personnel.

However, we question the advisability of shifting the South Hills unit to a cover-up position at San Jose headquarters. This is brought to mind by the fact that there are as many, if not more, fires answered from the South Hills unit as from Headquarters itself. During the patrol action, the pumping equipment on the fire, although used to advantage, could have been sent to another fire in the Headquarters District almost as quickly as the South Hills unit, which had been moved up, should the necessity have arisen.

Another point of possible criticism is the use of the chemical hose. While it is true that a few minutes may be gained by the immediate use of the rubber hose, nevertheless, its unwieldiness on a long lay and possible loss of time entailed thereby would not warrant its being adopted as a standard practice.

While it is admitted and recognized that Asst. Carter was familiar with the conditions and probability of danger in the path of the fire, and used his own judgment in his plan of attack, yet it seems that it would have been advisable if he had established some sort of line of attack on the ridge immediately above the fire. The fact that the wind was carrying the fire front toward the ridge, with the possibility of spotting on the other side, would bear out this contention, and conditions were such that men would not have been endangered.

The use of water was evidently both effective and utilized to good advantage. This applies to the entire equipment brought into action on the fire.

Mopping up and patrol compares very well with control time and there is no criticism relative to this.

The cost of the fire, both as a total and in its breakdown, was reasonable, no particular item having been found to be excessive.

Discussion did not bring out satisfactorily that the fire was not of incendiary origin. Therefore, there is a possibility that there could have been more effort made in Law Enforcement.

We find that, taken by and large, the action of Assistant Carter on this fire was commendable.

Arroyo Seco Division
Fire No. 5
Oakmont Canyon
April 9, 1932

The Arroyo Seco Division is to be commended on its presentation of this fire, and the map accompanying it. Both were excellent and showed that considerable interest had been taken and effort expended.

One important consideration to be borne in mind concerning this fire is that it occurred in a period before the beginning of our regular fire season. This perhaps explains some of the apparent weakness or lack of concerted action. The fact that the fire occurred in a very dangerous and hazardous area but was suppressed without great loss is commended. While the entire action was generally satisfactory, certain details were brought out which should be considered. The first is the apparent delay in Report Time to the responsible agency. It was not determined why Deputy Lang took so long (22 minutes) in getting this report through to Headquarters. Apparent confusion at Headquarters relative to proper dispatching is evident. It is reasonable to suppose that if the Dispatcher had really tried, although it did happen to be his day off, he could have gotten some kind of conveyance to take him to Headquarters, considering that a serious fire was occurring in his Division.

Another point of criticism is the action of Deputy Noller in not returning to Headquarters with the pumper direct from the fire.

While the fire was under discussion, the question arose as to whether or not the proper use was made of tank wagon and water equipment. A survey in the field shows that there is no criticism justified, as in this case the distance was altogether too great.

The committee holding these critiques was made up of individuals in top staff positions. This first year's group included Spence D. Turner, forester and fire warden; Joseph J. Davis, chief assistant forester; L.G. Smith, assistant fire warden; J.E. Pemberton, assistant forester; and B.H. Paul, Engineer, Intelligence Division.

Exit "Ethel" — Enter "Cobra"

For the few years that the Fish and Game Patrol Boat "Ethel" remained in service, it never performed more than a stop-gap service. This was due primarily to its small size and small engine. It had no firefighting capabilities, a feature that could have been useful on many occasions, as boat fires occurred with regularity in county-protected waters. The impetus to replace Ethel with a more adequate craft received a boost in an unexpected manner.

From the Forestry Annals comes this report:

"For many years the need was recognized that a patrol boat be permanently stationed in Los Angeles County waters, as the several boats belonging to the State Fish and Game Commission rarely were stationed here. The desirability was forcefully brought out in a prior year when the Forester, (Turner) recuperating at Catalina Island from injuries received in an explosion, and seeing the great amount of violations being perpetuated by the commercial fishermen, chartered a speed boat and made wholesale arrests.

"On October 29, 1929, the Board of Supervisors consummated the purchase, for the sum of $6,000, of the Patrol Boat 'Cobra' used for law enforcement purposes in the Los Angeles Harbor, Channel Islands and shoreline waters.

On November 15, the Cobra had a trial run, on board being the Forester and several Assistants. The run to Point Vincent proved the worth of the vessel.

"The Cobra was scheduled to have two bases, one in Los Angeles Harbor at Wilmington, and the other at Avalon, Catalina Island, at the newly-constructed Patrol Station. Immediately upon the boat's commission into service, law enforcement measures were taken against the commercial fishermen who for years had their way."

Assistant Warden Lester G. Smith was assigned to the Cobra at a wage of $6 per day. Several excerpts from his diary serve to show the variety of duties his craft performed.

"July 25, 1931, 110-foot yacht 'Westward' burned in Avalon Bay. I could not make any headway in fighting it with the 38 gpm Pacific Pump.

"October 11, 1932, towed disabled fishing boat 'Santa Lucia' to safe anchorage off Topanga Canyon and called the Coast Guard to pick them up.

"May 21, 1932, while patrolling for net boats in the closed district around Catalina Island, we came upon the disabled sailing sloop 'Sea Hawk,' which had lost all her canvas. Crew was wet and cold. We towed them to Avalon, for which they were thankful.

"Starting May 27, 1932, we patrolled five days for the body of William Sherwood, who capsized and was drowned off of Italian Gardens, Catalina Island, but the body was not found."

The Cobra was a wooden craft, some 40 feet long. It required considerable maintenance, due to its heavy use. Warden Smith's diary continues:

"On June 14, 1932, we put the Cobra up on the ways for overhauling of its Hall-Scott engine, this being the first overhaul since the engine was installed. Replaced main and connecting rod bearings, piston rings, cleaned out circulating water passages and ground the valves. We put her in the water again on June 26, 1932."

Two small entries in Lester Smith's diary will show the origin of a "tempest in a teapot" scandal, the details of which were published briefly in the Los Angeles Times. Smith writes:

"August 22, Mr. Turner caught his first Marlin.

"September 15, took eight Marlin to Wilmington to be distributed among the needy."

The Times questioned the forester's use of county equipment for sport fishing, even though the catch was given to the destitute in the harbor area.

The March 10, 1933 Earthquake

Earthquakes occur regularly along the Pacific Rim and adjacent states. At unpredictable intervals, moderate to strong temblers can be expected to shake some portion of Southern California. Until 1933, no

The Cobra proceeds through Los Angeles Harbor waters. A. Muench photo.

Forester Ed Medaris uses the "Hauck" torch during a demo of backfiring technique, circa 1930. This torch was also used during roadside weed clearance in the spring of each year, prior to fire season. LACo Forestry Dept. photo.

Forestry field personnel demonstrate the field telephone during fireground operations. These units were in use throughout the 1930s, until the advent of the walkie-talkie radio, after WW II. Jas. Foote photo, LACo Forestry Dept.

Survivors stare in awe at the remains of a home the day following the Long Beach quake. Forestry Dept. members assisted with the demolition of such structures for several days following. A.A. Blakeslee photo, from the collection of Charles Blakeslee.

L.A. County Forestry Dept. motorcycles ready to serve, as sailors from Long Beach Naval Station march to their duty stations. A.A. Blakeslee photo, from the collection of Charles Blakeslee.

quake of any destructive magnitude had affected the county of Los Angeles since the beginning of its rapid urbanization in the 1890s. Much of the commercial and public assembly construction during that 41-year period was of the standard brick and mortar type – totally unreinforced, often with stone facades.

Exactly how many such structures existed was discovered rather suddenly at 5:56 p.m., March 10, 1933, when the Newport-Inglewood Fault moved.

The fault, which runs parallel to the famous San Andreas system, lies partially under the Pacific Ocean. It starts on land at Newport Beach and extends northwestward through Signal Hill and the Baldwin Hills, ending north of Culver City.

The epicenter of the quake was located offshore, three miles southwest of Newport Beach. Particularly hard hit were the cities of Long Beach and Compton, and about half of the total area affected was at the time within unincorporated Los Angeles County. The quake's magnitude was eventually calculated at 6.3 on the Richter scale, which is considered a moderately strong earthquake. But the damage was extreme, due in part to the nature of the subsoil in the area, and because of some substandard building construction.

The estimated number of deaths was about 120; the damage to property about $50 million.

In the unincorporated county territory, Forester and Fire Warden Spence Turner was placed in charge of fire control, rescue, body search, pulling down badly-damaged structrues vulnerable to aftershocks and general emergency operations.

Battalion 1's Chief W.B. Klinger and his staff set up headquarters at Fire Station 9 in the Florence District. All available Forestry personnel were pressed into service. Motorcycle patrolmen acted as

Four automobiles that were never again the same after taking simultaneous blows from the parapet wall of the building on the left. A.A. Blakeslee photo, from the collection of Charles Blakeslee.

A lone sailor guards against looting along a block of buildings that suffered heavy damage. A.A. Blakeslee photo, from the collection of Charles Blakeslee.

A Red Cross shelter in Lincoln Park the day after the quake. First aid equipment is at lower right. A.A. Blakeslee photo, from the collection of Charles Blakeslee.

A fireman stretches in a 2½" line at a Signal Hill refinery explosion near 27th and Atlantic. A.A. Blakeslee photo, from the collection of Charles Blakeslee.

This American LaFrance pumper from an unknown jurisdiction has laid out all its hose as its crew prepares to go to work on this side of the fire. A.A. Blakeslee photo from the collection of Charles Blakeslee.

message runners: the combination water tanker/pumpers were utilized not only for firefighting, but as sources of safe drinking water. Some Forestry personnel were loaned to other agencies to act as liaison or in whatever capacity was needed, often using department motorcycles.

Districts with only slight damage were Downey, Clearwater-Hynes, Belvedere Gardens and Howard. Moderate damage was reported in the Norwalk, Belvedere, Lennox and Laguna districts. The heaviest damage occurred in the Miramonte-Florence-Graham and Bellflower districts. Bellflower Station 23 was a total loss. Temporary headquarters were found at 906 Maple until the station could be rebuilt six months later.

In 1933, the fire protection district had 31 engine companies located in 29 stations, manned by 172 men. Many of these companies saw duty in the earthquake areas, and many were recalled to perform duties on an as-needed basis over the 10 days that followed. A total of 504 men from the Forestry Department and the fire protection districts were utilized in county territory and provided assistance to other cities.

Less than a month after the Long Beach earth-

Debris, missing pieces of automobiles and utter devastation attest to the power of the explosion which wracked Signal Hill. A.A. Blakeslee photo from the collecton of Charles Blakeslee.

This 1934 Ford received little protection from its shelter as the flood proceeded through this La Crescenta property. From the collection of John Whelan.

quake, another catastrophe . . . this one man-made . . . visited the vicinity of Long Beach. The Signal Hill, Long Beach, Los Angeles City and Los Angeles County fire departments joined forces to fight a massive petroleum fire which resulted from a gas explosion at the Meader gasoline refinery of the Richfield Oil Co. on the morning of June 2, 1933. All fire and rescue forces involved had their hands full for the two-day duration of the incident, as the initial explosion and resulting fire ultimately involved a ten-acre area of the refinery. Oil derricks, tanks, and office and housing structures were either immediately destroyed by the force of the blast, or subsequently set on fire by the rapidly spreading flames. Twenty persons were killed, and dozens injured by flying debris.

While precise details of the actions of Los Angeles County Fire units are not available, newspaper accounts of fire service action during this incident indicate that aside from rescuing injured persons, the main concerns were surrounding the fire to keep it from involving any more property, and the removal of excessive amounts of oil spilled from the ruptured storage tanks into dikes which were filled to overflowing by sudden surges of the product.

Twenty-five years later, Los Angeles County Firemen would find themselves repeating their actions in the same vicinity.

The "Pickens" Fire and La Crescenta-Montrose Flood

Occasionally throughout the brief history of Los Angeles County, an event has occurred which was both predictable and classic in form (such as the yet-to-come 8.0 + earthquake.) On New Year's Eve 1933, the district of Fire Station 19 (La Crescenta Valley) suffered the results of a brush fire-flood sequence which has yet to be equalled locally in intensity and life loss within the county.

Late in the evening on November 21, 1933, a brush fire began near the mouth of Pickens Canyon above Foothill Blvd. in the northeast corner of Station 19's territory in the La Crescenta Fire Protection District. Very dry Santa Ana weather conditions allowed flames to spread rapidly away from Engine 19's crew. The fire quickly entered the Angeles National Forest and territory protected by the L.A. County Forestry Department. General assistance was requested from both of these agencies.

Gusty and erratic winds allowed the fire to spread in several directions simultaneously. Engine 19 personnel worked with Pumper "G" from County Forestry District Headquarters in La Canada (now Sta. 82) to halt the flames along the south flank near Foothill Blvd. County Forestry District Pumper "M", from the San Jose Division (now Sta. 64), protected homes along the west flank near New York Drive. Pumper "J" from the Soledad Division Headquarters (now Sta. 73) worked along the east flank above homes near Earl & Hall-Beckly Canyons. Good structure protection was achieved, although a few structures were lost.

The main fire progressed to the north over the next two days, and burned Dunsmuir, Shields, Eagle, Pickens, Winery and Gould Canyons. It then burned west as far as Haines Canyon and east as far as the upper Arroyo Seco.

An interesting variety of equipment from several different agencies was used on this fire. The County Forestry Annals disclosed that "extensive use was made of Pacific Pumps and the C.C.C. boys in the canyon areas." Eventually the cities of Pasadena, Glendale and Los Angeles each sent pumpers to assist with this incident.

The use of L.A. County Forestry equipment was in excess of the county's share of the acreage burned. So, according to the agreement of 1924, the U.S.F.S. paid the county the sum of $1,481.07 to cover the imbalance.

By November 24 the "Pickens" fire was contained after consuming some 4,830 acres of prime front-country watershed south of the 5,000 ft. Sister Elsie Mountain (now called Mt. Lukens). Eleven major and minor canyons were denuded of vital protection from rapid run-off of water and topsoil in the event of a heavy rain. No flood control facilities had

The Pickens fire of November 1933, allowed heavy rainfall to inundate La Crescenta, center, and Montrose, lower right with mud and debris on January 1st, 1934. Large peak, top center, is Mt. Lukens. LACo Forestry photo.

as yet been constructed in this area of the county, so the intensity of the winter's rainfall would determine the likelihood of life or death and severe property loss for hundreds of persons in the Crescenta Valley.

December's rainfall had been about normal, totalling four inches in one two-day storm on the 14th and 15th. Then, on New Year's Eve, an intense storm moved into Southern California from the Pacific. Since this particular system moved slowly through the area, more rain was allowed to fall as the front passed. Abundant moisture was available in this storm, and as the bands of intense rainfall approached the slopes of the mountains, the uplifting action condensed copious amounts of precipitation from the clouds. In many foothill rain gauges, nearly one-half of the normal annual rainfall drenched the area in a 48-hour period, with peak rates reaching 1.30 inches per hour. Total rainfall in La Crescenta for the storm totalled 10 inches, with 14 inches recorded in the mountains to the north.

Los Angeles County Forestry and Crescenta Valley firemen had this scenario to contend with, as described by Mr. E.C. Eaton, then the Los Angeles County Flood Control Engineer.

"Starting at midnight of December 31, and lasting for an hour, there were a series of debris flows which destroyed or damaged 483 homes (property loss $5 million in 1933). Forty people were known to be dead, and 45 more were missing.

"The great volume of rain falling on the denuded drainage basin caused a large number of slides to occur from the mountainside and the steep slopes of the canyons. These slides were projected into the bed of the canyons. The flood waters apparently tended to accumulate behind this debris and push it out from the canyons onto the debris cones. These pulsations of water and debris are said to have occurred in waves as high as 15 feet, flattening as they progressed across the cones. It is estimated that these flows contained 70% saturated debris and 30% water by volume, and that the average velocity of this mass was five feet per second. This mass carried boulders of almost unbelievable size. One that was projected onto a paved street (Foothill Blvd.) at the mouth of Dunsmuir Canyon weighed just under 60 tons. Following this flood of water and debris, surveys were made to determine its volume, which was found to be 659,000 cubic yards."

Once again the County Forestry Department and District personnel were called upon to ameliorate a disaster in the Crescenta Valley. Immediate searches were begun for missing persons. Bodies of flood victims were retrieved. (The American Legion Hall was used as a temporary morgue.) Utilities to damaged homes needed to be severed, or otherwise rendered harmless to occupants and rescue personnel. A 3,000 foot 2½-inch hose lay was accomplished from central La Crescenta to western Montrose to act as a temporary water supply for that town.

Trucks from the Forestry Department were assigned

This home has a large load of mud and rocks against its north wall. From the collection of John Whelan.

This 1926 Chevrolet peeks out from behind a 60 ton boulder on Michigan Ave. (Foothill Blvd.). The completely bare Mt. Lukens is the large mountain at top, center. The mud flow was unimpeded due to lack of any ground cover following the "Pickens" fire. From the collection of John Whelan.

The 1935 Las Flores Cyn. Fire approaches the top of Lincoln Ave. in Altadena, burning downslope against the wind. A.A. Blakeslee photo, from the collection of Charles Blakeslee.

to this project; some of the personnel involved were actually detailed to the Sheriff's Department for the duration of the incident.

The severity of this incident inspired a complete investigation by the Los Angeles County Conservation Association, Mr. George Cecil, President. He stated in part:

"the 'Pickens' Canyon fire in November of last year, and the heavy rains of the first of January, have again brought forcibly to the attention of everyone the relationship between fire and flood. It has proved again, as it has repeatedly in the past, that the cover on the mountain sides surrounding the Los Angeles Basin cannot be trifled with. All of those who have been responsible for fire prevention activities have prophesied such calamities for many years, but the memory of man is short – he forgets easily. The necessity of protecting and renewing the watershed cover is increasingly apparent."

Thirty-five years later, the City of Glendora would hear the echo of these words.

Mission at Malibu

Over the years, the Los Angeles County Fire Department has responded to many types of emergencies. Wildland fires, impinging on structural development, continued to be a major source of fire loss, not only within the county, but throughout all of Southern California. Prior to 1934-35, several large fires of this type had been fought, each under its own individual set of circumstances. The summer of 1935 brought with it one of the major challenges in the life of the young department.

In the early morning hours of October 23, 1935, a fire broke out in an area north and east of Latigo Canyon in the Malibu Mountains. As is often the case in the fall and early winter months, strong winds out of the northeast prevailed, blowing at speeds estimated at over 50 miles per hour. These "Santa Anas," or "Devil Winds," were accompanied by corresponding low humidity and fuel moisture. The fire spread rapidly to the south and west, in the direction of dozens of homes and cabins in and near Latigo Canyon.

Past experience had shown that a direct attack during a high wind on a rapidly-moving flame front over 50 feet high was an exercise in futility. Lacking the water-dropping helicopters and fixed-wing, retardant-dropping airplanes of today, the department could only use the few bulldozers that it then possessed, along with a number of water-tanker pumping engines. Men armed with hand tools and backfiring were also utilized. The pre-cut firebreak-motorway could often provide the final control boundaries – if everything went according to plan.

The "Latigo Fire" burned rapidly toward the coast, and was controlled along this line by late the first night. To the east, at the mouth of Malibu Creek, a firing out operation was begun, extending to the north as far as Malibu Dam, a distance of approximately one mile. This was successful, and on the morning of October 25th, the winds died down as control was being achieved along the Mesa Peak firebreak from Malibu Dam west to the Castro Peak Lookout. Control of this sector of the fire seemed likely within the day.

During the afternoon of the 25th, the Devil Winds began anew, this time from a more northerly direction. This caused the fire to jump the Mesa Peak firebreak and hook around slightly toward the east –

Eleven chimneys and fireplaces represent all that is left of 11 cabins. Loss was approximately $500,000. A. Muench photo. LACo Forestry Dept.

A crew of hand firefighters work with shovels and tanker hoselines on the 1935 Latigo Fire in the Malibu Hills. Note the complete absence of any work-related safety gear. LACo Forestry Dept. photo.

A structure fire in a Santana wind destroyed 11 homes in a row in the Malibu Beach colony (currently Station 88's district) in 1929. Forestry Dept. tankers, which had no hydrants available, were unable to save the structures. LACo Forestry Dept. photo.

threatening once again to jump Malibu Creek and burn east toward over 1,000 homes and cabins near Topanga Canyon.

With careful coordination, firing out commenced, extending north from Malibu Dam to the junction of the Mesa Peak firebreak. Nine portable Pacific pumps were used to draft water from Malibu Creek at a point where the canyon narrowed. This operation was ultimately successful.

During the course of the fire, plans were being made to fire out the control line along the north and west flanks, using the firebreak that ran west from Castro Peak to the ridge above Latigo and Dume canyons and then turned southward. Adverse wind conditions held this operation in abeyance until the afternoon of the 26th. To aid in the operation, a long hoselay was made from the 5,000-gallon water tank atop Castro Peak. It was extended downward and along the control line. Seven Forester and Fire Warden tankers were used to resupply the Castro tank. By a shuttling procedure, the tank was kept full. One pumper was used to regulate the pressure in the lengthy hoselay.

Once again, careful coordination was employed. Chief Spence Turner described the action: *"On several occasions, particularly when the main fire made runs and met the backfire close to the firebreaks, a strenuous fight was necessary to keep the flames from crossing the emergency firebreak. Without the use of water lines it is doubtful whether the backfire would have been successful. Backfiring was first started from the lower end of the hoselay at the 2,380-foot elevation point. From this point to the Latigo Canyon Road, a distance of 2,500 feet, backfiring had been accomplished the previous night because topography and available water enabled us to do so with safety. Backfiring then proceeded down into the saddle, and once the saddle was reached, backfiring was started on the top of the main ridge at the 2,700-foot point. Simultaneously with this, backfiring was also started east along the main ridge; by noon of the 27th, this backfire crew tied in with the backfiring being done west of Mesa Peak. On this long run, only one breakover (slop-over) occurred, which was quickly controlled by the use of water lines from the tank trucks keeping pace with the backfiring crews.*

"Although backfires to the layman are the desirable thing, it is this department's practice never to use a backfire unless absolutely essential. This fire, however, was practically controlled by the use of backfires. The total mileage of backfiring from the ocean at Malibu Creek and along the main ridge between Mesa and Castro Peaks, then down into Dume Canyon, a few miles above the ocean to the west of Malibu Creek was 16.7 miles."

The hose lay used to back up this operation consisted of 2,600 feet of 1½-inch hose, with two 1-inch lines wyed off at 400-foot intervals. The total amount of hose used was 4,100 feet. Water consumption was calculated to be 13,500 gallons. The nine Los Angeles County rigs were assisted by a tanker from Beverly Hills, two U.S. Forest Service tankers and a voluntary tanker from Malibu Colony. The U.S. Forest Service and the California Division of Forestry also provided overhead and fire camp staff and equipment.

During the operations connected with the Latigo Fire, another blaze broke out 5 miles to the northwest, near Lake Sherwood. This fire burned south, and eventually joined the Latigo Fire along a common border. Both fires were eventually controlled after an infusion of additional men and equipment from other field divisions.

Of the 2,000 fire suppression men used on these fires, the large majority were from many Civilian Conservation Corps (CCC) camps, then in full operation through the county. Many of the men were released from a large brush fire in the Arroyo Seco Division that had consumed over 2,000 acres between Las Flores Canyon and the Arroyo Seco. This fire, located just north of Altadena, destroyed several homes in addition to the La Vina Sanitarium in Engine 11's and Engine 12's districts.

Other fires of a lesser magnitude were also burning elsewhere at this time, and men and equipment were released from them to join the efforts at Malibu, as allowable.

The fire operations at Malibu proved to be the forerunner of other campaigns utilizing similar techniques and provided an opportunity for the Forester and Fire Warden Department to hone its skills. The incident helped establish the Los Angeles County Fire Department as a leader in the art of wildland firefighting in both the eyes of the public and other professionals in the field.

A remarkably similar set of fires occurred 21 years later in the same area of the Malibu Hills. At that time, some personnel, such as Chief Harvey Anderson, could clearly recall the successful strategy used in the 1935 incident.

A Fatality in the Florence District

On August 11, 1938, a serious fire in the Western Candy Box Company at 1243 E. 63rd Street proved to be the final run for Fireman Bert F. Hancock, age 36, of Engine Company 9.

The two-story metal-clad frame structure was fully involved upon the arrival of Los Angeles County Fire Department units and was vigorously fought by Engines 9 and 16 for a period of two hours.

During the later stages of the fire, which was attacked mainly from the exterior, Fireman Hancock attempted to enter the second floor by means of a 24-foot ladder. He fell from the window sill to the concrete sidewalk below and was killed instantly.

Fireman Hancock became the second fireman to die in the line of duty with the L.A. County Fire Protection Districts.

Further Statistics and Data

A very thorough annual report was published by the Forester and Fire Warden for the period ending June 30, 1937. This report in several cases referred to statistical information from the preceding 10 years.

A chart in this report shows the severity of the 1927-28 fire season for the F&FW, due largely to a fire in the area adjacent to the Leona Valley as well as a rash of serious fires throughout the county. The 1935-36 fire season showed a large brush loss also, due primarily to the Latigo Fire in the Malibu area.

A rare photo taken on Feb. 7, 1939 showing the acceptance test of the "Galloping Ghost," Engine 20's 2,500 gallon tanker/pumper by Seagrave. Left to right: BC Glenn Griswold, Master Mechanic W.E. Powellson, designer of the apparatus, and Asst. Forester Adolf Heinzmann. Carson photo, LACo Forestry Dept.

Data on the pages that follow show the rolling stock assigned to the entire Fire Warden Department as of the summer of 1937. Most of the original tanker/pump equipment was still in service at that time. Some of the older automobiles used as staff cars and patrol cars had been replaced. The apparatus listed as "combination squad trucks" had their water tanks removed during the winter months and were used to transport personnel or cargo. Some of the patrol car (pumper) units carried Pacific portable pumps, and a few had the "Panama Pump," which was a small pump driven off of the vehicle's fan belt.

The Law Enforcement report and the list of field division structures showed that the use of horses and pack animals (mules) were still prevalent.

Also indicated is the extent to which the county telephone network had grown. Each field division, as well as Los Angeles headquarters and the Pacoima warehouse, operated its own switchboard with its own dispatchers.

Not reflected in these official reports is the fact that the Norwalk Fire Protection District placed in service a 2,500-gallon tanker/pumper fire engine. This was the largest capacity tanker west of the Mississippi, carrying 2,500 gallons of water. Designed by Master Mechanic Wallace Powellson, this unit required a special Department of Motor Vehicles permit to operate on California highways. It was built by the Seagrave Corporation, and left that company's Columbus, Ohio plant in January, 1939. It was assigned to Norwalk Engine Company 20, which was an area of few fire hydrants. As can be imagined, 2,500 gallons of transported water were welcomed at any fire scene! Dubbed "The Galloping Ghost," the big tanker served the county in several locations over a 20-year span.

Also not shown on any of the equipment lists is the Fish and Game Patrol boat "Cobra." The reason for this is unknown. By 1937, Cobra had seen much service, and her superstructure could have told many tales, could it but speak, such as the few times it was run off by armed Russian fishing trawlers whose crews were having no part of American fishing regulations.

While the superstructure might not have spoken, the Cobra's hull was making itself known by leaking from general deterioration and rot. Therefore, in the spring of 1938, she was laid up for the installation of running gear into a new hull and superstructure.

The motor and plumbing were again refurbished before the installation. The now practically-new craft was then recommissioned as the "Grey Gull" and launched in June of 1938. It remained in service until 1942; however, that's another story.

Warden "Captain" Lester G. Smith takes a sextant reading aboard the "Gray Gull" Fish & Game patrol boat somewhere in the Catalina Channel, circa 1938. This craft had a crew of two. LACo Forestry Dept. photo.

A 1939 view of Bn. 2's dispatcher switchboards in Station 17 in Santa Fe Springs. This equipment was typical of that used until the early 1970s in some locations. A Muench photo, LACo Forestry Dept.

An interesting ¾ view of the Galloping Ghost. The 55' aluminum ladder was later replaced with a 35' wooden ladder. Note four-1½" preconnected hose lines, and two 1" lines. Two long fog applicator nozzles are mounted high on the side. LACo Forestry Dept. photo.

The 300,000 gallon Owen Catchment Basin above Topanga Canyon in the Malibu Hills. This was specifically designed to catch rain water for use in supplying fire hydrants all along Topanga Canyon, circa 1935. Arnold Muench photo, LACo Forestry Dept.

Foresters demonstrate the use of Indian back pumps at Henninger Flats, circa 1937. A. Muench photo, LACo Forestry Dept.

The Forestry Department men gathered at San Dimas Park in May, 1934, following the annual forestry school. Warden Roland Percey, 2nd from left, shows that a softball game might be in the offing. From left: J. Trout, Frownfelter, Black, Gehr, Turner, Daries, Bollman, Carter, Thurston, Loggins, Kinsell, Huffman, Davis, Siegrest, Ireland, Ozanke, Kerton, Williams, Gardner, Van Wagner, R. Percey, Wertz, Hooper, Currier, Thompson, Cheney, Cesear, Kleinsmith, Hall, Barnes, A. Santa Maria, Clark, W. Santa Maria, Gibson, Cuthbert, Des Barton, Priest, L. Knowles, Anderson, Sam Trout, Taylor, Thrapp, Paul, Finn. LACo Forestry Dept. photo.

The 1936 pre-planning horseback cross-country trip conducted by Chief Turner for his top staff and field division supervisors. He did this each year from 1931 until 1941. This trip began in Newhall, then south via Oat Mountain through the Chatsworth Hills and into Bell Canyon (location of photo). After an overnight campout, the party terminated their trip at Brewster Ranch in the Malibu mountains, covering 25 miles.. Chief Turner insisted that all top staff personnel be intimately acquainted with the topography and fuel conditions of the County. From the collection of John Whelan.

The Trippet Fire

While the Latigo Fire of 1935 was still fresh in the minds of the residents of the Malibu Hills, those living further south and east along the range soon shared in the trauma and loss as they experienced their own wind-driven conflagration. This time, a prime residential neighborhood of Los Angeles was threatened. Before it was over, several prominent residents would owe much to the area firefighters.

On the last Wednesday of November 1938, David Trewitt, an employee of the Trippet Ranch of north Topanga Canyon, threw another binful of ashes into a leaf dump along the south edge of the ranch property. On this day, he had not waited long enough for the ashes to cool. The leaf dump soon ignited. A prevailing and sustained 35-mile-per-hour Santa Ana Wind spread the fire into the nearby grass and brush. Due to the increasing wind and extremely low humidity of that day, in no time the fire was off and running toward the coast.

Trewitt, as he later stated to the press, attempted to fight the fire himself. The ranch had no telephone, and thus he was unable to report the fire. At 12:30 p.m., the Los Angeles City San Vincente Lookout spotted the fire from its easterly position. At 12:31 p.m., the L.A. County Oat Mountain Lookout, located 17 miles to the north, reported the smoke. Cross referencing placed the fire almost due north of the L.A. County Forester and Fire Warden's Fernwood Station (presently Fire Station 69). Assistant Warden Cecil Gehr and his crews immediately responded to the scene.

Winds were now gusting through the canyons from the north at speeds reaching 60 miles per hour.

The new Malibu Division H.Q. building (currently Station 65) just prior to occupancy in 1936. This poured concrete and frame station is still in use. This was also the later site of the Malibu dispatch center. A. Muench photo, LACo Forestry Dept.

Warden Gehr placed his crews in a position that would protect the many homes and cabins in Fernwood. Fortunately, an adequate water supply was available after the installation of the Owen catchment basin and Topanga water tank.

Gehr and his crews were successful in keeping the fire out of the Fernwood area. The fire burned past them to the south, taking out the south end of Topanga Canyon. On the second day of the fire, flames hooked into the west and burned Tuna Canyon and the east slope of Las Flores Canyon.

The main head of the fire had not altered its course during the first day, rapidly burning south and east toward Los Angeles City territory located north of Pacific Palisades and Beverly Hills. It eventually reached Sunset Boulevard along a one-mile stretch – just inland from the Roosevelt Highway (now called Pacific Coast Highway).

The Topanga Patrol Station, Topanga Canyon, Malibu Division, circa 1938. From left: Harvey Anderson, warden in charge, William Santa Maria, unknown, unknown, Cliff Riggs, Connie Upham. The tanker in the photo is the last Moreland delivered to the department in 1936, Pumper "R." Carson photo, LACo Forestry Dept.

During the first day of the fire, almost all of the structural losses occurred in county territory. This amounted to 116 cabins in Topanga and Santa Ynez Canyons. The City of Los Angeles faced the potential of losing many estates near and above Temescal, Rustic, Sullivan and Mandeville Canyons. L.A. City Fire Department Chief Ralph J. Scott had fire hydrants available to his forces along Sunset Boulevard, as well as up some of the canyons for a short distance. He utilized them in making several 2,000 and 3,000-foot hose lays up the threatened canyons.

The Will Rogers estate, located in the path of the fire, had its own hydrants. Two engines and 100 men saved all of the structures on those grounds as well as neighboring structures.

While Los Angeles County forces had most of the windward-lying control lines secured by the second day of the fire, Los Angeles City had committed a "999" general alarm force of some 600 men and all available equipment to the east flank, which was still advancing. The fire was stopped by this force in Mandeville Canyon on the third day. The Santa Ana winds had diminished.

Final control was declared at midnight on the fourth day, Saturday. Some 14,820 acres of heavy watershed and 118 homes had been consumed by the fire. The total loss was set at $3 million, and of that, almost all of the structures and 6,000 acres of brush that burned had done so within the first two hours of the incident. According to veteran fire personnel at the scene, this was the fastest-spreading fire observed within Los Angeles County to that date.

The San Jose lookout south of the town of San Dimas was unique in that it had an aircraft beacon atop its cabin to warn aircraft approaching Brackett field about three miles to the west. Carson photo, LACo Forestry Dept.

A second generation lookout tower in place on Oat Mountain. During the 1940s and early 1950s, several towers were built or replaced with such structures. They had considerably more room in them and were more stable in strong winds than the earlier steel and glass models. LACo Forestry Dept. photo.

The rear view of Pumper "K," location unknown, in 1937. This is one of the later Morelands with a 600 gallon tank. A. Muench photo, LACo Forestry Dept.

Arroyo Seco Warden Roland W. Percey, on stairs, and observer Chester Kanoff on balcony of the San Rafael lookout, summer of 1938. Verdugo Peak, site of another lookout, is the tallest peak in the Verdugo Hills, right center. Carson photo, LACo Forestry Dept.

San Rafael lookout Chester Kanoff stands ready to observe the Flintridge Hills, north side of the Verdugo Mountains, and the south side of the San Gabriel range, circa 1938. This was one of the first towers closed due to the increase in industrial haze, or "smog" during the early 1950s. Arnold Muench photo, LACo Forestry Dept.

A classic photo showing the equipment and manning of San Jose Division H.Q. in San Dimas (currently Station 64). Equipment from left: middle 1930s Harley Davidson motorcycle, 1935 Chevrolet patrol, 1934 Moreland pumper, 1932 White tanker/pumper, and the newly arrived 1938 Seagrave 500 gpm pumper/tanker, pumper "V." LACo Forestry Dept. photo.

The Arroyo Seco Div. HQ (presently Station 82) proudly display its personnel and newly-delivered 1938 Seagrave pumper/tanker. Carson photo, LACo Forestry Dept.

The "Last Outpost," the Lechuza Patrol Station, currently Station 72, at the west end of the Malibu Hills. Its 1937 Chevrolet patrol/pumper and 1930 Moreland tanker/pumper were identical to the equipment found at Pine Canyon Station at the same time, circa 1938. Left to right: unknown, Adrian Willard, Robert Etz, Leonard Cesena, Paul Russell. Carson photo, LACo Forestry Dept.

Patrolman H. Allen Gibson poses next to his 1937 Chevrolet patrol pumper at the Escondido Patrol station in Malibu in 1938. This station boasted the only subterranean garage in the department. These patrol trucks were painted a forest green with black fenders.
Carson photo, LACo Forestry Dept.

A 1929 Moreland pumper/tanker in 1937, when assigned to the Pine Cyn. patrol station (currently Station 78). A 1937 Chevy patrol truck is in the apparatus barn; water well windmill turns slowly in the southwest wind. Morelands, such as these, served the F&FW through the WW II years, and then as reserve equipment, after being painted red. A. Muench photo, LACo Forestry Dept.

The War Years And Beyond

The crews of engines 15, 17 & 40 pose in front of Station 17 in Santa Fe Springs on March 3, 1939. Several key men can be seen: (l. to r.) (front row): Murray Bell, George Willingham, Orlo Pederson, Glenn G. Griswold, E. Johnson, Kenny Oker, Ray Hodges. (second row): Loy Estes, Duke Horn, Joe Zabaldano, Cecil Conley, Jess Bartlett, Bob Clark, Bob Schaffer. (back row): Joe Busch, Keith Klinger, Earl Dorning, unk., Byron D. Robinson, Bill Hayes, unk., unk. Carson photo.

During the year 1940, Los Angeles County attempted to conduct business as usual, despite the "national emergency" declared by President Franklin D. Roosevelt in 1939. Already, numerous plants engaged in the production of war material were springing up throughout the county. Many of these were located in the suburbs surrounding the City of Los Angeles, including the unincorporated areas.

To support these industries, additional workers and their families relocated to Southern California. Between 1940 and 1943, it was estimated that 310,000 people moved into Los Angeles County. Of these, 135,000 moved into Los Angeles City, with the balance settling in the outlying suburbs. This rapid and tremendous growth had a profound effect on the Los Angeles County Forester and Fire Warden Department, the fire protection districts and all other emergency service agencies.

Beginning in 1943, the rate of growth of the unincorporated areas each year was twice that of the City of Los Angeles. Services of all sorts commensurate with the growth had to somehow be provided. The County of Los Angeles entered into a lengthy "make-do" period, performing as well as it could under the circumstances. Surmounting problems of shortages of every description, from fire engines to firemen, to paper upon which to write reports, the Los Angeles County Fire Department was in no different a position than any other fire department in the nation at that time.

Ever since the fateful morning of December 7, 1941, the forester and fire warden, like many other officials, feared that Japan would soon attempt an attack on the West Coast of the United States similar to the raid on Pearl Harbor. All Fire Warden lookouts were called to man their towers, watching for Japanese aircraft.

AIR GUARDS ATTENTION!
To Chief Observers: All observation posts:
AWS (Aircraft Warning System)

You are directed to activate your observation posts immediately and to see that the post is fully manned at all times.

    By order of Brig. Wm. O'Ryan
Commanding Gen., 4th Interceptor Command

Although the towers were not normally manned during the winter, constant manning would be provided until June 30, 1944. Everyone waited for an attack to come. But, since one never transpired, the general hysteria gradually faded away.

Many large defense plants were built or expanded throughout the Los Angeles County region during this period. To disguise these as merely being parts of their surrounding neighborhoods, huge camouflage nets were strung over the buildings. It was hoped that this would hide them from enemy aircraft. To supply foliage for the top of the nets, the Los Angeles County Forester and Fire Warden had its Forestry Division deliver tons of waste forest products. Live, fast-growing trees and climbing vines were also planted and maintained alongside many

The second Construction Camp #2 in Deer Canyon in the Verdugo mountains south of La Crescenta. Note partial ship-lap wood frame construction on some buildings, portable construction on others. Circa 1941. LACo Forestry Dept. photo.

A classic two-tone green 1938 Seagrave 600-gal. tanker/ pumper after being bumped down to the Eaton Cyn. patrol station in late 1941. A different-style hood with large openable louvers had replaced the original, to relieve overheating problems common to older Seagrave apparatus. From the collection of Dale Magee.

A strikingly-beautiful 1940-41 Mack 500 gpm pumper/ tanker after delivery to the Soledad Div. at Newhall. It was the first of many purchased through 1950. The distinctive two-tone green paint was painted olive drab when WW II broke out. From the collection of Dale Magee.

The crews from Station 17 cool down a scorched wood oil derrick following a pumphouse fire in 1940. The remains can be seen at left. LACo Forestry Dept. photo.

Warden Barney H. Paul, head of the Intelligence Div. of the F&FW, poses beside his 1939 Studebaker Champion in front of his home. Vehicles like this had to last through WW II. Unknown photographer.

The hub of the LA County mutual aid system for fire defense during WW II was the back room of HQ at 524 N. Spring St., Los Angeles. Here, Chief Spence Turner, center, talks it over with a dispatch supervisor on Dec. 12, 1942. LACo Forestry Dept. photo.

of the buildings to supply additional camouflage.

Experiments were conducted to find a way to speed the growth of the trees and vines. They were discontinued after 1943, as the experiments had failed and it was becoming increasingly obvious that the Japanese Navy no longer had the capability of delivering carrier-borne aircraft close enough to the West Coast to launch an attack.

With the exception of a Japanese submarine firing a few shells at oil storage tanks north of Santa Barbara, the war never came to Southern California.

However, the pressures brought on by World War II markedly affected the County Fire Department's ability to serve the public in many ways. One of the truly lasting results was the development of a far greater level of intra- and inter-departmental cooperation – what we now term "mutual aid."

Manpower Shortages

One of the greatest wartime shortages to affect the Los Angeles County Fire Department was that of manpower. A paragraph from the Forester and Fire Warden Annual Report of 1942-43 outlines the problem in detail:

"The 1942-43 fire season proved comparatively successful, considering the manpower situation. Not only has the Department lost trained personnel to the armed forces, but also to defense industries because of its inability to compete with the high wages now paid in this essential work. Furthermore, the position of forest fireman [(auth: as well as in the Fire Protection Districts)] has always been rated as an arduous and hazardous occupation, and the young men with these qualifications are not available, having been absorbed by the military."

During 1941, many women participated in firefighting training being given by the Office of Civil Defense (OCD). By 1943, 350 women had been given training and were assigned to industrial plant fire brigades or with the Los Angeles County Auxiliary Fire Service engine companies. Training was conducted by the local fire station captain or someone from the OCD on a weekly basis. The collective opinion of the results of this training can be found in the 1943 report on the activities of this section:

"The auxiliary firemen program was given the utmost attention. Enrollment was increased 62 percent, this growth being due in part to the inclusion of women as auxiliary firemen. Every possible medium has been resorted to in order to increase the number of auxiliary firemen, not only to reach a goal of 1,400, but to replace those who have moved from their original district."

Since women did not have to meet standards for "arduous" labor to join the program, some were hired to replace male dispatchers at field division dispatch centers, thereby releasing those men to work in the field. The first woman dispatcher was Evelyn Mae Halsey, assigned to Arroyo Seco Division HQ.

This partial solution to the manpower shortage worked well. The department continued to hire women as dispatchers until the early 1950s. They were assigned to the same 24-hour-shift schedule as the men.

An Increase in Equipment

During this trying period, the fire department's regular equipment was augmented by the delivery of 12 OCD trailer pumpers, Coventry type, with 500 gpm pumps. Seven trucks were provided, each with a 500 gpm skid-mount pump and 400-gallon water tank. These OCD allocations nearly doubled the number of pumpers available in the fire protection districts.

An extensive amount of OCD equipment was also furnished to the Forester and Fire Warden: three "crash" trucks, Ford-American LaFrance with 500 gpm pumps and 400-gallon water tanks, went to Arroyo Seco Headquarters Station (Station 82), South Hills Patrol Station (Station 61) and Zuma Patrol Station (Station 71).

Two trailer pumpers, Coventry 500 gpm powered by Chrysler six-cylinder motors were located at Malibu headquarters (Station 69) and San Jose headquarters (Station 64).

Two one-and-one-half-ton GMC trucks with 75 gpm power takeoff pumps and 120-gallon water tanks went to Arroyo Seco headquarters (Station 82) and Castaic Patrol Station (Station 76).

There were now 48 engine companies operating out of 33 fire protection districts in the valleys. The Howard District and the Downey District each received new 900 gpm Seagrave triple combination pumpers. The Altadena District began construction of a new station (#52) in the east end of the district. Engine 52 was temporarily quartered in a leased market building and was equipped with a 1924 American LaFrance relief rig. In 1944, 52's received a new 500 gpm Mack triple combination pumper, and shortly thereafter moved into Engine 11's quarters until completion of their new fire station on Allen Avenue at New York Drive.

For the first time, the battalion chiefs in charge of district battalions were moved away from Los Angeles headquarters into fire stations in their respective

A national defense auxiliary fire station at 106th and Budlong streets was leased and assigned as Engine Co. 14. Photo is circa 1944. Seen in the bays are a 1929 Ford Model and a 1938 GMC. A. Muench photo.

Capt. Keith E. Klinger trains WW II civilian defense auxiliary firemen just south of Station 5 in San Gabriel. All of these trucks were homemade by the volunteers, with the assistance of regular firemen. Six trucks and 90 men received training at this station alone. LACo Forestry Dept. photo.

This middle 1920s Roamer tow truck pulling a 500 gpm Coventry trailer pumper was yet another attempt to beef up civilian defense fire protection in the Crescenta Valley during WW II. The photo was taken looking northeast at Pennsylvania and Foothill Blvds. LACo Forestry Dept. photo.

An amazing example of a civilian defense fire engine, homemade by personnel connected to La Crescenta Dist. Station 19. This 1929 Chevrolet, like other equipment, received its serial numbers from the Office of Civil Defense, and records were kept there of its activities. LACo Forestry Dept. photo.

battalions. They remained on a 40-hour week. Battalion 1's chief, W.B. Klinger, was quartered at Fire Station 38, Angeles Mesa; Battalion 2's G.G. Griswold was at Fire Station 17, Santa Fe Springs; the new Battalion 3, headed by V.T. Keys, was at Fire Station 3, Belvedere Gardens. It was felt that, in case of enemy bombing or sabotage, the chiefs in involved districts would be more immediately available to their areas. Fire protection district battalion chiefs were never again stationed at Los Angeles headquarters.

Whither the Grey Gull?

A common practice of government agencies in time of war is to clamp down on the public dissemination of information that could possibly be deemed "sensitive" – having value to the enemy. Perhaps that is why the ultimate fate of the "Grey Gull" Fish and Game patrol boat is not easily found in print.

Word-of-mouth reports from several retired mem-

In 1943, callmen were still a very important part of the crew at Engine 29. The only fulltime firemen were Capt. Arnspiger, A shift, and Capt. Tucker, B shift. Two of the callmen came in as fire foremen on alternate nights. They were paid $25 per month. There were nine men on call from Baldwin Park, three of whom – Heth, Marron and Heidt – had worked as callmen for 20 years. The callmen were paid $1 for attending a drill held once a week, and $2 for a fire. On special occasions, they would prepare a sumptuous meal that always ended with homemade ice cream. Unknown photographer.

In front of the station: (sitting): Walter Heidt and Tony Foto. (Standing, l. to r.): Merwin Heth, Art Thomas, Paul Skidmore, Capt. Charles Tucker, Earl Marron, Ray Strohmeyer and Acting Capt. Just Arnspiger. The same crew is shown in their turnouts with the REO truck. Missing from the picture are callmen Jason Harris and Chuck Craigmile and Fire Foreman Roberts. Unknown photographer.

The F&FW's first mobile food dispenser in 1942. It was built onto a 1942 Dodge pickup truck. The men in the field no longer had to depend on hit-and-miss meals from provisions stashed on their pumpers or donated by kindhearted local citizens. This rig fed up to 100 persons, and was supplied from one of the construction camp kitchens, the same system extant today. LACo Forestry Dept. photo.

bers of the F&FW concerned with that craft indicate that she was quietly impounded by the U.S. Navy after having proceeded outside the Long Beach breakwater on an unauthorized "submarine hunt" during one of the first dark nights of WW II. Interestingly, she evidently *found* a submarine, and quickly returned to report it to the authorities. However, after having been previously warned not to go outside the breakwater after sunset, the Grey Gull was summarily impounded for the duration of the war, never to sail again in her Fish and Game capacity for the county.

The Woodland Hills Fire

Another event that is not often discussed in print was nonetheless well known at the time because of its severity and size. On November 6, 1943, a brush fire ignited during a strong Santana wind near Chatsworth, just east of the L.A. City/County line. Wind direction and velocity carried it rapidly into county territory. All of the hills to the south and west were quickly scoured of flammable vegetation, as well as 114 structures, mostly dwellings and outbuildings. This 15,000-acre fire was notable not only for its size and severity, but also for the fact that the *primary* means of communication during fire operations were the only-recently-installed A.M. radio units of the Malibu Division.

It seemed that the major county fire telephone trunk lines were burned beyond immediate repair during the early stages of the fire. By placing the few units with radio receivers/transmitters in strategic locations, coordinated operations could be instituted, and aid requested from L.A. HQ as needed. The Woodland Hills Fire became the first fire handled exclusively by radio in Los Angeles County.

Mutual Aid Expands

World War II provided the impetus for expanding interjurisdictional assistance in time of "great public calamity such as extraordinary fire, flood, storm or other disaster." This expansion was the outgrowth of a meeting of the fire chiefs of the greater Los Angeles area, called by Chief E.F. Coop of Pasadena in the summer of 1940. The result was the Mutual Aid Act, drafted by the attorneys of the League of California Cities. It was enacted into law at the next session of the California State Legislature.

Mutual aid was rendered on an as-needed and as-available basis all during World War II. It is basically still operative today. Recently, other systems of interjurisdictional assistance have also been placed in operation, some of which had been developed even prior to World War II.

The F&FW A.M. field transmitter/receiver was mounted in a 1937 Chevrolet panel truck. The second view shows antenna setup and relationship to the field command trailer. LACo Forestry Dept. photos.

This photo shows F&FW radio equipment located on Castro Peak in the Malibu Mtns. circa 1941. LACo Forestry Dept. photo.

The Fire Dept's basketball team, circa 1935. From left: Firemen Heisterman, unknown, Johnson, Hayes, McCls, Clark, Maddux, and three unkonwns. Carson photo, from the collection of John Whelan.

As far back as 1914, the California State Constitution was amended to " . . . allow Charter Cities to insert provisions in their fundamental documents for the performance of municipal functions by counties . . ." The 1909 contract for forest fire assistance to the Angeles National Forest from the State Forestry Division via Los Angeles County, and the 1921 statute permitting ". . . one or more municipalities or one or more counties to exercise jointly by agreement any powers common to all of them . . ." were also early examples of empowerment to assist. The second example was seldom utilized, however.

In 1927, the City of Manhattan Beach contracted to provide fire service for the Los Angeles County El Porto District at a rate of $25 per call. In 1936, a contract was signed with the City of Pomona to provide fire protection services for the L.A. County Fairgrounds, which were located within Pomona city limits. In 1939, a new contract was drawn up with Los Angeles County for fire protection by the Forester and Fire Warden for the townships of San Dimas and West Covina. Both townships were essentially rural areas, each with populations of about 1,000. In 1934, the Verdugo Peak Lookout Tower was constructed. This was under a contract with the City of Glendale, which paid for the observer during each fire season. A contract for brush firefighting with Glendale and Burbank was also signed in 1938.

Thirty years later, economic conditions encouraged the use of existing contract-for-services statutes to a degree never dreamed of by anyone, least of all the smaller incorporated cities within Los Angeles County.

However, for the duration of World War II, the threat of enemy air attack served to coalesce the various fire agencies into a state of mutual interdependence.

A Wartime Test

With whatever crews they could muster, the Fire Warden field divisions were put to a test on October 20, 1942 in and around the Las Flores Canyon area of the Malibu Mountains. At approximately 0300 hours, a brush fire began near the head of Las Flores Canyon. Due to high Santana winds and low humidity, the fire spread rapidly down-canyon through the heavy brush, involving many cabins in flame.

This fire followed the same pattern that so many serious fires in these hills have taken, burning rapidly toward the coast with a large flame front and limited accessibility. This time, however, due to reduced manpower in the Fire Warden Department, Chief Turner called upon several companies from the fire protection districts, just as he had during the Pickens Canyon Fire of 1933. Although the records do not

Arroyo Seco Div.'s 1942 Mack 500 gpm pumper/600-gal. tanker after having been painted olive drab for the duration of WW II. All field units were not similarly painted. Following the war, the olive drab units were painted red. This rig became Eng. 82. LACo Forestry Dept. photo.

Heavy smoke from the Las Flores Cyn. Fire approaches Pacific Coast Hwy. in Malibu, July 1942. LACo Forestry Dept. photo.

reveal which districts responded, their equipment was used for structure protection along Roosevelt Highway.

Statistically, the fire was certainly large, but not *huge* when compared to others in later years. It is noted that "several" members of the department received burns while fighting this fire. It is not revealed whether this was due to inexperience or the difficult terrain. The fire was controlled in three days. It consumed some 5,900 acres and caused $100,000 in structural damage and $1 million in watershed damage.

Of particular interest concerning this fire is a quote from the record that reveals the sign of the times:

> "The Department was indebted to the men of the Armed Forces, from the Army Base at Point Dume, among others, who rendered valuable assistance in extinguishing this fire. Army officers cooperated enthusiastically, as they felt the experience to be excellent training for the men, under conditions somewhat resembling combat."

The 1942 Las Flores Cyn. Fire burns south towards the coast. The small motorway just left of center may have allowed tankers to save these homes in the heavy brush. Virtually none of them had any brush clearance to speak of. LACo Forestry Dept. photo.

A Life Too Short

The name of Glenn G. Griswold, battalion chief, Los Angeles County Fire Departmet, is one that many fire service "old timers" well remember. Griswold became, within his lifetime, synonymous with individual experimentation for the betterment of the fire service.

Born in Goldfield, Colorado in 1899, Griswold developed an early interest in the fire service. He joined the Colorado Springs Fire Department at the age of 20. After five years there, he moved to Los Angeles. There he found employment with the Los Angeles County Fire Department. Griswold soon found he was welcome to put to use his education as a hydraulic engineer – and to experiment with more efficient ways to use water to extinguish fires.

By 1929, he began initial experiments in the effectiveness of finely-atomized water droplets – "fog" – in extinguishing all types of fires. The results of these experiments, as well as other facts

Having been evacuated from Las Flores Cyn. ahead of a fire, this family arrives safely at Pacific Coast Hwy. with their 1930 Ford loaded with whatever they could hastily pack. LACo Forestry Dept. photo.

about Griswold's life, were published in the March 1944 issue of *The California Fireman*, the official publication of the California State Fireman's Association. A short excerpt follows:

> *"From the technical standpoint, there are the following principles behind Griswold "Fog-*

nozzls" (sic) which are the only type that produce fog by the impingement of two or more solid streams of liquid outside the nozzle, and which engineers claim is the only method possible to produce full atomization):

1. Materials of low flash point are extinguished with waterfog.
2. The extinguishing ability of water is increased up to 30 times over the conventional solid streams.
3. More efficient extinguishment and better personnel protection are secured by the fact that the liquid zone of waterfog is a homogeneous mass.
4. Reduced water damage is secured . . .
5. The large area of heat absorption, together with the convecting air currents, induces fire to bring about its owned restriction when waterfog is applied.
6. Waterfog aids in preventing dust explosions.
7. For detection of arson fires, materials are left undisturbed because of the waterfog way."

A short time after joining Los Angeles County in 1924, Griswold was assigned to Engine Company 17 in Santa Fe Springs, the heart of the oil drilling and refining industries of the county at that time. He was soon appointed captain, and in August 1932 was appointed battalion chief, replacing the recently-promoted Chief Heinzman. The balance of Griswold's service time was spent in a continuation of his experiments with fog as an extinguishing agent.

The California Fireman wrote:

"As to his record of accomplishments in the Fire Service, few have equalled, and none have surpassed, his contribution to its progress. For, mainly to his knowledge, skill and energy is due the adoption of the fog principle of fire extinguishment and the invention of the Griswold "Fognozzl,' now in universal use. He was considered a world authority on oil fire and wrote several text books on the subject."

Griswold's methods did not go unnoticed by the U.S. military during this time. His techniques and equipment were eventually adopted by the United States Navy for use in shipboard firefighting during World War II.

In June of 1943, Griswold was granted a military leave of absence and was commissioned a captain in

These two photos, taken circa 1941, show four styles of fog/straight-stream nozzles constructed using principles developed by BC Glenn Griswold and adapted for use by the U.S. Navy during WW II. A. Muench photo, LACo Forestry Dept.

the U.S. Army Corps of Engineers. After training, he was sent to Europe, shortly after the invasion of Italy. He was appointed fire chief of the city of Naples immediately after its capture. It was here that his life ended while in performance of duty.

From *California Fireman* comes this account:

"It was characteristic of him that when a chemical storage dump became involved in fire, and the potential hazard appeared to be great, that he would order all civilian and military personnel out of the area and himself make a personal investigation. While thus engaged, a violent explosion occurred that resulted in his death alone, owing to his foresight in having the area evacuated, and himself, making the investigation personally. He was awarded the Soldier's Medal, posthumously, by President Roosevelt, and his wife, Mrs. Lucille Griswold, was presented with it at Fort MacArthur, California, on March 10, 1944.

Many organizations connected with the Fire Service also received his interest and attention. He was never too busy to give his attention to any problem brought to him by any member of the service, regardless of rank.

Santa Fe Springs Station 17 was the location for a training program in how to use fog applicators on petroleum tank fires, circa 1947. LACoFD photo.

Station 17's monitor was used for large or long-term oil field fires. The nozzle could produce 1,000 gpm with three 2½" hoselines installed. LA CoFD photo.

The LACoFD district chiefs in 1944. (L. to r.): T.C. Loggins, asst. chief; K.E. Klinger, BC; his father, W.B. Klinger, BC; G.A. Bartling, BC; P.A. Clark, BC. LACo Forestry Dept. photo.

Belvedere Gardens Fire Station 3 appears quite secure from bombing attacks in this 1942 photo. Not all stations were so protected. A. Muench photo, LACo Forestry Dept.

Altadena Dist. Engine 52 (with relief eng. 35 in use) was pressed into service in this rented market building during the war year of 1944. This station was on Allen Ave. just south of New York Dr. The permanent station was just north of there; it's now a nursery school. LACoFD photo.

The Chatsworth patrol station's Moreland pumper had just extinguished a fire involving the cab of the Southern Pacific cab-ahead "Mallet" freight engine just outside the railroad tunnel through Santa Susana Pass on this summer evening in 1941. The Forestry Dept. firemen were expected to do the best they could handling a myriad of unusual incidents in the more remote areas of the county. LACo Forestry Dept. photo.

Located in the County's El Monte Dist., Five Points Station 43 needed a few good men to bolster its forces in this 1942 photo. Note the air raid warning horn on the pole in line with the flagpole. All stations had such horns installed. A. Muench photo, LACo Forestry Dept.

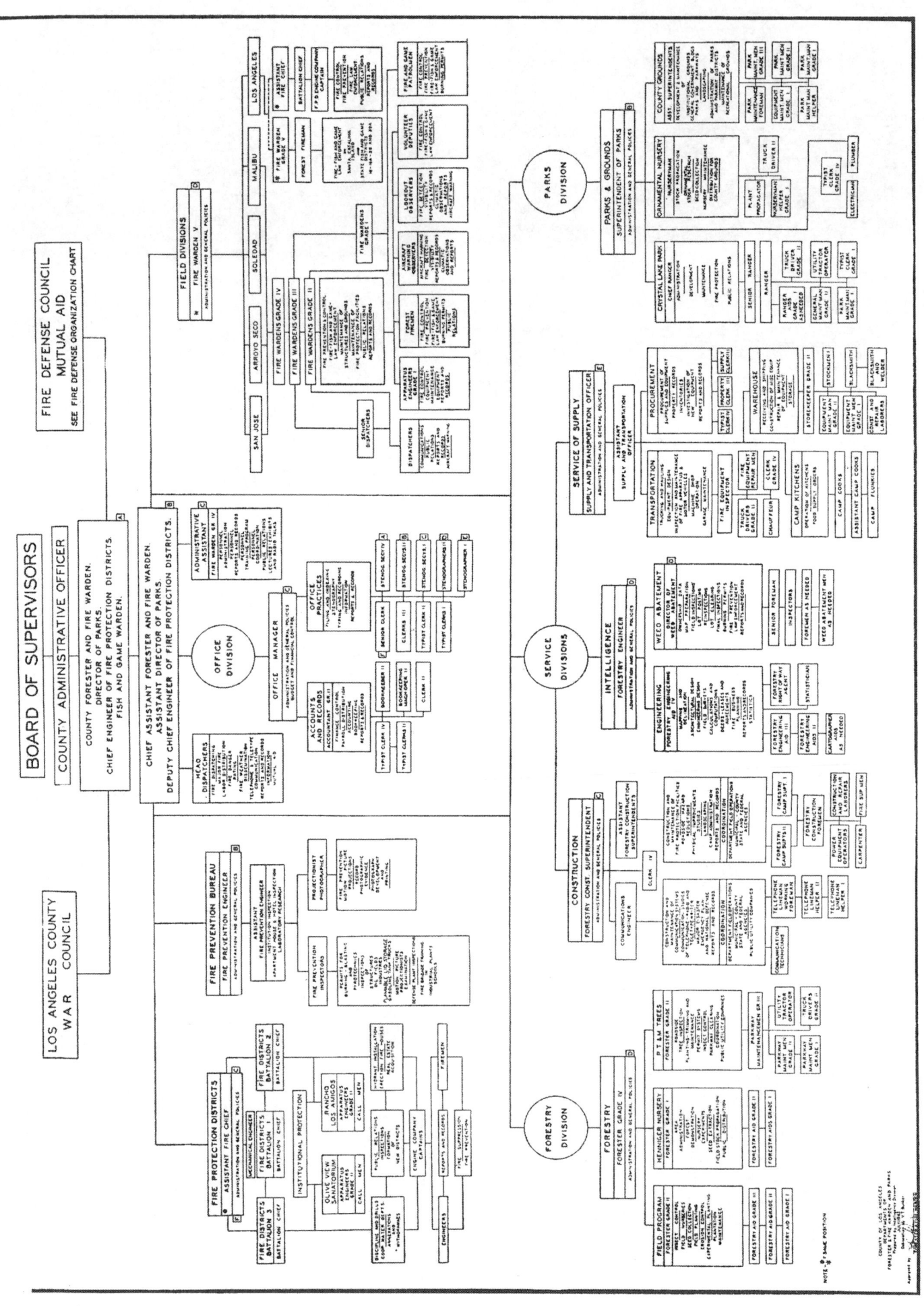

Some Improvements and Better Ratings

Fire departments and fire districts are rated by insurance companies to determine the fire insurance premium rates to be assigned to the area served. Deficiency points for items and conditions below a set standard are applied, placing the department in a classification from one to nine, one being the best.

As the war neared an end, the average rating for the Los Angeles County Fire Districts was a Class 6, with 743.5 deficiency points assigned. This was due largely to the irregularly-distributed water districts throughout the areas served by the department. The incorporated cities averaged 880.2 deficiency points.

Due to sharp economic inflation during and after World War II, property values soared, and along with them insurance rates and premiums. Clearly, the department needed to improve its rating, provide better fire protection, and, in so doing, bring the insurance rates down.

Fortunately, the increased property values brought more property tax revenues into county coffers. This financial improvement allowed for a gradual upgrading of the fire districts by the addition of more manpower, stations and fire hydrants. Several of the districts, such as Hollywood-Sherman and Miramonte-Florence-Graham, were soon brought up to a Class 3 rating.

The first F.M. radio installation, on Engine 41's 1943 Mack, can be seen in the large box behind the driver's seat in this 1947 photo. LACo Forestry Dept. photo.

On the other hand, those living in the unincorporated areas outside of a fire protection district were protected only by the F&FW, with its green brushfire apparatus, limited personnel and long response times. Nothing much could be done to help those persons with their insurance rates unless *one* county fire department could be formed from the two organizations, allowing regular county-wide responses by *all* apparatus.

Some advanced thinking along these lines was being done during the middle '40s. The clock governing this eventuality was ticking loudly. As if in anticipation, the F&FW radio network was enlarged. The installation of two-way transmitters/receivers at Malibu and Arroyo Seco headquarters was accomplished during 1943. The number of sets in use gradually increased, and with these new additions, the configuration of radio equipment by 1945 was as follows:

★ L.A. HQ: One 250-watt F.M. radio station.
★ Castro Peak Transmitter, Malibu Division Dispatch office at Station 65, call letters KMA 733.
★ 50-watt A.M. transmitter for Arroyo Seco Division. Dispatch office at present Station 82, call letters KMA 734.
★ 50-watt A.M. transmitter for the Soledad Division. Dispatch office at present Station 73, call letters KMA 735.
★ 111 two-way radio sets installed in appropriate chiefs' cars and pumper or patrol apparatus.
★ 26 Handi-Talkies and five walkie-talkies used in conjunction with construction camps on projects and fireground operations.

(As one might assume, the F&FW A.M. sets could not communicate with the districts' F.M. sets. See Chapter 8 for the resolution.)

The L.A. County Fire Department had been a leader in the use of radio communications. Other departments in the area would soon follow its example.

The Los Angeles County Fire Department Ladies Auxiliary

In 1948, a large group of women composed of the wives, mothers, daughters and sisters of active county firemen in Battalion 4 organized a group that would be known thereafter as the "Ladies Auxiliary." It was the purpose of this group to support the men while they were on extended, active fire duty, by providing refreshments, clothing and general moral support at the scene.

Founded by the wives of Chief Wesley Rowell, Captains Harold Jackson, Carl Burkhart, Robert McCarty and Engineer Rudy Alpi, this group served

Members of the Battalion 4 Ladies Auxiliary and a pleased Chief Keith Klinger pose next to La Crescenta Engine 19 at the February 15, 1956 dedication of the new station at 1729 W. Foothill Blvd. The value of these women's efforts at such occasions was appreciated enormously. LACoFD photo.

A raging structure fire involves sheds, oil tanks, piping, grass and assorted trash, exact location unknown. The Fire Prevention Bureau was hard pressed to eradicate substandard conditions such as these during and after WW II. LACoFD photo.

as an inspiration for others like it that were to follow. It is still active today.

When it was formed in the early '50s, the auxiliary consisted of 45 women headed by Mrs. Harry Muench of Glendora. They rallied at Battalion 2, East San Gabriel Valley. The group purchased and refurbished a 1936 Chevrolet to be used as a "canteen car," complete with propane stove and water tank.

The Battalion 4 group, also with 45 members, headed by Mrs. Edmund Reed, served the area of the Northwest San Gabriel Valley to Newhall Pass. Battalions 5 (Malibu) and 6 (Newhall-Palmdale) each had 35 members in their auxiliary, headed, respectively, by Mrs. Ed Fernandez and Mrs. George Reichart. These groups were stable in their organizational functioning, for it was still common for many of the firemen to live in or near the district in which they served. The present system of freeways and general socio-economic changes over large areas of the county have altered this pattern.

Many retired firemen still remember being served by the ladies auxiliary pending and during the establishment of fire camps. A sense of "family" was indeed nurtured by the presence and functioning of these unique support groups.

The Training Manual

Over the years, a series of "general orders" were issued by Chief Turner to the various divisions. These orders formed the general operating procedures of the department. General Order Number 20 was the drill manual used by fire protection personnel.

Each hose evolution had a drill number, which each firefighter on the crew was expected to remember when the captain called it out, for example, "Drill #3." (In current practice, each evolution is called by name, such as "single reverse lay, fire on the right.")

While the districts had their drills in writing, F&FW personnel used verbally-described procedures. Since F&FW apparatus carried no 2½-inch hose through WW II, hose evolution procedures were simple and few in number. Now, as the consolidation of the two departments drew nearer, knowing the F&FW apparatus would be utilized to provide more and more structure protection, a general move toward a printed "drill manual" was made. This is reflected in the following letter:

Battalion 7 HQ
March 1, 1947

To: Mutual Aid and Training Officer George Taylor
From: Captains Hall and Kleinsmith
Subject: Training Manual

We feel that ways and means should be set up to put together and publish a training manual for the Mountain Battalions. This manual should be in loose-leaf form, printed on good quality paper, and adequately illustrated with actual

Operations in front of the Swanee River Cafe fire in 1943. Located on Valley Blvd. in the county area of El Monte, it was fought by Valley Fire Protection Districts engines 43, 26, 42 and 4. Note Bn. 2 Ladies Auxiliary canteen car just left of center. This revamped 1936 Chevrolet responded to all large fires throughout the San Gabriel Valley. From the collection of Martin Rippens.

Capt. Kenneth Bicksler and fireman Martin Rippens wet down the ruins of the Swanee River Cafe fire. The metal Forker helmets worn in this picture would only be used for another few years. From the collection of Martin Rippens.

The 1938 Seagrave pumper/tanker assigned to Soledad Div. HQ following its being painted red and given the number 96. It was now a member of the Mountain Bn. 6. From the collection of Shawn Ryan.

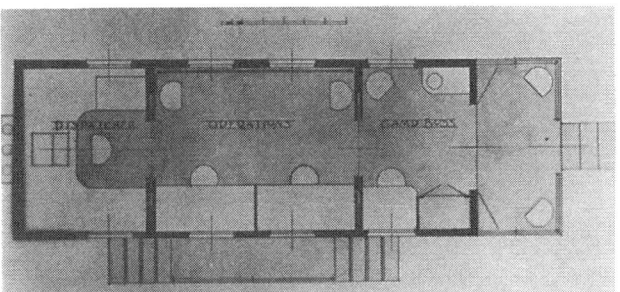

Interior schematic of the F&FW command trailer, taken in February of 1945. A. Muench photo, LACo Forestry Dept.

The latest in fresh air masks for structure firefighting, circa 1939. Fresh air is supplied through 50-ft. hoses using the hand pump. A. Muench photo, LACo Forestry Dept.

photographs. These photographs are to be on separate pages and show key points of each drill evolution. Then, in case of alterations in the printed matter due to changes in technique, the photographs would not necessarily have to be discarded, thus reducing the cost of keeping the manuals up to date.

The Mountain Battalion Personnel concur in this idea, so they will have something to guide them when drilling.

WMKWH:em
cc: Ch. J.J. Davis
    Ch. O.M. Thurston

Captains Hall and Kleinsmith had only recently returned from a two-day exposure to the fire college of the Los Angeles City Fire Department and were

Type B automatically-retransmitting box alarm equipment from Station 3, East Los Angeles, during the 1940s and 1950s. This equipment, greatly expanded, was later relocated to Fire Station 27 in the Central Mfg. Dist. when that station was constructed. LACoFD photo.

Altadena F.P.D. Engine Co. 11's 1948 "High Reeler" Seagrave 1,000 gpm pumper shortly after delivery. The hill-climbing ability of these rigs left much to be desired, as the 245 hp V-12 engine was required to haul 3,000' of hose and 500 gal. of water. Summertime overheating was common. Photo by Dale Magee.

A wartime 1943 Mack used at the Las Flores Patrol Station in Malibu. The number 92 in the circle indicates that this rig had been renumbered to conform to the Mountain Battalion numbering system used just prior to the F&FW and districts combining. From the collection of Dale Magee.

Engine Co. 5 of the Valley Fire Protection District takes delivery of a new 1942 "1000 gallon Mack" tanker/pumper. LACoFD photo.

no doubt impressed by the amount of material presented to LAFD personnel. Through communications to Chief Turner, they indicated the value of upgrading the level of training in the Los Angeles County Fire Department.

With the formation of the East Los Angeles Fire Protection District in 1947, a "Type-B" (automatically-retransmitted) fire alarm box system was installed. The power source and transmission equipment for that system were located at Fire Station 3.

When new Fire Station 27 in the Central Manufacturing District was constructed on Sheila Street during 1951, the system would house its equipment there. Gradually, during the 1970s and early 1980s, the system would be phased out entirely, due to the proliferation of the telephone and excessive false alarms being turned in on the box system.

New Fire Apparatus

During World War II, many permanent employees of the department were inducted into the armed services. At the close of the war, most returned to their positions with the districts or the F&FW. While they were away, the fire apparatus that they had left behind continued to serve – and to steadily wear out.

The four Mack pumpers that had been ordered in 1939-1941, the two Macks and one American LaFrance that came in 1943 and the eight Macks received in the years between 1947 and 1952 were the newest rigs the F&FW had. Except for six Macks and seven 1938-1939 Seagrave pumpers ordered by the districts, most of the district apparatus in service were the original 1924 American laFrance 750 gpm chain-drive models. A few Seagrave pumpers had been received from 1928 through 1931 when new districts were formed. The need for massive apparatus replacement orders was very apparent.

Bids were set in 1948 for ten 1,000 gpm pumpers built to district specifications. The order called for centrifugal pumps, 500-gallon water tanks, two 1-inch hose reels, power takeoff road pumps, adjustable drivers' seats, divided hose beds for laying two 2½-inch hoselines simultaneously and dividers for 800 feet of preconnected 1½-inch hoselines.

Beginning with these apparatus, at least 1,500 feet

Altadena 12s brand new 1949 General Pacific arrives for the grand opening of a supermarket on Fair Oaks Avenue. Photo by Dale Magee.

of 2½-inch hose would be carried. Of the 800 feet of 1½-inch hose, two or three "pulls" of varying lengths were carried; the configuration and lengths depended on the needs of the particular district, to be determined by the station captains.

The contract was awarded to the Seagrave Corporation of Columbus, Ohio. From late 1948 through early 1949, deliveries were made to the following stations:

★ Station 11, Altadena, FD-46
★ Station 13, Commerce (Central Mfg.), FD-52
★ Station 16, Graham, FD-49
★ Station 39, Bell Gardens, FD-50
★ Station 47, Temple City, FD- (new station)
★ Station 56, Rolling Hills, FD-45 (new station)
★ Station 63, La Crescenta, FD- (new station in 1950)
★ Station 86, East Los Angeles, FD-48 (new station)
★ Station 90, South El Monte, FD-53 (new station)
★ Station 105, Dominguez, FD-51 (new station)

(The "FD" designation refers to the fire department shop number.)

This equipment was powered by a 268-hp Seagrave V-12 engine and had vacuum-assisted brakes. Also included were three-way F.M. radios. The rigs' gearing suited flatland operations, but left much to be desired with respect to hill climbing. They were the last units delivered to the county without air brakes.

The first equipment received with the Hall-Scott engine was the result of a bid for nine more pumpers. The contract went to the General-Pacific Corporation of Los Angeles. General-Pacific did not build the complete components, but, rather, assembled the parts made by other manufacturers. The rigs were composed of a Kenworth chassis, a Hall-Scott engine, 1,000 gpm Hale centrifugal pump and a Coast body. All had 500-gallon water tanks. Two of the rigs were exceptions, coming with Waukeshaw engines and 750 gpm pumps. Assignments were as engines 6, 7, 12, 22, 54, 60, 70 and 233.

Central Mfg. Dist.'s Engine Co. 13's 1948 Seagrave. This particular rig had no hose reels, but did have considerable preconnected 1" hose in the right rear lower compartment. Note the "Haley" tips on the tailboard nozzles. These were the latest in adjustable straight stream nozzles in the 1950s. From the collection of Dale Magee.

District's Asst. Chief Ted Loggins demonstrates the two-way radio in his car, circa 1946. At this time, the districts and the F&FW could not communicate with one another, as the district's radio was F.M., and the F&FW's was A.M. LACo Forestry Dept. photo.

Senior Warden Cecil Gehr testing a WW II army style flame thrower for possible use as a backfiring tool for the Dept. It was probably a case of overkill, for it was not adopted. LACo Forestry Dept. photo.

James W. Simons, Tractor Operator and Hero

Just after noon on November 4, 1948, during a moderate Santana wind condition, a brush fire broke out in the Malibu Mountains. It was quite similar to the Trippet Fire of 1938, occurring in the same Topanga Canyon, only nearer to the head of the canyon and slightly farther to the west. Since both the population and the number of homes and cabins had increased during the intervening years, more lives and real property were in immediate danger. As the flames advanced towards the Post Office Tract, Topanga Woods and the Fernwood Tract three miles to the south, approximately 1,250 homes and an unknown number of lives lay in its path.

Apparatus and manpower were assembled to attempt to save the homes and, at the same time, establish a control line to stop the southerly spread of the fire. It soon became apparent that even a high concentration of tankers and numerous hoselines would not be able to save many of the dwellings. In fact, all three tracts stood a chance of being lost.

The newer Calabasas Patrol Station (currently Station 68) with a new apparatus barn, in 1950. The 1944 Ford LaFrance pumper was one of several acquired by the Dept. from the military near the end of WW II. LACo Forestry Dept. photo.

The official report from the office of Spence D. Turner, L.A. County Forester and Fire Warden, on what followed best describes what became one of the more notable occurrences in the history of the deppartment.

"Tractors were called for and one of the Department's veteran operators, James. W. Simons, responded with a D-7 tractor and bulldozer. At the time Mr. Simons arrived with the tractor, the fire was just starting to burn into the Topanga Woods and Topanga Post Office Tracts, containing several hundred homes, and was threatening to spread into the Fernwood area, which was even more densely populated. Due to the (fire's) rapid rate of spread and the inaccessible terrain, direct attacks with hose lines had been unsuccessful, and it appeared that the head of the fire at this point was impossible to control, and that many homes would be lost in that area.

"Because of the extreme hazard, the officer in charge of the fire was reluctant to order a frontal attack on the fire with the tractor, but Operator Simons volunteered to make an attempt if at all possible. As the strong winds made any lines constructed ahead of the fire useless, it was necessary for him to operate directly on the fire line. Cutting through heavy brush, and at times through flames that almost completely enveloped the machine, he was finally successful in cutting completely around the head of the fire and checking its forward progress.

"Many reports from officers on this fire, as well as comments and letters of commendation received from residents of the area, indicate that Mr. Simons' performance on this fire went far beyond the line of duty, and that he risked his life to control the fire at the most strategic points. When he came off of that particular part of the line, his clothing had been burned full of holes, his hair had been singed and his face blistered.

"Only through Mr. Simons' heroic work was it possible to keep the fire from burning through the tracts mentioned above, and particularly in the case of the Fernwood Tract, (for) had *the fire swept through these areas, tremendous property losses would have ensued, with inevitable loss of life."*

As brush fires in Los Angeles County go, this fire's size was unremarkable. "Only" 3,155 acres were consumed and 124 cabins and homes destroyed. However, Mr. Simons' action *helped save over 1,000 structures*. A total of 30 pieces of fire equipment from Los Angeles County, Los Angeles City and Ventura County and a total force of 650 firefighters worked on the fire during the two-day battle.

The letters of commendation from the public poured in:

". . . especially the capable work of Mr. Jimmy Simons, who in the face of very grave danger risked his good health, and possibly his life to stem the conflagration. The manner in which he operated his bulldozer was the greatest exhibition of efficiency and the bravest display of cool nerve I have ever seen. In the face of certain defeat, Mr. Simons, time and time again, reentered the burning area and fought the fire to a veritable standstill . . ."
Chris B. Miller, Topanga

". . . I hope you have an opportunity to really see where the 'cat' was driven, because any operator who has guts enough to go up and down the slides the operator of that 'cat' went, certainly deserves commendation entirely apart from the fact that he did it right in front of an oncoming brush fire."
Oscar A. Trippett, Los Angeles

"I know upon one occasion he was surrounded with fire, and that his clothing caught on fire . . . How much we are indebted to this man, we shall never know, but the very least we can do is to tell you that I consider him worthy of our everlasting gratitude."
Harold Z. Davis, Santa Monica

". . . Right here let me say that you have one man on your side who I will have to shake hands with mighty soon. I stand at awe at his prowess. He is your own Jimmy Simons, the 'cat' driver, a hero of the highest order. We owe him the deepest sort of gratitude for what he did . . . If I were passing out medals, he would get the gold one for sure."
Darrel B. Foss, Venice

And get one Simons did, although it was only made of bronze. On April 3, 1949, James W. Simons was awarded the James McLachlan Bissell Medal for heroic service. The award was presented annually, and was developed by Harvey Bissell of La Crescenta, a conservationist who had lost a son to a rattlesnake bite. It was presented at the annual meeting of the Southern California Association of Forester and Fire Wardens in Bakersfield.

Immediately after this award was presented, Simons was called to Washington, D.C., where a special award for heroism was presented to him by President Harry S. Truman. The publicity surrounding these awards brought great credit to Simons and

Jim Simons and his D-8 Caterpillar dozer arrive under Highway Patrol escort and offload before going into action on the 1948 Topanga Cyn. Fire. Pacific Press photo, from the collection of John Whelan.

These four photos were taken during the 1948 Topanga Cyn. Fire. James Simons is operating the D-7 dozer. The massive size of the Malibu brush is illustrated by the view of the hoseline going up the hill from the Seagrave tanker/pumper. In the next photo, crewmen catch a nap on the motorway near two Moreland pumpers. The last scene is an aerial view of the fire as it rolls toward the coast. LACo Forestry Dept. photos.

to the Los Angeles County Forester and Fire Warden.

The following is a chronology of significant tractor (bulldozer) purchases made by the Department until the present time:

1925 first tractor, a gasoline-powered Caterpillar model 30. Bulldozer blade added - 1929.

1938 first diesel tractor w/blade, a Caterpillar model D-4.

1946 first D-6 and D-7 tractors purchased; also received one Allis Chalmers HD-10 from the military as war surplus.

1953 first Caterpillar model D-8 purchased.

1960 purchased one International model D-24.

With the exception of the TD-24, all bulldozers purchased since have been D-8's. The department currently has six in service. During the fire season, three of them are placed on standby at Fire Station 85 in Glendora (San Gabriel Valley); Station 73 in Canyon Country; and Station 125 at Brent's Junction in the Malibu area. The balance are kept at the Pacoima warehouse.

Departmental Consolidation

By 1949, Forester and Fire Warden field divisions had been reorganized by labeling their jurisdictions "mountain battalions," similar in organization to the fire protection districts. The number of mountain battalions had increased to four, and would continue to increase almost yearly as the two departments grew and began continued steps toward consolidation.

A second type of consolidation took place at about this time. The separate fire districts and county governments began to feel that, by joining several districts together, the cost per district could be spread among the several districts. This would result in a net savings to the taxpayer, while at the same time increasing service efficiency.

Tractor Operator James Simons and his swamper (on top) cut a firebreak ahead of a brush fire, location unknown, in 1950. Pacific Press photo.

On April 12, 1949, the *Consolidated* Fire Protection District was formed from the following *separate* fire districts:

1. Angeles Mesa
2. Downey (which had absorbed Bell Gardens in 1940)
3. Bellflower
4. Clearwater-Hynes
5. Florence-Southwest (which was formed in 1947 from Miramonte-Florence, Southwest, Coast, Howard, Lawndale, Lennox, Lomita, Clifton Heights, El Porto and Willowbrook)
6. Hollywood-Sherman Arnaz
7. Norwalk
8. San Gabriel Valley (composed of Baldwin Park, Santa Fe Springs, East Montebello, Puente, Rosemead, Temple City and Duarte)
9. Southeast (composed of Artesia and Lakewood)
10. Walnut Park

La Canada-La Crescenta joined on June 13, 1950, followed by Belvedere-Laguna on September 25, 1951, San Dimas on December 16, 1952 and Newhall on December 3, 1953.

In the midst of this transition period, proposals were requested from various top staff members to suggest ways to amalgamate corresponding ranks in the two departments. At the time, F&FW ranks consisted of five grades of fire wardens, lieutenants and patrolmen/firemen. The districts called their corresponding positions captain, engineer and fireman. The two departments' rates of pay were also noncorresponding. A solution was needed whereby 24-hour, two-platoon captains' positions could be funded in place of the 44-hour-per-week fire warden Grade II positions. Other ranks needed to be brought into parity as well.

Some excerpts from an eight-page proposal by Senior Fire Warden Harvey Anderson (Malibu Division) show the complexity of the problem:

"The recent absorbing of Battalion 7 by the Consolidated Fire Protection District (into Battalion 4) has pointed up the problem faced by Fire Warden personnel in the immediate future. It is evident that Mountain Battalions 9 and 2 are ripe for similar consolidation with a little realignment of battalion boundaries.

"In the near future in the Malibus, the prospects are that the Consolidated Fire Protection District will be extended along the coast to include Point Dume and possibly to the Ventura County line; also Topanga Canyon and perhaps some portions of the Calabasas and Malibu Lake areas will be taken in. The recent drastic savings in insurance rates on the coast, due to the Fire Protection Districts' (arrival) and the National Board of Fire Underwriters' survey,

James W. Simons (r.), receives a special scroll from the County Board of Supervisors for his heroic firefighting efforts in Topanga Cyn. Others (from l.): Chief Asst. Fire Warden L.A. Percey, Chief Spence Turner, Supervisor Raymond V. Darby. LACoFD photo.

have given the people tangible results of their having joined the Consolidated Fire Protecion District.

"If 72-hour Captains are going to be necessary and appointments made as district funds become available, then it would seem that it would be better to have all 44-hour Captains made into 72-hour Captains. Then, as the Fire Protection Districts spread, the jobs would already be filled and there would be no quarreling over whether Fire Protection District personnel should get the jobs."

Anderson followed with a lengthy and detailed proposal for dropping one fireman's position from some of the "slower" stations such as Lechuza (72), Monte Nido (67), Eaton Canyon (66) and Padua (62) in order to help fund the 43 captain positions needed. As district funds increased over the years, the firemen's positions could be restored. He then continued with some additional reasons favoring consolidation.

"From the personnel standpoint, there would be a net loss of two positions when compared with the present budgeted salary positions. With (pending) retirements and promotions, it is positive that no one need lose a job under this proposal.

"When it is seen how fast the Fire Protection Districts have expanded with job opportunities, and contrasted with the present slow or practically stopped expansion of Fire Warden personnel positions, it can be seen that there would be great improvement in morale.

"Surely the Fire Warden and the Fire Protection Districts can be merged into one County Fire Department with less friction if all men holding like positions are working under the same conditions and with the same responsibilities."

An historian's dream photo – three generations of fire protection for station 6 in the Lomita Dist. captured by the photographer in 1949. Left, a 1949 General-Pacific 1,000 gpm pumper; center, a 1924 American LaFrance 750 gpm pumper; right, an early 1920s Ford Model T chemical car. LACoFD photo.

Fireman Martin Rippens of Engine Co. 42 performs overhaul work during this 1946 basement fire in the Chapman Woods district of Station 5. From the collection of Martin Rippens.

An assortment of Valley Fire Protection District equipment picking up after a basement fire. Foreground: Engine 52's 1944 Mack; to the right: Engine 42's 1938 Ford LaFrance; partially hidden behind that: Engine 5's 1942 Mack. From the collection of Martin Rippens.

Newly-delivered Truck Co. 8 sits in front of its yet-uncompleted new station on Santa Monica Blvd. in West Hollywood, March 7, 1950. This apparatus was quartered at a nearby movie studio shed pending the station's completion. V. Boergadine photo, LACo Forestry Dept.

Dispatcher Al Bouton at the fire dispatchers' facility at L.A. HQ, 524 N. Spring St., circa 1949. Note log book on the right. A written record was kept of all significant radio traffic. LACo Forestry Dept. photo.

Two views of Pine Cyn.'s 1948 Mack tanker/pumper after receiving its first number – 78 – with the county seal under the number. This series of apparatus was among the first F&FW rigs to be painted red. Evidently, 2½" hose was not loaded at this time. The N number was the shop I.D. number of the F&FW. LACoFD photo.

The radio field communications van, seen here circa 1948, was battery operated. LACo Forestry Dept. photo.

The tools of a patrolman's trade – the "Dead Horse" 5,000-gal. tank and callbox in Pico Cyn., Soledad Div., circa 1947. Hiram Swallow's Jeep patrol unit is at right. Hiram Swallow photo.

Patrolman Hiram Swallow performs maintenance on the Dead Horse callbox in Pico Cyn. This was one of the system of wildland callboxes provided until the widespread use of radio dispatch in the station and vehicles. Hiram Swallow photo.

EMPLOYEE'S STATEMENT — COUNTY OF LOS ANGELES

FORM 59 P Ⓟ · R — PLEASE DETACH AND RETAIN FOR YOUR RECORDS

DATE ISSUED	EMPLOYEE NAME	PAY LOC.	DEPT.	DIV.	SUB.	AMOUNT EARNED
5 10 46	HIRAM H SWALLOW		27	1		221 00
4 30 46 (ACCRUAL DATE)	INCOME TAX					6 30
COMPENSATION FOR PERSONAL SERVICES	F F W RETIREMENT					11 16
	MISCELLANEOUS DEDUCTIONS					203 54
						NET AMOUNT

NOT-NEGOTIABLE

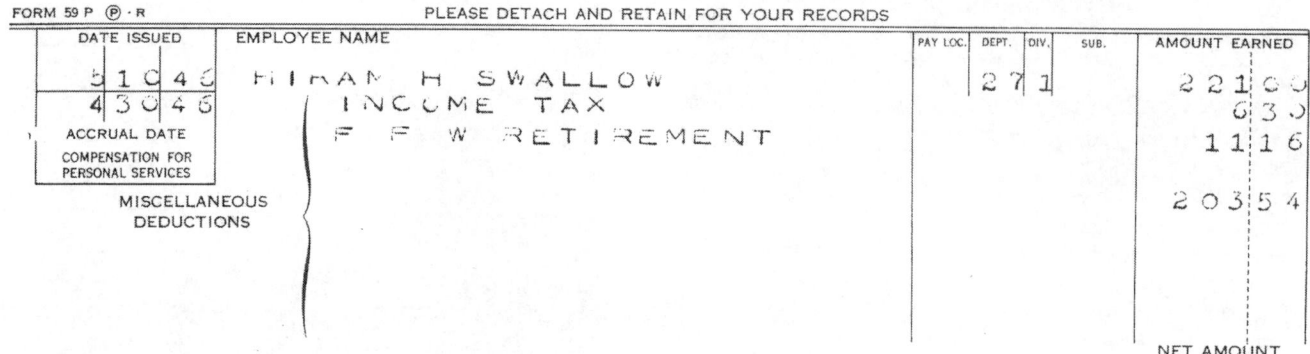

The check stub of Forest Fireman Hirman H. Swallow, Soledad Div. of the F&FW for the date of 5/10/46. The only deductions were federal income tax (no state) and F&FW retirement.

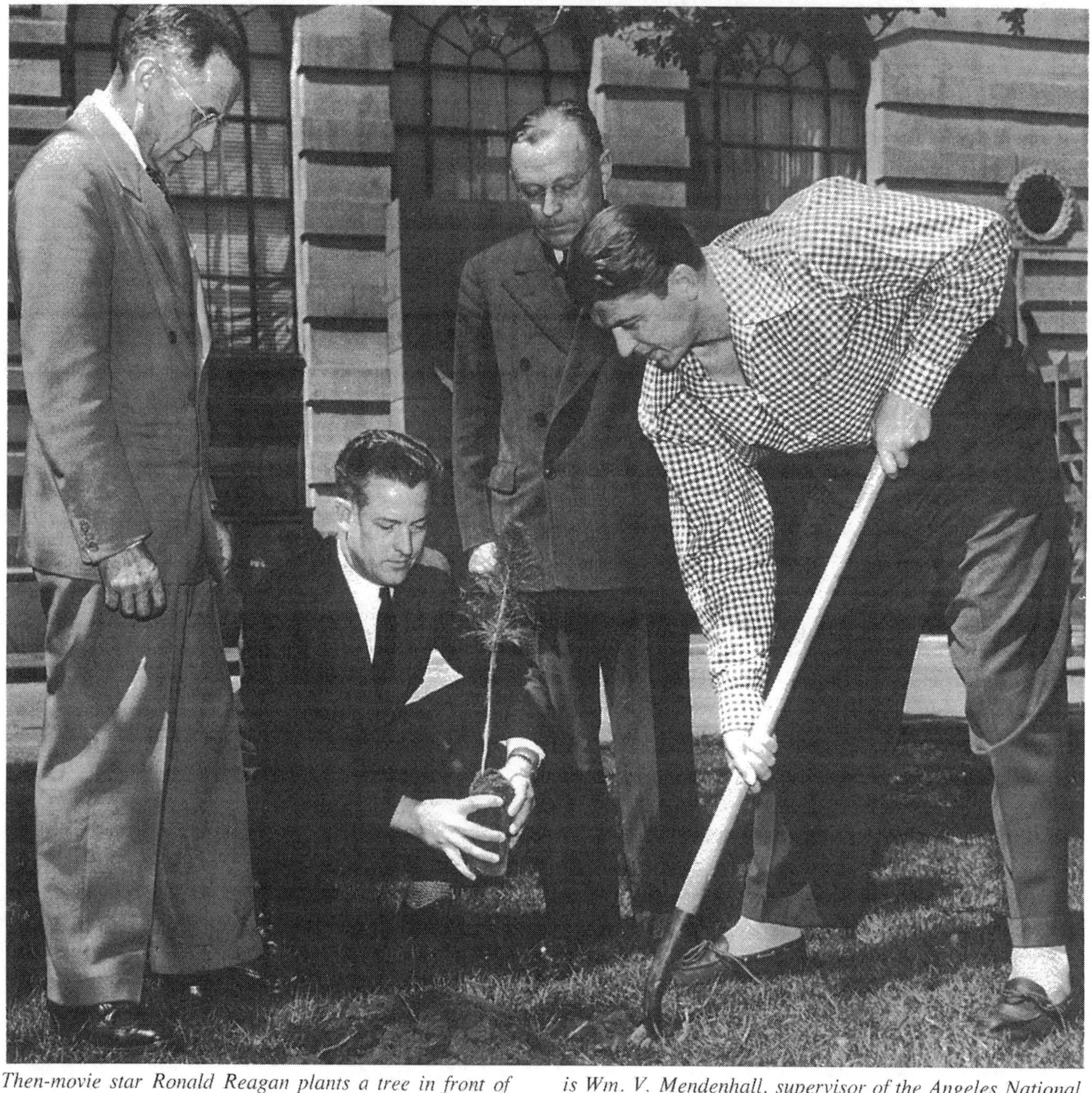

Then-movie star Ronald Reagan plants a tree in front of the Federal Building in downtown L.A. in 1950. Chief Spence Turner (l.) looks on; the man to the left of Reagan is Wm. V. Mendenhall, supervisor of the Angeles National Forest. LACoFD photo.

Altadena FPD Engine 52's Fireman Alfred Pederson, Capt. Bill Sadring and Eng. Rex Schull pose in the district's work uniform, circa 1947. By 1953, the bow ties and long-sleeve work shirts had been abandoned. The dark-blue wool uniform remained until 1969, and was worn by all hands. From the collection of Dale Magee.

Heavy dark brown to black smoke indicates the type and density of brush burning in the San Rafael (Flintridge) Hills on the border of Pasadena on a November day in 1949. This was the last day of a "Devil Wind," with very low humidity but little wind. This 100-acre fire threatened many mansions in the vicinity. From the collection of John Whelan.

The Dept.'s second ladder truck, a 1951 American La-France 85-ft. aerial, delivered to Fire Station 27. The first ladder truck was an identical 1950 model, delivered to Station 8 the year before. LACoFD photo.

A typical LACoFD district rescue squad. This 1949 Ford was placed at Station 47 in Temple City and manned with one fireman when responding with one of the surrounding engines, or with two men when responding in its own district. LACoFD photo.

Engine 46's classic 1950 Mack 1,000 gpm pumper. With less than 15,000 miles on the odometer, it was retired in the late 1960s and sent to a fire department in Mexico under the Bomberos program. From the collection of Dale Magee.

On a bright winter's day in 1949, the men of the newly-opened Fire Station 47 in Temple City polish their apparatus for the photographer. The 1948 "hi-reeler" Seagrave 1,000 gpm pumper is accompanied by a 1949 Ford ½-ton panel rescue squad and BC Keith Klinger's 1949 Ford. Maxeiner photo, from the collection of Dale Magee.

On Aug. 3, 1948, Engine 54's 1924 American LaFrance struck a truckload of scrap metal. Engineer Raymond Pytlewaski was badly injured, but, miraculously, no one was killed. LACoFD photo.

This 1947 fire involving the Beverly Blvd. bridge of the Rio Hondo River was typical of several that plagued the Dept. The creosote-soaked timbers burned with vigor. LACoFD archives.

Aftermath of a large fire in the Normandie Apartments, in Engine 7's district, circa 1948. LACo Forestry Dept. photo.

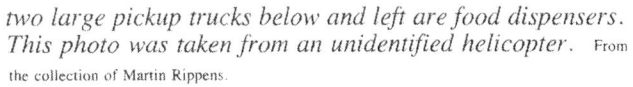

Duarte District Station 44 being used as a base fire camp for the Fish Cyn. Fire of July 4-5, 1953. Apparatus in center is a Ford LaFrance, one of those received during WW II. Ladies Auxiliary canteen car is to the left. The two large pickup trucks below and left are food dispensers. This photo was taken from an unidentified helicopter. From the collection of Martin Rippens.

Close inspection of William Santa Maria's collar insignia will reveal one trumpet, indicating that he is a lieutenant in the F&FW "Mountain Battalion" covering the Soledad Division. He poses next to his 1941 Ford patrol at the Mint Cyn. Patrol Station (81), circa 1947. Hiram Swallow photo.

Chief Spence Turner and Head Forester Ralph Van Wagner pour rye grass seed into the hopper of a leased helicopter prior to reseeding the 1948 Topanga Cyn. burn. Party at right is unidentified. LACo Forestry Dept. photo.

Changing Command

When considering the growth of the Los Angeles County Fire Department and the reputation it had achieved by 1952, it may be difficult to appreciate the fact that most of the time since 1920, when the fire warden was absorbed into the L.A. County Forestry Department, the entire combined department had been under the supervision of only one chief – Spence D. Turner. Allowing for present-day hiring and promotional practices, it would be virtually impossible for this to ever occur again.

Spence D. Turner was the chief of the department for 27 of his 32 years of service.

Chief Turner had used the original 1920 Ford Model T for his Forestry and related administrative duties. There were 21 Forestry employees during that time. By contrast, at the time of his retirement, Turner was in charge of 1,300 employees working out of 80 fire stations, fire prevention offices, lookout towers, nurseries, construction camps and dispatching centers.

Chief Turner retired on Easter Day, April 1952. A civil service examination determined his replacement later that spring, and another career member of the Forester and Fire Warden Department moved into the top position. Chief Cecil R. Gehr had joined the F&FW as a forest fireman in 1924 after attend-

Chief Cecil R. Gehr with two of his main staff members at the time of Gehr's promotion to top post. Asst. Chiefs Ted Loggins (l.) and Clarence Thrapp are in attendance. Chief Gehr wears the new-style badge of the combined F&FW and districts. LACoFD photo.

ing the University of California School of Forestry. He was appointed apparatus engineer in 1926, captain in 1927 and battalion chief in 1940. After a tour as chief deputy from 1949 to 1952, he assumed the position of chief engineer.

This was a man who had all of the qualifications to perform as well as Turner, but a person whom fate had declared would have by far the shortest term as County Forester and Fire Warden.

It was left to Chief Gehr and his staff to complete the "nuts-and bolts" work required to consummate

A classic publicity photo advertising the 1953 LACoFD Benefit and Welfare Assoc. dance. Posed on newly-restored Ford Model T Engine ½ are (l. to r.): Roberta Lynn (champagne lady for the Lawrence Welk Band), Chief Cecil R. Gehr, LA Co. Supervisor Darby and Capt. E.E. Queitsch. LACoFD photo.

Engine 82's newly-delivered 1951 International Harvester "cornbinder," following a brushfire hoselay drill in the Verdugo Hills. International photo by E.B. Hershberger.

the joining of the two departments. Common ranks, positions, pay scales and retirement systems were developed, as well as a standardized uniform. The work uniform was worn prior to 11 a.m., except during the summer fire season, when it was worn all day. It consisted of blue cotton pants and a matching zippered jacket. The material was a medium-weight "Levi-style" denim. The "fatigue uniform" worn in the station after 11 a.m. consisted of a navy-blue wool long-sleeved shirt, matching pants and black six-inch (minimum) work boots.

All parts of all uniforms, including "turnouts" (heavy canvas coats, pants, rubber boots and helmets) were purchased by the men themselves when they were hired. (After 1957, state law required that all safety equipment be purchased by the employer.)

The two-tone green of the F&FW fire apparatus was painted red. Stations were renumbered, as the "mountain battalions" were dissolved and absorbed into the Consolidated Fire Protection District *organization*. However, *funding* for the F&FW station remained the same, with monies coming from the county general fund, various state funds and Clarke-McNary funds.

More New Apparatus

A major apparatus purchase was made during the 1950 to 1952 fiscal years, as old equipment was either sold to salvage or placed in relief (reserve) status. A fleet of eighteen 1,000 gpm pumpers was built by the International Harvester Corporation. Powered by Hall-Scott six-cylinder gasoline engines, they were of a conventional open-cab design. The bulk of these rigs served in active duty until the late 1960s, and a few even into the early 1970s. Their rugged disposition and ancestry earned them the nickname "Cornbinders." These engines were assigned as follows:

Engine 18, Lennox; Engine 21, Lawndale; Engine 24, Walnut Park; Engine 25, Pico Rivera; Engine 26, La Puente; Engine 28, Flintridge; Engine 41, Willowbrook; Engine 42, Rosemead; Engine 52, Altadena; Engine 63, La Crescenta; Engine 80, Vincent; Engine 209, Florence; Engine 217, Santa Fe Springs; Engine 245, Lakewood; and Engine 282, La Canada. (The 200-numbered series indicated the apparatus as being a completely separate engine of a two-engine house.)

Chief Cecil R. Gehr inspects a recruit class in 1952 at the Santa Fe Springs training facility (Station 17). The dungaree uniform worn by these recruits was also the work uniform worn during the brush fire season until 1969. LACoFD photo.

This photo was taken July 5, 1953, during the final stages of the giant Sulphur Springs Fire in the mountains south of Little Rock-Juniper Hills. (L. to r.): BC Harvey Anderson, Chief Cecil R. Gehr. Angeles Forest Rep. Sim Jarvi, County Fire P.R. Officer Robert Singleton, Dep. Chief Keith E. Klinger and Chief's Driver Willard Miller. From the collection of John Whelan.

Chief Cecil R. Gehr and BC Harvey Anderson mull over progress during the Fish Cyn. Fire of early June 1953. This is probably the last photo taken of Chief Gehr before his death. LACoFD photo.

A Leader Is Lost

During the first week of July 1953, Chief Engineer Cecil R. Gehr had personally directed Los Angeles County fire forces in a multi-agency effort to control the huge "Sulphur Springs Fire." This fire burned 40,000 acres of brush and timber along the north slopes of the San Gabriel Mountains in the Angeles National Forest south of Palmdale, Little Rock, Pearblossom and Juniper Hills. It had extended south to the Cloudburst Summit-Mount Waterman area. This beginning of what was to be a busy fire season had left Chief Gehr with little rest.

On July 13, a fire in Topanga Canyon, with Chief Harvey Anderson in charge, claimed Gehr's attention. Upon his return to L.A. headquarters on July 14, Chief Deputy Keith Klinger offered Gehr his new car to use. News had just come in of another fire starting in Little Tujunga Canyon, north of Pacoima, with Chief Roland Percey in charge.

Chief Gehr responded northward, out of the San Fernando Valley area, on Hollywood Way towards Pacoima. He was alone, responding "Code R" – red lights and siren. Attempting to pass through the intersection against the red light at Verdugo Avenue in Burbank his car was struck broadside and crashed into a light standard. The offending car was driven by James Heinrich, who, witnesses stated, was traveling "about 50 miles per hour."

In those days, without benefit of seatbelts, Chief Gehr suffered massive injuries. He died shortly after arrival at St. Joseph's Hospital in Burbank.

This fine man was paid tribute by his fellow workers in the July 1953 edition of *Straight Streams*, the department's official Benefit and Welfare magazine:

Accident scene at Hollywood Way and Verdugo Rd., Burbank, on July 3, 1953 that claimed the life of Chief Cecil R. Gehr. His car is the 1953 Ford facing the Royal Triton sign (door open). As a result of this accident, all field chief officers and the Chief Engineer were assigned drivers. LACoFD photo.

"Chief Gehr had served as Chief Engineer of our department for a little over one year. In that time, many changes were made and new policies inaugurated. His responsibilities were tremendous. Many were the long hours he spent at his desk, in the field, and in conference, straining to bring about a reorganized and unified department.

"His first and constant thought was that no individual in the department was ever to be hurt through the proposed changes, and his secondary endeavor was to continually build a better department, improve efficiency and render better service to the community.

"He was a kindly man, and a considerate one. Through his persuasive personality, he was able to achieve help and cooperation from individuals and organizations that might not have been forthcoming under different circumstances.

"The Chief was a man's man and a fireman's fireman. He loved his job as few individuals are privileged to do. He particularly loved the business of fire fighting, the planning, the strategy and the physical contact with the fire.

"Although his term as Chief of the department was beset with tremendous problems, he maintained his fine sense of good humor throughout. He was always available to any member of the department who needed help or advice, and his callers were invariably greeted with a hearty smile, and few, if any, left his office dissatisfied. In short, Chief Gehr was the kind of man you seldom meet, and never forget."

Ironically, at 3 p.m. on July 18, as the 1,500 persons attending Chief Gehr's funeral in Inglewood filed out, the largest structure fire ever to strike the Altadena Fire Protection District was in the process of destroying one million board feet of lumber at the Johnson Lumber Company at Lincoln Avenue and Atlanta Street (now Woodbury Road). This $750,000, three-alarm fire brought out Engines 12, 11, 52, 82, 282, 28, 66, 63, 19, 5, 47 and Pasadena Engine 6. Since the majority of the chief officers were attending the funeral 25 miles away, for the first half hour or so, this fire was under the command of District Captain Marion Smith. Chiefs Victor Petroff and Roland Percey soon arrived to take command. Chief Percey was named first assistant chief two days later.

After barely a year as forester and fire warden, Chief Gehr was gone. The County Board of Supervisors adjourned for a day in his honor. The following day, Chief Deputy Keith E. Klinger was appointed acting chief engineer of the department.

Chaplain Edward Spruill leads staff officers from the funeral of Chief Cecil Royal Gehr, July 18, 1953, as off-duty department members salute. The sudden loss of this great leader came as a shock that was felt for several years. LACoFD photo.

The Klinger Era ...Part I

Keith E. Klinger, Chief Engineer, from 1953 to 1969. Unprecedented and coordinated growth took place under his leadership. LACoFD photo.

Chief Klinger's first groundbreaking ceremony as chief engineer was for the replacement for Altadena Station 11, in the spring of 1954. He watches over the shoulder of Mrs. E. Reed, a member of the Bn. 4 Ladies' Auxiliary. Looking on are (l. to r.): David D. Cox, Wilbur Stoops, Engineer Carroll V. "Cack" Foy, Fm. Watson, Capt. Harold Jackson, Capt. Sam Hancock and an unidentified fire prevention inspector. LACoFD photo.

On January 23, 1954, Keith E. Klinger completed his six-month probationary period and was permanently appointed as Los Angeles County Forester and Fire Warden and Chief of the Los Angeles County Fire Protection Districts. The combined agencies were now officially known as the Los Angeles County Fire Department. As a direct result of the death of Chief Gehr, all field chiefs, as well as Chief Klinger, had their own full-time fireman-drivers.

Under Chief Klinger's leadership, the Department entered one of its greatest growth periods. This growth was not only in size, but in professional stature. It was Chief Klinger's goal to continue to improve and upgrade the department's image and effectiveness through expansion of the training and fire prevention inspection programs, modernization of firefighting methods, apparatus replacement and new station construction. Working conditions for department personnel were also improved. That Klinger succeeded in his efforts is a historical fact.

The selection of Chief Klinger's top assistants was an item of prime importance to him. After the examination process it was decided that John Duncan would be appointed as his chief deputy. Roland Percey, by now well known nationally as an expert in brush firefighting, was chosen to be head of the firefighting division. His new rank was first assistant chief. The chief of Field Division I was Harvey Crutchfield. Division II remained under the command of Harvey Anderson.

The Forester and Fire Warden patrol stations and personnel now had equal status in every respect with their consolidated fire protection district counterparts. However, joining the two agencies resulted in some interesting changes for the personnel. Many wondered where the members of the newly-combined departments would prefer to work. Would the "Stumpies" (as they were called) of the F&FW rush to transfer into the valleys and towns as vacancies occurred? As a matter of record, just the opposite took place. As positions became available in the mountain and desert F&FW stations, district personnel transferred to these outlying areas in a steady stream. Not only were land and homes less expensive there, but the infamous Los Angeles Basin smog had already become intolerable in the valleys and towns, especially during the summer months. Even if they didn't choose to live in the outlying districts, firefighters figured that at least they could work in the fresh air for 12 shifts per month. Certainly not least of the considerations was that the "Flatlanders" (as the district firefighters were called) could gain brush fire experience – many for the first time.

The method devised to enact transfers within the county fire department was agreed upon through the cooperation of the administrative staff and the now-merged labor unions of the two departments. The method, called the "bid system," is still in effect. It continues to be a very important and valued feature of all labor contract negotiations. Simply stated, the system fills vacancies as they occur by written bid submitted by the personnel vying for the opening. The bids are processed once a month and awarded on a seniority basis. Except for firefighters who, after being employed for 10 years, receive longevity pay, seniority in the department has no other value. Those at the rank of battalion chief or above are considered to be management, and may not bid.

At the time of the merger, F&FW Union Local 1425 and the district's Local 1014 were united into one – Fire Fighters Local #1014, International Association of Fire Fighters. Jim Thompson was elected president. Membership was, and still is, voluntary. No-strike constraints prevail. There have been some stormy periods within the union local itself as well as between it and the L.A. County government. However, support has historically remained strong among the members. It is notable that a retired former Local 1014 president and L.A. County fire captain, Alfred K. Whitehead, went on to assume the presidency of the International Association of Fire Fighters of the American Federation of Labor.

To say that the period of growth of the L.A. County Fire Department during the late '40s and early '50s was rapid and sustained would be an understatement. Another surge in the population's exodus to the suburbs was in progress. Adequate fire protection necessarily had to follow. All along the new system of freeways that were just beginning to be constructed, small towns expanded into small cities. Hundreds of tract homes were being built on what was once prime agricultural land. People who had come to Southern California during the war years to work in defense industries were staying on. The population of Los Angeles County was increasing at a rate never before experienced.

More than any other fire agency in the county, the L.A. County Fire Department grew to appreciate the freeway system. Now apparatus could be quickly sent to distant incidents and "moved up" to cover empty stations in much less time.

However, on the negative side, it also became necessary to deal with high-speed auto and truck accidents. The freeways allowed traffic – except, of course, during peak rush hours – to move swiftly. Thus, traffic collisions were commonly both spectacular and violent, requiring an increasing amount of expertise in the extraction and removal of accident victims.

Current style badge reflects combining the Fire Protections Districts and the F & FW. It was phased in from 1947 through 1953. LACoFD photo.

The Monrovia Peak Fire

Chief Klinger did not have to wait long to come face to face with his first major incident as chief engineer. It happened almost in his own back yard, give or take a few miles. This incident would fully occupy his time, and that of his newly-appointed staff, for a full seven days.

The 27th of December, 1953 was the sixth continuous day of Santa Ana wind conditions. A light rain measuring 0.31 inches had fallen at Mount Wilson 23 days earlier. The rainy season, to date, had certainly not been very productive.

On Sunday, December 27, northeasterly winds over the mountain ridges and passes increased in velocity, with 70 mile-per-hour gusts recorded.

At 3:59 p.m., U.S. Forest Service Patrolman Don Starr was proceeding south along the Mount Wilson Road, which led from Red Box to Mount Wilson. Off to his left he spotted a smoke column looming up from the next large mountain to the east, Monrovia Peak. He immediately notified his dispatcher in Arcadia by radio. The dispatcher initiated a response composed of the few winter fire crews commonly found in the Angeles National Forest at that time of the year. Forest Supervisor William V. Mendenhall and Fire Control Officer Harry Grace were informed of the incident. A short time later, the Los Angeles County Fire Department dispatched a full brush assignment of six engines, one bulldozer, four camp crews and the local battalion chief. This assignment was rapidly increased over the next three days to a force of 61 engine companies from all agencies. The bulk of these were utilized along the south and west flanks along the foothills and in the Mount Wilson area.

Chief Klinger had seen the initial smoke column rising up from Monrovia Peak while he was working in the garden of his home in Arcadia. After calling and conferring with First Assistant Chief Roland Percey at the USF Headquarters on Santa Anita Avenue in Arcadia, mutual concern was directed toward saving the hundreds of homes located in the foothills in the towns of Monrovia, Arcadia, Sierra Madre, Pasadena and Altadena. The fire was moving rapidly toward these heavily-populated areas.

As darkness fell this first night, spectators by the hundreds lined Foothill Boulevard in the San Gabriel Valley to watch the flames sweeping across the foothills toward the west. Since there were practically no paved roads leading into the mountains in this area, and the terrain was very steep and covered with heavy brush, it was considered far too danger-

Chiefs Harvey Anderson, Roland Percey, Keith Klinger and Ch. Newcombe talk over strategy at Mt. Wilson during the Monrovia Peak Fire, Dec. 1953. Gene Hackley photo. LACoFD.

A final control line about three dozer blades wide leads down into upper Eaton Cyn. from the Mt. Wilson Toll Rd., Dec. 28, 1953. The old Mt. Wilson-to-LA T.V. cable can be seen on the poles on the ridgeline above. This is about as steep a terrain as a bulldozer may operate safely on. LACoFD photo.

Capt. Radke of the LA City FD observes hose being laid with a city bulldozer up a canyon during the Monrovia Peak Fire of Dec. 1953. As a result of this operation, the County Fire Dept. ordered a similar unit. Gene Hackley photo. LACoFD.

Norwalk Engine Co. 20 pumps at the Monrovia Peak Fire of Dec. 1953. Since the F&FW and districts were now one department, the "flatlanders" began to go to brush fires more frequently. B.N. Landrum photo. LACoFD.

ous for personnel to attempt any entry into the narrow canyons leading into the fire area. The only paved roads allowing ingress were the Chantry Flats Road, which led into Big Santa Anita Canyon, and the road up Sierra Madre Canyon. This historic area of the San Gabriels was crowded with dozens of original Forest Service-leased cabins and a store. It was during this first night that 33 of these rustic homes in Santa Anita Canyon burned to the ground. All residents had been evacuated, and no one was injured.

The perimeter of the fire eventually reached 36 miles. Almost all of it was in rugged canyon country, necessitating very heavy emphasis on the use of hand crews. The crews, called in by the USFS, from as far away as Arizona and New Mexico, were comprised of specially-trained Zuni Indians, masters of the brush hook and Pulaski tool. Also responding were local paid fire crews, juvenile probation camp crews, 400 paid volunteers and dozens of unpaid volunteers. To assist the hand crews, 16 bulldozers were utilized, 12 of them from seven private construction firms in the San Gabriel Valley region and one from the Los Angeles City Fire Department.

On the fifth and sixth days, the fire crept toward 5,700-foot Mount Wilson, the location of one of the famous Hale Observatories – and seven television transmitters. By this time, the wind had died down and shifted to the southwest, giving all crews along that flank of the fire some relief, since the fire in this sector was now burning into the wind. The Mount Wilson facilities were saved, as was the fire camp that had been established there. Additional fire camps were set up at Henninger Flats, Spring Camp, Deer Park, Arcadia County Park and the USFS warehouse and headquarters in Arcadia.

The Monrovia Peak Fire was declared controlled on January 3, 1954, after it had consumed 16,135 acres of watershed located above hundreds of homes in six cities. There would most assuredly be flooding if heavy rains fell within the next three months.

As it happened, heavy winter rains began shortly after the fire was controlled. The dreaded fire-flood sequence was set in motion. Debris-laden waters cascaded down the hillsides and into the canyons, carrying mud, rock and ash through streets and yards and into dwellings in the northern sections of Sierra Madre and Arcadia. Property damage was extensive.

A secondary, less visible, aspect of the fire-flood sequence was also taking place: the water lost down storm drains and concrete washes eventually found its way to the sea, rather than to percolating slowly into the ground to replenish the water tables under the San Gabriel Valley.

Fire equipment from Kern Co., LA Co. and the USFS stages in the parking lot near the Mt. Wilson Observatory on Jan. 2, 1954, at the end of operations for the Monrovia Peak Fire. A substantial rain fell a few days later, helping complete extinguishment. Gene Hackley photo, LACoFD.

A simulated brush fire operation staged for Channel 11 KTTV somewhere in the Montebello Hills, near HQ. A 1951 International pumper is at left; a 1950 International tractor and lowboy arrives with a bulldozer as the T.V. camera rolls. Engine "1/2" is almost lost in the dust, right center. Rothschild photo, from the LACoFD.

135

An Attempted Remedy

The Los Angeles County Board of Supervisors responded to this unhappy chain of events by creating the L.A. County Watershed Commission. Chief Klinger, Angeles National Forest Supervisor William V. Mendenhall, and representatives from the County Flood Control District, Army Corps of Engineers and California Division of Forestry, as well as the mayors of 12 foothill cities met on March 20, 1954 at the Arcadia City Hall, and several times a year thereafter. The committee attempted to determine the amount of additional funding that could be acquired from affected local, state and federal governments in order to mount a meaningful campaign to prevent and control large mountain fires. Other counties in Southern California also developed such commissions. Collectively, they were known as the Southern California Watershed Council.

By the end of 1954, the L.A. County Watershed Commission concluded that $515,000 per year should be spent for additional fire stations, crews and engines. The stations were to be manned year-round in the national forests. The sum of $195,000 was recommended for new heliports, water tanks and firebreak maintenance, along with increased funding for hand crew camps, especially juvenile probation camps. The "juvy" crews had been very successful in tree planting and construction projects. It was felt that they could be further utilized for very little more than the cost of additional camp quarters, crew trucks and foremen's salaries. The "juvies" received 50 cents per day, plus food and lodging. Each inmate was assigned to a crew under the auspices of the L.A. County Probation Department.

Despite these optimistic plans, by the end of the 1957-58 fiscal year, only one-third of the minimum recommended dollar amount had actually been funded. Although better than nothing, it was not really a meaningful amount. More serious brush and forest fires would no doubt occur and would likely not be controlled before becoming unmanageable. Although no one could have predicted it at the time, the next four summers would be among the warmest and driest ever seen in Southern California. In fact, the summer of 1955 would hold the record for almost 30 years.

Enter Aircraft

A method of fighting wildland fires that would certainly have assisted in combating the giant Sulphur Springs fire and the destructive Monrovia Peak fire of the same year was tested extensively during the fall of 1953 at Muroc Dry Lake, near Mojave in the California desert. At the suggestion of Donald W. Douglas, test director of the Douglas Aircraft Company, attempts were made under controlled conditions to "bomb" fires with water from the air, using large,

A guided tour of the L.A. Co. Forester and Fire Warden main nursery facility at Henninger Flats is conducted by Head Forester Ralph Van Wagner (sixth from r.). The occasion was the Oct. 1954 meeting of the L.A. Co. Forest and Watershed committee. LACoFD photo.

A Douglas DC-7 makes test water drops at Muroc dry lake bed in the Mohave Desert on Nov. 17, 1953. These tests helped prove the feasibility of using such fixed-wing aircraft during brush and forest fire operations. LACoFD photo.

fixed-wing aircraft. (Smaller planes had been tested sporadically since the mid-30s.)

Chief Engineer Klinger, along with other top California chiefs, observed the tests of the four-engined DC-7s. The aircraft made successive passes at various altitudes, dropping 1,600 gallons of water on pre-set fires.

James K. Mace, deputy state forester, summarized the feelings of those in attendance: "Obvious procedures entail the use of such ships over rugged terrain difficult to reach by ground routes. Research has just begun, but we may well be on the threshold of a new era in fire control."

Within three years, regular use of leased, converted World War II aircraft in firefighting operations began. Commonly-used planes included the Grumman TBF or TBM torpedo bomber, the Consolidated PBY-5 patrol plane, the Grumman F7F fighter-bomber, the Douglas DC-6 and DC-7 transport, the Boeing B-17 bomber and the North American B-25. There was initially also occasional use of the Stearman N5N bi-plane, which was often used for cropdusting.

The L.A. County Fire Department was not far from developing its own "air force." The type of aircraft utilized has changed over the years, but the underlying principle has remained, having proven itself many times over to be of incredible value as a major tool in the fight against wildland urban interface fires.

The Rothschild Fire

To say that oil refineries are inherently dangerous as far as their capacity for enormous-potential fire hazards is an understatement. In spite of various automatic shut-off systems, vents, dikes and onsite fire brigades, mishaps do occur. On May 18, 1954, the Rothschild Oil Company refinery in Santa Fe Springs was the site of one such mishap. In retrospect, this ranks as one of the greater petroleum-related incidents ever faced by the Los Angeles County Fire Department.

It began when a stuck vent on a 2,500-gallon tank of casing-head gasoline allowed vapors to accumulate and, eventually, migrate. A gentle sea breeze carried the heavier-than-air fumes to the north side of the plant, where they found an open flame in a gas-fired boiler. At 3:45 a.m., the vapors ignited and flashed back to the tank, setting it and everything in between on fire. The scene was a mass of flames.

A first-alarm assignment from the Los Angeles County Fire Department was quickly sent by the Battalion 2 Dispatching Office, then located at Fire Station 17. The L.A. County firefighters and the onsite brigade attempted to confine the fire to the area of origin, which, in this case, was especially important, as the fire was adjacent to a tank farm contain-

The engineer on Engine 22's General-Pacific pumper prepares to charge the monitor during the Rothschild Oil fire in Santa Fe Springs, May 18, 1954. Note salvage cover on far side of the rig to protect it from radiated heat. LACoFD photo.

ing 45 42,000-gallon gasoline storage tanks.

The fire burned for several hours and was almost at the point of containment when gases leaking from damaged piping, later identified as carrying butane, ignited. This spread the fire to additional gasoline facilities. The tremendous heat caused adjacent tanks to rupture, spill and ignite. Reacting to the sudden increase in the size and intensity of the fire, the firefighting crews were forced to retreat, some in great haste.

A second alarm and a third alarm assignment were requested, bringing eight additional engine companies and a truck company, plus staff personnel. Two truckloads of mechanical foam were transported to the scene from headquarters, and numerous 2½" lines were laid and siamesed into foam eductors.

The fire began to spread from tank to tank. The contents of the leaking tanks began to fill the dirt dikes designed to contain such leaks, but in this case, because so much water and foam had been pumped into the fire area, some of the dikes began to overflow. Firefighters, under protective water-screen sprays from fire hoses, entered the area and proceeded to raise the height of the dikes, using shovels and whatever soil was available. One firefighter, Captain Tom Showers, received burns on his feet when some of the involved liquid overflowed as he was working on the dikes.

After a valiant day-long struggle, the fire was controlled. Seven tanks of gasoline were lost, totalling 350,000 gallons of product, along with considerable related piping and other refinery structures. Due to adequate hoselines that protected the expansive exposure and the holding ability of the augmented dikes, 40 tanks of gasoline were saved from destruction. Two hundred exhausted firefighters picked up their equipment and returned to quarters after a tremendous and relatively successful struggle.

Operation Firestop

All during the summer and fall of 1954, the Los Angeles County Fire Department, along with Los Angeles City, the U.S. Forestry Service, the California Department of Forestry, the U.S. Weather Bureau and the University of California, participated in a series of experiments using all manner of new approaches and devices to help control wildland fires. The bulk of the experiments were held at the U.S. Marine Corps base at Camp Pendleton in Oceanside, California, and were labeled "Operation Firestop."

Among the significant devices and methods used for the first time were a lightweight television camera to observe a fire from a helicopter or other aircraft, laying of 1" and 1½" hoselines from a pumper truck to the fire scene using a tray mounted in or under a helicopter and using a helicopter for water drops on wildland fires. The helicopters utilized built-on water tanks as well as "helitanks." Helitanks were 35-gallon canvas tanks carried under the helicopter. Water was released through a long tube at the rear of the canvas bag. Portable 100-gallon tanks equipped with a small gasoline motor and pump could also be delivered by helicopter into remote areas and used for final overhaul of brush and forest fires.

The finale of the events was the dropping of 600 gallons of water from a torpedo bay of a U.S. Navy TBM torpedo bomber flown by the famous test pilot Paul Mantz. A ground pattern 90 feet wide and 250 feet long was drenched.

A similar series of experiments had been carried out during the previous year at a dry lake in California's Mojave Desert. At that time, Chief Engineer Klinger commented, "The water did not completely extinguish the fire, but we did not expect it to. However, it did allow the men to go in and work on the fire, whereas before (the drop) they were unable to get anywhere near it."

After these tests, the die was cast. Chief Klinger had been a champion of airpower to fight fires, and

An AG-2 makes a practice 300-gal. water drop during experiments connected with "Operation Firestop" at Camp Pendleton. From this time on, use of fixed-wing water-dropping planes increased rapidly throughout the West. B.N. Landrum photo, LACoFD.

the tests served to further his enthusiasm, as well as that of the other fire service agencies represented. Klinger further stated, "... most of us have concluded that there is a tremendous potential in the use of helicopters and other aircraft by firefighting agencies, not only for day-to-day work or in forest and brush fires, but in civilian defense and other major disaster operations. You simply cannot appreciate the value of these aircraft until you see them in action."

These words would be prophetic, for within three years the County of Los Angeles was to have two helicopters in use by its sheriff's department, and one in its fire department. This proved to be a breakthrough in firefighting technology that spelled widespread use of aircraft by progressive fire agencies involved with wildland firefighting operations.

A Quiet Fadeout

During Operation Firestop, some experiments were conducted in which television cameras were installed in lookout towers, their electronic eyes perhaps eliminating the need for human observers. While the concept worked in principle, the industrial haze (smog) throughout the Los Angeles Basin precluded such use in that area. In fact, visibility had decreased to such a point that, even by the middle '40s, there were many days in the summer when the lookouts were totally useless.

One by one, the county lookout towers along the foothills of the San Gabriel Mountains were closed down. Temple Tower, San Jose, San Rafael, Verdugo Peak, Pacoima Peak Tower – all but one fell by the wayside by the early 1950s. (See Chapter 11.)

Although most of the towers were demolished, the San Rafael Lookout may still be seen, intact. Located at the end of Sugarloaf Drive in the extreme south end of Fire Station 19's district in the Flintridge Hills, it is covered with transmitting dishes and FM radio transmitter antennae, but is still recognizable as having been a lookout tower.

The Castro Peak Lookout is also still intact, including all interior furnishings. It is located at the Henninger Flats Nursery, 3½ miles up the Mount Wilson Toll Road, at the extreme north end of Fire Station 66's district. It was moved to its present location from Malibu in 1986, and is available for public viewing.

Presently, there are no operational lookout towers in the mountains surrounding Los Angeles, including the Angeles National Forest. Due to the spread of smog beyond greater Los Angeles, as well as cost factors relating to upkeep and manning, it is doubtful that lookout towers will ever again be used in these areas.

New Rolling Stock

During the 1953-54 fiscal year, provisions were made to continue replacing the older Seagrave and Mack pumpers that had been purchased prior to and during World War II. In addition apparatus was needed to equip the series of new fire stations that had been constructed through the mid- and late '50s.

An order for 18 new cab-forward 1,250 and 1,500 gpm pumpers, powered by Hall-Scott engines, was placed with the Crown Coach Company of Los Angeles. A manufacturer primarily of school buses and a few pieces of commercial chassis fire apparatus, Crown began its new line of "Firecoaches" in 1951. Winning the bid from Los Angeles County marked a major move into fire apparatus manufacturing for Crown.

Most of the early Crowns were 1,250 gpm units. The larger-capacity pumps were to follow in later orders, since many areas of the county were experiencing heavy construction of commercial and manufacturing buildings and facilities that required heavy-duty fire equipment for adequate fire protection.

Regardless of pump capacities, all Crown apparatus

Head Dispatcher Owen Couey keeps track of the status of the "Bootlegger Fire" on the blackboard of the F&FW command trailer on Aug. 19, 1954. The data on this map places the fire in Station 80's district. Chiefs Barton and Manchester are in charge. B.N. Landrum photo, LACoFD.

City Terrace Engine 32 and Copter 2 practice a hose laying technique that was not widely used. Photo was taken at the training center in 1959. LACoFD photo.

Former Engine 17's 1930 1,000 gpm Seagrave pumper in service as Central Mfg. Dist.'s hose wagon – the first "hog." This rig would remain in service until the arrival of the first Crown pumpers in 1954-55. Shawn Ryan collection.

Office of Civilian Defense officials, Chief Klinger and the chiefs of five smaller towns in the San Gabriel Valley pose in front of Fire Sta. 64 on the occasion of the arrival of the first shipment of state-owned civilian defense fire engines. All were 1954 GMC 1,000 gpm pumpers, completely equipped. LACoFD photo.

Angeles Mesa Engine Co. 58's brand-new 1959 Crown 1,250 gpm pumper. These rigs featured a two-stage Waterous pump, 500-gal. water tank, 1,600 ft. of 2½" hose and two hose reels. This model apparatus was well received, and served the dept. satisfactorily for 25 years. Warren Bowen photo.

Stock LA Co. FD photo shows typical engine co. equip. LACoFD photo.

One of only two of a kind, a 1957 F.W.D.-Calavar 500 gal. tanker/pumper assigned as Engine 382, the 3rd engine operating out of Station 82. Its four-wheel drive feature enabled it to travel many places an ordinary pumper could not. An identical rig was stationed in Newhall at Station 73. LACoFD photo.

Typical truck company equip. circa 1958. LACoFD photo.

Glendora Engine Co. 85's brand-new 1959 "Toyophet" Crown, so named because of undecipherable Oriental writing found on the dashboard. This apparatus featured a 1,000-gal. pump instead of the usual 1,250, and a shorter wheelbase, though it did retain the 500-gal. tank. Due to a too-small engine, however, it did not perform well in hill country. Warren Bowen photo.

On June 7, 1955, Supervisor Burton Chace and Chief Keith Klinger pose with the prototype of the revised and enlarged sign that would be placed at the entrance to all hazardous fire areas in the county. These signs were, and are, hung about May 15 of each year, as the fire season opens, and pulled down for maintenance and storage at the close of the season. The signs are constructed of ⅝" plywood. B.N. Landrum photo, LACoFD.

was equipped with Waterous centrifugal pumps and rotary gear road pumps. Power steering and standardized compartments were initiated with this order. Their shorter wheelbase allowed a 37-foot turning radius – a vast improvement.

On June 1, 1954, the first Crown Firecoach was delivered to Fire Station 40 in the Pico District. This unit had a 1,250 gpm pump, a 500-gallon water tank and a 295 hp Hall-Scott gasoline motor. The second rig was delivered immediately thereafter to Fire Station 27 in the Central Manufacturing District. This unit had a 1,500 gpm pump and a 320 hp motor, but was otherwise similar to Engine 40's Crown. Additional 1,500 gpm units went to Station 8, West Hollywood; Station 9, Florence District; and Station 17, in Santa Fe Springs. These units also had 320 hp motors.

One of the regional battalion dispatch offices, this one at Fire Station 82 in Battalion 4. Dispatcher Harriet Nepil talks on the public service phone. Six months hence, the new Central Dispatch for the San Gabriel Valley opened at 5710 Peck Rd. in El Monte, adjacent to Fire Station 57. Photographer unknown.

The primary difference between 1,250 gpm units going to the fire protection districts and those delivered to the hill and desert areas of the Forester and Fire Warden was the size of the water tank. Consolidated Fire Protection District rigs were equipped with 500-gallon tanks, while the F&FW rigs had 600-gallon tanks.

The first 18 Crowns delivered throughout 1954 and 1955 were well received by all concerned. Having proved themselves, an additional order was placed with Crown for 22 units to be delivered throughout 1956 and 1957. For the next several years through 1977, many more Crowns were ordered as the need arose, usually five or six at a time.

With the exception of two 1963 sedan-cab Seagrave pumpers and two Coast pumpers delivered in 1958, the department ordered Crown Firecoach apparatus exclusively until 1971-72, when, once again, a major replacement program commenced.

1955

By July 1, 1953, the consolidation that had begun under the command of Chiefs Turner and Gehr had been completed. The energies of the department were now directed toward keeping up with the continuing phenomenal growth of the county. The Los Angeles County Fire Department was conceded to be the second-largest fire department in the western United States – and the fastest-growing in the nation.

Of the total 4,000 square miles in the county, the L.A. County Fire Department by 1955 protected almost half of this area. The population in the unincorporated areas had risen to 1.3 million, protected by 87 L.A. County fire stations, most of which had a single engine company. As industrial and commercial districts continued to enlarge, the need for specialized fire apparatus became apparent. Two American LaFrance 85-foot aerial ladder trucks were delivered in 1951 and 1952 to Stations 8 (West Hollywood) and 27 (Central Manufacturing). These were the first truck companies placed in service by the LACOFD. The number of rescue squads continued to increase, with 11 in service by this time. With consolidation came the necessity of establishing a combined headquarters building that would house the ever-growing support staff. During 1952, property at 1320 N. Eastern Avenue in East Los Angeles had been purchased, and for $320,000, a two-story concrete office structure and basement dispatching center was constructed on the crest of a hill overlooking the City Terrace area for then Chief Gehr and his staff. In addition to housing Clief Klinger and his top staff members, the new facility was also home to a portion of the now-30-man Fire Prevention Bureau, the Forestry Division, Research and Planning, Business and Payroll divisions, Public Information Office, Photographic Section, Chaplain's office, stockroom and conference rooms.

Of particular significance was the dispatching office. Prior to 1955, most dispatching had been done at a battalion or division level. It was felt that a dispatching office having jurisdiction over a larger area would be more efficient. This led to combining several centers into one central office in the new headquarters building basement. Head Dispatcher Owen Couey and his staff dispatched for the entire county east, south and west of Los Angeles, except for the Malibu mountains. All of the dispatchers were male, as were the remaining dispatchers at the Malibu Dispatch Office at Fire Station 65 in Malibu and Soledad Dispatch at Station 73 in Newhall. Women dispatchers were collectively transferred from the other battalions' dispatching centers to a new facility constructed behind Fire Station 57, located on North Peck Road in the Norwood (now El Monte) area. This new facility, called Valley Dispatch, opened on September 20, 1954. It became the alarm center for the entire San Gabriel Valley, as well as the Crescenta-Canada Valley, and remains so today.

New FM three-way radio equipment with up to 600 watts of power was installed at both L.A. and Valley dispatch centers. However, initial dispatching was still done mostly over county telephone lines and through the original switchboards. The first 12 "selective-calling" units for dispatching by radio were soon installed at the L.A. office. This initial selective calling system was gradually expanded throughout the department, leading to 100 percent radio dispatching by 1972 (unless the alarm originated from one of the fire alarm boxes in East Los Angeles, Commerce or Marina Del Rey.)

The short-lived Station 86 was eliminated as several annexations occurred in the East Los Angeles-Central Manufacturing District areas. The desert areas adjacent to the Antelope Valley, especially Palmdale, Lancaster, Quartz Hill and regions to the east, began to grow along with the rest of the County of Los Angeles. Aircraft plants were constructed near the Palmdale Airport. Several necessary adjustments in fire protection facilities were made during the 1954-55 year. Among these were the installation of paid firefighters at Station 84, Quartz Hill. At Palmdale and Lancaster, call men were replaced with paid personnel supplemented by call men. New stations 92 and 93 were constructed at Littlerock and Pearblossom and staffed with call men. Station 79, at Valyermo (Big Rock) received a Mack 500 gpm pumper and two additional firefighters, upgrading that station from a one-man patrol station.

The F&FW Pine Canyon Station Number 78 in the western Leona Valley also received a Mack pumper and larger crew, as did Station 81 in Mint Canyon.

All of this growth resulted in the formation of Battalion 11 and increased the number of field divisions to three. Division I now encompassed the central and southern county areas. Division II was composed of the San Gabriel Valley and adjacent areas. Division III included the mountain and desert areas to the west and north.

Co. Supervisor Burton W. Chace, Chief Engineer Keith Klinger (on tractor) and crews of Station 3 and Engine 32 watch as Norma Duarte turns the first shovelful of earth as construction commences on the Cecil R. Gehr Training Center on Aug. 19, 1954 B.N. Landrum photo, LACoFD.

Engines 3 and 32, Truck 27 and Rescue 3 perform multiple hose lays in a demonstration marking the dedication of the Cecil R. Gehr Training Center, Nov. 14, 1954. LACoFD photo.

Growth was rapid and continuous. So rapid in fact, that the system could barely keep up! Although the planning for expansion had been carefully coordinated with the National Board of Fire Underwriters and Klinger's staff member Virgil DeLapp, some field facilities were taxed to the limit. Training facilities were but one example. As a fitting climax to the banner year of 1955, the five-story, $200,000 Cecil R. Gehr Training Center, located just north of the HQ building on Eastern Avenue, was completed in June. It was dedicated on November 14, 1955, by Chief Klinger, Supervisor John Anson Ford and Mrs. Cecil R. Gehr, widow of Chief Gehr. One hundred new men had been trained there by the time of the dedication. The staff, consisting of captains Rex Schull and James Furber, continued to train new firemen on a two-platoon basis. The old facility at Station 17 in Santa Fe Springs was temporarily retained for the use of its oil firefighting equipment.

At this time, the County Forestry nursery program was in need of expansion as well. Three juvenile probation camps were selected as sites of new branch nurseries to assist the by-now-overtaxed Henninger Flats seedling production program. By the time of Chief Klinger's retirement, four more branch nurseries would be established, bringing the total to seven, in addition to the Henninger facility.

During 1955, one of the greater threats to the continuity of the Los Angeles County Fire Department presented itself in the community of Lakewood. The county fire and sheriff departments had protected this area since the district formed in 1941. Now, the area was due to be developed into a planned community of 18,000 homes and 70,000 people. Should this area incorporate and develop its own public services, a large gap would be created in the county's sphere of influence.

Sheriff Peter Pitchess and Chief Keith Klinger met with Lakewood officials during early 1956, and together they formulated a plan. Los Angeles County would continue providing services to the new city by having it join the Consolidated Fire Protection District via a contract, and, in a similar manner, retain the Sheriff's Department. In so doing, the new City of Lakewood kept its county fire station (45) and availed itself of the services of other county stations surrounding the city, as well as gaining another station near the border of Long Beach – Station 94. (This engine, a 1943 Mack, was housed in a tent pending the outcome of an annexation attempt by the City of Long Beach. The attempt ultimately failed.)

This contract plan example was followed, upon incorporation, by dozens of other small cities in Los Angeles County in years following, as they attempted to retain a high level of service at a minimum cost. From 1956 on, a contract for service from the county sheriff or fire department, by any city, was referred to as the "Lakewood Plan."

The Turnbull, San Dimas and La Habra Heights Incidents

The dates of August 31 to September 2, 1955 were to be long remembered in the Los Angeles County Fire Department. Due to the long-term drying ef-

The LACoFD has, on occasion, inherited some amazing fire apparatus upon contracting with a city to provide fire protection. This 1938 Ford tanker and 1929 Cadillac pumper and equipment transporter were in place in Lakewood when the county took over. Their fates are unknown. Glen Alton photo, from the collection of Dale Magee.

fect of this, the hottest summer in recorded history in Los Angeles, and in particular, the dry conditions on these three days, it was obvious that major problems would plague the department if a fire were to start anywhere, and fire conditions were worsening with each successive day.

On August 31, a serious but short-lived brush fire had flashed through a portion of Turnbull Canyon in the Whittier Hills, located south of Hacienda Heights and north of Whittier. Burning in heavy brush, the fire had threatened homes in that area.

On September 1, a far more serious fire burst out of the barrancas and orange groves south of the township of San Dimas and threatened to burn into the heart of the town itself. The local railroad station and several homes were destroyed. This was due, in part, to a woefully inadequate water supply in that area.

September 2 brought with it a continuation of the 100-plus-degree heat, accompanied by humidity readings in the 10 percent range, similar to the previous two days. Had Santa Ana wind conditions also prevailed, it is likely that the city of Whittier would have suffered serious damage from a brush fire that began in the Whittier Hills on that infamous third day. The fire erupted near Skyline Drive and Hacienda Boulevard in La Habra Heights.

At 1:10 p.m., the City of Whittier fire dispatcher informed the Los Angeles County fire dispatcher that a fire was threatening structures in the vicinity. A normal first-alarm assignment of six engines, one camp crew, one tractor and a battalion chief was dispatched.

Fire conditions were so extreme that when Chief Klinger, the field division chief and two additional battalion chiefs responded four minutes later, they were closely followed by three more engine companies, a second camp crew and a 1,200-gallon tanker from the Pacoima Warehouse. Full second and third alarm assignments were filled out soon thereafter. A concentrated effort was made to save homes and lives and stop the easterly spread of the fire.

Chief Harvey Anderson was also dispatched from Malibu, at Chief Klinger's request, to contribute his expertise. First Assistant Chief Roland Percey was called from home to the Los Angeles headquarters to cover the rest of the county should another fire break out.

Although the fire subsequently burned only 900 acres of brush and caused little structural damage, a most unexpected and tragic occurrence took place during the height of operations. It was the first of its kind in the history of the department. Excerpts from the official report submitted by Chief Klinger to the Chief Administrative Officer Arthur J. Will and the Board of Supervisors perhaps best describe what occurred:

"So that your honorable board may be apprised of the tragedy which occurred on the La Habra fire of September 2, 1955, which took the lives of one Los Angeles County Fire Captain and five members of Probation Forestry Camp 5-1, and injuries to seven other persons, the following report is submitted.

"The first reports at the fire indicated that it was imperiling homes and lives in La Habra Heights. The La Habra Heights Volunteer Fire Department was on the scene at the time L.A. County units arrived. Due to the extremely adverse weather conditions, which the U.S. Weather Bureau called the worst in the history of Southern California, and because of the experience of the L.A. County Fire Department on fires in Turnbull Canyon two days previous, and in San Dimas the day before, more equipment was dispatched to the La Habra Heights fire than is usually dispatched under ordinary circumstances.

"Considering the locale of the tragic accident, it was the opinion of the county fire captain and his crew, as well as the County Forestry foreman in charge of Crew 5-1, that the firemen and the camp crew could work there safely. Firemen directed their attention to extinguishing a small, isolated fire in a corral with their hose lines. This was done. The Camp Crew was then to build a small firebreak in preparation for laying hose in case it became necessary to fight the fire at that point. (Such assignments on the outer periphery at the scene of a fire are normal assignments for a Camp Crew.) The crew formation extended from a point 25 feet from the lawn of the nearest dwelling to a point 175 feet to the south.

"According to the statements of eyewitnesses, and all survivors of the fire, there was no active fire in the vicinity observed by any of them just prior to the apparent blow-up. Each person interviewed stated that immediately prior to the accident they felt a strong wind, followed immediately by smoke and what appeared to them to be an explosion. This phenomenon is a behavior of fire which experts find to be unpredictable, and is not well understood. As the members of your Honorable Board are aware, this is one of the problems that 'Operation Firestop' is attempting to solve through study and research.

"The synopsis of statements of eyewitnesses expresses the concurrence as follows: The fire was in a very quiet condition (at that location) and there was no visible flame, and only a few remaining embers in the vicinity of the corral. Suddenly, flames exploded out of the top of the draw into a number of eucalyptus trees which deflected heat and flames down upon the men and engulfed them instantly."

The heaviest loss of life, five men, was to Crew 5-1, under the command of Foreman Lewis Randall. Also killed was Fire Captain Glenn Rockey of Engine Company 4, South San Gabriel. Rockey, a 15-year veteran of the department, witnessed the flashover, grabbed the 1-inch reel line from his engine and attempted to run downhill into the area of flames in order to save the boys. He gave his life in the effort. Seven other men received burns.

Chief Klinger's report continues:

"In almost 24 years of such (camp crew)

duties, several thousand young men have participated in the Probation Camp programs. In this time prior to September 2, 1955, there had been no serious injuries. This is a remarkable record. The results of extensive inquiry fail to reveal any basis on which this unfortunate accident could have been anticipated and avoided. It appears that all normal precautions were taken not to place the men assigned to these duties in places of danger or foreseeable disaster. The Departments of Probation and Forest and Fire Warden extend deepest sympathy to the bereaved families of the firefighters and the members of Probation Camp 5, all of whom were giving highly creditable service in the protection of life and property. They gave their lives in the public service."

Camp 5, located in Sycamore Canyon north of San Dimas, was renamed "Camp Glen Rockey" in honor of Engine 4's fallen leader.

The End of Stage Eight

A type of fire problem peculiar to the area in and around Los Angeles is the "movie lot." Large structure house "sets," are fabricated for use during a movie and then disassembled or stored away. These sets are often stored in the same building, which may itself be a movie set. Since all construction, except for the building itself, is temporary and designed to be easily moved around, the finished products are often quite flimsy. They are usually made of light wood and canvas. Since the material is reused, many coats of paint may cover its surface. All of these features are conducive to rapid fire spread.

During the 1950s, sprinkler systems were not required in these structures. Consequently, an occasional mishap did occur, almost always with disastrous results.

Cities with the potential for studio fires were (and still are) Universal City, Burbank, Culver City, West Los Angeles and the Sunset Strip district, which is now incorporated as the City of West Hollywood.

On May 16, 1952, Los Angeles County and Los Angeles City had assisted Burbank with a large soundstage fire at Warner Brothers Studios that caused $5 million damage. In May of 1957, a far-less-serious fire occurred at Universal Studios, destroying two sound stages.

At 4:11 a.m. on July 21, 1958, an American District Telegraph Alarm rang in West Hollywood stations 7 and 8, indicating a fire at the Sam Goldwyn Studios, Santa Monica Boulevard and Formosa, north

A fire burns downhill and against the wind during the La Habra Heights Fire of Sept. 2, 1955, with another three or four crews such as the one in the foreground, considerable progress might have been made along this line. B.N. Landrum photo, LACoFD.

The scene where five perished on Sept. 3, 1955. Explosive heat from the fire roaring up the deep canyon on the right focused on the grass and eucalyptus trees, center, igniting them under the men, foreground. They were instantly engulfed in flames. LACoFD photo.

In April 1955, Chief Keith Klinger traveled to Washington, D.C. to stump for more funds for wildland fire protection for So. Calif. watershed areas. Here he meets with then-Vice President Richard M. Nixon. The mission was largely successful. White House staff photo.

side, center. Engines 8 and 208, Truck 8, Rescue 8, Engine 7 and Battalion 1 responded. Upon arrival, they requested simultaneous second and third alarms. The second alarm brought engines 38, 82, 14 and 209, along with Battalion Chief Bennett, Assistant Chief Barton, Assistant Chief Weyant, Chaplain Ross Barb and Public Information Officer Robert Singleton. The third alarm consisted of Los Angeles City engines 51 and 27, Truck 27, Squad 27, Engine 41, Truck 61 and Battalion Chief King. Upon arrival, the LAFD also requested a second alarm, increasing the assignment level to four alarms and bringing engines 52, 61 and 82, Truck 29 and Assistant Chief Thad Whippo.

The southern portion of the building was across the county into the City of Los Angeles. The building, measuring 200 feet by 400 feet by 65 feet, was fully involved upon the arrival of the first engine companies. City-county boundary lines were completely ignored. The involved structures and exposures on both sides of the boundary contained flammable set storage, sound stages and related motion-picture equipment.

Firefighter tactics consisted largely of preventing the fire's spread. Heavy streams generated by monitors and ladder pipes were employed. Additionally, 2½" handlines were used wherever feasible. Close cooperation between the city and county units was fully in force – and it paid off. The fire was confined to the building of origin. The damage totaled $2 million.

Mutual aid operations had assisted all parties involved and would do so for years to come. In 1974, this entire scenario was repeated when the Sam Goldwyn Studios again suffered the loss of a sound stage and extensive damage to adjacent buildings, as well as in May of 1967, when a huge fire at Universal Studios destroyed several sound stages.

The next logical step in cooperation came about in the early 1980s when automatic aid procedures were inaugurated. Here, requests for aid are agreed upon in advance and dispatched on the first alarm as a part of the initial assignment.

Paid Fire Camps — A Major Upgrade

Over the years, paying crews to fight forest fires with hand tools has been a customary procedure in Los Angeles County. As the Forester and Fire Warden merged with the fire protection districts in

July 17, 1955 saw a department tractor laying a 1½" hoseline up a firebreak to be "wyed off" into smaller 1" lines for final overhaul of the Switzer Fire north of La Canada.

Since their advent in 1925, bulldozers have always been utilized to the maximum by the LACoFD. G.Hutchinson photo. LACoFD.

1953, this vital function was carried over into the present-day department.

A large and important camp had been built for a firefighting and construction crew during the WPA-CCC Depression years, at first located in the Arroyo Seco area. It was later moved to Deer Canyon, south of La Crescenta in the Verdugo Hills. When the time came to increase the number of paid camps during the early 1950s, consideration was given to rebuilding and reopening this facility as paid Camp Number 2. After a lengthy inspection by Chief Klinger, in the company of various county officials with the power to influence decisions, it was concluded that the camp was inadequate for then-present day use. An alternate site was chosen, north of the Arroyo Seco District headquarters of the USFS, in Oak Grove Park, east of what is now known as La Canada-Flintridge.

The new site placed the fire department in direct competition for the use of the land with the California Institute of Technology's famous Jet Propulsion Laboratory, which was situated just to the north. Through the influence of Pasadena City Manager Donald C. MacMillan and Pasadena Fire Chief S.H. Edmondson, this land, belonging to the City of Pasadena, was leased to the Los Angeles County Fire Department for use as paid Fire Camp Number 2.

Built during the 1954-55 fiscal year at a cost of $192,000, Fire Camp No. 2 is considered to be the "hub" of the camp system. Strategically located near the center of the county, this facility has housed as many as four paid 10-man crews. Camp 2 houses the principal kitchen facility that provides food for the portable food dispensers on major brush fires. Camps 11 and 13 maintain similar cooking facilities.

The number of paid camps has varied from year to year, depending upon the availability of funds in each budget. As of 1990, there are three: Camp 2 in Oak Grove Park; Camp 9 near Los Penitos Peak north of Sylmar; and Camp 8 in Malibu. A large helicopter is quartered at Camp 2 during the fire season. Camps 8 and 9 each also house a large copter which is equipped as an air squad, with appropriate EMT 1's, paramedics and volunteer medical doctors on board. (See Chapter 11.)

On September 22, 1957, two new Bell 47G-2 two-place helicopters were delivered to Los Angeles County, one for the sheriff's department and one for the fire department. Each craft cost $40,000. The fire department helicopter was housed with the sheriff's department copters and used their repair and

A scattering of equipment at Clear Creek on the Angeles Crest Hwy on July 17, 1955. (L to r. against the embankment): A USFS GMC Marmon-Herrington tanker, three stakeside trucks from the Pacoima warehouse, Engine 28's 1952 International, Engine 57's 1951 International, a small grasshopper tanker (probably leased), a D-6 dozer, *Engine 74's 1948 Mack, a tanker and stakeside from the Pacoima warehouse. Foreground: an unidentified International, the dozer's tractor and lowboy, a Ford staff car, Dodge utility truck and 1955 Chevrolet food dispenser.*
G. Hutchinson photo, LACoFD.

The annual inspection of July 28, 1955 at Fire Station 74, Bn. 4, in Kagel Cyn. Chief officers (from left): First Asst. Chief Roland W. Percey, unk., BC Orlo Pederson, Ch. Dep. John Duncan and Chief Keith Klinger. Engine crew members are in their summer brushfighting heavy cotton dungarees. Note the captain's very-popular Caterpillar watch fob hanging from his belt. Valley Times photo, from the collection of John Whelan.

During an "off-season" brush fire in Big Tujunga Cyn. in March of 1956, Engine 82 is refueled by the Dept.'s International fuel dispenser. Extended fire operations kept the fuel tenders busy. B.N. Landrum photo, LACoFD.

maintenance facilities. Roland Barton, a former sheriff's department pilot, was named as the Los Angeles County Fire Department's first helicopter pilot.

Further Developments — 1956-1957

The public's demand for rescue services continued its steady climb during the mid-1950s. By 1956, 12 rescue squads were in service as a part of the Los Angeles County Fire Department. They were located at fire stations 3, 8, 9, 10, 11, 18, 19, 29, 31, 40, 45 and 47. One or two rescue units were added with almost every year that followed.

In January, 1956, Chief Klinger began a public campaign through the Los Angeles Times to bring about the creation of a helicopter fleet for the Los Angeles County Fire Department.

On September 8, 1956, a brush fire erupted on the south side of the San Gabriel Mountains, near the mouth of Dunsmore Canyon at the north end of Pennsylvania Avenue at the base of Mount Lukens. La Crescenta Engine Co. 63 was first due. Under the command of Captain Alfred Pedersen, the crew came within only a few yards of stopping the fire before it made a run up the steep slopes, racing into the Angeles National Forest. Although little note was made of it at the time, this fire provided two landmark events.

First, two state helicopters were used to haul equipment and to carry some manpower to and from the firelines, marking the first such use of this type of craft at a Los Angeles County Fire Department incident. (1st USFS use – Big Tujunga Cnyn., 1947.)

Second, a Stearman biplane from Varney's Flying Service in Willows, California made several 120-gallon water drops on the fire, marking the first time that this method was used to help extinguish a wildland fire in Los Angeles County.

During 1956, replacement Fire Station 42 was constructed at 9319 E. Valley Boulevard, Rosemead, replacing the station at the corner of Valley Boulevard and Muscatel, which had been taken over from the volunteers in 1941.

During November of that year, much fanfare surrounded Chief Klinger's naming Walt Disney as the first honorary fire chief of Los Angeles County. This event continued Chief Klinger's policy of drawing public attention to the Los Angeles County Fire Department.

Also during the month of November, the lone Bell 47G-2 helicopter belonging to the sheriff's department was used by the Forestry Division to re-seed the fire-denuded slopes of the Verdugo Hills to the north of the City of Burbank.

On Sept. 14, 1956, Chief Klinger continued his policy of calling attention to the department and worthy public figures by naming Walt Disney the honorary fire chief of LA Co. The mouseketeers observe the proclamation approvingly. LACoFD photo.

This 120 gallon water drop by a Varney Flying Service Stearman Biplane was the first ever in L.A. County. It occurred on Mt. Lukens, Sept. 9, 1956. USFS photo.

The 1956 fast-pitch softball team, as fielded by the LACoFD. This team won the Alhambra Div. championship four years in a row. The 1955 team had a 23-0 record. Members (l. to r.) (top row): Harry Beardo, mgr.; Walt Goodwin, 2b; Jim Enright, 3B; Bob "Tonto" LaFoya, OF; Orlo Pederson, c; Ken Ertel, 1B; Andy Waroff, OF; Bottom row: Jim Cervantes, OF; Phil Curinga, OF; Les Cox, C; Cal Sanders, SS; Don Vucetich, P. Other members of the team were Gene Vrooman, P; Jack Simmons, 2B. LACoFD photo.

Aug. 8, 1957: a landmark day for the County Fire Dept.! On hand to celebrate the delivery of the department's first helicopter, a Bell 47 G, were (l. to r.): Pilot Roland Barton, Pilot Mechanic Sewell Griggers, Chief Keith Klinger, Mechanic Lindell Griggers and Bernie Rollinger. LACoFD photo.

Pilot Roland Barton tests a canvas bag holding 50 gal. of water for dropping on brush fires, Sept. 6, 1957. By 1961, the first all-metal 100-gal. tank would be designed by the department, vastly improving the effectiveness of this method. J. Homuller photo. LACoFD.

The L.A. County Fireman's Assoc.'s Ford Model T. "Engine 1/2" participated in the Dec. 1956 Hollywood Christmas parade down Hollywood Blvd. This apparatus always pleased the crowds. A.E. Smith photo. LACoFD.

The Klinger Era ..Part II

The "Newton" Fire approaches Pacific Coast Highway on the morning of December 27, 1956. The dark mass of heavy smoke, left, is dangerous for anyone entering due to wind driven embers, dust and lack of visibility. Roads such as this are commonly closed for the duration of the fire to allow fire equipment to operate freely. B.N. Landrun photo, LACoFD.

The Newton-Hume-Sherwood Disaster

On December 25, 1956, the Malibu Hills exuded a freshness that only a Santana wind can create. The Devil Winds had arrived a bit early that fall, blowing intermittently since October 24th. Due to a strong, cold high-pressure cell that was moving into Utah and Nevada, the winds increased out of the northeast to a sustained velocity of from 40 to 50 miles per hour on Christmas Day.

Locally, stronger wind gusts, measuring over 80 miles per hour, demolished the roof of the USFS Sierra Pelona Lookout tower some 40 miles northeast of the Malibu Hills.

Rainfall for the season had been only 0.46 inches since the first of July, about nine percent of normal. Moisture in living fuel, such as sumac and chamise, had dropped to 58 percent – just enough to barely sustain plant life. Relative humidity readings approached the zero mark. Thus was the stage set for a major fire disaster. All that was needed was source of ignition. That source was only a matter of hours away.

At 2:40 a.m. on December 26, an airliner headed towards Los Angeles International Airport was flying in a westerly direction over Fontana, some 75 miles to the east of the Malibu Mountains. The pilot radioed the control tower, commenting, "Say, that's quite a fire they have in the hills up the coast!"

The message was relayed from the airfield to the Los Angeles County Fire Department Dispatcher. Moments later, the Malibu dispatcher at Fire Station 65 received a telephone call from near Zuma Beach, which, coupled with a sighting by the USFS Mendenhall lookout north of Pacoima, corroborated the fire's general location.

Evidently, a smouldering ember in a dump at the head of Newton Canyon had been blown into the

155

nearby grass. A fire quickly ignited that commenced burning rapidly south and west in brush 15 to 20 feet deep. It was headed for the coast. Dispatcher Toni King immediately dispatched most of Battalion 5, consisting of engines 65, 265, 67, 68, 70 and 270, along with six patrol units from those stations, two hand crews and two bulldozers. Personnel totalled 50 men. Division III Chief Harvey T. Anderson and Battalion Chief Frank Zalaha were also dispatched. At 0349 hours, a request for 13 additional engine companies, six patrols, six hand crews and three bulldozers – and a total of 132 more men – was initiated. Chief Engineer Keith E. Klinger responded at approximately the same time, after being notified of the fire by the head dispatcher in Los Angeles.

Chief Anderson had helped fight a similar fire in this area in 1935. He knew this fire could reach the coast, and in no time involve many homes in the coastal canyons and beach areas. He also knew that, with such adverse Santana conditions, stopping the head of the fire was out of the question. It would be necessary to "parallel" the fire on the east and west flanks, using bulldozers, hand crews and tankers. Protecting the homes to the south would require additional help.

By 0430 hours, 38 more engines, including 15 from Los Angeles City, six patrols, six hand crews and three bulldozers were on scene or responding, adding an additional 224 men to the operation.

The head of the fire reached the Pacific Coast Highway at 0500 hours, leaping and spotting forward, traveling the four miles in approximately two hours. It easily jumped the 100-foot-wide coast highway, burning several homes on the south side next to the beach. Now, daytime weather conditions would indeed influence the fire's path of devastation.

As often occurs during brush fires, the daytime heating of the south slopes of the hills began to counteract the flow of the Santana winds, lessening their velocity. The fire began to burn to the west to some extent, and also "backed into" the wind and burned toward the east. This phenomenon was caused by the wind crossing ridge tops and broad canyons, making large eddy currents, just as it had in the fire of 1935.

At night, nocturnal cooling of the slopes occurred. This allowed the Santana wind flow to increase once again, causing the fire to sweep through new sections of unburned brush, igniting homes to the south. This pattern repeated itself for two days, making accurate fire behavior forecasts difficult along the active fire fronts.

By 0950 hours, 7,000 acres of watershed had been consumed. By 1700 hours, the maximum commitment of resources amounted to 87 engines, 25 patrols and 24 hand crews. Of the 27 bulldozers utilized, most were leased or borrowed from other agencies. By now, 1,195 men struggled with the inferno. Organizationally, it had been divided into two divisions and several sectors.

The fire displayed all of the characteristics that one could expect during such dire conditions. Smoke and heat from the massive flame front were driven horizontally, reducing downwind visibility to nearly zero. Embers blew downwind for hundreds of feet to start spot fires that threatened to trap anyone caught in between.

Even when fire equipment could approach a home in an attempt to save it, inadequate vegetation clearance frequently compounded the problem. No ordinances *requiring* brush clearance had as yet been passed, so such homes were invariably lost. This was especially true for those houses having untreated cedar shake shingled roofs. Nonetheless, there were a few instances where a homeowner who had the recommended brush clearance around his property saved it from destruction by refusing to evacuate and staying on to wet down the roof with a garden hose. However, these instances were few and far between.

Late on December 26, the Encinal Canyon Pump House burned, followed shortly by the Trancas Canyon Pump House. Reservoirs could now no longer be filled, cutting off the water supply for the engines and tankers. Both canyons burned out, including five homes on the sand at Trancas Beach.

By nightfall, 1,000 people had been evacuated from their homes along the Malibu Coast and nearby canyons. Latigo, Decker, Encinal and Escondido canyons, as well as Paradise Cove, were cleared of homeowners. Fifty homes were destroyed in these areas.

Conditions on what was now called the "Newton Fire" continued unchanged for 30 hours. By 1700 hours on December 27, some 27,000 acres of heavy brush and trees had been consumed. Some degree of control was achieved along the northeast and northwest flanks, where bulldozers were able to gain access. Work was begun to cut new firebreaks, where needed, and widen existing breaks.

One of the primary tasks for the dozers was the construction of a firebreak above Corral Canyon to the east. It was hoped that a large firing-out operation could be initiated from this ridge, in order to stop the easterly advance of the fire. At 2000 hours on the 27th, the firing-out operation began. It was completed along the McReynolds Motorway at 0700 hours on the 28th. The line held.

At the time of peak resource commitment on the Newton Fire, another situation arose to challenge the exhausted and thinly-spread firefighting forces. At 1741 hours on December 27, there was a telephone report of a fire in the Hume Tract, two miles north of the Malibu Sheriff's Station and seven miles east of the Newton Fire.

The first-alarm dispatch included five Los Angeles County engines from the base camp at the Newton Fire, three engines from the City of Santa Monica and two camp crews from the Newton Fire with Chief Klinger in direct command. The second alarm, called at 1758 hours, brought seven additional L.A. County engines and one bulldozer from the Newton Fire. A gradual buildup of forces over the next four hours brought State Office of Civil Defense (OCD, now known as OES) engines from as far away as San Luis Obispo and San Diego. One hundred eighty one off-duty L.A. County firefighters were also called to duty.

Flames 40' in length lick at fire personnel and photographers seconds before jumping an unknown road in the Malibu Hills during the "Newton" Fire on December 26, 1956. 1½" hose lines are useless against flames of this length. Windspeeds during the beginning of this fire rendered backfiring impractical and dangerous. LACoFD photo.

Tractor 1 cuts line during the final stages of the great Malibu Fire of 1956. Malibu is ideal country for bulldozer operations, having a large percentage of the terrain as rolling hills. B.N. Landrum photo, LACoFD.

Manpower for "overhead" supervision in L.A. County was heavily taxed by this time. The United States Forest Service was requested to take over this function for the "Hume Fire," as it was now called. Supervised by Jay Peterson and Stubby Mansfield, sector teams were developed, using OCD engines and L.A. County firemen for manpower. The USFS also supplied the main fire camp. This included kitchens, telephone communications, a motor pool and the field dispatching of newly-arriving equipment.

While the cause of the Hume Fire was never determined, it behaved very much like the Newton Fire. Fuel, topography and burning conditions were identical. This fire did begin much closer to the ocean, thus not as much acreage was involved. A total of 4,000 acres were burned, including 26 homes and outbuildings.

While both the Newton and Hume fires were being contained on December 28, an arsonist-set fire burst into life south of the Ventura County community of Thousand Oaks, in the vicinity of Lake Sherwood. This new fire burned in comparable territory, with weather conditions similar to the previous two fires. It moved rapidly toward the community surrounding Lake Sherwood.

The first alarm at 1050 hours brought Ventura County engines 31, 32, 33, 41 and 42, and their dozer, under Chief Pete Little. An additional six engines from Los Angeles County and 11 bulldozers from the L.A. County road department followed. The fire quickly consumed 25 homes and outbuildings around Lake Sherwood, although many were saved by a valiant stand by first-responding engine company crews.

After burning rapidly to the south and consuming Ventura County's Triumfo Lookout tower and several barns in Little Sycamore Canyon, the head of the Sherwood Fire joined the existing Newton burn along Decker Road. There it self-extinguished. The flanks were picked up by the bulldozers, various firing-out operations and the hand crews. A total of 9,450 acres had been burned over.

On December 27, Governor Goodwin J. Knight, responding to a request by L.A. County Supervisor John Anson Ford, declared a "state disaster area" in both Los Angeles and Ventura counties. On the following day, as the Sherwood Fire raged on, President Eisenhower proclaimed a "national fire emergency," the first ever so declared, qualifying the State of California and the counties of Los Angeles and Ventura for help of all kinds. This included low-cost loans to fire victims and reimbursement to local governments for damage to public facilities.

All told, the Newton, Hume and Sherwood fires consumed 35,500 acres within a perimeter of 90 miles. A total of 136 engines, 27 bulldozers, 25 patrols and 1,518 personnel had been utilized to fight these fires. These figures included 225 men and seven bulldozers from the Navy base at Port Hueneme in Ventura County. Practically every city in California south of San Luis Obispo either sent equipment to the fires or moved to cover empty Los Angeles County fire stations. The Red Cross, sheriff's department, road department and flood control district were all heavily called upon.

One man, a civilian, was killed when he drove his car into a ravine during a period of zero visibility caused by smoke. This individual, Frank L. Dickover, had been fleeing from his home. Additionally, 15 persons required hospital attention.

Total federal disbursements to Los Angeles County for damaged property were $552,688.

It had been eight years since a major fire had visited the Malibu area, but it would not take that long for another occurrence.

The Woodwardia Fire

One of the more serious fires to occur in Los Angeles County as the 1960s approached need not have occurred at all if USFS crewman William Grader had been given his scheduled day off. On the morning of October 13, 1959, moderate Santana conditions required that the crew of the Angeles Crest Ranger Station tanker remain on duty for an extra day. Upset at this news, Grader left the station, which was on the Angeles Crest Highway north of La Canada, and traveled up the roadway until he came to Woodwardia Canyon. At this point, he threw a burning paint brush over the side of the road near the canyon bridge. He then returned to duty quarters.

The resulting fire jumped the roadway, as it raced up the hill to the southwest, igniting heavy brush and timber. The fire at once became inaccessible to ground firefighting units because of the extremely steep and rugged terrain.

Later that day, wind velocity increased, causing concern over whether the fire might reach into the northern section of La Canada, a community of large and expensive homes. As night approached, the fire also began burning southward down the large canyon to the east, the Arroyo Seco, in the direction of the California Institute of Technology's famous Jet Propulsion Laboratory. County and U.S. Forest Service units massed on the Gould Mesa area to the north. Pasadena Fire Department units were moved in by Chief T. William Heidner to protect homes along the east bank of the Arroyo Seco.

During the night, the fire crept over the last ridge above La Canada, coming under the full force of the down-canyon effect in the south slope canyons, thus increasing its rate of spread. Chief Klinger and Chief Percey held a conference and concluded that the fire would indeed reach the homes closest to the brush. Action was taken to dispatch engine companies and camp crews along Alta Canada Road, El Vago Street and La Canada Boulevard. One home on Alta Canada was destroyed. Some fire damage was suffered by a few other homes and outbuildings, but dozens were saved in the threatened area.

Due to ameliorating wind conditions and increasing humidity, the fire made only moderate progress west of this area. However, the following day, a USFS attempt to fire out the Arroyo Seco along the west canyon bottom allowed embers to spot to the east. The resulting fire eventually burned out Big and Little Bear canyons, Grand Canyon and Brown Mountain to the east.

On the third day of the fire, the pilot of a contract Grumman TBM fixed-wing bomber lost his life when his borate load failed to discharge in time. His aircraft struck a ridge immediately north of Millard Canyon, across from Chaney Trail. In addition, a Zuni Indian hand crew member working under Captain Richard Houts died when he didn't react quickly enough to the "drop" command and was struck by a 600-gallon borate drop from another TBM aircraft.

The Woodwardia Fire had all the earmarks of a major disaster waiting to happen. And it would have happened if the wind had not decreased and the humidity had not risen the next morning. County Supervisor Warren Dorn, whose district lay in the path of the fire, prevailed upon the Board of Supervisors to declare Chief Klinger a "fire czar," enabling the chief to order whatever he felt was required to quell the flames – no questions asked. Since the State of California soon declared the fire area a state disaster area, Klinger's position was enhanced in this regard.

The Woodwardia Fire burned 14,000 acres during its three-day existence, claimed two lives and destroyed or damaged a number of structures. The arsonist who set the fire in a burst of pique received a $1,000 fine and one year in jail for his act – the maximum sentence then allowable.

A TBM making a low drop on a ridge during the Woodwardia Fire above the Altadena-LaCanada area. One craft crashed along such a ridge during these operations when its 600 gal. load failed to release from the tank. LACoFD photo.

Engine 54's 1949 General Pacific 1,000 gpm pumper on a long pump job during the Norumbega fire. The food dispenser has been by with supper. LACoFD photo.

Field-mixing of borate fire retardant for use by the Dept. helicopter at George's Gap near the junction of Angeles Crest Highway and the Angeles Forest Highway (Palmdale cutoff). A USFS tanker and crew supply the hose line. Such cooperation during large brush fires was, and is, commonplace. LACoFD photo.

Marking the Spring of 1958

Oftentimes, it is easier for members of a large organization such as the Los Angeles County Fire Department to remember specific incidents by the year in which they occurred. Such is the case with two memorable emergencies that transpired in February and May of 1958. Both events took place in the southeast section of Los Angeles County, and directly involved battalions 2, 7, 8 and 9.

On February 2, shortly after the dinner hour, two military aircraft from two different facilities met in midair, approximately 2,000 feet above the community of Norwalk. A Douglas DC-6 military air transport plane with 40 men on board was struck by a Navy Lockheed P2V Neptune patrol plane. The Neptune had just taken off from the Los Alamitos Naval Air Station with a four-man crew.

The collision ruptured the fuel tanks of one of the planes, causing an aerial fireball that was seen as far away as Pasadena, some 20 miles to the north. A cascade of burning fuel and debris plummeted out of the night sky.

As the planes broke apart, the major portion of the DC-6 fell into the parking lot of the L.A. County Norwalk Sheriff's Station on Firestone Boulevard.

The Neptune fell into a Santa Fe Springs field several miles northeast of Norwalk, near Fire Station 17. All on board both the planes perished, but, miraculously, no one on the ground was killed or even seriously injured. Firefighting efforts consisted of controlling scattered blazes caused by falling debris and burning aviation fuel.

While there had been, both before and after this incident, aircraft crashes in and around Los Angeles County, a mid-air collision was at that time an almost unheard-of occurrence, for the odds of two planes colliding in the then-much-less-crowded skies of the 1950s were slim indeed. This tragedy was judged as being unlikely ever to occur again. Actually, 32 years were to pass before Los Angeles County again had to deal with this type of incident, and, in fact, in almost the same vicinity.

The Hancock Fire

May 22, 1958 marked the first day of a three-day struggle to control one of the largest oil refinery fires ever to strike Southern California. At 2:06 p.m., the Hancock Oil Company facility, located near the top of Signal Hill, was rocked by an explosion and fire in its petroleum storage facilities, killing two employees. The fire became immediately uncontrollable, overpowering the Signal Hill Fire Department and a three-alarm-plus force from L.A. County and Long Beach. Sixteen oil storage tanks and a cracking tower soon became fully involved.

As the fire spread throughout the 10-acre facility on the second day, a primary concern was the ability of the dikes surrounding the storage tanks to contain the burning fuel as it combined in volume with the thousands of gallons of water and foam being used for fire suppression.

Here on "The Hill," any burning product that overflowed the diking would flow into the Long Beach Airport and the business district along Lakewood Boulevard. Consequently, evacuation of a portion of those two areas as well as an area near Termino Avenue and Willow street was ordered.

The Photo Section of the Los Angeles County Fire Department was soon on the scene, filming in sound and color the massive firefighting effort. The resulting film was shown county-wide to members of the department and a number of public groups. Battalion Chief Noel Manchester of the Fire Prevention Bureau later made frequent presentations of the spectacular production. The firefighters' valiant struggle to control the conflagration by wading in the burning mixture of petroleum and water was clearly documented. It could be seen how these men, working at the point of near exhaustion, could not let up in their efforts, or the result might well have been their demise.

Extensive use of tractors to improve the diking around the involved area was employed along Termino Avenue, and on the third day, thanks to suppression and exposure protection by L.A. County, City of Long Beach and Signal Hill fire crews, as well as diminished fuel sources, control was achieved. The gigantic column of black smoke that had hovered over much of the Los Angeles Basin began to dissipate.

Damage to the Hancock Refinery amounted to $15 million. When translated into today's dollars, the loss would approach 10 times that much. Most significantly, the fire was not allowed to spread toward the airport facility and Lakewood Boulevard, and, with the exception of the two employees killed in the initial explosion, there was no further loss of life.

A heavy stream from an unidentified engine appears ineffective in this aerial view of the northeast quadrant of the Hancock Oil fire. Refinery equipment at left has been damaged in the initial blast and fire. Long Beach airport in background. B.N. Landrum photo, LACoFD.

Another aerial view of the Hancock Oil Fire. Note that the dikes designed to contain any spill-over of product have functioned well. Note also how the force of the original blast has scattered automobiles like toys in the field, foreground. B.N. Landrum photo, LACoFD.

Heat from the initial blast has practically melted the cars in the foreground as the Hancock Oil Refinery fire rages on. Many parts of this fire were unapproachable. B.N. Landrum photo, LACoFD.

Lakewood Engine Co. 245 pumps through a dual forward lay to Engine 9 somewhere off to the right of this picture during the Hancock Oil Fire of March of 1958. Equipment such as this 1952 International pumped for two to four days during this fire. LACoFD photo.

Continuing County Growth

The Woodwardia Fire furthered the impetus of fire service agencies to create and enforce legislation requiring the clearance of flammable brush from around structures in fire-prone hill areas. During the period just prior to the 1960 fire season, such legislation appeared in Los Angeles County. The required distance, as stated in the fire code, for vegetation clearance away from structures (cut down to mineral soil) was 30 feet. Vegetation also had to be cut down to 18 inches for 100 feet. (In later years, these distances were nearly doubled in areas where extra-hazardous conditions prevailed.) Those not complying with the fire code would have the required clearance performed by the department's Weed Abatement Section. A fee for this service was then placed on the owner's property tax bill for that year.

The fire department had been without a patrol boat of any kind since the Grey Gull was impounded by the U.S. Navy in 1942. By 1960, the small boat harbor at Marina Del Rey had increased in size and use, requiring the services of a fire-rescue craft. On April 1, 1962, the Consolidated Fire Protection District assumed the responsibility for fire and rescue services at the marina by building and installing a jet-powered craft with a 2,500-gallon-per-minute pumping capacity, manned by a crew of two firefighters. A facility to house the fireboat and an engine company was built and occupied by 1965, becoming Fire Station 110.

The department's field divisions had increased to five by the 1961-62 fiscal year, with the number of battalions standing at 12. The south portion of Battalion 2, in the San Gabriel Valley, formed the new Battalion 12. The desert area, north of Vincent Gap and from the Leona Valley to the east had been separated from Battalion 6, forming the new Battalion 11. In the west San Gabriel Valley, the east end of Battalion 4 and the west end of Battalion 2 were combined, forming the new Battalion 10.

While the paramedic program had not yet come into fruition in Los Angeles County, the number of one-man rescue squads had proliferated over the years, increasing to 21 by 1963. These venerable squads, with their heavy, suitcase-like E. and J. Resuscitators, rolled with the engine companies throughout the county, assisting them with oxygen therapy, first aid and general rescue. The number of rescue calls was, even then, on a steady increase, having risen to over 10,000 during the fiscal year 1962-63. This accounted for a quarter of all emergency responses.

The need for more help in this field prompted Chief Klinger to press for more resuscitators to be installed on every engine and truck company in the department, thereby providing backup protection for both the public and firefighters during firefighting operations. Of the 127 engine companies and seven truck companies in the department, 85 had placed

The kitchen set-up in the fire camp used for the "Norumbega" Fire behind Monrovia in the San Gabriel Mountains, October 2, 1958. It is late in the fire, and a few acres of brush are being fired out to clean up a control line. LACoFD photo.

E. and J. "Lyteport" units in service during 1962-63. By 1964, all companies were so equipped.

On April 1, 1960, the City of Commerce was incorporated, using the basic boundaries of what had been known as the Central Manufacturing District. The city wanted its own fire protection equipment, but did not wish to staff it, preferring to leave that to the county. In order for this to occur in a legal manner, the city first had to withdraw from the East Los Angeles Fire Protection District. A state legislative action elminating technicalities prohibiting such a move, sponsored by Union Local 1014, was passed. Thus Commerce was able to provide itself with as much, or as little, fire protection as it desired at any given time.

Not until 1988 did Commerce abandon its arrangement with the county, finally joining the Consolidated Fire Protection District.

In the Construction and Maintenance Division, the number of fire camps had risen to 15, which included

Nursery Operator Ezra Miller, Forester Ralph Van Wagner, Helicopter Pilot Roland Barton and Chief Engineer Keith E. Klinger make estimates of seed coverage needed to replant the Laurel Canyon burn for the City of Los Angeles, October of 1959. The sowing of rye grass and/or mustard seed on bare slopes following a brush fire was an attempt to slow the erosive effect of heavy winter rains.
LACoFD photo.

A display of the equipment carried in the standard county rescue squad, circa 1958. Rescue 3's 1958 Ford is being used. LACoFD photo.

LA City Fire Chief William Miller, right, arrives at the training center for Fire Service Day, May 2, 1960, and poses with Co. Chief Keith Klinger. As the county's helicopter fleet grew, LA City would also develop its own 'copter fleet. E. Wagner photo, LACoFD.

Auxiliary Fireman Dale Miller on ground and Fireman Don Wisinger demonstrate the E & J resuscitator used in the 1950s and 1960s by Rescue Squad personnel at a school assembly. LACoFD photo.

all three types – paid, juvenile probation and adult prisoner. Their services continued to be of high quality and were greatly valued in all phases of construction and firefighting. It became increasingly common for these crews to be "special called" by other fire agencies throughout the county that did not maintain such crews. Their services were requested from time to time by Los Angeles City, Burbank and Glendale – all of which had brush areas within their city limits. This procedure remains extant today, and is occasionally extended to other counties or states.

With the growth of the fire department phone system, the development of a common system of signal codes for the bells naturally followed. Various combinations, all controlled at the dispatcher's switchboard, were developed over the years. In some stations, such as Station 5 in County San Gabriel, a relay was located. This allowed a call from the Battalion 2 dispatcher to pass through the station and continue on the line to reach the Battalion 4 dispatcher in La Canada, where it could then be redirected if necessary. A special ring code was used to indicate to the captain at 5's to throw the relay.

With the enlarging of each dispatch center's jurisdiction and the realignment of battalion boundaries, these relay stations were eliminated. Through the late '50's, '60s and very early '70s, bell codes were reduced to four basic signals:

One long ring: fire call or move-up
Two short rings: business call
Three short rings: rescue call
Four short rings: call for the battalion chief

In addition, the captain in the station could ring the bell system manually – five rings – to tell the crew to line up for inspection.

During 1963, Chief Klinger had succeeded in winning acceptance from the Board of Supervisors for his "10-year program" of watershed station construction, replacement and relocation of 16 stations. New residential construction was rapidly extending onto hillsides and up canyons in the mountainous areas of the county. With the growth, brush fire starts were increasing, placing these new homes and other structures in ever-mounting jeopardy. Response times needed to be improved for these areas.

As public use of wildland areas continued to increase during the middle '60s, the number of call boxes installed in these areas peaked, with 140 in service by 1966. Thereafter, they began to be removed, as housing tracts began to encroach into these areas, eliminating their usefulness. With the coming of the selective calling radio dispatch system in the early '70s, and the subsequent removal of the "county line" phone system, all of the boxes were eliminated.

During the years from 1960 through 1965, several stations were either rebuilt or added onto, and new sites were picked for others. These included stations

June 7, 1961 saw the dedication of Fire Station 109 at Fox airfield in Lancaster. The Yankee FWD crash truck was painted yellow, and saw limited service. This was also the last assignment of the 1939 Seagrave rig 2,500 gallon tanker/pumper "Galloping Ghost," originally from Station 20. L. to r.: unknown, Capt. Peterson, Chief Klinger, Supervisor Warren Dorn. LACoFD photo.

44 (Duarte), reestablished 2/1/65 for $135,000; 70 (Malibu), 7/1/64 for $250,000; 125 (Agoura), which cost $140,000; and 123 (east of Newhall), for $100,000. Two station sites were chosen for Battalion 6: one at the mouth of Big Tujunga Canyon, the other near the present junction of Interstate 5 and Highway 14, south of Newhall. Neither station was ever built; funding sources diminished before this could happen. One additional station, 108 in Sierra Madre, was eventually constructed, only to be closed in 1975 due to lack of funds for continued manning.

Two especially noteworthy station openings occurred during the summer of 1961. The sorely needed Station 107 at Solemint Junction east of Saugus opened with a Crown pumper and a patrol truck. It was the first station constructed with a heliport adjacent to the building.

The second station opening was found at Fox Airfield near Lancaster, as Fire Station 109 opened with a new, yellow, FWD Yankee 10-wheel-drive crash truck. The station opened on June 7, 1961, at a cost of $77,000. The FWD engine cost $67,987. This station was the last regular field assignment for the 2,500-gallon Seagrave tanker "The Galloping Ghost."

Two consolidated stations were replaced during this time: La Puente Station 26, build for $75,000 and opened July 1, 1965, and Baldwin Park Station 29, built for $97,000 and opened October 11, 1964. In addition, two 75-foot snorkels (truck companies) were delivered to Station 29 and Station 127 in Dominguez on May 1, 1966. These were the second and third snorkels delivered to the department.

Solemint Junction Station No. 107 was dedicated on April 12, 1961. Present for that occasion was 'Copter 2, trying out the station's heliport, the first such facility built next to a county fire station. Engine 107's new Crown 1,000 gpm pumper on right. R. Bird photo, LACoFD.

Improved Working Conditions

Working conditions for firefighters across the United States continued to improve after World War II. Many departments were adopting a 72- or 84-hour workweek, with the 67.5-hour week becoming more common by the mid-50's. Los Angeles County was one of the departments eventually instituting the latter. A system of relief personnel, called "Suitcasers," filled in for men taking vacation days, holidays and sick days. These Suitcasers became quite adept at traveling lightly on their "suitcase routes."

On January 1, 1960, the C Platoon (third shift) was established. The former suitcasers formed the nucleus of the new C shift, with newly-hired men and those working overtime filling the empty positions. Promotions needed to be made to cover the many additional engineer, captain and battalion chief positions created by the new shift. Many men began studying diligently in order to pass with high marks the examination that would place them on the lengthy promotional eligibility lists.

A concerted drive to bring the work schedule more in line with the standard 40-hour week enjoyed by most blue-collar workers throughout America picked

Capt. Foster of Marina Del Rey jet fireboat 110 (1st model) issues a citation to this boat owner for leaking fuel from his craft into the channel. This craft was soon displaced by a more adequate boat as the marina area grew into a small city unto itself with hundreds of boats at anchor. From the collection of Chief Keith E. Klinger.

As the desert areas surrounding Lancaster continued to grow, Fire Station 117 was dedicated on April 13, 1960, and many key local citizens were on hand. Left to R: Chief Keith E. Klinger, Mr. & Mrs. Walter V. "Pappy" Dorn (father of Co. Supervisor Warren) and Lee Berriman, Saugus District Supervisor for the Angeles National Forest. R. Bird photo, LACoFD.

Supervisor Warren Dorn, left, and Chief Keith Klinger, right, honor First Assistant Chief Roland W. Percey on the occasion of his retirement after 40 years with the Los Angeles County Forester & Fire Warden and Fire Department. Ch. Percey, as much as anyone, helped establish the County as a world class wildland firefighting organization. His knowledge of the topography of the county and firefighting tactics is legendary. LACoFD photo.

up some momentum during the mid-'60s. In 1964, the 56-hour schedule, without the hours reduction, became standard in the Los Angeles County Fire Department. However, this number of hours per week was gradually phased in over a two-year period. The first year, 13 "payback" shifts were worked gratis for the county before overtime could be earned for extra shifts. The second year, six shifts were "paid back."

The 56-hour-per-week schedule has been firmly in place ever since. Because of its on-and-off shift arrangement, there has been very little impetus to diverge from this schedule.

Santa Fe Springs and Del Valle

For the many years that the Los Angeles County Fire Department served the area of Santa Fe Springs, an oil firefighting training facility was maintained adjacent to Fire Station 17. It was utilized as part of the overall training program for all new firefighters.

When the area incorporated, on May 15, 1958, becoming the City of Santa Fe Springs, it formed its own fire department. After the departure of this area, the Los Angeles County Fire Department expanded an existing training facility at Del Valle, two miles west of Fire Station 76, just north of Highway 126, not far from the present "Magic Mountain" amusement park. With the cooperation of the LPG Gas Association, 12 "props" were constructed for the opening in October 1962. The number of props has since been reduced to eight. All are used for training and retraining Los Angeles County firefighters. Actual petroleum fires are set during the training sessions.

In addition, thousands of members of other governmental agencies and firefighting organizations statewide have utilized the Del Valle facility over the years.

The department, under Chief John Englund, was

Marking the delivery of the new E & J "Lyteport" resuscitator to Fire Station 14 are, top l. to r., A. Fowler, Bn. Chief R. Fry, Div. Asst. Ch. Mabie. Holding the head of the resuscitator are Supervisor Kenneth Hahn and Chief Engineer Keith E. Klinger. The entire department was outfitted with these units during 1963 and 1964, making oxygen therapy as close as the nearest fire station. Photo from the collection of Keith Klinger, courtesy of the office of Kenneth Hahn.

able to engineer the purchase of Del Valle and the surrounding 160 acres during the 1987-88 fiscal year. Plans for extensive new facilities to be constructed on the site are underway.

The Arsonists' Reign

One of the difficulties by the Los Angeles County Fire Department during the fire season each year is its vulnerability to the random and/or pathological firesetter. There exist several plausible scientific theories concerning what it is that makes these persons act as they do. But whatever the reason, all fire agencies are from time to time required to deal with the result of the "firebugs'" untoward activities. Due to the normally dry conditions found in the wildland areas of Southern California during the fall months, the departments in these areas routinely prepare themselves for any eventuality along these lines.

With weather conditions similar to those of 1956, the fall of 1958 was unusually dry throughout Southern California. Only 0.57 inches of rain had fallen between July 1 and October 31. Numerous small fires had occurred during that summer and early fall. As the Devil Winds began in November, the first of a series of intentionally-set fires commenced to plague the county, especially in the Malibu Mountains.

Assistant Chief Harvey Anderson in his Levis jeans, dress cap and carrying an early model portable radio coordinates a firing out operation on the Liberty fire as it approaches a single blade bulldozer line. Due to an apparent lack of wind here, this control line has a chance of holding. Pre-laid hose lines would add insurance. LACoFD photo.

At 2:21 p.m., November 29, a brush fire broke out near the Warner Brothers Movie Ranch near Calabasas (Engine 68's district). The standard Malibu response of six engines, six patrols, one dozer and two camp crews was unable to make a dent in the fire's progress. The flames made a run toward the Malibu Canyon area and showed every sign of extending as far as the Malibu Colony on the coast.

Massive mutual-aid requests went out immediately, and after a day-long struggle, 61 engines from L.A. County, the California Division of Forestry and USFS managed to keep the fire out of the Colony.

This 4,000-acre fire was only an indication of things to come. Four days later, December 2, at 10:35 a.m., a fire was ignited near Las Virgenes (Malibu) Canyon Road and Trycross Street. Extreme fire weather had caused Chief Anderson to increase the first-alarm assignment to eight engines. Both Battalion Chief Frank Zalaha and Division Chief Anderson responded on the first alarm, and, as anticipated, the fire got away. Engine 67 reported from the scene that two acres were involved in high winds. Chief Anderson requested a second alarm at once, bringing the department helicopter and engines 82, 382, 66, 50

COUNTY OF LOS ANGELES FIRE DEPARTMENT *Organization*

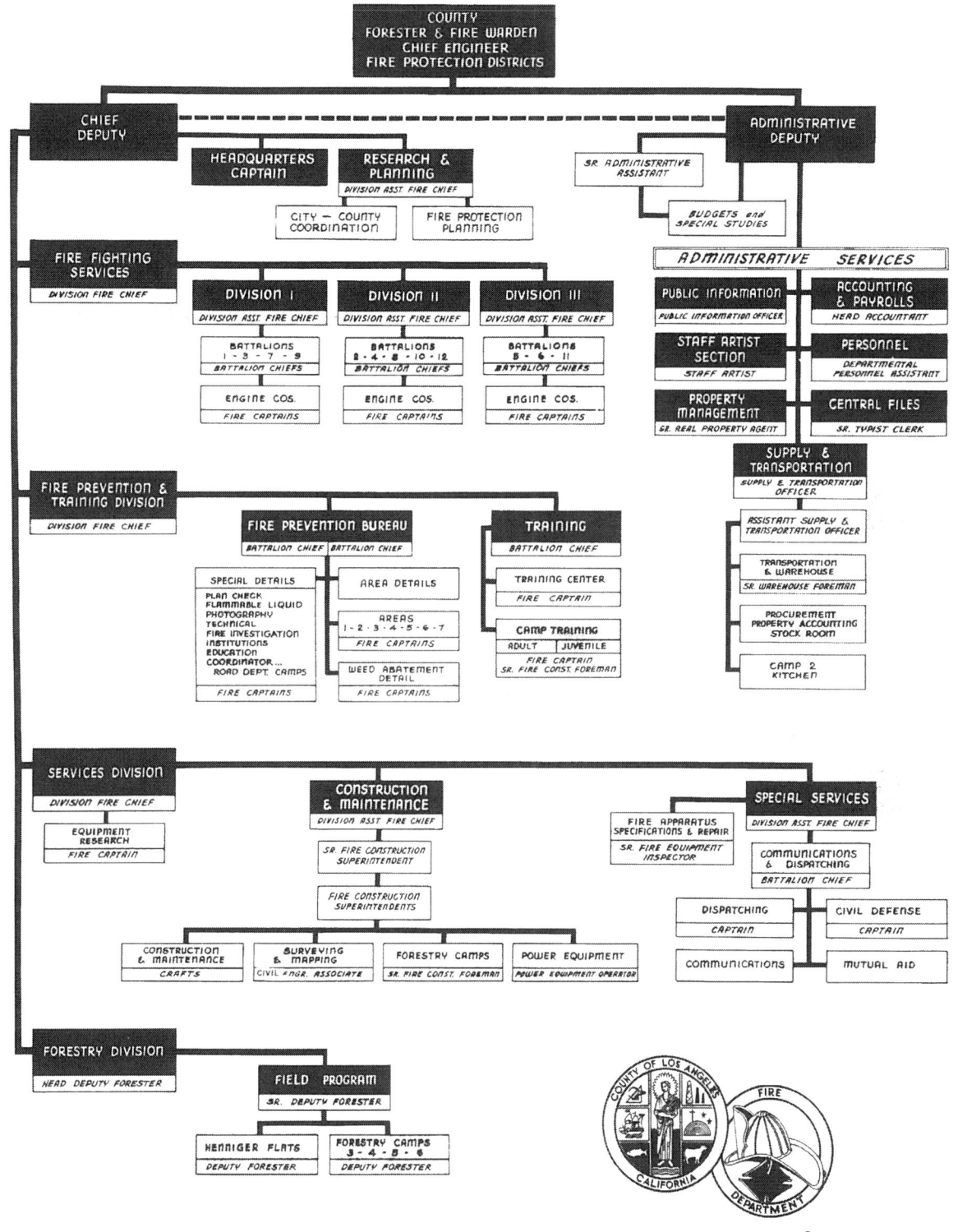

The Organization of the L.A. County Fire Department   circa 1961.   LACoFD photo.

Members of a juvenile probation department Camp Crew perform vigorous overhaul following a brush fire, location unknown, circa 1958. Embers in and around smoldering stumps must be exposed and cooled down, lest they flare up later. From the collection of Jerry Meehan.

and 7, along with five additional patrols, a second dozer and six more camp crews.

As the battle lines were being drawn on this fire, another blaze was reported an hour later, this time in the Agoura area, near Ventura Boulevard and Liberty Canyon Road. This 11:22 a.m. alarm was north and west of the current blaze in Malibu Canyon. Move-up companies from the valleys covered Malibu stations, and engines 245, 209, 17 and 25 responded, along with First Assistant Chief Roland W. Percey, who was in the area due to the initial fire. As the spread of this fire was equally as rapid and uncontrollable as the first, Chief Percey at once requested 21 additional engine companies and five more tractors.

Mutual aid was then instituted. Los Angeles City sent 10 engines, the USFS sent four and Ventura County sent six. These engines were placed well ahead of the fire's front, massed in the Malibu Colony area. No structures burned in that vicinity. However, the second fire did join with the first near Malibu Lake, and, as it traveled toward the coast, it burned the telephone line connecting the Malibu Division with the Castro Peak Lookout radio transmitter, as well as several miles of other phone lines.

Communications in the immediate fire area were now severely hampered. Trouble might reasonably be expected.

Engines 13 and 58 were responding under these difficult conditions into the head of Corral Canyon. As they were proceeding around a curve, the fire swept over the road ahead of and behind them, cutting off any avenue of escape in either direction. The men gathered around and under their apparatus and wet themselves down. In spite of these efforts, two men were burned seriously enough to require ferrying out by helicopter to Santa Monica Hospital after the fire had passed. Six other received lesser burns.

Engine 13's 1948 Seagrave pumper was burned beyond repair. Engine 58's 1955 Crown pumper received $15,000 in damage, but was eventually rebuilt. All of the men recovered from their burns, and considered themselves fortunate, indeed, to have survived.

This 17,000-acre fire was controlled on December 6, after destroying 42 structures. In addition to 75 engines and nearly 1,900 men, 23 patrols, 18 bulldozers, one helicopter, two PBY and three TBM tankers from Van Nuys Airport were utilized.

While this fire was in progress, several more small fires were set in the Malibu area of Los Angeles and Ventura counties. These were handled by move-up

Unidentified fireman, Capt. Lester Maddux and Capt. John Whelan demonstrate the equipment found on a rescue squad for some local daycare school children at the Cecil R. Gehr Training Center in East LA. Public Relations contacts such as this did much to instill an appreciation for the fire service. LACoFD photo.

companies filling in at empty stations, many from departments of the 10 smaller cities that provided engines under mutual aid.

The Santana winds continued during the month of December, and, on December 31, caused a fire similar to the "Liberty Fire." This one wreaked havoc in another area of the Malibu Mountains. This fire was discovered by patrols 68 and 69 while looking north from Mulholland Drive toward the San Fernando Valley.

The 9:30 a.m. fire sprang into life east of their position near Canoga Avenue in the City of Los Angeles. A first alarm from L.A. County brought engines 68, 69, 65, 265 and 75; five patrol units; two dozers; and six camp crews. Los Angeles City also received the alarm, and sent two engines, a Mountain Patrol tanker and a dozer.

The fire began burning rapidly southward along Topanga Canyon, heading toward the Fernwood Pacific Tract and Big Rock and Tuna canyons. Chief Harvey Anderson ordered second and third alarm assignments within 10 minutes. This brought engines 7, 209, 25, 22, 245, 73, 373, 382 and 81; an additional six fire patrols; an unrecorded number of camp crews; and three additional bulldozers.

As the county's major fire plan again went into effect, Chief Klinger responded to the incident and took command. In addition to coverage from smaller local communities, Ventura and Kern counties each sent five engines, and one engine each came from Santa Barbara, Santa Barbara County, Montecito, Glendale and Santa Monica. Fifteen OCD engines were manned and sent into the area along with military units from the naval base at Port Hueneme. In all, 118 engines, 16 patrols, 18 bulldozers and three helicopters were engaged in this incident.

In comparing this fire's aerial support with that sent to previous blazes, a substantial increase is apparent. In addition to the three helicopters, four TBMs, two PBYs and one PB4Y tanker were also utilized, along with a "Bird Dog" fire-spotter plane. A common Bird Dog plane of the time was the single-engine Beechcraft "Bonanza," but there is no record of which type was actually used at this fire.

Fine Tuning the Support System

With the occurrence of each major incident such as the Malibu fires of 1956 and 1958, the capacity of the department to supply the armies of men with equipment and supplies was heavily taxed. Over the previous years, the Service of Supply Division had developed regular procedures for providing extra food, tools, cots, fuel, dozers, communications equipment and other support services for the main camp and various spike camps that were established during each firefighting campaign.

A feature of the Klinger era in this regard was the formalization of enlarging such services, using what was renamed the Supply and Transportation (S&T) Division. Increases were tiered into two levels, referred to as "Plan I" and "Plan II." Plan I was designed to be used with a 10-to-15-engine, or battalion-sized, incident. Plan II was designed for 15-engine, or a division-sized incident – and beyond. In later years, a "Plan III" was added. With these plan increments, consistency in organization and supply for the entire incident was achieved.

Support equipment dispatched on a Plan I was as follows:
Operational Chief
Camp Boss
Line Mapper
Gas Dispenser
Food Dispensers (2)*
Radio Communications
Truck and Operator
Dispatcher
Fire Equipment Repairman
Water Tenders 1 and 2
Camp Crew Coordinator
Tractors (as needed)
Tractor Supervisor
Tractor Spotters (swampers)
Photographer
Refrigerated Truck
Safety and Welfare Officer
Timekeeper
"P" Kit from warehouse**
Fire Investigator***
Chemical Unit
Aircraft (number and type as needed)
Helitack Truck w/three men
Public Information Officer
Telephone Line Repairman

*A food dispenser fed 100 hot meals. Meals were prepared in the kitchen of Camp #2 in La Canada. They usually consisted of roast beef, potatoes, vegetable, salad, bread and butter, juice, milk and coffee.

**A "P" kit, delivered on a stakeside truck, consisted of 4,000 feet of 1-inch hose, four adaptor kits, five 10-gallon water cans, two 100-foot lengths of rope, a 100-man hand crew kit and two cases of flares.

***The fire investigator was ordered only if the fire began in county territory.

Whenever a Plan II incident occurred, a full fire camp was established, and a Plans section added to the overall structure. Until the advent of Plan III, this Plan II structure was merely expanded for incidents of Plan III size.

Support equipment dispatched on a Plan II, in addition to that already sent on a Plan I, was as follows:
Division Chief (5)
Line Chief (5)
Service Chief
Sector Chief and Crew Leaders
Assistant Dispatchers
Backfiring Crew (5)
Air Officer
Tractor Coordinator
Auxiliary Firemen (CD)
Fire Camp Set-up:
Supply Officer
Transportation Officer
Communications Officer
Tool Boss
Kitchen Boss
Radio Repair Crew
Telephone Repair Crew
Checker
Plans Chief
Operations Trailer
Timekeeper Assistant
CD Communications Trailer, as needed
Red Cross or Crescenta-Canada Emergency Corps

Quoting Chief Klinger:

"We can appreciate that no one fire department, however large, can hope to have immediately available all of the fundamentals that may be required to meet a single major emergency, let alone several different types of disaster. In the Los Angeles area, fires, floods (and earthquakes) are what may be termed 'recurring emergencies.' Therefore, we have found it expedient to maintain certain reserves which can be thrown into action with a minimum loss of time."

All purchases relating to any emergency incident were confirmed by and coordinated with the Business Division of the department. This division kept track of all the incident's budgetary, fiscal, personnel, procurement, contractual and warehousing concerns, as well as those occurring on a daily basis within the normal functioning of the department.

LA HQ (Klinger Center) bottom, and the Cecil R. Gehr Training Center, circa 1962. Located at 1320 N. Eastern Ave. in East LA, this facility continues to be the hub of the entire department. LACoFD photo.

1990 WORK SCHEDULE

☐ Holidays ☐ A Shift ▥ B Shift ≡ C Shift

The 56-hour per week 3-platoon work schedule utilized by the LA Co FD. Each shift is off-duty 24, 48 or 96 hours between 24-hour shifts. An example of the scheduling appears in the month of January.

The Klinger Era, Part III

Demonstrating the 100 gal. aluminum drop tank under the Dept's Bell 47-G helicopter on August 24, 1961. This tank was a vast improvement over the 50 gal. canvas bag previously used. E. Wagner photo. LACoFD.

Air Attack and its Development

By 1961, the County of Los Angeles had at its disposal four Bell 47 G2 helicopters. Three were assigned to the sheriff's department, and one was assigned to the fire department. The sheriff's mechanical and repair facilities for the aircraft were shared. One sheriff's pilot, Lyndell Griggers, was cross-trained in fire department operations.

After extensive research and development by pilot Roland Barton, the Jeb Aircraft Company was given the contract to construct the first aluminum drop tank for use with 'Copter 2. The tank could carry 105 gallons of liquid of any type, and could be attached to the helicopter in two minutes. It was first used during the 1961 fire season, with good success.

In order to familiarize the entire fire department with air operations in general, an air attack manual was compiled and placed in each fire station and administrative site. The manual delineated the helicopters' official functions. Examples of duties for this rapidly-developing fire control weapon were as follows:

1. Initial fire attack; holding spot fires, lightning strikes, etc.
2. Fire prevention patrol during periods of severe fire weather
3. Fire suppression activities such as initial attack, manpower transportation, fireline reconnaissance and transporting cargo
4. Directing firefighters via radio and megaphone
5. Rescuing trapped firefighters and/or transporting the sick and injured
6. Specialized equipment use
7. Search and rescue in isolated areas

Off-season specialized uses included:

1. Re-seeding fire-damaged areas (brush)
2. Hauling special equipment into remote areas
3. Experimental undertakings
4. Apparatus drills
5. Aerial surveys and mapping
6. Public demonstrations and public relations
7. Transportation, on an "as-available" basis, of top department officers, members of the Board of Supervisors and visiting dignitaries

All of these duties are still carried on. Other duties have been added, as the helicopter fleet has grown and the capabilities of the larger craft have increased.

During Operation Firestop, carried out in 1954, a need to develop certain specialized functions was realized. In the ensuing years, standard equipment available for the Bell 47 G2 helicopters included:

1. Hose tray and attachments (4)
2. Four cargo carriers with electric sling releases
3. Two 105-gallon water/retardant drop tanks (three 35-gallon tanks were held in reserve)
4. Two helitack jump suits (for jumping from 10 feet or less at 10 mph or less)
5. Two rescue "horse collars," one life raft, one set of pontoons
6. Two seeder kits; two sump tanks
7. Four 1,000-gallon folding reservoirs (canvas), to be filled at the fire scene by means of hovering, low-level water drops

All of this equipment was either developed or modified by regular fire department personnel. Pilot Roland Barton, Captain Frank Hamp and Chief Mechanic Bernie Rollinger all contributed their expertise. Equipment related to firefighting and rescue operations was stored on an air attack vehicle that was located at Fire Station 104 (near Claremont, since closed), and then at Fire Station 47 in Temple City. This specially-equipped apparatus and crew

Roland "Bart" Barton, the LACoFD's first helicopter pilot, and co-pioneer of much of the early technology attached to helicopter operations, much of which was patented. LACoFD photo.

A consolidated Vultee PBY-5 making its 1,000 gal. borate drop during the Woodwardia Fire in the fall of 1959. This high-lift and slow moving aircraft was used extensively for this purpose throughout the west during the late 1950s and early 1960s. LACoFD photo.

responded in support of the helicopter to whatever heliport the copter was utilizing for a given incident. All of the crew members were hand-picked according to standards of experience, and, as the manual stated, were to be ". . . fully conversant with the special techniques the operation demands, highly skilled in the safe use and installation of all accessory equipment, well advised as to flight performance of the aircraft and properly oriented to the situations and problems the pilot must face." It was an *honor* to belong to this crew!

During this period, the Los Angeles County Fire Department also took full advantage of the progress being made in fixed-wing aircraft. A lease was signed with A-J Tankers, Inc., out of the Van Nuys Airport in the San Fernando Valley. Pilots Jack Hennessey and Lou Leach flew their converted Navy AJ-1 Savages, numbered 77 and 88, out of the Van Nuys location until 1966, at which time operations were moved to the Lockheed Airport in Burbank.

These planes were powered with two R-2800 engines capable of moving the aircraft at a speed of 180 miles per hour when fully loaded. Each plane carried a 2,000-gallon payload in four tanks. Drops could be made all at once (salvo), 500 gallons at a time or in sequence until all the tanks were empty. The planes were equipped with both L.A. County and L.A. City fire frequency radios, and could also operate on the U.S. Forest Service radio net when necessary.

Both "77" and "88" were a common sight over

Roland Barton, right, assists in bringing out the first aluminum drop tank designed specifically for use under the Dept.'s Bell 47-G helicopter. This unit, developed at JEB Aircraft in Burbank, was the forerunner of many and larger units which would be utilized by the large craft of the future. R. Bird photo, LACoFD.

The two leased AJ-1 Savages assigned to the LACoFD during the mid 1960s flying across the face of 10,000 ft. Mt. Baldy. Both aerial tankers performed yeoman service with the Dept. and other agencies who requested their service. Their large 2,000 gal. capacity was a welcome assist during difficult fires. LACoFD photo.

Loading a Grumman TBM borate bomber at Van Nuys Airport during the Woodwardia Fire in the fall of 1959. This type of plane was one of the workhorses of retardant dropping operations in the west for several years. LACoFD photo.

Fm. Jim Lonsbury loading borate solution into the PBY-5 at Van Nuys Airport during the Woodwardia Fire. Borate was a sterilant of plant life but not toxic to humans. LACoFD photo.

Borate mixing operations in full swing at Van Nuys Airport during the Woodwardia Fire. The two firemen facing the camera are Jim Lonsbury and George Murray. This was very hard work under almost brutal conditions that often went on from sunrise to sunset. LACoFD photo.

Flames race over a ridge during the 1964 Flintridge Hills fire. Note the roll eddy current in the smoke, center, caused by the fire being driven by high winds over the ridge line and then dropping into an area of relatively lower air pressure, pushing smoke and embers downwind and setting numerous spot fires – a dangerous location during such a fire. Photo source unknown.

Los Angeles County during the 1960s, lumbering across the valleys and hills, occasionally dripping water or pink Phoscheck from their tanks. The Phoscheck, made by the Monsanto Chemical Company, was a fertilizer as well as a fire retardant. (The white borate mixture that it replaced was a soil sterilizer.)

After moving from a temporary facility at the Van Nuys location to Lockheed Airport, a more-permanent facility was established. Designed and fabricated by now-Battalion Chief Frank Hamp and Engineer Belford "Dick" Welsh, a 1938 Seagrave pumper engine and pump were mounted on a steel frame. This was interconnected with an incoming water supply and mixed with the powdered Phoscheck.

The Phoscheck came packaged in 100 lb. bags. The bags were opened by an attending juvenile camp crew by dragging them across the fixed blade of a table saw. The resulting mixture was then pumped into holding tanks where a specific gravity of 1.08 was maintained. From there it was pumped through 2½-inch hoselines with camlock attachments into the tanks of the waiting air tankers.

In addition to the juvenile camp crew, Engine Co. 63 (La Crescenta), and later, Engine Co. 28 (Flintridge), along with the driver of Utility 4 from Station 12 (Altadena) were utilized as manpower to operate this facility whenever the planes flew.

The Twin Holocausts of March

During the two days of March 16 and 17, 1964, Los Angeles and surrounding counties were visited by extremely strong Devil Winds. High-velocity air currents roared down the Mill Creek and Arroyo Seco canyons of central Los Angeles County. These winds blew the anemometer off the roof of the Montrose sheriff's substation during a 100-mile-per-hour gust. The blasts of dry air caused high-voltage electrical transmission lines to arc or snap in many locations. In two places in particular, real damage ensued as the arcing went to ground in areas of heavy grass and brush, immediately starting fires.

At approximately 7 a.m., one of these fires started south of Fire Station 28, near Inverness Drive and Chevy Chase in the Flintridge area. It burned rapidly south toward the Chevy Chase Country Club and threatened the numerous, expensive homes that surrounded the club grounds.

About four miles to the west, La Crescenta Engine 63 was just backing into quarters on Ramsdell Avenue, returning from a "wires down" call. The crew observed a flashing arc and ignition due south of the station in the Whiting Woods Canyon area. This fire immediately raged southward, up the rugged canyons and hillsides of the Verdugo Mountains that lead to the crest near Mount Tom. The fire was burning away from any homes, at least for the time being.

Both of these fires were in the City of Glendale, whose eight-engine company department quickly became overwhelmed by the size of the conflagrations. Mutual aid was rapidly initiated, sending units from Burbank and Los Angeles County racing up the winding canyon roads south of the fires in an effort to save whatever homes they could.

By the afternoon of March 17, both fires had

crossed their respective mountain ranges and began entering the south slopes, which were dotted with numerous hillside homes. In the easternmost area of the "Chevy Chase Fire," parts of Pasadena began to be threatened, near Scholl Canyon and along Patrician Way. Homes in Glendale's Glenoaks Canyon were simultaneously threatened. Shortly thereafter, the fire began what was to be its final run – down the slopes of the hills into the Los Angeles area of Eagle Rock. Numerous Los Angeles City Fire Department units were dispatched up the streets north of Colorado Boulevard, meeting the fire head on and managing to save dozens of homes.

At the same time, to the west, on the south slope of the Verdugo Mountains, the Whiting Woods Fire began to consume some homes between the Rossmoyne section and the north end of Pacific Avenue. Efforts to save homes here were generally successful. As in the Chevy Chase Fire, the Whiting Woods Fire was prevented from burning from roof to roof beyond the southern limits of the grass and brush areas. A marked decrease in wind velocity aided this effort, as well.

Of the hundreds of homes that were threatened, 20 burned to the ground and 10 were badly damaged. In all, 11,650 acres of watershed were destroyed. Fortunately, heavy rains did not occur until the fall of 1965, reducing flood damage from runoff.

Two notable factors affected these incidents. First, the cause of the fires was *unusually* strong Santana winds. Second, the rapid spread of the fires was aided by near-drought conditions during the preceding six weeks. With only half the normal rainfall during the months of December and January, the vegetational fuel returned to near summer-like conditions under the influence of the dry winds.

Considering these circumstances, it is apparent that the combined efforts of all mutual aid entities, largely coordinated by the Los Angeles County Fire Department, saved millions of dollars of high-value property – without a single loss of life.

The Watts Riot

The area in the south-central portion of greater Los Angeles known as Watts was, at one time, an independent city. It had its own city hall and fire and police departments, and acted as a major rail junction for Southern California's rapid transit system known as the Pacific Electric. The PE's "big red cars" stopped at the Watts Station on their way to Long Beach, Redondo Beach and the distant Orange County community of Santa Ana.

In May of 1926, the City of Watts was annexed to Los Angeles. However, bordering the newly-annexed area were portions of other communities that were also known as "Watts." Some areas that were considered to be part of Watts were actually parts of independent cities such as South Gate, Lynwood and Compton. Other areas known as Watts were within the jurisdiction of Los Angeles County, depending upon this governing body for fire and police protection.

Originally a small, primarily "blue-collar" residential suburb, the general area of Watts gradually became an economically and socially depressed community.

It was within this setting that the Los Angeles County Fire Department, Sheriff's Department, California National Guard and the Los Angeles fire and police departments were exposed to as arduous and dangerous a task as they would ever face in their professional lives.

Beginning on Friday, August 13, 1965, some segments of an already disturbed Watts population destroyed a major portion of its business community. Long-standing social and economic frustrations surfaced, aggravated by an extended heat wave featuring unusually high humidity. The riot-triggering incident was reportedly a dispute between a California Highway patrolman during the arrest of a citizen, Marquette Frye. This event, observed by a number of bystanders, was just enough to set off a wave of general unrest and vandalism that rapidly spread throughout the area.

Despite a personal plea at the scene for calm by comedian Dick Gregory and others, conditions continued to deteriorate. A totally misinterpreted and frequently repeated slogan, "Burn, baby, burn!" over radio station KGFJ did not help matters at all.

Negative crowd reaction spread throughout the community during the afternoon of August 13th, quickly escalating into riot proportions. Groups of people began breaking into stores in Los Angeles

LA policemen advance toward riot area and burning building, exact location unknown. Towering smoke column, left, indicates probable roof collapse with sudden venting. LACoFD photo.

Fires burn along Avalon Blvd. in Watts as seen from LA Co. 'Copter 2. Downtown LA upper left. Harbor Freeway lower left. LACoFD photo.

Fire units converge on fully involved structure during Watts riot. Tactics were simply to extinguish each fire and move to the next one as quickly as possible. LACoFD photo.

Brand new Truck 43 preparing to go to work on Stanley's store, unknown location, during the Watts Riots of August 1965. Fires such as these popped up by the dozens during the five days of the riot. LACoFD photo.

City territory, along 103rd Street near Avalon Boulevard. The mob looted the contents of the shops and then set fire to many of the structures, often with "Molotov cocktails." Structure fires began to be reported faster than the beleagured Los Angeles City Fire Department could handle them. To make things worse, firefighters found themselves being pelted by bricks, rocks, bottles and anything else that could be thrown by the crazed mob.

As the affected area spread, it quickly spilled into the jurisdiction of the Los Angeles County Fire Department. By evening, County Fire Chief Klinger and LAFD Deputy Chief Raymond Hill faced identical problems of strategy, logistics and personnel safety. It was necessary to use extreme caution in entering the airspace above the area – as Chief Klinger observed the riot zones from the department's helicopter, gunfire was directed at his craft from below.

Klinger knew that County fire stations 9 and 16, located near the heart of the riot area, were no longer habitable. While his firefighting forces became more and more involved with handling structure fires, he ordered all the department's utility trucks to report to L.A. headquarters on Eastern Avenue. From there, these 12 units responded to Fire Station 24 in Walnut Park, an area just northeast of the riot zone. Then, they were divided into groups of four or five and dispatched "Code R" under the protection of two sheriff's cars – each with four men armed with shotguns – to stations 9 and 16. While the sheriffs stood guard, the utility crews literally stripped the stations of anything of value that would move. This included the contents of the men's lockers. Everything was loaded into the utility trucks, the stations secured and they proceeded back to Station 24, again Code R. Station 24 became the County command post, and all of the goods from 9 and 16 were piled onto the apparatus floor for safekeeping.

By the morning of the 14th, the County had dozens of units committed to the Watts incident. Reserve engines were now being manned and sent into action. The department's first snorkel, Truck 43, was rushed into service directly from the fire shops.

During that day, the rioting and destruction showed no signs of ebbing. Therefore, it was decided to develop a central staging area just outside the riot area. This was to be at Firestone Plaza, located between Alameda Street and Santa Fe Avenue. From here, engines in groups of four or five were dispatched to fire calls, each group returning to the Plaza to await another assignment. No forces entered the riot area without a two-car sheriff's escort, one leading; the

A carload of LA Co. Deputy Sheriffs guard two engines and Truck 43 operating on a fully involved store during the Watts riot. LACoFD photo.

other following. Additional protection came from the California National Guard, which had sent 13,000 troops into the area the night before. All firefighters were issued "flak jackets" for additional protection.

Approximately 40 percent of the riot zone lay within Los Angeles County Fire Department jurisdiction, and the remainder lay within the City of Los Angeles. One Los Angeles City fireman was killed in the line of duty. One Los Angeles County Sheriff's Department deputy was killed. Numerous members of the fire and law enforcement agencies suffered injuries as a result of firefighting and riot-control activities.

The wrath of the mob that created the destruction in Watts began to taper off late on Monday, August 16. Personnel and equipment were slowly withdrawn. Damage estimates to property approached the $50 million mark. Civilian deaths were placed at 32.

Much of the area where the riots had taken place remained vacant for many years afterwards. Many of the owners of the ruined properties and businesses vowed never to return. Vacant patches of land in the riot zone still can be seen today. One entire street is now often referred to as "Charcoal Alley."

After conferring with County Supervisor Kenneth Hahn, in whose 2nd District much of the damage occurred, it was decided to allow Los Angeles County Fire Department camp crews to enter the area to clear a public right-of-way and eliminate health and safety hazards. After two weeks, fire department operations in the area returned to normal.

Reserve Engine 25, a 1948 "High Reeler" Seagrave, supplies a 2½" hand line during the Watts riot. LACoFD photo.

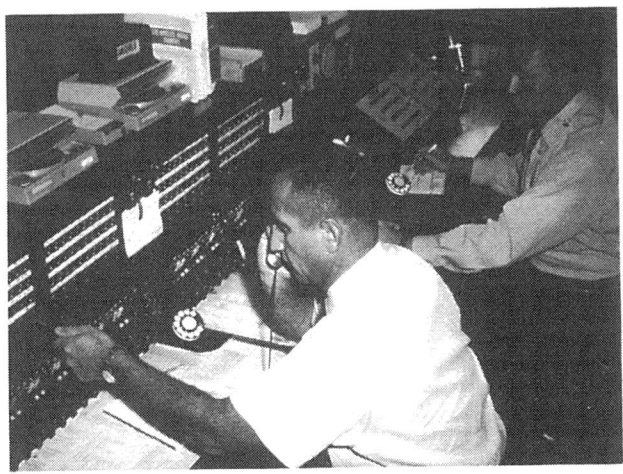

Two photos showing Capt. Norm LaVigne and dispatcher Jerry Dwyer operating the telephones, switchboard, and street and area code card searching in the hanging file.
LA Dispatch, circa 1960.

F&FW Engine Co. 66 (east Altadena) as received in 1963. These split-rear-ended Sedan-Cab 1,000 gpm rigs, powered with the 1091 Hall Scott gasoline engine, were much appreciated during campaign fires in the late fall and winter, and on responses in the rain. Dale Magee photo.

August 4, 1961 marked the arrival of the nine "400" series rigs to the Dept. Designed for use on motorways during brush fires, they were a throwback to the smaller Morelands and Whites used by the Forestry Division during the 1920s and 1930s, even though the latter had more power and better maneuverability. Moldonado photo, LACoFD.

Developed during the middle 1960s by the Thiokal Co., this "Snowcat" type vehicle, nicknamed the "Sprite," was used to haul 400' of 1½" hose and 800' of 1"hose up steep hills and other difficult terrain. The coming of the larger Bell 204 model helicopters beginning in 1967 usurped the function of this machine. LACoFD photo.

The first of the closed cab brush engines; Engine 82's 1963 Crown being delivered to Station 82, Bn. 4, August 1, 1963. L. to r.: Capt. "Bud" Hund, Chief Keith Klinger, Co. Supervisor, 5th District Warren Dorn and Red Wilmore of Crown Coach of Los Angeles, CA. The closed cab provided protection for the crew from fire and the elements. All County fire apparatus is now closed-cab.
LACoFD photo.

"Big John" Griffiths of Engine Co. 12 prepares to complete a counter payoff salvage cover throw during an attic fire in Engine 11's district. Good salvage work often saves much property loss during a fire, and has always been emphasized by the LACoFD.
LACoFD photo, from the collection by John Whelan.

On March 21, 1966, truckies from CMD Truck 27 squeegee water following an incident into a pool for removal by the new Scott "Water Vac" vacuum. This device is still in use, in other sizes as well, throughout the dept. LACoFD photo.

The August 1965 recruit class going through rudimentary calisthenics on a cloudy and probably humid day. This was the 10th year of this facility's operation. LACoFD photo.

Engine 17's new Crown pumper and Truck 43's new Crown-Pitman Snorkel posing for the camera during shakedown tests at the training center, summer of 1965. Warren Bowen photo, from the collection of Keith Klinger.

The City of Industry's Truck Co. 43, a 1965 Crown-Pitman "Snorkel" as delivered in the summer of 1965. It was pressed into service during the Watts Riot of August that year. Warren Bowen photo, from the collection of Keith Klinger.

Having the BC over for a Sunday meal was a periodic, pleasant custom throughout the history of the Dept. In the days before air conditioning, T-shirts were allowable as an inside uniform only. Taken at Fire Station 12, Bn. 4 in July of 1966. L. to r.: Capt. Dennis G. Stangland, Eng. Ralph Angel, Fm. David Boucher, BC Hubert T. Lynch and a portion of Fm. Richard Atkins From the collection of David Boucher.

Events of 1966-67

The fire department's growth in jurisdiction and staff seemed to reach a plateau during 1967. In the previous 18 months, the large new Fire Station 110 at Marina Del Rey opened, housing an engine company and a fireboat. The department received three additional 75-foot Crown "Snorkel" elevating platforms, and two 2,000-gallon-per-minute Crown pumpers for assignment at Fire Station 8 (West Hollywood) and Fire Station 27 (City of Commerce). These were soon nicknamed "The Hogs."

One area of growth that did continue at a fast pace during this period was new station construction and replacement. Glendora Fire Station 86 opened with an engine and patrol on August 1, 1966. A 75-foot snorkel was added in 1968. Station 127 in Dominguez and Station 36 in Carson opened on February 15, 1967 and April 6, 1967, respectively. Replacement Station 33 in Lancaster was established on April 12, 1967, followed on November 5, 1967 by Station 49 in La Mirada. During the summer of 1968, new Station 48 in Irwindale and replacement Station 90 in South El Monte were dedicated.

In one of the first of several "fund reallocation" moves to follow, Fire Station 52 in east Altadena was closed, and Station 146 in Walnut was opened on July 1, 1969. Stations 28 in Flintridge, 2 in Laguna and 13 in Commerce also closed soon thereafter, due to fund restrictions.

The new, enlarged Antelope Valley Dispatch Center opened north of Palmdale, closing its previous facility at Station 37 and eliminating the center at Station 73 known as "Soledad." The topography of the territory covered by Antelope Dispatch is highly irregular, containing three major mountain ranges, four valleys and the coastal strip along Malibu Beach. In order to reach all areas with a dependable radio signal, six separate transmitter sites have been established over the years:

KMG 941 Rolling Hills
KMB 352 Castro Peak
KEY 816 Portal Ridge
KMD 778 Oat Mountain
KBG 521 Hauser Peak
KGP 458 Tejon Peak

During the period of the 1960s, a very unfortunate incident occurred involving one of the pilots of the leased AJ-1s. Pilot Jack Hennessey was killed while piloting his aircraft during a landing attempt at Burbank Airport on September 17, 1966. He lost power and directed his falling craft between two buildings adjacent to 7943 Coldwater Canyon, in North Hollywood, narrowly avoiding persons on the ground. Lacking a seat belt, he struck his head on the instrument panel and died instantly.

In March 1967, the department received its first large helicopter. This was a turbine-powered Bell 204 B, capable of carrying 4,000 pounds of payload, whether in the form of a 10-man hand crew or 360 gallons of water in the drop tank. This was the first in a series of highly successful copters of this type utilized over the years by the department.

The pilot of this new helicopter, Roland Barton, received high praise and an award from the Helicopter Pilots' Association as a result of his skillful flying during the USFS "Loop Fire" in the fall of 1967. It was here, in the central San Gabriel Mountain foothills, that 12 members of the USFS El Cariso hotshot hand crew lost their lives when overrun by flames near the mouth of Pacoima Canyon.

The largest class of new firefighters ever to begin training at the Cecil Gehr Training Center, 90 men, began their schooling in the spring. The 84 men who graduated were initiated into a three-platoon, 56-hour-work week system.

These graduates, as well as the entire department membership, had a new duty added to their job requirements. All members were trained to become deputy registrars of voters for Los Angeles County during the fall months – a duty that remains intact today.

The department continued contracting for services with additional, newly incorporated cities within the county. The 29 cities contracting for the services of the Consolidated Fire Protection Districts by the end of 1967 were:

Artesia Station (Station 30)
Baldwin Park (Station 29)
Bellflower (Station 23)
Bell Gardens (Station 39)
Bradbury (Station 44)
Cerritos (Station 30)
Commerce (stations 13, 22, 27, 50 and 89)
Cudahy (Station 39, Station 147 [during 1971 only])
Duarte (Station 44)
Hawaiian Gardens (Station 34)
Hidden Hills (Station 68)
Industry (stations 43 and 87)
Irwindale (Station 48)
Lakewood (Stations 45 and 94)
La Mirada (Station 49)
La Puente (Station 26)
Lawndale (Station 21)
Lomita (Station 6)
Norwalk (Station 20)
Palmdale (Station 37)
Paramount (Station 31)
Pico Rivera (stations 25 and 40)
Rolling Hills Estates (Station 106)
Rolling Hills (Station 56)
Rosemead (stations 4 and 42)
San Dimas (Station 64)
South El Monte (Station 90)
Temple City (Station 47)
Walnut (Station 146)

Glendora joined the following year, with stations 85, 86, 151 and 152. The two-man Station 152 located close to Station 86, which had been left open for political reasons, closed one year after the Glendora contract was consummated.

By 1967, several organizational changes had been completed within the Fire Prevention Bureau. As a comparison, the organization of the previous 10 years showed the bureau being headed by an assistant

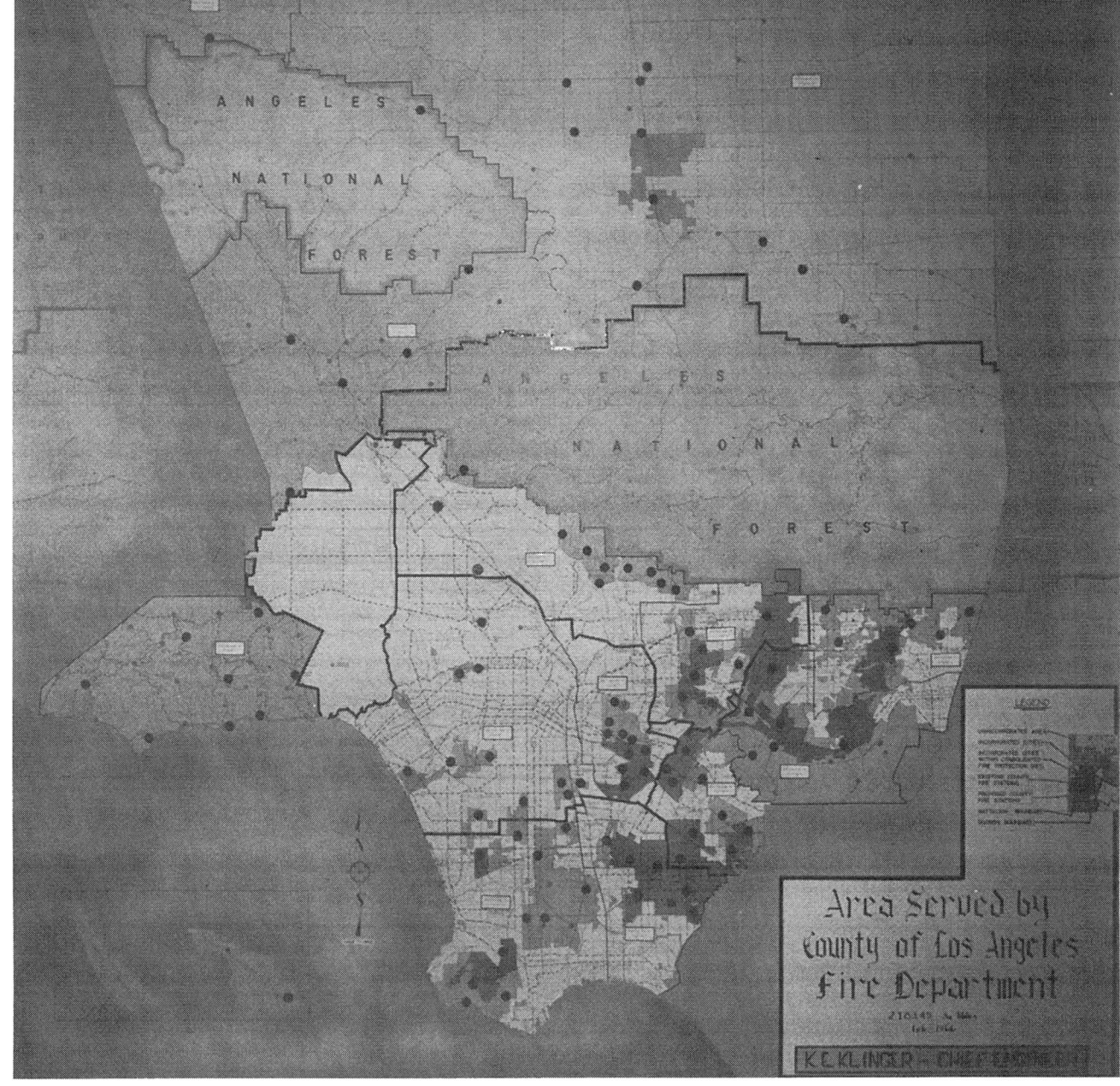

The area served by the LACoFD in 1966. Each round dot is a fire station. The city of Los Angeles in the lightest color, lower center. Note many county "islands" in this area. From the collection of Keith Klinger.

chief, assisted by a battalion chief. These men were in charge of a two-section organization containing the Fire Prevention section, comprised of the Education, Licensing and Permits, LPG and Tank Trailers, Petroleum institutions and Junior Fire Department details. Seven captains were also assigned to the field battalions for selected building inspection purposes. In the Weed Abatement section, four foremen and 65 weed abatement men were employed part time during the spring and summer months, under Battalion Chief Dean Russell.

The changes during 1967 were numerous. One additional battalion chief was assigned in charge of the Weed Abatement Section. A Technical Detail was developed to handle certain exotic and hazardous fuel situations. Such fuels were being developed by the Rocketdyne Corporation (located in Engine 75's district). Explosives were being used extensively in numerous freeway construction projects and at the Feather River Canal system, which was under construction through Battalion 11's district. LPG and Petroleum details were combined, becoming the Flammable Liquids Detail. A School Safety and Public Education Detail was added as well as an Institutions detail. A Fire Investigation Unit under captains Milan Priest and Bob Greer, worked hand in hand with the sheriff's Arson Detail. The Junior Fire Department program, which continued its efforts in the public school assembly system, remained intact under Captain D'Arce "Buck" Hooper.

A major addition in 1960 had been the assignment of the Fire Photography section to the Fire Prevention Bureau. By 1967, the section contained a captain and three firemen or civilian photographers, a far cry from the single warden assigned in 1926. These men worked continuously at producing fire photography, fire investigation photography, slide programs and motion pictures.

The captain-photographer, Charles McCraney, was replaced in later years by Captain John Taylor, a County Fire Department history buff in his own right, who held the position until his untimely death from heart disease in 1978. (Currently, the Photo Section is staffed by one civilian photographer and one video technician, the latter hired in 1989 to assist with training materials, the monthly newletter and special projects.)

The Chaplain's Office

A key ingredient in maintaining a high level of personnel morale within the Los Angeles County Fire Department, as with any such vast organization, is the existence and proper functioning of the chaplain's office. Non-denominational in character, this office has assisted countless hundreds of department members through both joyous and difficult times in their personal and professional lives.

During the late 1940s and into the 1950s, an engine company captain from the San Gabriel Valley, Edward C. Spruill, served as chaplain on a part-time basis. After Captain Spruill's retirement, two full-time captains were appointed to the position. Captain Roy Hinger replaced Spruill, and was soon joined by

During the early 1960s, the filming of incidents and training procedures whenever possible came into vogue. Capt. Cleveland and helicopter pilot Roland Barton simulate filming from the helicopter. LACoFD photo.

Marina Del Rey in the early 1960s when practically no craft were as yet occupying the facility. This area became a small city in itself and required the department to install an engine, truck, and a fireboat. LACoFD photo.

A large fog stream, two smaller hand lines and the Hi-expansion foam unit in operation when a flammable liquids tanker overturned. Off-duty Capt. Larry Hamilton rescued the driver before the tanker exploded into flames. LACoFD photo, taken from the dept. helicopter.

One of the three large fires which have struck Universal Studios. This fire in 1967 was plagued by low pressure due to inadequate mains. The water system has been extensively upgraded since then. LACoFD photo.

Engine 1/3, a size-reduced working model of a Crown pumper of the early 1960s. Here a group of Cub Scouts, Co. Supervisor Warren Dorn and Chief Keith Klinger take it for a demonstration ride. LACoFD photo.

Captain Ross Barb. Both worked out of L.A. headquarters. They were also known as "headquarters captains." Hinger and Barb were eventually replaced – Roy Hinger in 1975, by Captail Bronelle Greer, and Ross Barb in 1976, by Captain Dale Cauble. They, in turn, were replaced by captains John Kuykendall and Don Upham.

All of these men provided spiritual and welfare guidance to any department member who desired such support. Attending members' retirement dinners, funerals and other department functions on request, as well as assisting personnel with retirement plans were all part of their regular duties.

The headquarters captain's position as part of the support staff at L.A. headquarters was later abolished. However, Captains Cauble and Kuykendall, as well as Captain Gerald Smith, David Coffman and Timothy Stromer now serve in the chaplain's capacity from their engine company locations.

As further assistance to department members, a "wellness" program is now in place. A committee is staffed by trained counselors whose primary responsibilities are assisting members with personal problems – including addictions to substances that

(L to r) Chaplains Roy Hinger, Bronnelle Greer, Dale Cauble and Ross Barb pose with retired Chaplain Ed Spruill, center. These "HQ Capt's." were of enormous service to any and all department members and families. LACoFD photo.

February 21, 1969 saw the graduation from a state and county sponsored training academy of another class from a fire department group from Mexico, part of the Bombero program. Here Ch. Klinger along with Ed Bent, director of State Fire Training, presents a certificate to a happy graduate. LACoFD photo.

can affect their job performance and personal relationships with the department and family members. With the adoption of this program, and the continuance of chaplains' positions from field locations, no department member ever need fear being without a place to turn in time of need.

The Forestry Division Changes Status

The original Forestry Division had become, over a 10-year period, a primary division of the Los Angeles County Fire Department. After the mid-'60s, funds allocated to this division gradually diminished. The Forestry Division then became a part of several different divisions of the fire department in the years that followed.

During 1971, the Little Tujunga and Encinal Canyon nurseries that had opened in 1954-55 were closed. This placed the primary stock-growing burden on the main Henninger Nursery, now supervised by Paul A. Downing. The Malibu Nursery, supervised by Forester Carl P. Fischer; the Saugus Unit, headed by

191

Forester Martin G. Gubrud; the San Dimas Unit, supervised by Forester Mike A. Wilkinson; and the Lake Hughes Unit, under Clyde H. Sims, remained open, but on a reduced scale.

It is ironic that what was the "forefather" of the entire County Fire Department in 1924 is now reduced to a subdivision of another bureau. In tribute to this "backbone" of the Forester and Fire Warden Department, a listing of Forestry Division heads is presented here:

Everett R. Stanford	6/1/24 to 8/8/29
John R. Wimmer	8/8/29 to 2/1/39
Carl O. Gerhardy	2/1/39 to 6/30/44
Ernest L. Lioret	7/1/44 to 1/31/46
Ralph M. Van Wagner	3/1/46 to 3/31/68
Arthur M. Arndt	4/1/68 to 1/23/83
Robert E. Johnson	4/1/83 to 3/31/87
Joseph Ferrara	7/1//87 to present

The Liebre Mountain Fire

Occasionally, in the late spring and early summer, a strong northwesterly wind will funnel cooler air down through the long valley in which lies Interstate Highway 5 leading from Gorman in the northwest, to the vicinity of Castaic, Saugus and Newhall. A true Santana wind is from the northeast. However, this northwest wind produces the same drying and warming effect here, as a result of compressional heating. Should a brush or forest fire ignite, its direction of spread will be considerably different.

On June 21, 1968, such a combination of meteorological events did occur. A fire subsequently started near Liebre Mountain, along a branch of Highway 138, the Quail Lake Road, about five miles due east of Gorman, in the extreme northwest corner of Los Angeles County. Captain Phil Goodell of Patrol Station 77 at Quail Lake and a full brush response of engines 76, 78, 73, 273 and 373, as well as a similar response by the USFS, were on the call. They were soon overwhelmed, as the fire spread rapidly down I-5 (then called Highway 99). It was headed toward Castaic, some 18 miles to the southeast. A second alarm was called. This was followed by a rapid buildup of forces until a Plan III was reached in conjunction with the USFS, in whose territory the fire lay.

At a point about eight miles south of Gorman, Captain Goodell and La Canada Engine 382 found themselves crossing ahead of the path of the fire on a dirt Edison Company access road. This road led to the "Old Ridge Route" highway, an abandoned two-lane road one mile to the east of Highway 99. The plan was to attempt to "fire out" ahead of the blaze if at all possible, in order to rob the advancing flames of consumable fuel. Unfortunately, the fuel volume was too large and the wind too strong for this plan to succeed. To make matters worse, the fire arrived much too soon for the crew to effect an escape in either direction.

The crew of Engine 382 crawled under their FWD pumper/tanker with charged hoselines and covered up as best they could. Captain Goodell threw fusees (backfiring torches), in an attempt to decrease the fuel supply, until the last seconds. Flames overcame him before he could get into the cab of his patrol truck. The crew of Engine 382 escaped with some small second- and third-degree burns. Captain Goodell suffered third-degree burns over much of his body, and was airlifted by Copter 10 to the County-USC Hospital burn ward soon thereafter. Chief Klinger accompanied him and the medical team on the flight, reassuring Goodell and comforting him as the chief was able to do so well. Sadly, Captain Goodell passed away soon after arrival at the hospital burn ward.

Captain Goodell was known to be a devoted fireman who fiercely defended his district responsibility whenever called upon to do so. His death illustrated a strong lesson for all county firemen – not only to avoid entering such a hazardous set of circumstances, but to always, when possible, get into the enclosed cab of the apparatus, air masks in place, when danger threatens. A fast-moving fire will pass by, probably damaging the apparatus, but without injuring the crew. Captain Goodell, if circumstances had been slightly different, might have gotten into his patrol truck's cab. But Engine 382 did not have an enclosed cab – like 98 percent of County engines at that time.

Relative to this occurrence and the experience of the Watts Riot in 1965, all County fire apparatus ordered in 1968 and thereafter was delivered with fully-enclosed cabs, and all apparatus in service (and not in reserve status) were retrofitted with enclosed fiberglass cabs during the early 1970s.

Wage Increases

During and shortly after World War II, the economic inflation rate in the United States increased dramatically. Wages were slow to catch up, but, by the late 1950s and early 1960s, substantial wage increases were being realized by Los Angeles County Fire Department personnel. Part of this was due to the ongoing efforts of Chief Klinger to "professionalize" the force, making the fireman worth more to the public. Part was also due to the firefighters' union capitalizing on this goal during wage and hour negotiations. Some examples of wages received by various ranks by the time Chief Klinger neared his retirement in 1969 are shown here:

Chief Engineer	$2,662/month ($31,944/year)
Chief Deputy	$2,142/month ($25,704/year)
Division Chief	$1,793/month ($21,516/year)
Division Asst.	$1,627/month ($19,524/year)
Battalion Chief	$1,380/month ($16,560/year)
Captain	$1,170/month ($14,040/year)
Engineer	$ 922/month ($11,064/year)
Fireman	$ 842/month ($10,104/year)

Since, at that time, the cost of housing was still being figured into the cost-of-living index, wage increases negotiated by Local 1014 were substantial, and usually matched or exceeded the cost of living. The most dramatic increase was the 16 percent realized from January 1, 1971 through July 1, 1971.

Nothing to compare with that has ever occurred again.

The Glendora-San Dimas Catastrophe

August 23, 24 and 25, 1968, saw a tragedy on the rugged brush-covered foothills north of the towns of San Dimas and Glendora. A major brush fire swept the hills and canyons of the San Gabriel Mountains north of fire stations 97, 64, 104 and 102, burning northward into the Angeles National Forest and eventually consuming 19,000 acres.

On the afternoon of August 23, Foreman George Thomas was leading his camp crew across a small ridge, cutting a fireline as they went. Suddenly, he found himself and his crew in the dangerous position of having considerable unburned groundcover downslope between their location and the fire, which hooked around and below them into a canyon near the bottom of the slope.

At that time, camp crew foremen did not carry handi-talkie radios. Foreman Thomas could not hear, above the din of activity around him, other firefighters shouting a warning as the brush below them suddenly ignited. By the time the crew was fully aware of the danger, it was too late. The fire swept rapidly upslope over the entire crew, sending all nine of them to their deaths.

Chief Klinger had been circling above the fire in the department helicopter and saw the danger these men were in. Klinger later stated, "I felt so helpless. There I was, screaming my head off at them from the copter, hoping they could hear me, and knowing they couldn't. It was terrible!" This, the "Canyon Inn Fire," took its toll of camp crewmen, and also profoundly affected Chief Klinger. During the following winter, an enormous flood swept the Glendora-San Dimas area, involving hundreds of members of the department in an often-futile struggle to save dozens of homes from the ravages of silt and fire debris. Troubled by the two tragedies, Chief Klinger's health began to be affected.

However, out of tribulation, progress sometimes is born. In this case, during succeeding years, all camp foremen, and anyone else who might possibly find himself in such a precarious position at a fire, were issued handi-talkies.

Chief Klinger Retires

Shortly after the Glendora fire/flood, Chief Klinger began to develop an irregular heartbeat. He was advised by his doctors that the emotional stress and strain of his responsibilities as chief engineer had begun to affect his health, and that it would be best for him to retire from the fire service. Klinger left his post on a disability leave on April 8, 1969, and retired effective June 30 of that year.

Since the formation of the Los Angeles County Fire Department, each long-term chief has made his mark on the department. Chief Keith E. Klinger was no exception. Thanks to his excellent working relationship with the Board of Supervisors, his staff and the press, Klinger was able to focus the public's attention on the need for fire prevention backed by a

Tractor 1 moves into position to widen a fire line as heavy brush explodes into flame, left. Good judgment by tractor operators avoids personal injury when operating near a hot fire line. B.N. Landrum photo, LACoFD.

superior firefighting force. History has recorded some of the ways in which he succeeded in his efforts.

The department *doubled* in manpower, to 2,500 personnel, during Chief Klinger's term. The number of fire stations increased from 80 to 113. Ten additional stations were under construction when he retired. By utilizing the law that allowed cities to contract for services, 31 additional cities followed the example of the "Lakewood Plan" and joined the Consolidated Fire Protection District. All contract cities realized substantial monetary savings as well as increased fire protection service. The major portion of the Consolidated Fire Protection District had improved its National Board of Fire Underwriters' rating to a Class II, thereby gaining reduced fire insurance rates for the citizens.

Conditions for members of the department improved substantially, as well. In addition to the reduction of the work week to 56 hours, the living/working quarters of fire station personnel had been upgraded. The majority of the Consolidated Fire Protection District stations, and many of the Forester and Fire Warden stations, were either newly-constructed, replaced or remodeled. Ninety new pumpers, five additional ladder trucks and 15 more rescue squads were placed in service. Three helicopters and supporting equipment, personnel and housing had been delivered, ordered or constructed. Two additional bulldozers were provided to the Construction and Maintenance Division for firefighting and fire road and firebreak maintenance. One of the dozers was equipped with a reel for laying 2½-inch hose up firebreaks.

Due to the rapid growth of the department during this period, it was impossible to keep the ranks fully staffed in any position. The retirement-promotion-

Division Asst. Chief Harvey Anderson, left, and Chief Keith Klinger pose informally at LA HQ, Dec. 22, 1967, two years before their retirements. LACoFD photo.

This simulated response by Patrol 73, Bn. 6 chief's car, Engine 273 and Engine 73 took place on February 5, 1968. This station housed 11 men and was the hub of Bn. 6 at the time. LACoFD photo, from the collection of Keith Klinger.

hiring sequence could not be kept in balance. As a result, the method used to keep the ranks fully staffed was to continue to hire off-duty men to work overtime in the vacant positions, as was the case when the 3rd Platoon (C shift) was formed. The number of men who volunteered to work was plentiful, even though overtime was paid at a straight time rate. The men realized an opportunity to raise their standard of living without taking on a second "side job." Consequently, morale soared, and the men received valuable additional experience in their profession.

At the time of his retirement, Chief Klinger was honored by the Board of Supervisors, during a regular meeting. Supervisors Warren Dorn and Kenneth Hahn eulogized him as having been a truly great fire chief, calling him "the county's most effective department head." The Board elected him "fire chief emeritus" of Los Angeles County. All those present gave him a standing ovation.

Appropriately, the Los Angeles County Fire Department's headquarters building on Eastern Avenue was renamed "Klinger Center."

Chief Klinger made it a point to make annual visits to selected Battalion HQ stations for purposes of keeping the men informed of the status of the department. Seated at the table are Mr. McLain, BC Stan Barlow, Mr. Mort Golden, Chief Deputy George Brunton, Chief Klinger, Div. Chief Walter Meagher and BC Noel Manchester during this 1968 visit to an unknown station. LACoFD photo.

The T.V. Channel 5 "telecopter" crew and owner Gene Autry were presented honorary Fire Warden badges by Chief Klinger on March 26, 1968. Gene Autry, left; Herb Greene, right. LACoFD photo.

195

FORESTER & FIRE WARDEN AND FIRE PROTECTION DISTRICTS
LOS ANGELES COUNTY FIRE DEPARTMENT

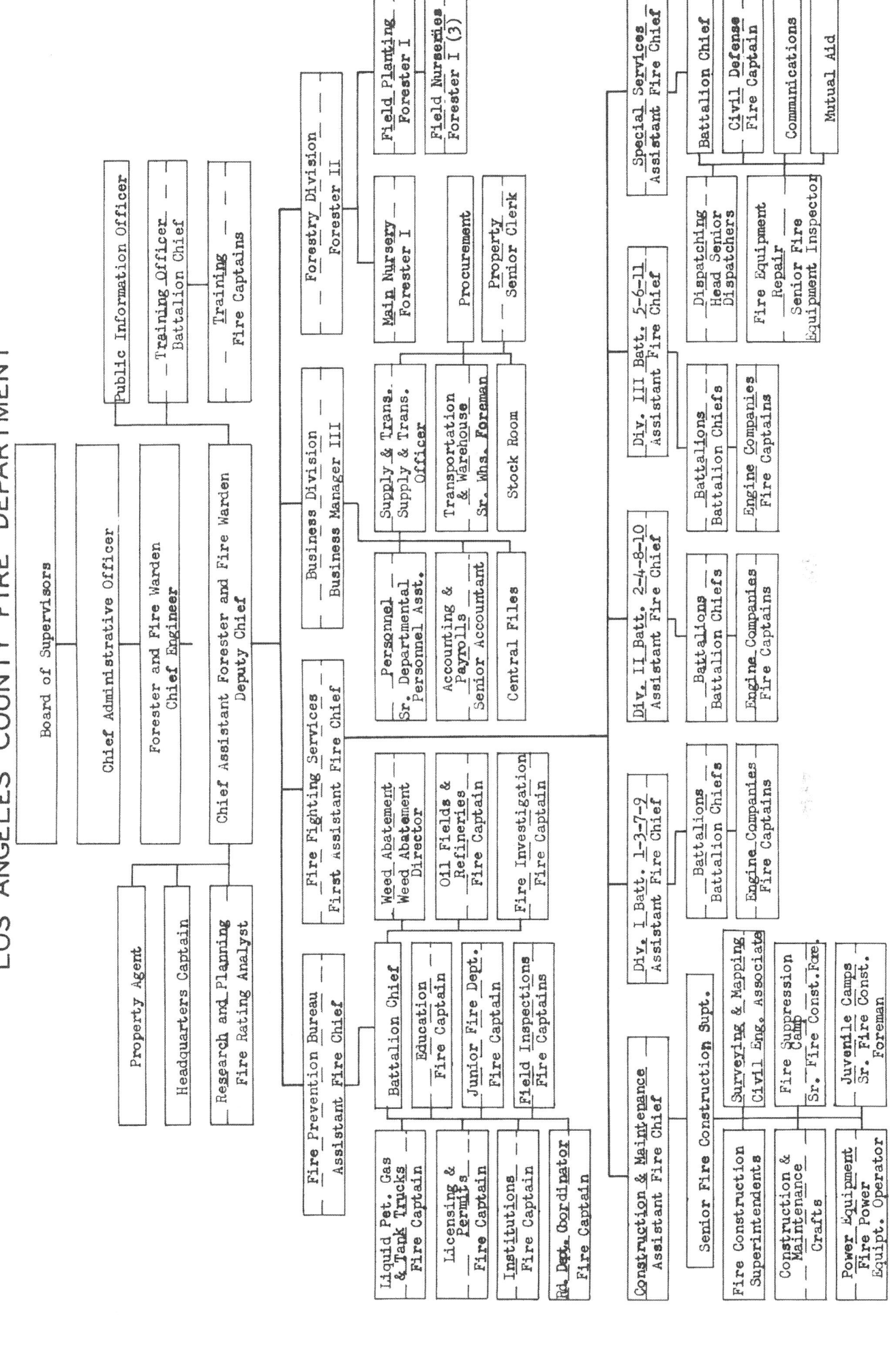

Adding To The Mission

Chief Richard H. Houts, LACo. Forester & Fire Warden 1969-77. LACoFD photo.

Richard H. Houts Assumes Command

After extensive civil service testing among several prospective candidates, the Board of Supervisors on June 10, 1969, appointed Division Chief Richard H. Houts to the position of chief engineer.

Almost as if to issue a challenge to the new chief, the fire department experienced its first highrise fire the evening before Houts' appointment. Captain James O. Page and his first-arriving crew of Engine 7 were greeted by falling and sailing shards of glass from the well-involved Playboy Club on Sunset Boulevard. This West Hollywood building erupted into flames on the fourth floor. The fire began lapping upward, floor by floor. Fortunately, the fire was readily accessible to a ladderpipe stream from L.A. County Truck 8 and an elevating platform stream from an L.A. City Fire Department unit, thus preventing further upward extension of the blaze.

Although his eight years as chief were filled with many good and productive times, Chief Engineer Houts also faced some difficult challenges during his tenure. Some of these challenges would be met, some would not. The mood of the taxpaying citizens was becoming more and more conservative, directly affecting the manning levels and equipment status of the entire department. Funding for the fire department was greatly reduced during this time.

The long period of construction and expansion that was initiated during Chief Klinger's term of office during the '60s began to level off during the '70s. However, expansion did continue as far as smaller, incorporated cities continuing to join the Consolidated Fire Protection District. A number of additions took place: Glendora, on November 29, 1967; Signal Hill, on February 6, 1968; Maywood on August 1, 1970; Bell, on September 21, 1971; Huntington Park, on January 1, 1972; South Gate, on May 1, 1975; Claremont, on August 1, 1975; and Whittier, on September 1, 1975.

Fire Station 147 in the new city of Cudahy opened in the fall of 1971 with a 1951 International pumper and a two-man crew. It closed exactly one year later, the area then being covered primarily by Station 39 in Bell Gardens.

As a side note, although little note was made of it at the time, County Supervisor Kenneth Hahn made a formal proposal on March 13, 1969 to develop a program of young potential firefighters through the Explorer Scouting program of the Boy Scouts of America. Although it would be several years before the program would actually come to fruition, the seed had been planted for the fire department to initiate the program.

The morning after the Playboy Club Fire in Engine 7's district on Sunset Blvd. Well-placed streams from ladder-pipe and snorkel units halted the fire's exterior "lapping" from floor to floor. Aggressive interior attack from the rear completed extinguishment. Photo courtesy James O. Page.

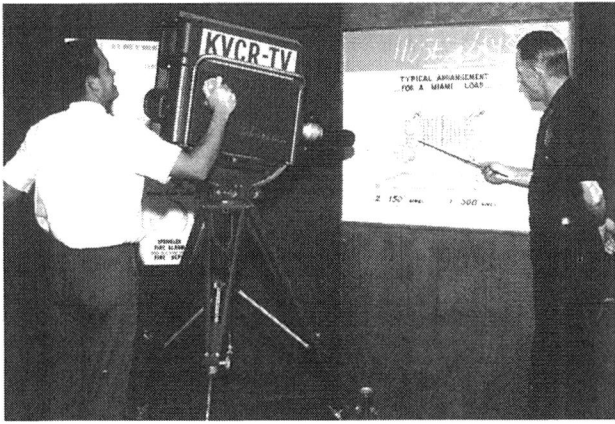

Capt. John Whelan of the Training Section explaining the fine points of the "Miami" 1½" hoselay for the television recording camera, circa 1969. Capt. Whelan was a stalwart of the Training Section for many years. From the collection of John Whelan.

The Malibu-Newhall-Chatsworth Fires

The Devil Wind tends to blow with a higher velocity during the winter months. This is partially due to a considerably colder air source moving in from Nevada. Occasionally, cooler air invades the area much earlier in the season. These early Santanas then reach higher-than-normal velocities. Such were the weather conditions throughout Southern California on September 25, 1970.

At 1031 hours, a motorist turned in a "still" alarm to Fire Station 125, just northwest of the intersection of Highway 101 and Las Virgenes Canyon Road, at Brent's Junction. The reported fire, in some illegally-dumped rubbish and grass, was burning to the south of Highway 101 and 500 feet east of Las Virgenes Road, about a quarter mile from the station.

As Captain Fred Dean and his crew started out the door on board Engine 125, Patrol 125 also spotted the fire and called for a full brush assignment. While engines 225, 65, 67 and 68, their patrols, four hand crews, a dozer and a helicopter were responding with 125's, Captain Dean called for 10 additional companies. The fire had already consumed an estimated 50 acres of light grass and brush, and was on its way over the first hill heading southward, down Las Virgenes Canyon.

Initially-arriving companies attempted to keep the fire from spotting to the west across Las Virgenes Canyon Road, south of Highway 101. They were unsuccessful. The fire began a run toward the 20th Century Ranch and the Monte Nido area. Sustained northeast winds, measured at the Oat Mountain Lookout, were blowing from 60 to 70 miles per hour. Humidity was below 10 percent. The staff at Los Angeles headquarters were alerted and plans were established to meet the worst possible situation.

A Plan I had been called. The base camp was set up at an elementary school one-half mile south of Station 125. Chief Houts soon amended this, since the fire could not be contained anywhere near that site. In fact, there was no doubt that the fire would reach the coast, some 18 miles distant, in a matter of hours if the wind continued at such a high velocity. Chief Houts had the fire camp moved to Fire Station 71 at Zuma Beach, eight miles to the southwest. He also raised the fire's status to a Plan III. Fifty additional engines, from both Los Angeles County and City, were requested. As was expected, the fire reached the ocean north of Malibu Colony at 1500 hours.

The command of the fire was split into two divisions. Assistant Chief Ben Matthews took the south and east sides. Division Chief Walt Meagher took the north and west. Tactics were simply to protect homes, evacuate areas that could not be defended and try to keep from losing lives. The incident was designated the "Wright Fire."

Chief Matthews' car proceeded south, toward the coast on Malibu Canyon Road, paralleling the fire to allow Matthews to size up its progress. Only three engines managed to make the trip from the north over this route to the coast to assist the companies stationed there, for on the return trip up the canyon from Malibu, Matthews' car met with a cascade of rocks plummeting down the vertical Malibu Canyon slope. The landslide rolled onto the road north of the dam and south of the tunnels. Fire and wind had loosened the rocks, creating a source of potential injury or death for anyone passing along the road. Chief Matthews immediately ordered the road closed to *all* traffic.

Additional responding fire units now had to go *around* the fire to reach the coastal canyons, which were threatened by the fire even sooner than anyone

Members of Glendora Engine Co. 86 remove bulky roofing material from a building during ventilation operations. This can be both difficult and dangerous when structural members underneath are partially burned through. LACoFD photo.

had originally expected. Topanga Canyon Road and Encinal Canyon Road were now the best available thoroughfares from the Agoura Valley to the Pacific Coast Highway, adding 10 to 20 miles to the trip.

During the time the Wright Fire was making its first run, those Battalion 6 engines to the north that were not already moving toward Malibu were dispatched at 1100 hours to a fire beginning east of Newhall. This fire was in the vicinity of the Newhall Refinery, near Highway 14, south of San Fernando Road. Weather conditions there were identical to those in the Malibu area.

Captains Ed French and Don Kanallakan and the crews of Engines 73 and 273 could do nothing except watch the fire as it spotted wildly ahead of them in light brush and grass. So began what would be the fire's long, continuous run south to Fire Station 125 at Highway 101 at Brent's Junction. It would go over Oat Mountain, covering a major portion of the Chatsworth Hills and Twin Lakes area. This 19-mile distance was traveled by the "Clampitt Fire" in a little over 14 hours. It would burn 107,000 acres and destroy 103 structures en route. Los Angeles County and Los Angeles City damage figures for this fire came to $7.4 million.

At the time the Clampitt Fire was doing its damage in Chatsworth, another fire in Battalion 6 had

Members of engine 89 lock in and tie off a 1½" hoseline during long-term overhaul operations, location unknown. LACoFD photo.

199

Located at 15721 Atlantic Ave., the Custom City Motorcycle sales building burns vigorously. Engines 31, 57, 105, 98, 41, 9 and 214 responded, along with Truck 31 and Light Unit 52. A passing civilian helps firefighters position a 2½" handline. Pat Olsen photo.

ignited. Located in Fire Station 81's community of Agua Dulce, this fire burned rapidly southwest down Mint Canyon. It destroyed 20 structures before being halted by 24 engines and patrols from the County and USFS and 160 men. It caused $584,000 damage.

The original fire at Malibu in itself would have been large enough to activate mutual aid for Los Angeles County. With the outbreak of additional fires, as well as several smaller ones the following day, *massive* mutual aid was requested and received. All equipment was coordinated by members of the Los Angeles County and Los Angeles City fire departments, the California Disaster Office, California Division of Forestry, United States Forest Service and various police agencies.

The Wright Fire was contained on Sunday, September 27, as a result of a massive stand made along the ridge west of Topanga Canyon and along the ocean on the south. The fire burned 28,000 acres, 123 structures and 25 automobiles. The dollar loss stood at $6.8 million.

Accompanying the Wright Fire and the Clampitt Fire were several less-severe incidents scattered throughout Los Angeles County. One grass fire, south of Colima Road in the Whittier Hills, caused burns to Captains Jim Hunter and Al Moore and Engineer Ron Dittmer of Engines 15 and 91. Engine 91 was severely damaged.

Mutual aid engines were utilized both on the various firelines and as move-up companies. As these units filed toward Los Angeles County, many stopped to fight fires along the way. A large fire was burning in San Diego County, and two smaller fires burned in Ventura County. The California Division of Forestry and the federal USFS pumpers were split and scattered, some being used on incidents in their own jurisdictions, others assisting Los Angeles County. In all, 57 cities sent personnel and equipment.

The scope of the fire problem in Los Angeles County for the weekend of September 25 and 26, 1970 is reflected in the following table:

FIRE	# OF ENGINES	MANPOWER
Wright	103	1,250
Clampitt	75	450
Agua Dulce	24	160
Brea	24	180 (bordering Orange Co.)
Val Verde	12	100
San Gabriel Cyn.	14	260 (USFS)
Lopez Cyn.	6	60
Liebre Mtn.	8	120 (USFS)
Hacienda	19	165
Colima Rd.	27	200
Palos Verdes	10	50

Incredibly, there were 375 engines in action in Los Angeles County within a three-day period! In all, 3,100 personnel manned them, assisted by a myriad of auxiliary rolling stock such as 'copters, patrols, dozers and camp crew equipment. Chief Houts credited southland fire agencies with the finest display of cooperation in history, with a nearly total commitment of first-line resources.

LA County and CDF personnel observe a measured test fire burning an acre of wild oats during Operation Firestop. LACoFD photo.

Operation Firescope

From the onset of the Firescope program, Los Angeles County was its active supporter. The program was developed as a direct result of the severe 1970 fire season in Southern California. Through it, the counties of Southern California, many cities, the CDF, and USFS, have a planned, coordinated system to support each other during times of severe fire occurrence. The new agency would coordinate all movement of emergency equipment to the affected area. It would also provide a common descriptive language to use when conducting business. Among other duties, the agency tracks weather contitions in order to forecast Santana winds. It implements the National Weather Service's "Red Flag" warning system, wherein a watch is issued a day or two in advance of a suspected wind episode, a "warning" when one is likely and an "alert" when one is imminent or in progress.

The program took several years to develop and become generally accepted. When Firescope became operative for the 1976-77 fire season, the County of Los Angeles was selected to be Firescope's temporary Southern California base, it being the geographical center of the strip of coastal counties. Quarters were established in a recently-closed L.A. County fire station – Engine 57's house at 5710 N. Peck Road in El Monte. (Most of this district had been annexed to the City of El Monte.) Then-Battalion Chief John Englund was assigned as Los Angeles County's representative.

The following year, Firescope's permanent headquarters was established at the California Division of Forestry headquarters at Riverside. Its first elected chairman also was Battalion Chief Englund.

An outgrowth of the organizational changes accomplished by Firescope was the transfer of many of those changes to a new type of command structure, the Incident Command System. This standardized method of command provided for a common method of management of resources by all fire organizations adopting and participating in it. While almost all fire departments now use the method, it was first field tested by Battalion 4, Division 5, during the fall of 1985. It was subsequently adopted by the entire L.A. County Fire Department on April 1, 1986.

Firescope now meets at the state level in Sacramento once a month. It continues to be an effective program, benefiting all cooperating fire agencies and, in turn, the public.

The Paramedic Program

Although the idea of offering medical care in the field had long been in the back of many people's minds, such services were provided only minimally, and the required technologies for widespread application did not exist. In general, persons suffering from life-threatening medical emergencies could not expect

Paramedic Squad 59, operating out of Harbor General Hospital, circa 1969. Nurse Carol Bebau, left, Paramedic Jerry Nolls and David Phillips stand ready to serve the South Central area of the county. LACoFD photo.

Paramedics "Rocky" Doke and Dale Cauble pose with their equipment next to their red Ford station wagon, which was being used as Squad 36 in 1969. This is one of the first two paramedic squads. LACoFD photo.

to receive rapid attention and stabilization of their condition unless they happened to be very near a hospital emergency room when the problem occurred.

According to retired Chief Harvey Anderson, the accidental drowning of a young girl in 1947 at Malibu Beach stimulated local support for rapid emergency medical care. However, 20 years were to pass before technology and governmental interest sufficiently increased to allow development of an acceptible program.

The City of Miami, Florida had developed a program in which a patient's heartbeat could be transmitted via radio from an emergency scene to a physician at an emergency hospital, enabling the doctor to relay instructions to medical aid personnel in the field.

During the mid-'60s, a program in Seattle, Washington attracted national attention. Hundreds of members of the public were given instruction in the technique of cardiopulmonary resuscitation.

After lengthy consideration by the Los Angeles County Board of Supervisors regarding public emergency medical care, it was determined that some sort of paramedic program should be developed. Supervisors Kenneth Hahn and Warren Dorn were the program's particular mentors. It only remained to be determined how the program might be implemented and delivered to the public.

Various ideas were put forth and discussed. After due consideration, the consensus was to use the fire department as the means of delivery. After all, its personnel were already on duty in the field with the rescue squads – such as they were. Rescue squad members were deemed trainable in advanced emergency medical techniques. The die was cast. The Los Angeles County Fire Department was going into the medical business.

As a start, six firemen – Robert Belliveau, Dale Cauble, Gary Davis, Gerald Nolls, Dave Phillips and "Rocky" Doke – began training at Harbor General Hospital. Upon graduation, they were stationed on Squad 59 at Harbor General Hospital and Squad 36 in Carson, beginning December 8, 1969.

The "paramedics," as they were now called, responded in their areas surrounding the hospital and in Carson in their Ford ambulances. An emergency room nurse accompanied them for purposes of starting intravenous injections (IVs) when needed.

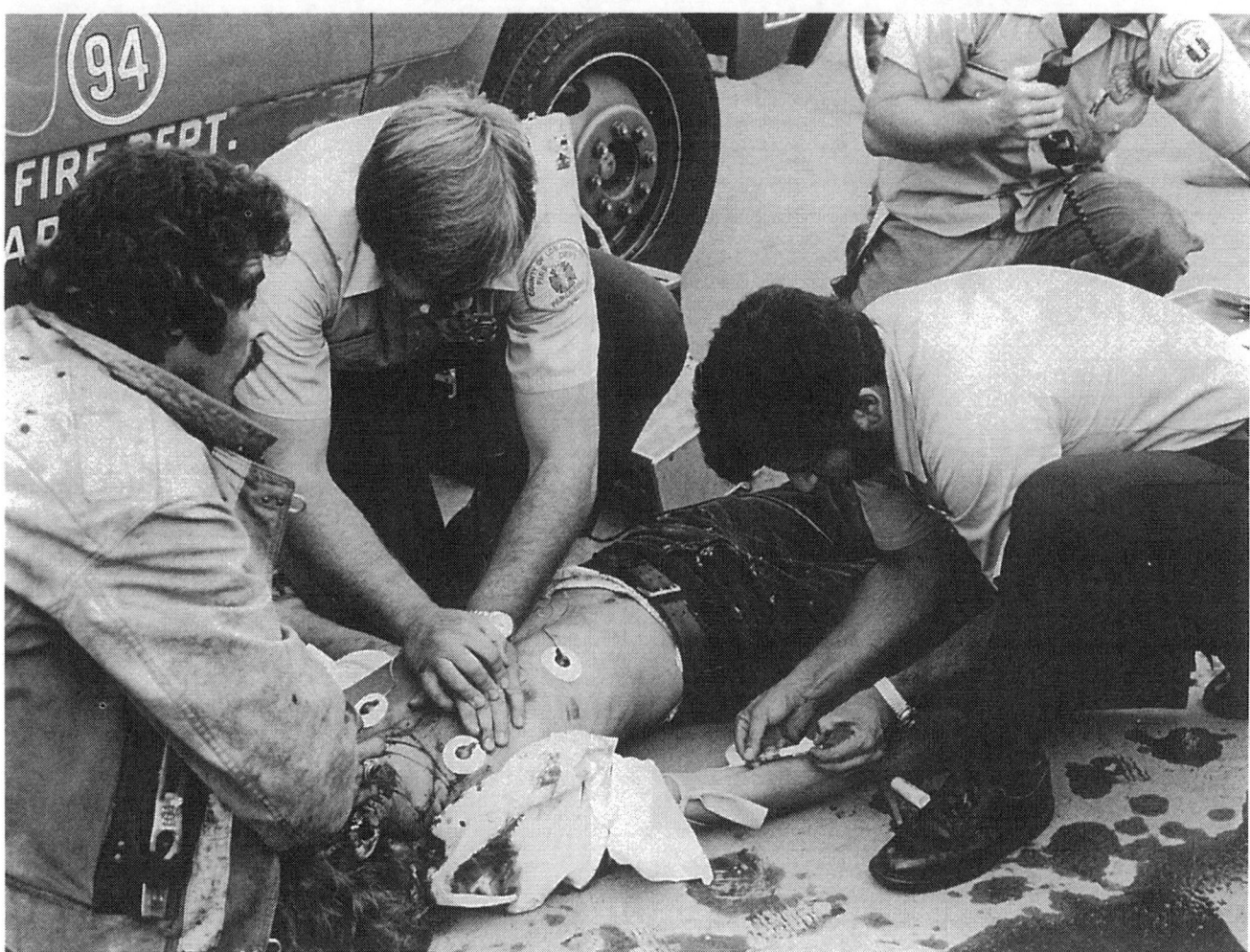

Paramedics of Squad 94 attempt to save a victim who was not breathing upon their arrival with a drug injection and CPR en route to the hospital emergency room. LACoFD photo.

The success of this experimental program cleared the way for the training of the next class of paramedics. They were assigned to Squad 38 in the Angeles Mesa area on October 1, 1970 and to Squad 14, South-Central L.A. area, on November 15, 1971. As more classes graduated and additional funds became available, squads proliferated throughout the unincorporated areas and in the contract cities served by the fire department.

Since the paramedics were still primarily firefighters, it was important that they be released from their medical duties as quickly as possible following a medical response. The county decided to contract with private ambulance services to transport patients to hospitals. In many cases, when paramedic follow-up to the hospital was not required, they could immediately "go available" at the scene via radio. This policy is still in effect.

The table that follows indicates the next 20 squads that were placed in service up to December, 1973. From that time on, single squads were added as demand and funds allowed. Eventually, the paramedic squads replaced the remaining rescue squads that were still in service. Both names were soon shortened to the designation "squad," and the other names phased out.

SQUAD #	ACTIVATION DATE	CITY
36 & 59	12/08/69	Carson & Harbor Gen.
38	10/01/70	Angeles Mesa
14	11/15/71	Watts
20	8/01/72	Norwalk
11	8/01/72	Altadena
7	8/01/72	Sherman (W. Hollywood)
94	8/01/72	Lakewood
3	2/16/73	Belvedere Gardens (East L.A.)
33	2/16/73	Lancaster
47	2/16/73	Temple City
43	3/16/73	Industry
29	4/28/73	Baldwin Park
40	4/30/73	Pico Rivera
31	5/25/73	Paramount
39	5/25/73	Bell Gardens-Cudahy
49	7/07/73	La Mirada
6	7/08/73	Lomita
37	8/06/73	Palmdale
151	8/06/73	Glendora
9	9/14/73	Miramonte-Florence (Watts)
165	9/14/73	Huntington Park
19	10/12/73	La Crescenta (La Canada-Flintridge)
64	10/12/73	San Dimas

The balance have been added piecemeal over the years.

An original publicity poster advertising the pilot episode of the "Emergency" T.V. series. This program enjoyed enormous approval ratings and kept the LA Co. Fire Dept. in the public's eye for several years. From the collection of James O. Page

Fireman Richard Zimmer extinguishes flames on the back of a stuntman after a scene called for him to fall out a window while on fire during 1972 filming of the program "Emergency" on Worcester St. in Pasadena. LACoFD photo.

The 1973 Ward LaFrance 1,000 gpm (rated) pumper delivered to Universal Studios for use in the television series "Emergency." It appeared during the season as a replacement for the 1965 Crown pumper that was initially used. The number 51 was not in use at the time, nor is it to this day. LACoFD photo.

The Department and Mr. Cinader

During the mid- and late 1960s, "Adam 12" and "Dragnet" were two very successful programs on national radio and television. Dragnet, a weekly 30-minute program, focused on the activities of two Los Angeles Police Department detectives. The co-producers of the show, the late Jack Webb and the late Robert Cinader, were apprised that paramedic services were being incorporated into the Los Angeles County Fire Department. Cinader became curious enough about its potential as an entertainment feature that he began to stop by Station 7, which had a paramedic squad.

After further contacts with the paramedics, Cinader also began to visit Station 36. After signing a special release of liability, he was soon riding along on paramedic responses.

It soon became apparent to Mr. Cinader that the potential for both a dramatic and informative television series about paramedics did, in fact, exist. But, in order to fully capitalize on the venture, it would be necessary to elicit the cooperation of the fire department staff. Contacts with Chief Engineer Richard Houts via Public Information Officer Richard Friend proved fruitful. Friend would later coordinate the show's writers, and review their scripts.

Captain James O. Page at Station 7 also offered general support and encouragement. All this departmental input did, however, have one very important stipulation: All emergency incidents portrayed must have actually occurred and must be presented in an authentic fashion. (A previous attempt by others in a similar program, "Rescue 8," had failed in this area.) Paramedic Dale Cauble was assigned to work directly with Cinader's office.

With plots for the shows a matter of historical research, there remained the selection of the two actors to play the paramedic leads. Randy Mantooth was recruited to play the younger, single John Gage. Kevin Tighe was selected to play the slightly-older, married Roy DeSoto.

So many different kinds of incidents were eventually portrayed in the series that episodes were shot almost everywhere in the county. Fire Station 127 in Dominguez was utilized for much "stock" exterior filming. A complete replica of the interior of Carson Fire Station 36 was constructed at Universal Studios for filming situation shots of internal station activities.

For filming on location, fire equipment and per-

Squad 51, vehicular star of the T.V. series "Emergency." This 1969 Dodge with a two-man cab is presently owned by the LA Co. Fire Dept. Museum Association. Photo by David Boucher.

Station 51 scenes for "Emergency" were filmed here at Station 127, in Carson. Photo by David Boucher.

A view of one of the main buildings at the Veterans' Hospital north of Pacoima, following the 6.5 earthquake of February 1971. Careful inspection will reveal workers from LA County, LA City, the USFS and various police units. The last survivor was located one week after the quake. LACoFD photo.

sonnel from the nearest adjacent battalion were utilized. Reserve equipment and off-duty regular personnel were hired by Universal for the day's shooting. All were required to join the Screen Actors Guild, at a special rate, in order to be hired. Either a captain or a battalion chief was tapped as a "technical officer" in order to determine the authenticity of every detail as each scene progressed. Realism was virtually assured.

The first pumper used in the program was an older Crown. It was replaced during the progress of the series by a brand new 1973 Ward LaFrance. This rig was driven across the country from the factory in 20 days, from Elmira Heights, New York to California, by PIO Dick Friend, Engineer Mike Stoker, Captain Mike Stearns and FFPM Ed McFaul to draw public attention to the new show and explain the paramedic program.

The show's paramedic squad was a 1969 Dodge with a two-man cab. Both the engine and the squad were purchased by Universal Studios. They were assigned the number "51," since that number was not being used by the fire department at the time.

The program was titled "Emergency." It brought fame and goodwill to an already highly-thought-of fire department. Not only was it an excellent public relations effort, it also helped to educate the public about the day-to-day duties of L.A. County firefighters and paramedics.

The program ran for seven seasons, 30 shows per season, including reruns. It was seen all over the world, with the language of the particular country in which it was shown dubbed in. Reruns are still seen today.

The 1973 Ward LaFrance that was known as Engine 51 currently serves Yosemite National Park.

The Shaker at Sylmar

By 1971, it had been 38 years since a strong earthquake had originated in Los Angeles County. The 7.7 Kern County quake of July 1952 originated on the White Wolf Fault near Arvin, and, although it was felt throughout Los Angeles County, only a modicum of damage occurred.

At 6:30 a.m., February 9, 1971, a temblor rated at 6.6 on the Richter Scale violently awakened the residents of the entire San Fernando Valley, as well as surrounding communities. Centered just south of Bear Divide, it became known as the "Sylmar" or "San Fernando" quake. It caused the ground north of Foothill Boulevard to rise three feet in a split second. Shock waves, arriving at Fire Station 74 in Kagel Canyon, four miles from the epicenter, tore the station from its foundation. The violent shaking threw Captain Scott Franklin and his crew out of their beds. They ducked for cover as various pieces of furniture hurtled past them. The right rear tires of Engine 74's Crown pumper left black rubber

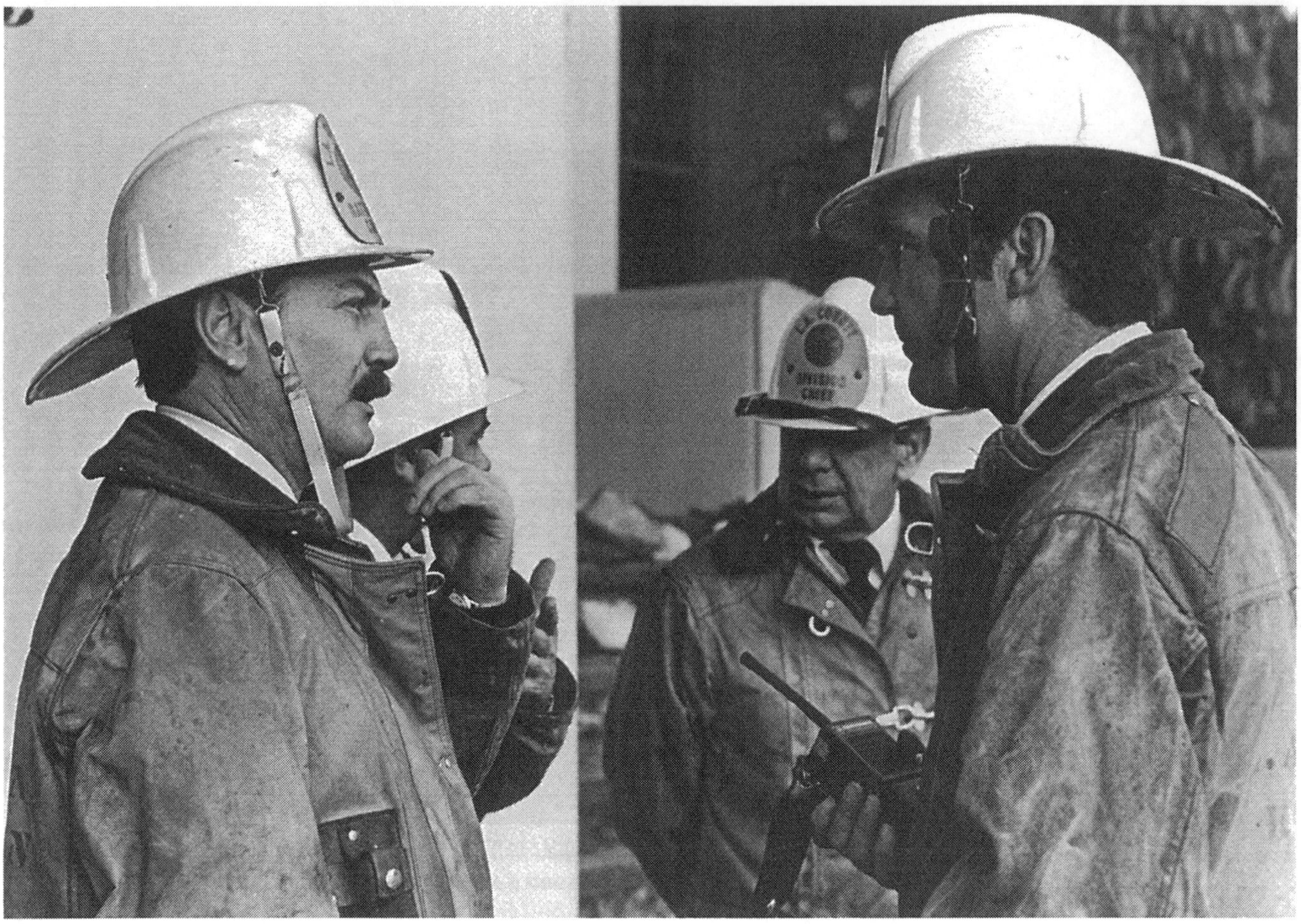

BCs Harold McCann, Ray Schackleford, Div. Chief Ron King and AC Earl Fordham discuss strategy during an unknown structure fire, circa 1970. Command posts tended to be less formal before the arrival of ICS in 1985-86. LACoFD photo.

Station 74 in its mobile home following the destruction of the living quarters portion of the station during the Sylmar Earthquake. Their 1963 Seagrave pumper and the apparatus barn shook and bounced violently, but somehow received little damage. The next photo shows the new station during 1972. LACoFD photo.

marks on the walls of the old apparatus barn three feet above the floor level (which subsequent crews have carefully preserved).

Seven miles to the west, Fire Station 46, at Olive View Sanitarium, was also affected. Constructed in 1926, prior to present building codes, it simply shook itself to pieces. The engine was jammed against the apparatus door, trapping the equipment inside until Captain Bert Buck and his crew could pry the door open.

Fire Station 80, at Vincent, 15 miles to the northeast, also suffered major damage. All three stations were replaced by new buildings within two years.

The Los Angeles City Fire Department handled the bulk of the earthquake-caused responses facing fire agencies in the area. It protects approximately 95 percent of the San Fernando Valley south of the San Gabriel Mountains. A large county hospital within the City of Los Angeles, the previously-mentioned Olive View Sanitarium, had only recently been completed and occupied. It lost its first floor, as the four floors above "pancaked" onto it in one piece. A

The LACoFD's air force, as of August 1971 – copters 2, 3, 4, 10 and 12. Copter 3 was eventually sold; Copter 4 crashed near Glendora Ridge north of San Dimas in 1988. Jerry Meehan photo, LACoFD.

separately-constructed staircase and smoke tower fell away to one side completely intact. Three lives were lost at the Olive View facility. Numerous pre-building-code, one-story buildings surrounding the main structure either collapsed or were badly damaged.

Fires caused by broken electrical and natural gas lines erupted throughout the northern valley area. Three miles to the east, the earthquake caused nearly-complete destruction of the Veterans' Administration Hospital, at the north end of Sayer Street. Several buildings toppled over, causing 47 of the total 58 earthquake-related fatalities.

Other hospital buildings, also constructed prior to strict codes, fell into numerous pieces, killing or trapping patients and staff in the concrete, masonry and tile rubble.

Los Angeles County and City fire crews, along with Construction Division personnel, used cranes and tractors throughout the next 48 hours to break concrete, drilling and probing for victims and removing bodies as they went. Survivors were given medical aid at the scene and were then transferred to other area hospitals via ambulances and by city and county fire department helicopters.

Since the Veterans' Hospital was in county territory, the large force of L.A. City firefighters was gradually withdrawn and replaced by County crews. The L.A. City crews were sorely needed in their own areas to fight fires and work in conjunction with other agencies to restore the water supply. The quake had, in several neighborhoods south and west of the epicenter, broken the water mains, which subsequently drained local reservoirs.

The damage from the earthquake would total slightly over $500 million.

Seventeen years would pass before the Los Angeles County Fire Department would be involved in a similar earthquake disaster operation.

Expanding the Helicopter Fleet

The Los Angeles County Fire Department placed Copter 2 in service in 1957, a new Copter 2 in 1964 and Copter 10 in 1967. Their service record was impressive, indeed, and it became apparent that the fleet should be expanded. Impetus was provided by a new program wherein the copters could be utilized to transport camp crews to remote areas to construct fire and fuel breaks. The copters would pay for themselves in both time and transportation savings for the crews. Therefore, from 1969 through 1973, a priority item in several budgets was the purchase of additional helicopters.

The following table shows the purchase record and subsequent disposition of the eight helicopters that were first processed through the system:

Bell 47 G2, purchased in 1957 (Copter 2). Sold in 1964.

Bell 47 G3, B-1, purchased in 1964 (Copter 2). Sold in 1969.

Bell 204 B, purchased in 1967 (Copter 12, originally Copter 10). In use.

Bell 206 B, purchased in 1968 (Copter 10, originally Copter 4). Destroyed 12/2/86.

Bell 47 G3 B-2, purchased in 1969 (Copter 5-2). Sold shortly thereafter.

Bell 205 A-1, purchased in 1971 (Copter 14).

Destroyed 7/24/77.
Bell 205 A-1, purchased in 1972 (Copter 15).
In use.
Bell 205 A-1, purchased in 1973 (Copter 11).
Destroyed 7/27/77.

In order to man these ships, several more pilots were hired over those same years. In addition to Pilot Roland Barton, hired were Allan MacLeod, July 14, 1967; Loren Patterson, September 8, 1968; Joseph Kelly, August 4, 1969; Frank Pino, August 18, 1969; Bob Dickens, September 9, 1970; Theodore Hellmers, April 15, 1971; Randall West, July 29, 1971; Richard Cearley, March 13, 1972; James Sanchez, July 13, 1972; and Jan Vinson, August 13, 1973.

The department screens pilots carefully and selects them through an oral interview and flight-check process. All pilots must meet the following requirements:

1. 4,000 hours of helicopter flight time.
2. 1,500 hours of the helicopter flight time must have been over terrain similar to L.A. County, at altitudes above 4,000 feet.
3. Substantial medium turbine time.
4. Previous firefighting experience preferred, though not required.

Of the department's copters, models 204 B and 205 A-1 are considered the "workhorses," because of their large carrying capacity of 360 gallons of water of Phoscheck or a nine-man hand crew plus pilot and air operations crewmember (firefighter/paramedic). When in air ambulance (air squad) configuration, two paramedics are on board. Frequently, an emergency-room physician may ride along also.

The End of an Era

One of the massive projects undertaken during the 1960s by the Forestry Division was planning and afforestation of the shoreline and related facilities of the new Castaic Reservoir. This huge dam and lake, along with Pyramid Lake a few miles north, form key holding sites for Feather River Aqueduct water from Northern California.

Near the Castaic Reservoir was the Castaic Lookout at Charlie Point, which opened when the dam was filled during 1965. It was manned by the Los Angeles County Fire Department.

A letter written to Chief Deputy Stanley Barlow by then-Division Chief Clyde Bragdon not only indicated the myriad of funding sources required to keep the department operating, but also marked the end of a system of fire warning devices finally made obsolete by a combination of improved communications, smog and fund depletion. Bragdon wrote:

"The Castaic Lookout Tower was required jointly by this Department and the United States Forest Service, funded by State Water Resources under contract and operated by this Department. The contract with State Water Resources expires September 3, 1971. Although we budgeted for a full year's manning, there will be no offsetting revenue after this date.

"I have contacted the Forest Service and they have indicated no desire to continue to require a lookout tower at this site. . . .

"It is therefore my recommendation that the Castaic Lookout Tower be closed at the end of the work day on September 3, 1971."

While the USFS continued to operate a few towers of its own in the high country of the San Gabriel Mountains, the Los Angeles County Fire Department ceased lookout tower operations on that Labor Day weekend in 1971.

Phantom Funding and Department Survival

The year 1972 saw the passing of state-level legislation that limited the taxing ability of local governments. Senate Bill 90 froze the property tax rate at 80 cents per $100 of assessed valuation, severely limiting the ability of the fire protection districts to meet increasing revenue demands. This measure was only one of three that served to hinder the funding ability of the fire department during the succeeding six-year period. As a direct result of SB 90, 39 chiefs' driver positions were lost. Field battalion chiefs returned to the pre-1955 custom of driving themselves.

The second measure, passed in 1976, determined that Community Redevelopment Agency property tax revenues were to be returned to the city in which the project was located for the 30 years following the project's completion.

In effect, both of these measures denied the fire department the ability to provide the additional service that the ever-increasing construction and population demanded. However, the potential damage caused by the third measure, state ballot Proposition 13, far exceeded the damage inflicted by the first two. Simply stated, Proposition 13 limited the property tax rate to one percent of the *market value* of the property. (See Chapter 12.) Budget hearings in 1972-73 were traumatic for all county departments, and especially for Chief Houts and the fire department. Another major apparatus replacement program was becoming necessary due to the aging of the large fleet of Crown pumpers purchased in the middle and late '50s. These fire apparatus were approaching the time when they should be placed in reserve status. The department's 1949 Generals and 1950-52 International Harvesters and Macks had, for the most part, already passed the point of qualifying for reserve status. Thus, it was most important that funds for a fleet of replacement pumpers be retained in the proposed budget.

After exhaustive effort by Chief Houts, the budget item including the new pumpers was retained. Forty-six Ward LaFrance 1,500 gpm pumpers (downrated to 1,000 gpm) with Waterous single-stage pumps, Allison automatic transmissions and 400-gallon water tanks were ordered from the Elmira Heights, NY factory in the spring of 1972. Each pumper cost $44,000. Assignments by 1974 were as follows:

Forestry personnel, Nov. 1974. (L. to r.) (front row:) Art Arndt, Ch. Houts, Ch. Barlow, Grant Brown. (second row:) Klaus Radtke, Ross D. Johnson, Paul A. Downing, Harold J. Johnson, Lawrence M. Rankin, Joseph Ferrera, Paul J. Okstad, Paul H. Rippens, Clyde H. Sims. (third row:) James R. Ross, Anthony R. Baal, George Veverka, Norman W. Cook, Ronald S. Mayer, Raymond C. Uterback, William F. Draper, Eldon C. Anderson, James M. Anderson. (back row:) Robert A. Dibala, John Haggenmiller, Herbert A. Spitzer, David K. Boyd, Carl P. Fisher, Robert E. Johnson, John R. Griffen, Larry Blackman, David L. Drennan, James R. Stallings. LACoFD photo.

Agoura Engine 65 upon delivery in 1972. This 1972 Ward LaFrance had two hose reels and a 500-gal. tank, indicating it is an F&FW rig. The transverse 1" hose rack to the rear holds about a dozen sections of double-rolled 1" cotton-jacketed hose for extended hoselays. Jerry Meehan photo, LACoFD.

A new cab, offering enclosed protection for firefighters, and a new engine and transmission extend the life of one of the original 400-Series brush engines. LACoFD photo.

The Department's Grumman command and control van. This unit is used for top staff and interagency planning and strategy conferences during major emergencies. It features a synthesizer radio unit, enabling the radio operator to dial in exactly the frequency desired, useful when working with aircraft or other agencies. LACoFD photo.

During the tenure of Ch. Richard H. Houts, the main county nursery at Henninger was re-dedicated as the Spence D. Turner Forest Nursery in honor of the strong guidance Chief Turner gave the Department during his 27 years as Forester & Fire Warden. LACoFD photo.

Another view of the nursery as it appeared during the early 1970s. LACoFD photo.

A retirement function held at FS 82 for Capt. Homer "Milt" Halsey. He was the last person to hold the old F&FW rank of lieutenant. His wife, Evelyn, was the first female dispatcher hired by the Department during WW II. (L. to r.) (first row): Al Rodgers, Milt Halsey, Evelyn Mae Halsey, Ch. Richard H. Houts, Danny Fleming, Louis Thomas. (second row): Ralph Van Wagner, Ezra Miller, Robert Parsons, Roland W. Percey, G. Truitt, Herb Thompson, John Whelan and K.C. Cites. Photo was taken in March of 1972. LACoFD photo.

The Los Angeles basin spills even farther into the Santa Clarita Valley as ground is broken for new fire station 111 on Seco Canyon Rd. near Boquet Canyon. This area continues to require additional stations as growth runs rampant. L. to r.: Div. Asst. Ch. Clyde Bragdon, unknown, Ch. Richard H. Houts, Capt. Scott Franklin, Eng. Trombley, Fm. C. Seder, Co. Supervisor Warren Dorn, Fm. Hale, unknown, Fm. Magita, unknown, Fm. Ketcheside. LACoFD photo.

CONSOLIDATED FIRE DISTRICTS:
3, 5, 9, 12, 19, 29, 30, 33, 37, 40, 41, 43, 53, 71, 83, 87, 90, 96, 98, 111, 115, 116, 141, 145, 146, 273, 282
FORESTER AND FIRE WARDEN:
46, 62, 64, 65, 67, 70, 72, 74, 78, 79, 81, 97, 99, 123, 125, 325, 507, 518, 539. (500 series engines are reserve engines.)

While funding for the fire department would be an ever-present consideration facing Chief Houts for the next few years, so would various court decisions involving the racial makeup of the department. The department was directed to develop and implement a program that would aim recruiting efforts at the ethnic minorities within the county. Still in effect, although with several modifications, this program was intended to ensure adequate minority representation when hiring new personnel.

The Board of Supervisors also took due note that the badges in use at the time were imprinted with the word "fireman." In keeping with the spirit of the times, the Board acted in December of 1974 to have the department reissue all badges of that rank with the word "firefighter," thus including women in the job description.

The first woman to meet all of the qualifications for entry into the recruit academy was Cindy Fralick, hired on February 12, 1983. She graduated from the Cecil R. Gehr Training Center and presently holds the rank of firefighter specialist (engineer).

The "Mill" Fire

There are times when the Devil Wind will strike a given area with little or no warning, even though weather forecasting techniques have steadily improved to almost preclude these occurrences. However, on November 23, 1975, such was the case in the Mill Creek area of the Angeles National Forest.

Some 15 miles north of LaCanada-Flintridge, two USFS hotshot crews (hand crews) were attempting to complete mop-up of an eight-acre fire that had burned the afternoon before. Neither they, nor the rest of the county, was prepared for a sudden appearance by the Devil Wind in such a vicious form that it would threaten an entire Los Angeles County ter-

The beginning of the Mill Fire, 11:50 a.m., Nov. 23, 1975. Note the USFS hand crew (right center), which was powerless to counteract the force of the wind when attempting to cut a line around the fire. Justin Griott photo.

ritory, as well as the cities of Glendale and Los Angeles. What occurred is best described by an eyewitness, Justin Griott, a member of the USFS Bear Divide hot shot crew that was working at the scene:

"As a member of the Bear Divide Hot Shot crew, I was dispatched at 4 a.m., November 23, 1975, for relief and mop-up on the previous afternoon's fire in Mill Creek near the narrows. We reached the fire at 7:30 in the morning and changed shifts with the overnight crews. We hadn't been working more than a half hour when the first 'sleeper' took off up the hill about 90 yards south of our position. We were able to stop that one at the top of the ridge to the west of the drainage that the original fire had been in. Another crew coming in for mop-up (the Oak Grove Hot Shots) was assigned to pick up the spots on the west side of this canyon while we continued to pick up spots on the east side.

"At about mid-morning, we had all of the various spots under control, and L.A. County air support had returned to base. It was at this point that I noticed another finger of flame on the east side of the canyon, a couple of hundred yards down canyon from us. I reported (this) to my supervisor, who immediately called the Oak Grove Hot Shots on his radio and informed them of the danger. There was very little smoke; in fact, Oak Grove reported to us that they could see the heat column rising, but not much else. I remember being impressed by the brightness of the flames.

"Oak Grove held their positions until we reached them, then together we started cutting a safety line toward the fire. At the fire's edge, we started cutting downhill in an attempt at keeping the fire from buttonhooking on us or jumping the bottom of the drainage. The flames were running uphill into a retardant line laid down by aircraft the day before for that spot. We felt confident that we were going to catch this fire, as well.

"It was about 11 a.m. when the first wind came up. My personal recollection was that the wind just came barrelling down the canyon. The first gusts of wind coming at us sounded like a freight train, or a B-17 making a water drop. When I turned to face the sound, all I saw was the brush being laid down by a wave of wind. We then stopped for an instant and watched as the flames whipped into the drainage below us and then across to the west side of

Assigned to Construction Camp 2 in Bn. 4, lead saw-man Reginald Lee poses with his chain saw, used to clear a path for the crew following him as a "line" is cut through the brush. LACoFD photo.

the canyon. In less than one minute we had lost it. We then pulled back to the Fall Creek Trail nearby and watched helplessly as the entire canyon blew up in our faces."

The wind increased in velocity and scope over the next 36 hours, driving the fire south and west through the San Gabriel Mountains at a very rapid rate. All of the watershed of Big Tujunga, Little Tujunga, Kagel and Lopez canyons (Engine 74's district) eventually burned out, consuming some watershed that had not burned since the Pickens Fire of 1933, the Big Tujunga ("Bryant") Fire of 1947 and the Woodwardia Fire of 1959. Herculean efforts by the USFS and Los Angeles County firefighters saved many cabins and homes in Big Tujunga Canyon. The second morning, the fire swept south, skirting the Briggs Terrace area of Engine 63's district. It extended into Goss Canyon, eventually burning nine homes in the Markridge area, along the north edge of the City of Glendale Annex, even in spite of pre-positioned fire department forces there.

The third day, after skirting the Sunland-Tujunga, Lakeview Terrace and Pacoima areas, the fire was halted along the east bank of Pacoima Canyon, just north of Engine 46's territory north of Sylmar.

In the end, this wild, wind-driven inferno had consumed 47,000 acres of prime watershed. It had traveled in a straight line for a distance of 20 miles, one mile more than the Clampitt Fire of 1970.

The bulk of the acreage burned in the Mill Fire has now returned to near normal conditions, with the exception of the area that burned in September of 1979 during the USFS-managed "Sage Fire."

Near Disaster, Recovery And A Bright Future

Chief Engineer Clyde A. Bragdon.

The Fire Department and Proposition 13

It has been postulated that California is the "trendsetter state." Many representatives in state government have come to strongly believe in that premise, for whatever they fail to accomplish, the citizens initiate themselves. One such November 1978 initiative, Proposition 13 – the "Jarvis-Gann Amendment" to the State Constitution came close to causing the disintegration of the Los Angeles County Consolidated Fire Protection District.

Proposition 13 was designed to fix the property tax rate in California at one percent of the market value of all real property. Property values were to be rolled back to 1976 levels for the purpose of tax computation.

The effects of such massive budget cutting would be daunting. Since the Consolidated Fire Protection District's portion of the fire department's budget was (and is) funded mostly by property tax revenues, 70 percent of the department's supporting funds would be affected. The fire station closures and layoff of personnel would be sweeping, setting back the level of fire protection and paramedic services some 50 years!

Clyde A. Bragdon, appointed Fire Chief of Los Angeles County on August 16, 1977, from Division Chief in the Fire Protection Districts, inherited this massive problem. Knowing the inevitability of continued increases in both medical and fire responses, the department made an appeal to the public to reject Proposition 13 or else face a massive loss of emergency services throughout the county. Chief Bragdon appeared on television at the scene of a moderate-sized brush fire in the Whittier Hills just prior to election time, showing the public "the total firefighting force available for such an incident in the entire county territory if 'Prop 13' were to pass."

Regardless of these stated consequences, the desire for property tax reform won out. The taxpayers called for relief from near-confiscatory tax bills. Proposition 13 passed easily in the November, 1978 election.

The Los Angeles County Board of Supervisors responded by instituting a temporary freeze on all hiring and promotions. Staff shortages soon appeared, especially in the captain, firefighter and camp crew ranks. Personnel were repeatedly recalled for unscheduled overtime in order to keep manning at minimum levels. Plot plans were developed showing which fire stations would be closed. Lists were drawn up indicating which special equipment and staff positions would be eliminated.

Since funding at the 1976 level was not adequate for most public agencies, Proposition 8 was proposed as a remedy. It was placed on the ballot in 1978 in order to utilize "augmentation funds" at the state level. These funds were a permanent feature and were to be given to the Board of Supervisors to use as they felt necessary. The fire department received some of the funds, which eased the way for additional personnel to be hired and promotions made during the following year.

Early in 1979, a temporary lifting of the promotional and hiring ban was allowed. A few men were promoted to captain, with the result that engineers were now recalled excessively. Firefighters experienced no real relief, either. However, a fortunate set of circumstances soon made themselves felt. It seemed that the state of California had a large surplus of funds in its coffers. It only lacked a mechanism to distribute the monies to local governments throughout the state. Many local government officials, Chief Bragdon included, made the trek to Sacramento to testify to the dire need for legislation allowing distribution of the funds.

An agreement was reached, and at least a one-year (minimum) "bail-out" of local governmental entities was achieved through the passage of Senate Bill 154, presented by State Senator William Campbell. The passage of this legislation allowed sufficient time for local governmental bodies to review how they could make up the losses in property tax revenues in order to restore their local financing.

A long period of recovery has since passed. Rapidly-rising property values and sales have revived county property tax incomes. As a result, the Consolidated Fire Protection District is experiencing its best financial condition in many years.

However, the General Fund Forester and Fire Warden Stations have become impacted by a shortage of monies received from various Federal and State programs. This has resulted in a complete reversal of the fiscal situation of 20 years ago.

Paramedics Assisted

While the paramedics on the new squads performed their duties adequately enough, it was generally felt that the assisting engine company personnel could be of much greater assistance to them if they possessed a more advanced knowledge of medical procedures, as well. Accordingly, all uniformed personnel in the department were required to pass the Emergency Medical Technician Level 1 course during 1979-80. With experience, these engine/truck company personnel, as well as chief officers and staff personnel, were able to evaluate patients' condition upon arrival, and cancel the responding paramedic squad when appropriate. This released that unit back to service as soon as possible.

EMT-1's are required to requalify in their craft every two years. There is no doubt that the medical aid program of the department has been greatly enhanced by the EMT-1 program.

A Rash of Incidents

The frequency and severity of the Devil Wind appears to vary seasonally, in a manner similar to rainfall. Such a cycle reached a notable peak from 1978 to 1982, being marked by a series of severe wind-whipped blazes that burned vast areas of brushland and numerous structures in the Malibu Hills, Verdugo Hills and the Bradbury area north of the City of Duarte.

The Kanan Fire of October 23, 1978, was set by an arsonist along Kanan Road, south of Highway 101, in Engine 65's district. It burned 25,000 acres, traveling south and west through the Malibus, arriving at the coast near Broad/Zuma Beach some two-and-one-half hours later, after burning 230 structures.

Division IV Chief John Englund was covering Division III that day, and was in the process of proceeding toward Malibu, having been alerted about the high winds in the area, when the fire broke out. After struggling to take off in the high winds in a department helicopter from Station 65's heliport, he was

Series of photos, taken in La Crescenta, January 1978, show the results of fire debris clogging flood control channels and then suddenly releasing. Heavy winter rains followed the 1975 Mill Fire for three years. Note that the hillsides have only stubble growth — not enough to retard the movement of topsoil and rocks. LACoFD construction crews worked for several days to assist where feasible. LACoFD photo.

Testimony as to the ferocity of the wind and high temperatures developed by the Kanan Fire, this home at Broad Beach virtually disappeared in flames. Jerry Meehan photo.

flown (or, as he maintains, blown) south to the coast to reconnoiter the fire's progress. His report to L.A. Dispatch was frankly not believed by the office staff, as he indicated the fire would be at the coast in about one hour, and it had only been burning just over one hour! Fifteen miles in two hours? Not a chance!

Nevertheless, Chief Englund requested all available help to Broad Beach/Zuma Beach. But, by the time the machinery could be put into motion, it was already too late. The fire did indeed set the all-time record for reaching the ocean.

In retrospect, it appears doubtful that enough fire equipment could have been massed in time to save very much property. Once again it had been demonstrated that mother nature is not always reasonable.

Because of the speed of this fire, it was thought by some that a second fire might have been set, halfway to the coast along the fire's path, and that it might have been the first to reach the Zuma area. One civilian died in this incident.

On September 12, 1979, Engine 66 in East Altadena was sent by Valley Dispatch to a "trash fire in the street" on Pinecrest Road, near the entrance to the Mount Wilson Toll Road. Nearing the scene, Captain Robert Wineman realized that there had been a mistake in the incident identification. He immediately saw that he had a "brush fire near the street," instead, and that he was alone with his three-man crew. Wineman immediately requested a full brush response, with Battalion Chief Robert Messall requesting a second alarm moments later.

Try as they might, 66 was unable to catch up with the fire as it charred through moderate brush alongside a home. It reached a small, narrow canyon at the rear of the house, whereupon the "chimney" effect took the flames rapidly up the steep slopes of Muir Peak, west of Eaton Canyon, and into the Angeles National Forest.

Designated as the "Pinecrest Fire," it was finally controlled four days later, after burning over 10,000 acres, including all of the Eaton Canyon drainage to the north, wildland that had not been burned over since 1897. Only last-minute backfiring saved the nursery at Henninger Flats. The loss was heavy, not only in terms of watershed and wildlife, but in dollars and cents.

It cost well over $1 million to extinguish this fire. Another million was spent to clean out the Eaton Canyon Dam, which had filled with silt, rocks and fire debris that had poured out of the canyon during the torrential rains of the following winter.

Much speculation arose concerning this fire. Might the fire have been stopped had a fourth man on 66's crew been present, or if the fire had been correctly identified by the caller to Valley Dispatch? There is no doubt that all those who responded to the incident in the 100-degree heat did everything that could be done to prevent the fire's escaping. This incident reinforces the concept that early and accurate notification, along with a rapid response with adequate manpower remains absolutely essential to an effective fire attack.

The "La Tuna Canyon" Fire burned 10,000 acres of brush and numerous homes and ranches in the Verdugo Hills on November 15, 1980. While primary responsibility for the fire area was shared by Los Angeles City, Burbank and Glendale, brush engines from Battalion 4 (engines 74, 63, 82, 12 and 66) responded under the command of Battalion Chief James Turner. This initial action response was requested by L.A. City because of the severity of the wind and the number of homes threatened. Beginning at 0230 hours, the fire had burned west, down the canyon, to Sunland Boulevard by sunrise. With a wind change the next day, the fire hooked around the west end of the Verdugo Mountains and burned south and east toward Burbank and Glendale.

The "Stable" Fire also began on November 15, 1980. It began from a wind-blown campfire near some corrals at the mouth of Fish Canyon, east of the city of Duarte in Engine 44's district. As the fire burned northwest along the foothills of the San Gabriel Mountains and into the Angeles National Forest, it was slowed in its advance as it approached the mesa-top community of Bradbury. This was due to vigorous firefighting efforts and a dying wind.

Fireline construction and mop-up operations by dozers and hand crews began. Several engines had been released to home quarters, and one strike team of five engines had been placed on standby at nearby Station 44 in Duarte as a precaution. Suddenly, at about 0230 hours, the same wind that caused the rapid spread of the "La Tuna Canyon" Fire some 20 miles to the west also hit the dying "Stable" Fire. The wind's velocity was estimated in the 60-70-miles-per-hour range.

The strike team being held at Station 44 was activated and all available engines in the San Gabriel Valley were rushed back into action. The fire roared into Bradbury, consuming 50 large estate-sized homes and ranches. This devastation was partially attributable to an over-taxed water system and a pump failure. Ironically, five fairly close engines from Battalion 4 that could have been used in this situation had just been dispatched with Los Angeles City to the La Tuna Canyon incident.

The following day, a massive brush fire, burning west along the Chino Hills in Orange County, began to approach Engine 120's district south and east of Diamond Bar. As rapidly as was practical, engines, crews and copters were released from the La Tuna Canyon and Bradbury fires and redirected to the "Orange County" Fire. They staged along Tonner

County San Gabriel Engine 5 gets first water on a fire in a large gun store and reloading shop at Rosemead Blvd. and Del Mar. This second-alarm fire was fought by Engines 5, 47, 66, 42, 4, Trucks 42 and 29 and Squad 47. Four civilians were trapped, and perished, in the initial basement explosion. Station 66 archives.

Commerce Truck 27, an American La France, prepares to put its ladderpipe into action during a building supply yard fire, circa 1982. Engine 163's monitor stream is being absorbed by the tremendous heat. Pat Olsen photo.

Ventilation crews retreat from the roof during the intermediate stages of the William Penn Hotel Fire. Flames had already begun to extend through the attic, and a general "blow-up" was feared, and rightfully so. Phil McBride photo, LACoFD.

Crews set up heavy elevated streams to begin exterior operations after the attic of this Whittier hotel became fully involved. Trucks 20 and 49 are seen in operation. LACoFD photo.

La Mirada Truck Co. 49 in action during the later stages of the William Penn Hotel Fire in Whittier. This fire crept through the old structure following numerous hidden spaces and a large open attic. Ventilation crews were pulled from the roof in the nick of time. LACoFD photo.

Crews attempt to stop fire spread through the interior of the National Lumber Co. in Bellflower. Heat mushrooming through the interior trapped one firefighter. Dave Carlson photo.

Canyon Road with numerous Orange County and California Division of Forestry units. Over 50 engines were then dispersed throughout the area. Along with a vigorous helicopter and camp crew attack, they succeeded in halting the flames along the first ridge one mile east of the 57 Freeway. No homes were lost in this area.

October 9, 1982 saw the ignition and rapid spread of a fire in the Bell Canyon area of the southern Chatsworth Hills. This arson-caused fire burned through many of the same areas as the 1943 "Woodland Hills" Fire and the 1970 "Wright" Fire. The blaze, fought in close conjunction with the Los Angeles City Fire Department, was termed the "Dayton" Fire. It burned rapidly south into the Malibu Hills and was controlled two days later along Malibu Beach. It scorched

Engine 39 prepares to put lines into action during the Federal Paperboard Fire. Wide-open storage yard fires of this type spread quickly with even a light wind, also starting spot fires downwind. Pat Olsen photo, LACoFD.

42,000 acres and consumed 85 homes.

The Dayton Fire was the last in this series of fires, and was the second-largest fire to occur primarily in Los Angeles County territory in 30 years. It was surpassed in size only by the "Clampitt" Fire of 1970. All were driven through heavy brush by the Devil Wind, consuming homes, watershed, and wildlife in their path.

There would be several more fires in the Malibu area, including the large "Piuma" Fire in the fall of 1985, but the cycle of very large and serious fires would take a downward turn that remains in effect today.

New Apparatus and Meager Dollars

During the last few years of Chief Bragdon's tenure as fire chief and the first year that Englund was chief, a few pieces of new pumping equipment were squeezed out of the meager post-Prop. 13 budgets. All new equipment had the now-standard (L.A. County-specified) 1,500 gallon per minute single-stage pump, downrated to 1,000 gallons per minute. (The downrating was to make certain that the annual pump tests were always passed.) Water tank capacities had returned to 500 gallons. A return to the pre-'68 Crown era occurred, as all apparatus from 1981 on were outfitted with six-speed Spicer manual transmissions.

The 1981-82 deliveries were all American La France pumpers, 22 in all, placed in service at the following stations: Fire Station 95, Compton, FS 28, Whittier; FS 20, Norwalk; FS 56, Palos Verdes; FS 163, Bell; FS 61, Walnut; FS 39, Bell Gardens; FS 37, Palmdale; FS 165, South Gate; FS 23, Bellflower; FS 49, La Mirada; FS 41, Willowbrook; FS 151, Glendora; FS 21, Lawndale; FS 84, Quartz Hill; FS 3, East L.A.; FS 18, Lennox; FS 35, Cerritos; FS 83, Palos Verdes; FS 110, Marina Del Rey; FS 22, Commerce; and FS 27, Commerce.

During the 1984-85 budget year, the maximum use of limited funds was made by replacing 21 first-line pumpers with new units manufactured by the P. E. Van Pelt Company of Oakdale, California. In order of their assignments, they were placed in the following fire stations:

Fire Station 38, Angeles Mesa; Engine 264, FS 64, San Dimas; Engine 214, FS 14, Watts; FS 40, Pico-Rivera; Engine 236, FS 36, Carson; FS 87, Bassett; FS 26, La Puente; Engine 244, FS 44, Duarte; Engine 273, FS 73, Newhall; FS 45, Lakewood; FS 57, South Gate; FS 164, Huntington Park; FS 94, Lakewood; FS 41, Willowbrook; FS 4, Rosemead; FS 9, Florence; FS 29, Baldwin Park; FS 111, Canyon Country; FS 15, Whittier; and FS 25, Pico Rivera.

A fire in the McCloskey Paint and Varnish factory caused thousands of cans of spray paint to fall on the area like a hailstorm. Photographer unknown

Truck Co. 127 from Dominguez sets up a water curtain in an attempt to cool adjacent occupancies during the height of the McCloskey Paint and Varnish Co. Fire. Heat of this magnitude requires tremendous volumes of water to effect containment. LACoFD photo.

Transport 7, its lowboy, and the powerful Caterpillar D-8 tractor with bulldozer, ready to respond anywhere in the county. Since 1978, the LACoFD has maintained six of these units in a ready state each fire season. Larry Cummings photo.

Dedication Day, June 7, 1980, at Fire Station 114, an all-volunteer house at Lake Los Angeles. "Nearby" engines 92 from Little Rock and 79 from Big Rock are also present for the event. This station is now full-paid, as the area has built up substantially. LACoFD photo.

Duarte Engine Co. 244's 1985 Van Pelt pumper after delivery and equipping. These Cummins-diesel-powered, stick-shifted pumpers have 1,500 gpm pumps rated at 1,000 gpm, as do all county apparatus delivered from 1972 on. LACoFD photo.

Seventeen Seagrave pumpers were delivered during the 1985-86 budget year and were assigned as follows:

Fire Station 12, Altadena; FS 17, Whittier; FS 30, Cerritos; FS 34, Hawaiian Gardens; FS 54, South Gate; FS 59, Whittier; FS 77, Gorman; FS 90, El Monte; FS 91, Hacienda Heights; FS 115, South Whittier; FS 117, Palmdale; FS 116, Carson; FS 120, Diamond Bar; and FS 127, Dominguez.

These pumpers were equipped with pre-plumbed Stang monitors, a slightly shorter wheelbase providing a smaller turning radius, a new tire size of 12 R 22.5 and stainless steel water tanks.

Fire Chief John Englund's Inheritance

Immediately following the March 27, 1984 retirement of Chief Bragdon, Chief Deputy John Englund received his temporary appointment as fire chief of Los Angeles County, a position he would retain for just over four years. His appointment was made permanent on September 24, 1984. When Englund first joined the Los Angeles County Fire Department, he was a firefighter at Fire Station 27 in the Central Manufacturing District. It was this station's replacement that he helped to dedicate a few months prior to his retirement.

Englund rose steadily through the ranks of the department. At the time of his appointment, he was the third top chief to come from the fire protection districts, with Chiefs Klinger and Bragdon before him. All the other chief engineers had come from the ranks of the Forester and Fire Warden Department.

Chief Englund inherited the constant funding problems that faced Chief Bragdon. Like Bragdon, Chief Englund spent a great deal of his time at the state capitol in Sacramento, testifying, "buttonholing" legislators and generally monitoring the precarious funding sources available to the department. Chief Englund estimated that he had spent, by the time of his retirement on November 1, 1988, an average of one day per week in Sacramento involved in such activities.

The Cerritos Plane Crash Disaster

During the mid-morning of Sunday, August 31, 1986, Flight 498 of AeroMexico prepared to approach Los Angeles International Airport from the southeast on its flight from Mexico.

Flying 6,000 feet over the City of Cerritos, the Douglas DC-9 was struck by a Piper PA-28 Archer on a flight to the east out of the L.A. area. The impact severely damaged the private aircraft, causing it to crash into a nearby elementary school yard, killing both occupants. The damaged airliner plunged to earth at a steep angle, striking the ground one block east of Carmenita Road at 183rd Street, in a residential area. This was in Los Angeles County Fire Station 35's district.

Upon being apprised of the incident, the L.A. Communications Center immediately dispatched a second-alarm assignment as well as all available paramedic

Fire Chief John F. Englund, chief of the LA Co. Forester and Fire Warden and Fire Protection Districts, 1983-1988. LACoFD photo.

squads and ambulances in the vicinity. Neighboring Orange County and Santa Fe Springs fire departments dispatched an "automatic aid assignment" after seeing the gigantic column of black smoke that was suddenly rising from the area.

Captain Larry Hamilton on Truck 30 was the first on-scene, soon to be relieved by Assistant Chief Steve Sherrill, passing by on the nearby 91 Freeway. Sherrill took over as incident commander. He was soon relieved by Assistant Chiefs Paul Delaney and Morris Gregory and Battalion Chief Matthew Kearns.

As the extinguishing effects of masterstreams from the engines at the scene began to allow some movement into the affected area, it became apparent that most of the paramedic squads and ambulances that had been dispatched would not be needed. Nearly all of those involved in the incident were deceased. Only a few residents of the nearby damaged homes were treated for injuries, many of them for shock.

Initially-responding equipment was faced with an inferno. Fifteen homes were involved in fire from burning jet fuel. Four of the homes and their occupants, including a dozen in one home attending a social gathering, simply disappeared in the blast at the time of the impact.

Strike teams 1104 and 1112 were dispatched to the training center in East Los Angeles for possible use at the incident. Team 1104 was chosen to proceed to the scene. The team arrived two hours after the impact, relieving now-exhausted first- and second-alarm crews, performing overhaul operations and completing the search for victims.

As darkness approached, final overhaul operations ceased and crews were gradually released. As a part of the department's "Critical Incident Stress Debriefing" program, Deputy Chiefs William Zeason and George Delaney arranged for all personnel, fire department and otherwise, to be interviewed by several on-call psychologists in order to determine if anyone might have been subjected to more gruesome sights than their particular mental state could tolerate. Each crew was interviewed before being allowed to return to the station. One month later, all were interviewed again in a mass "rap session" under the guidance of a psychologist. The tendency for delayed, long-term mental distress as a result of viewing large disasters such as this plane crash had become well-known. The department wanted each person to know that he or she could seek aid at any time – then or in years hence.

The real loss in a disaster such as the Cerritos plane crash is, of course, human life. A total of 82 persons died in this incident. The Los Angeles County Fire Department, with the much-appreciated aid of its neighboring jurisdictions, held the fire resulting from this crash to the area first involved after impact. There was little else it could be expected to do.

Members of Engine 66, 12, 63, and 82 pause to reflect during overhaul operations following the Cerritos plane crash. They were members of Strike Team 1104, which arrived to relieve the first and second-alarm crews. David Boucher photo. Station 66 archives.

A 5.9 for Whittier

At 7:42 a.m., on the morning of October 1, 1987, a 16-year-long spell during which virtually no noteworthy earthquake activity in Los Angeles County had occurred came to an abrupt end. An earthquake rated at 5.9 on the Richter Scale struck the southern San Gabriel Valley and northern coastal plains. The temblor was centered some eight miles underground, on the recently discovered Elysian Park thrust fault. The epicenter was located southwest of the intersection of Rosemead Boulevard and Garvey Avenue. It caused the land in the vicinity to thrust upward several inches in a split second, sending shock waves rolling throughout the county and beyond.

The L.A., Valley and Antelope dispatch offices immediately transmitted the "all call" signal to all stations. Each station left quarters to survey its respective district for property damage, fires and injuries.

The fire stations closest to the epicenter (Stations 1, 3, 4, 17, 25, 28, 40, 42, 43, 47, 59, 87, 90, 91 and 103) all reported violent shaking with immediately-apparent property damage in their districts.

The older city of Whittier, with its numerous pre-building-code structures of unreinforced brick, was most severely hit. Neighboring towns of Santa Fe Springs, Rosemead, San Gabriel, Monterey Park, Montebello and East Los Angeles were also affected. Within the City of Whittier, a command post was established in front of Fire Station 28, and on-duty Battalion Chief James Rounds began to coordinate activities. Liaison was instituted to help coordinate the activities of the Whittier Police Department and Building Department in order to determine which buildings needed to be abandoned.

Many emergency fire department responses were made from the Whittier stations upon direct reports from the citizens. One estimate indicated that less than half of all emergency incidents were logged through the L.A. Dispatch Center. Over 200 incidents were "still alarms" to the Whittier stations.

Ground Zero at Cerritos. The small crater in the foreground is where the nose of the DC 9 struck the ground. Four homes stood in the immediate foreground and distant center. View is looking southwest. David Boucher photo, Station 66 archives.

As occurs in all earthquakes, a rash of structural fires ensued, along with reports of broken natural gas lines, water mains and downed electrical lines.

Only two deaths occurred in Whittier. Elsewhere, rolling shock waves toppled a block wall at California State University, Los Angeles, near Engine One's district in City Terrace, crushing a female student. In Engine 66's Altadena district, 12 miles north of Whittier, a Union Construction Company foreman was trapped 30 feet inside an Edison tower footing shaft that he had been excavating. It was almost miraculous that only these four persons died as a result of this earthquake.

Estimates of responses made by the fire department related to this earthquake totaled over 700 throughout the immediate area. Many additional calls for broken gas and water lines were not answered until the following day, due to delayed discovery and further damage as a result of aftershocks. Initial damage figures quickly reached $100 million, and then slowly tapered off. The two strike teams of engines from Orange County and one from L.A. City which had been sent into the area around Whittier were gradually released. The long task of surveying the surviving buildings relative to their safety and salvageability began.

The Los Angeles County Fire Department proved equal to the task at hand. Field reports indicated that the two-frequency VHF-UHF (white-blue) radio systems proved invaluable, being utilized along with the Incident Command System of management.

It remains to be seen how the department, and in fact all other emergency agencies, will be prepared for the 8-plus magnitude earthquake that is predicted (and expected at any time!) within the next 30 years in Southern California.

Lives in the Balance — A Summation

Between the years of 1955 and 1968, several members of the Los Angeles Fire Department lost their lives during large and notable incidents. Following the death of Captain Phil Goodell during the Liebre Fire, the remaining fatalities took a random pattern, scattered over the years and in locations often far removed from one another. However, each situation served to remind all department members, as well as the public, that the firefighting profession is indeed a dangerous one. Terminal trouble can strike at any time.

The following is a brief summation of the circumstances surrounding the death of department members due to external, violent causes, from January 1, 1969 to September 1, 1989:

Stanley Schnabel, firefighter, Engine 23, Bellflower —trapped and overcome by a mushrooming interior fire at the National Lumber Company, April 24, 1972.

Wellesley Hartman, camp crew foreman — struck on the head by a rock that was loosened by a bulldozer while working on a hillside above him during a brush firefighting operation, July 4, 1976.

Thomas Grady, helicopter pilot — during night flying operations on the "Monte Cristo Fire" with the USFS, struck by another helicopter during a landing attempt, July 24, 1977.

James Michelli, firefighter-paramedic, Engine 29, Baldwin Park — trapped and overcome by a mushrooming fire inside an appliance store on December 18, 1979.

Gary Maiben and Salvador Torres, fire shop foreman and mechanic (respectively) – traffic collision in their department vehicle when struck head-on by another vehicle whose driver was purportedly committing suicide. The tragedy occurred on the City Terrace off-ramp of the San Bernardino Freeway immediately north of Los Angeles headquarters, June 30, 1982.

Jerald Hiesel, construction camp foreman, Camp 11 — electrocuted by current going to ground from overhead powerlines, through a crane and drainpipe being installed, December 14, 1983.

Raymond Eichert, firefighter, Engine 62, Padua Hills — fell while working in the hose tower of that station, on August 10, 1984. (The cause of this death was not considered external or violent, and therefore may not be included in all lists of this type.)

Additional Helicopters

Heavy usage of all copters, and the destruction of two of them, made it necessary to purchase additional replacement craft during the late '70s and the '80s. Severe budget constraints at this time dictated the purchase of used aircraft.

The brand new, twin-engined Bell model 412 Helicopter 17 on arrival at Cecil Gehr Training Center in the spring of 1989. Larry Cummings photo.

A near mid-air collision between a USFS leased helicopter and the LA Co.'s 'copter killed pilot Thomas Grady during the Monte Cristo or "Middle" fire. Steve Meramble photo.

Still in service:

Bell 205 A-1, purchased in 1977, presently Copter 14

Bell 205 A-1, purchased in 1980, presently Copter 16

Bell 206B III, purchased in 1987, presently Copter 10

Bell 412 (twin engined), purchased in 1988, presently Copter 17.

Copter 17 and one other copter can be utilized in the mode of an air squad. The pilot program, federally funded, began in 1970 on a six-month trial basis. Since proving successful, the program has continued to be expanded. The following "fact sheet," published by the Air Operations Section, lists all of the pertinent facts concerning this program:

To replace pilots who had died, resigned or retired, several additional pilots were hired during this period. They were:

Richard D'Andrea and Gary Lineberry, hired in 1977; Thomas Grady and Wayne Lanin, 1976; Gary Bertz, 1977; John Finnerty and Virgil Benson, 1981; Charles Moreno, 1982; Wayne Wright, 1983; and Robert Dunbar, hired in 1986.

County of Los Angeles
FIRE DEPARTMENT
AIR OPERATIONS

Air Squad Helicopters

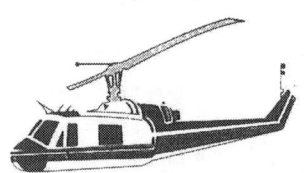

AIR SQUADS

1. —Base: Barton Heliport
   —Air squad 9: available 24 hours per day, 365 days per year
   —Air squad 8: available 10 hours per day, 365 days per year

2. Crews include:
   —2 Firefighter Paramedics
   —Board Certified Emergency Medicine, Reserve Physician (weekends and holidays)
   —Helicopter Pilot (Emergency Medical Tech I)

3. Designed to provide life preserving treatment, extrication of victims by rescue hoist with a 250 ft. cable. Transporting victims to the nearest hospital.

4. Can be airborne within three (3) minutes of dispatch. Will accommodate three patients lying down, and two patients sitting. Air squads are configured to allow maximum access to patients for treatment in flight. Helicopters are also available for Neo-natal transfer with incubator, plus a medical team.

5. —Single engine Bell 205 helicopters
   —Can fly and land in marginal weather conditions
   —Cruises at a speed of 118 miles per hour

6. Serve approximately 2165 square miles of Los Angeles County. Air squads are deployed daily to Fire Suppression Camp 8, located in Malibu, and Fire Camp 9, located in Sylmar.

7. Equipped with standard L.A. County MICU
   —Cardiac monitor/Defibrillator
   —Anti-Shock Trousers
   —obstetrical Drugs and supplies
   —Advanced airway maintenance equipment

8. Responds to all appropriate calls.

9. Air Squads have water / retardant for firefighting, as well as emergency medical response.

10. All flight crew personnel given special training in aero medical physiology and in-flight patient management.

FACT SHEET

A series of photos showing a chemical drop by a Douglas DC-6 on a small fire burning near Acton. LA Co. works in conjunction with the U.S. Forest Service in this area of Bn. 11. Mike Meadows photo.

An LA Co. fire helicopter makes a 360 gal. water drop at the head of this small fire near Acton. The camp crew has a "scratch hand line" already cut. Mike Meadows photo.

Truck 127, Dominguez, displays its 1968 Crown 85' Snorkel. Larry Cummings photo.

Fire Prevention — A Different Approach

One of the ways to prevent a wildland conflagration is to burn out vulnerable areas ahead of time. Although the Indians and ranchers of the late 1800s might not have cared particularly whether a fire was ever controlled, present-day techniques allow wildland areas to be burned out under carefully-controlled conditions. Weather, topography, fuel type and fuel moisture are all taken into consideration. This method, called "prescribed burning," allows a given area to be partially burned out while retaining its flood prevention characteristics. Ideally just the types of fuel that resist fire control measures are removed. Prescribed burning is a part of the Coordinated Resource Management Program instituted in 1984.

The Los Angeles County Fire Department's "prescribed burning" program, under the command of Captain Scott Franklin, has pre-burned hundreds of acres over the past several years. Some of this has been under contract arrangements with other jurisdictions such as the City of Los Angeles. The on-going program functions on a year-round basis. As proper burning conditions present themselves, pre-selected projects are burned out. Engine Company, Patrol, Camp Crew, and Helicopter equipment and personnel are utilized to prevent the burn from escaping. The IC system of command is utilized during each burn.

Since 1983, 11 fires have occurred adjacent to earlier prescribed burns. All have been more easily controlled as a result. Three of the fires were stopped when encountering those areas, even though they occurred during severe burning conditions.

To date, the results obtained from the program have warranted its continuance.

Los Angeles County Fire Department — Truck Companies

Due to the essentially rural, residential and ranching characteristics of the County of Los Angeles prior to the 1950s, the need for aerial ladder service was minimal. From that point on, however, the need for truck companies increased, as both commercial structures and manufacturing plants multiplied. By 1952, two 85-foot American La France aerial ladder trucks were in service, one at Fire Station 8, West Hollywood, and one at Fire Station 27, in the Central Manufacturing District. Bellflower's Truck 23, a 1953 Seagrave, was next, followed by East Los Angeles American La France Truck 3 in 1954, and Rosemead's Seagrave Truck 42 in 1961.

The following table shows the ladder trucks and snorkels in service as of September 1989:

Year & Model	Station Number	City/Area
1964 Crown 85' Snorkel	49	La Mirada
1965 Crown 75' Snorkel	86	Glendora
1966 Crown 75' Snorkel Reserve	502 @ 58	Angeles Mesa
1966 Crown 75' Snorkel	82	La Canada-Flintridge
1968 Crown 85' Snorkel Reserve	501 @ 48	Irwindale
1968 Crown 85' Snorkel	127	Dominguez
1971 ALF 100' Aerial	42	Rosemead
1971 ALF 100' Aerial	20	Norwalk

Truck Co. 31, Bn. 9, Paramount one of the first 100' aerial ladders delivered in 1989. These Seagrave Cummins-powered diesels marked the first use of a tillered aerial by the department. Note the vertical arrangement of the ground ladders. AFJ photo.

Transport 8 hooked up to the 6,500 gal. mother tanker used to supply water reservoirs at remote construction campsites, nurseries and fire scenes requiring an extended water supply. LACoFD photo.

1971 ALF 100' Aerial	45	Lakewood
1971 ALF 100' Aerial	28	Whittier
1973 ALF 100' Aerial	110	Marina Del Rey
1973 ALF 100' Aerial	8	West Hollywood
1977 ALF 100' Aerial	3	East Los Angeles
1977 ALF 100' Aerial	164	Huntington Park
1977 ALF 100' Aerial	116	Carson
1977 ALF 100' Aerial	106	Rolling Hills
1977 ALF 100' Aerial	30	Cerritos
1966 Crown 75' Snorkel**	24	Palmdale

**This truck was "inherited" from the City of Azusa when that city contracted for county fire protection. A Quint, originally painted white, it was repainted red for LACoFD service.

1984 Van Pelt 100' A/pltfrm	118	Industry
1984 Van Pelt 100' A/pltfrm	27	Commerce
1987 LTI 100' Aerial	31	Paramount
1987 LTI 100' Aerial	29	Baldwin Park
1988 LTI 100' Aerial	73	Newhall
1989 Seagrave 100' Aerial	28	Note: These five
1989 Seagrave 100' Aerial	3	trucks are the first
1989 Seagrave 100' Aerial	164	tractor-trailer models
1989 Seagrave 100' Aerial	31	for the LACFD.
1989 Seagrave 100' Aerial	49	

Engine 127, Dominguez, Seagrave 1,000 gpm (rated) pumper shortly after delivery, circa 1986-1987. The slightly-shorter wheelbase, pre-plumbed Stang monitor, larger tires, and very adequate power from its Cummins diesel have been well received. LACoFD photo.

This Chevrolet light unit, Mobile Air Cache Unit 52 operates out of Bn. 13 in South Gate. It is one of two in use by the department. The 12 quartz lights provide enormous quantities of light for emergency scene operations. LACoFD photo.

A Ford diesel crew truck from Construction Camp 8 in Malibu Hills. These newer trucks provide enclosed protection from heat, smoke and the elements for crews traveling through otherwise untenable conditions. LACoFD photo.

Fireboat 110 during a test run just off its docking location at Marina Del Rey. LACoFD photo.

Patrol 66, a 1989 G.M.C. one-ton unit having a 100 gal. water tank and a 100 gpm "slip-on" pumping unit. This was the first unit delivered with the new fully compartmentalized utility body holding medical equipment, "over the side" rescue gear, and an assortment of fire-fighting and forcible entry tools. Larry Cummings photo.

Engine Co. 66, Bn. 4, Div. 5, a 1974 Crown triple combination pumper with a 1,000 (rated) pump, 500 gal. water tank, and repainted in 1989. This was one of the first Crown Cummins-powered diesel delivered since 1968. Larry Cummings photo.

Engine Co. 39 of Bell Gardens 1981 American LaFrance 1,000 gpm (rated) triple combination pumper. These were the first pumpers delivered following the advent of Proposition 13 budget reductions. Larry Cummings photo.

Engine 118's (Industry) 1989 Kovatch (KME) 1,000 gpm (rated) pumper. Larry Cummings photo.

Haz Mat Squad 87, from the City of Industry, and its equipment and various stages of suiting available for haz mat incidents. Haz Mat Squads 105 in Dominguez and 76 in Valencia are similarly equipped. LACoFD photo.

Hazardous Materials — A Growing Problem

By 1979, governmental agencies concerned with such matters had agreed that a serious threat to the health of the general public existed in the storage and transportation of toxic and otherwise hazardous materials. It was clear that the situation warranted special attention. The average fire department engine or truck company lacked the proper equipment and technical knowledge to protect its personnel from harmful effects, both short and long-term, due to exposure at emergency scenes. Meaningful solutions were rapidly becoming necessary.

The County Board of Supervisors moved into action. After receiving extensive training at the National Fire Academy, two squads were stationed within the Los Angeles County Fire Department's jurisdiction. On March 1, 1982, these squads went into service at Fire Station 87, City of Industry, and Fire Station 105, Dominguez. A third squad was soon deemed necessary, because of the truck traffic on Interstate Highway 5 and the growth of the Valencia Industrial Park located nearby. On December 1, 1985 this third squad was placed in service at Fire Station 76 at Castaic Junction, Valencia.

All three squads initially utilized converted two-seat crew-cab paramedic squad trucks. Permanent, custom-made GMC vans were soon placed in service. These were truly complete "laboratories on wheels," able to determine the nature of any unknown substance that might be encountered during an emergency incident. Once the material was identified, plans could then be made for handling it. Four levels of protective clothing were provided for each member of the crew, which was composed of a captain and four firefighters. Their resources included extended-time breathing apparatus and equipment for decontaminating clothing and equipment after each incident in cooperation with assisting engine companies.

Regular firefighters received an annual "first responder" drill to familiarize them with the operation of the hazardous materials squads. They drilled in specific procedures to follow when working with them. A careful record is kept of each person's hazardous materials exposure history. Such records should prove invaluable if any health problems develop in later years as a result of possible exposure to carcinogenic materials.

The haz-mat squads respond on any second alarm or greater structure fire in their region of the county, in order to provide additional manpower. Their service is provided to nearby incorporated cities on an as-needed, as-available basis. These squads have presented frequent demonstrations to both the public and to interested governmental agencies.

By 1986, the three haz-mat squads had an annual response total that reached 500. Any increase in the number of haz-mat squads will depend upon available funds and demand for the service that they provide.

Nineteen homes under construction in Engine 24's district in Palmdale were razed by fire in a high wind. Heat here is too intense for equipment to approach the scene. The summer of 1989 saw three similar fires occur in Bns. 6 and 11. Jerry Meehan photo.

Eighty foot flames race south through Liberty Cyn. in the Malibu Hills. Fires of this severity are common during Devil Winds. LACoFD photo.

The Present Outlook

Even as the final phases of *Ride the Devil Wind* are being written during the last months of 1989, the Los Angeles County Fire Department is in the midst of one of its more serious brush fire seasons, due in part to an extended drought. Historically, these months of October, November and December are the most demanding, for they are the time of the Devil Wind.

The 1989 fire season was the first one not participated in by Fire Chief John Englund, as his retirement became effective on November 1, 1988. A few salient accomplishments during Englund's administration include the graduation of 300 Explorer Scouts with a firefighting specialty, and an Explorer Advisor in each battalion; the elimination of a difficult-to-administer fire district by arranging for the City of Long Beach to contract with Signal Hill, thereby eliminating County Fire Station 154; the blending of all remaining small fire protection districts (Wrightwood, Dominguez, Universal City) into Consolidated; the rebuilding of Fire Stations 4, 18, 27, 30, 61, 77 and 79, and the beginning of construction of new Stations 119 and 121 (Diamond Bar).

Fiscally, he was able to eliminate all debt service owed by the department, and was subsequently able to pay cash for all new apparatus purchased during his tenure. Through a combination of General Fund money and District bond sales, the $36 million Command and Control Dispatching Center was assured.

During this general time period, the following cities within L.A. County incorporated and contracted for fire/paramedic services from the county:

Hidden Hills — October 19, 1961, Station 68
Westlake — December 11, 1981, Station 144
Agoura Hills — November 2, 1982, Stations 65 and 72
Palos Verdes Estates — July 1, 1986, Station 2
Santa Clarita — December 15, 1987, Stations 73, 107, 111
Diamond Bar — April 18, 1989, Stations 119, 120, 121

The new fire chief, P. Michael Freeman, has served in office just long enough to begin to come to grips with the full scope of his position. Having come to Los Angeles County from the City of Dallas, Texas, on February 5, 1989, it was his first desire to travel to as many county fire facilities as possible in order to better grasp the massiveness of the organization he now led – and to better understand the spirit that drove it.

After his first six months, he and his administration have developed a new mission statement for the department – a statement that will assist in motivating every action of its members. It is:

> "To proudly protect lives and property by providing prompt, skillful, cost-effective fire protection and life safety services."

Construction of the new $36 million computerized "command and control" dispatching facility adjacent to Klinger Center continues, supervised by Deputy Chief James Hunt and Assistant Chief John Cummings. Construction continues on schedule, with

Fire Chief P. Michael Freeman, chief of the LA Co. Forester and Fire Warden and Fire Protection Districts, Feb. 1989. LACoFD photo.

initial field tests of station-level equipment in Battalion 7 successfully accomplished. Completion of the entire project is anticipated in early 1991, at which time the Los Angeles County Fire Department will operate the most advanced dispatching system in the entire United States.

In conjunction with this new dispatching facility, a "tiered dispatch system" is slated to be inaugurated. This system will adjust the level of response according to the need of the caller, thereby no longer necessitating the dispatching of an engine company, paramedic squad and an ambulance on every medical incident. Dispatchers will be required to screen each call and judge the severity of each case.

New Kovatch pumpers continue to be placed in service. Locations for five new articulated 100-foot aerial ladder trucks are being chosen. (See table, this chapter.)

On July 1, 1989, Fire Station 46 was closed permanently. Engine 64 in San Dimas was reactivated at the same time. Captains have been placed on Trucks 82 and 86, and a new Fire Station 121 in North Diamond Bar was opened on August 1, 1989.

A new firefighter exam is anticipated for the fall of 1989, and the hiring of civilians as fire dispatchers is almost complete.

Cardiac defibrillators are being placed on several engine companies.

The entire department is moving forward in a spirited manner, the better to meet the increasing demands for service.

The 1989 graduating class of Fire Explorers, taken at the training center's main auditorium. A reserve of interested young persons is maintained in this program, each of whom may be used in non-hazardous functions. Many of these young people go on to become professional firefighters. LACoFD photo, courtesy of Jim Henson.

Viewed from Highway 14 near Escondido Summit, the "Sage" fire explodes toward the southeast. This fire has "blown up," creating its own draft. Mt. Gleason, right center. Mike Meadows photo.

A Capt. on Engine 307, Bn. 6, sets a backfire with a "fusee" along this fire line, then makes a hasty retreat. Mike Meadows photo.

Always in sight is the fact that the population of Los Angeles County is increasing day by day. Territories served by the department that were once open country — containing only brush-covered hills and canyons — are now growing cities.

It has been said that there is no way of judging the future but by the past, and the past is whatever the records and memories agree upon. The records have now been searched and memories reviewed, setting forth the rich heritage of the Los Angeles County Fire Department.

Whatever else the future may bring, Los Angeles County firefighters will certainly continue to "Ride the Devil Wind."

A typical sign erected by grateful homeowners following the summer of 1989 "San Fran Fire" in Bn. 11, in the vicinity of Green Valley and Elizabeth Lake in the Leona Valley. Such expressions of gratitude are common following the saving of neighborhoods during wildland operations. Jerry Meehan photo.

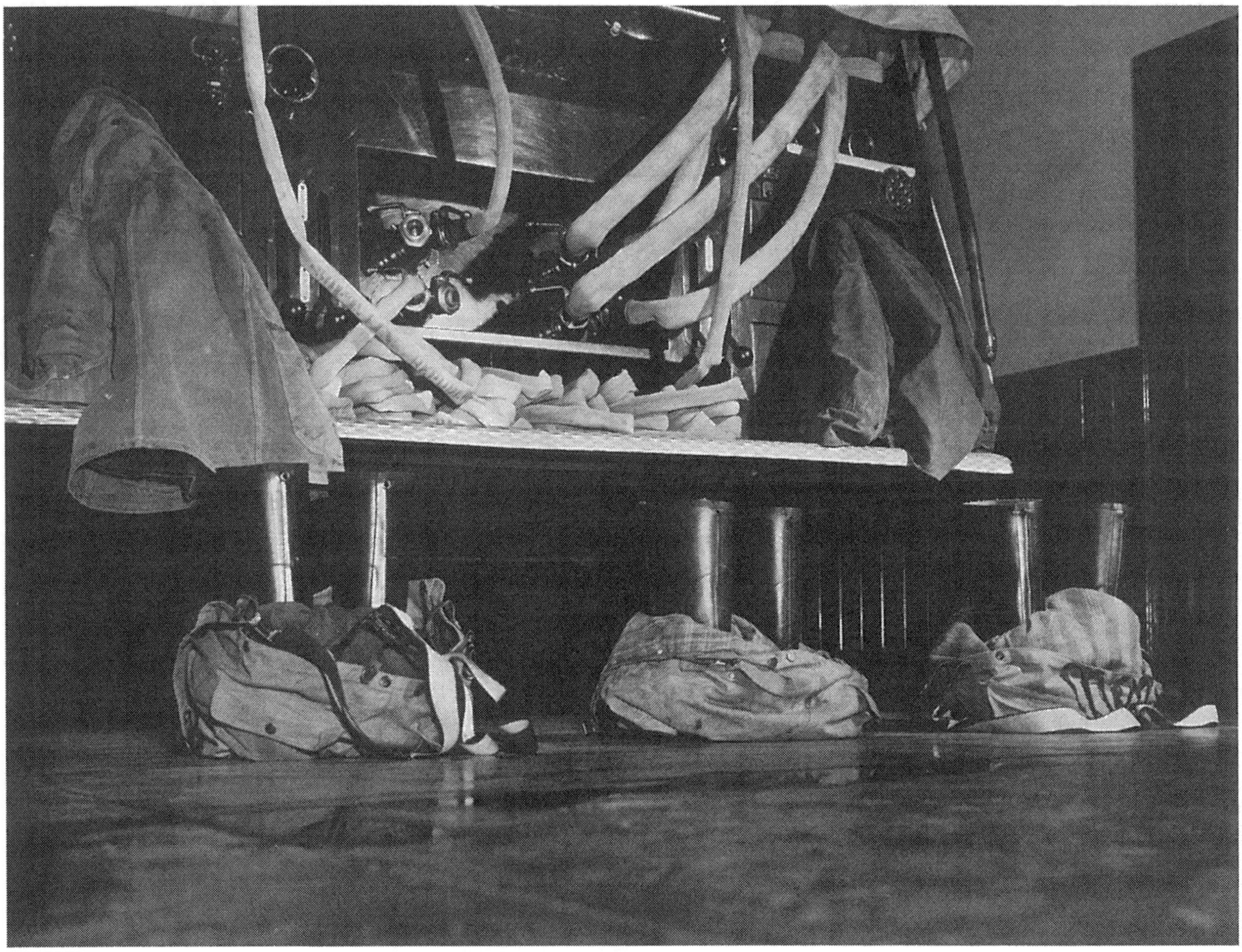

Bibliography

Anderson, Harvey. *Firebreak Study of L.A. County*. L.A. Co. Dept. of Forester & Fire Warden, 1936.

Anderson, Henry W. *Forests and Water*. USDA Forest Service Technical Report, 1976.

Bodine, R.C. *Notes on Early Reforestation Activities in L.A. County*. Henninger Flats, 1933.

Bonelli, Frank G. *Watershed Protection in Los Angeles County*, 1962.

Bowers, Peter M. *Western Flying*. March 1958.

Bragdon, Clyde A. *L.A. Co. Fire Dept. Emergency Operations Procedures*. 3rd edition, 1980.

CCC News. Fort McArthur District, October 28, 1935.

Cecil, George H. *Forest Protection in Southern California*. 1932. (pamphlet).

Clar, Raymond C. *California Government and Forestry, Vols. I and II*. California Division of Forestry, 1969.

Cooperative Forest Fire Control, U.S. Forest Service, 1966.

Countryman, Clive M. *Burning Conditions on the Hacienda Fire*. California Forest and Range Experiment Station, 1955.

Crump, Spencer. *Ride the Big Red Cars*. Trans-Anglo Books, 1972, 5th edition.

Davis, Joseph J. *Annals of the Forestry Department of the County of Los Angeles*. L.A. County Forester & Fire Warden, 1931-1934.

Dektar, Clifford. *Fire Engineering Magazines*. Various 1952-1960.

Ditzel, Paul. *History of the Los Angeles Fire Department*. Fire Buff House, 1986.

Donoghue, James R. *Intergovernmental Cooperation in Fire Protection in the Los Angeles Area*. U.C.L.A. 1943.

Earl, Howard. *Civil Defense Report of Malibu Fire Operations*, 1957.

Grapevine, The. Los Angeles Fireman's Relief Association, January 1930.

Greenwood, Capt. Harold W. *Los Angeles Brush Area Conflagration*. L.A. Fire Dept., 1962.

Hanson, P.D. *Aerial Bombing of Forest Fires*. U.S.F.S., 1947.

Hollywood News, June 7, 1928.

Kimball, Warren Y., L.A. County Fire Dept. *N.F.P.A. Fireman Magazine*, May 1955.

Klinger, Keith E. *Report on the La Habra Heights Fire*, 1955.

——————. *Air Attack Manual*. Los Angeles Co. Fire Department, 1963.

Lippincott, J.B. *Some Past Floods of Southern California*. L.A. County Flood Control, 1934.

L.A. County Dept. of Forester & Fire Warden. *Fire Plan*. 1932 & 1950.

L.A. County Fire Department. *Annual Reports*. 1924-1982.

Los Angeles Examiner. June 8, 1928.

Los Angeles Times. Various editions from 1924 to 1959.

MacLeod, Allan. *Air Operations of the Los Angeles Co. Fire Department*, 1987.

Malibu Fires, The. December 26 to 30, 1956. U.S.F.S., 1957.

O'Tolle, Marvin. *Box 15 Club Newsletter*, various, 1975.

Pasadena Star News. Various editions from 1920 to 1959.

Peavy, George W. *Various letters to Stuart J. Flintham and Spence D. Turner*, 1919 to 1930.

Sherman, E.A. *1924 San Gabriel Mountain Fire Review*, U.S.F.S. 1924.

Straight Streams. L.A. County Fire Dept. Relief Association, 1953-1976 (various).

Test of Television for Forest Fire Detection. Pamphlet, State Division of Forestry, 1956.

Tillotson, Clarence. *1929 Annual Dance Pamphlet*. L.A. Co. Relief Association.

Turner, Spence D. *Fire Break Study of Los Angeles County, 1935*.

——————. *Backfiring to Control Chaparral Fires*. L.A. County Department of Forestry, 1936.

——————. *Report on 1938 Floods in L.A. County*. L.A. County Forester & Fire Warden, 1939.

——————. *Rules and Regulations of the L.A. County Fire and Rescue Disaster Services, 1946*.

Watts, Lyle F. *Clarke-McNary Forest Fire Control Manual*. U.S. Forest Service, 1948 (revised).

Western Fire Chiefs' Association. Western Fire Journal, June 1969.

The author is deeply indebted to the Central Libraries of the cities of Glendale and Pasadena, California for the use of various facilities during the research and writing of this book. He is also very grateful for the donation to the author of four boxes of research material which had belonged to L.A. County Fire Department Captain John W. Whelan (deceased), by his widow, Jeanne.

FORESTER & FIRE WARDEN DIVISIONS CIRCA 1937

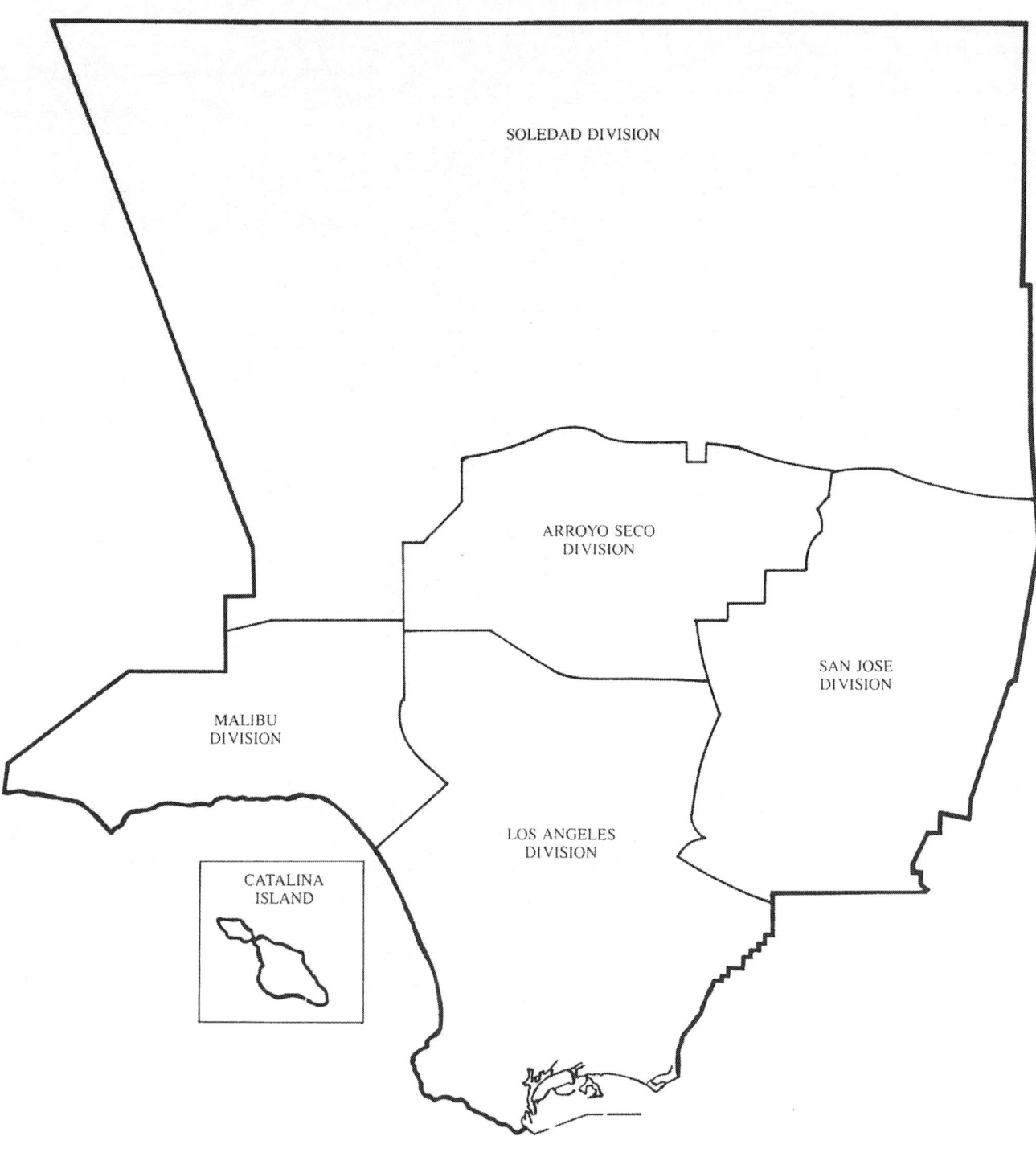

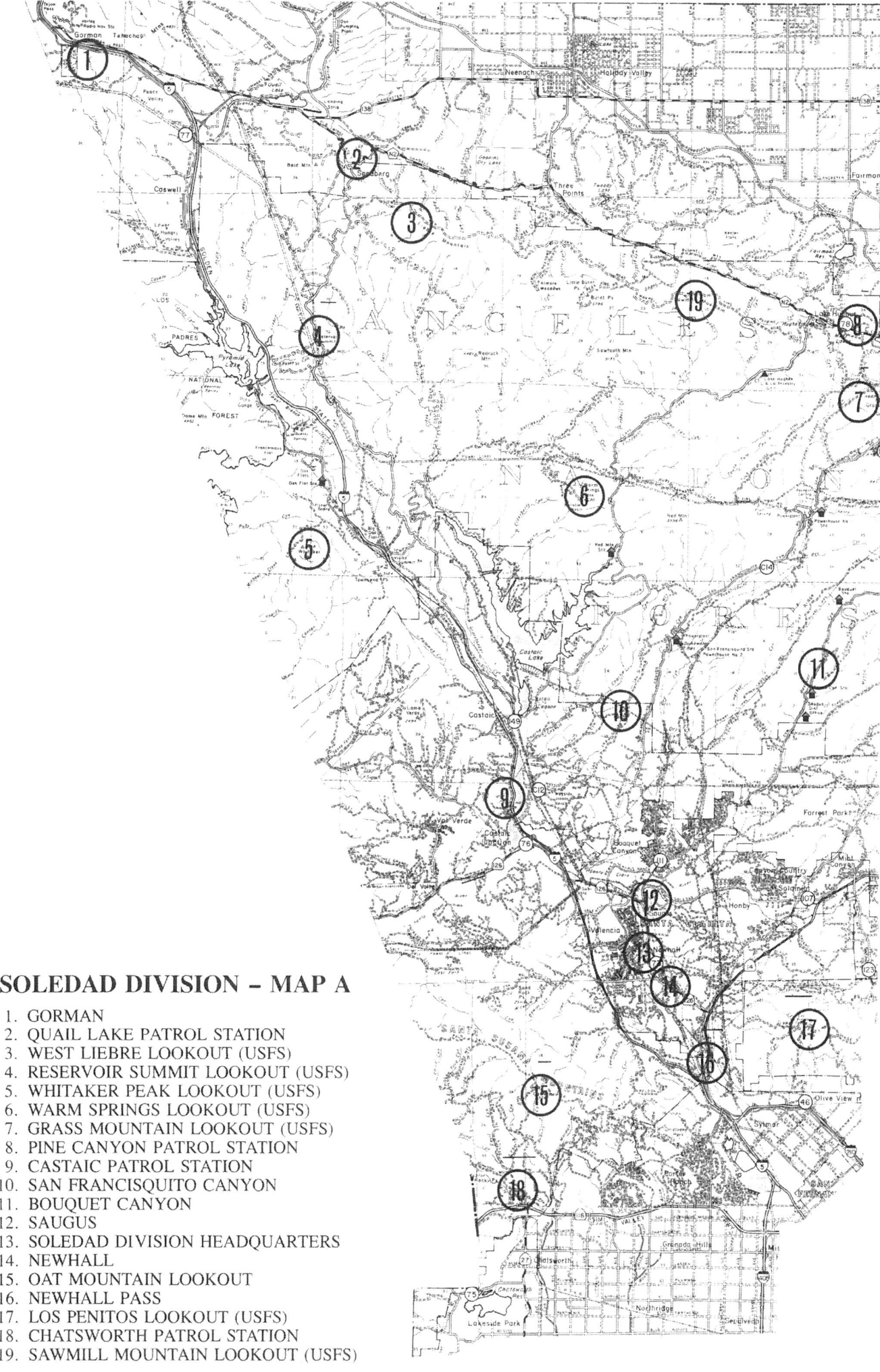

SOLEDAD DIVISION – MAP A

1. GORMAN
2. QUAIL LAKE PATROL STATION
3. WEST LIEBRE LOOKOUT (USFS)
4. RESERVOIR SUMMIT LOOKOUT (USFS)
5. WHITAKER PEAK LOOKOUT (USFS)
6. WARM SPRINGS LOOKOUT (USFS)
7. GRASS MOUNTAIN LOOKOUT (USFS)
8. PINE CANYON PATROL STATION
9. CASTAIC PATROL STATION
10. SAN FRANCISQUITO CANYON
11. BOUQUET CANYON
12. SAUGUS
13. SOLEDAD DIVISION HEADQUARTERS
14. NEWHALL
15. OAT MOUNTAIN LOOKOUT
16. NEWHALL PASS
17. LOS PENITOS LOOKOUT (USFS)
18. CHATSWORTH PATROL STATION
19. SAWMILL MOUNTAIN LOOKOUT (USFS)

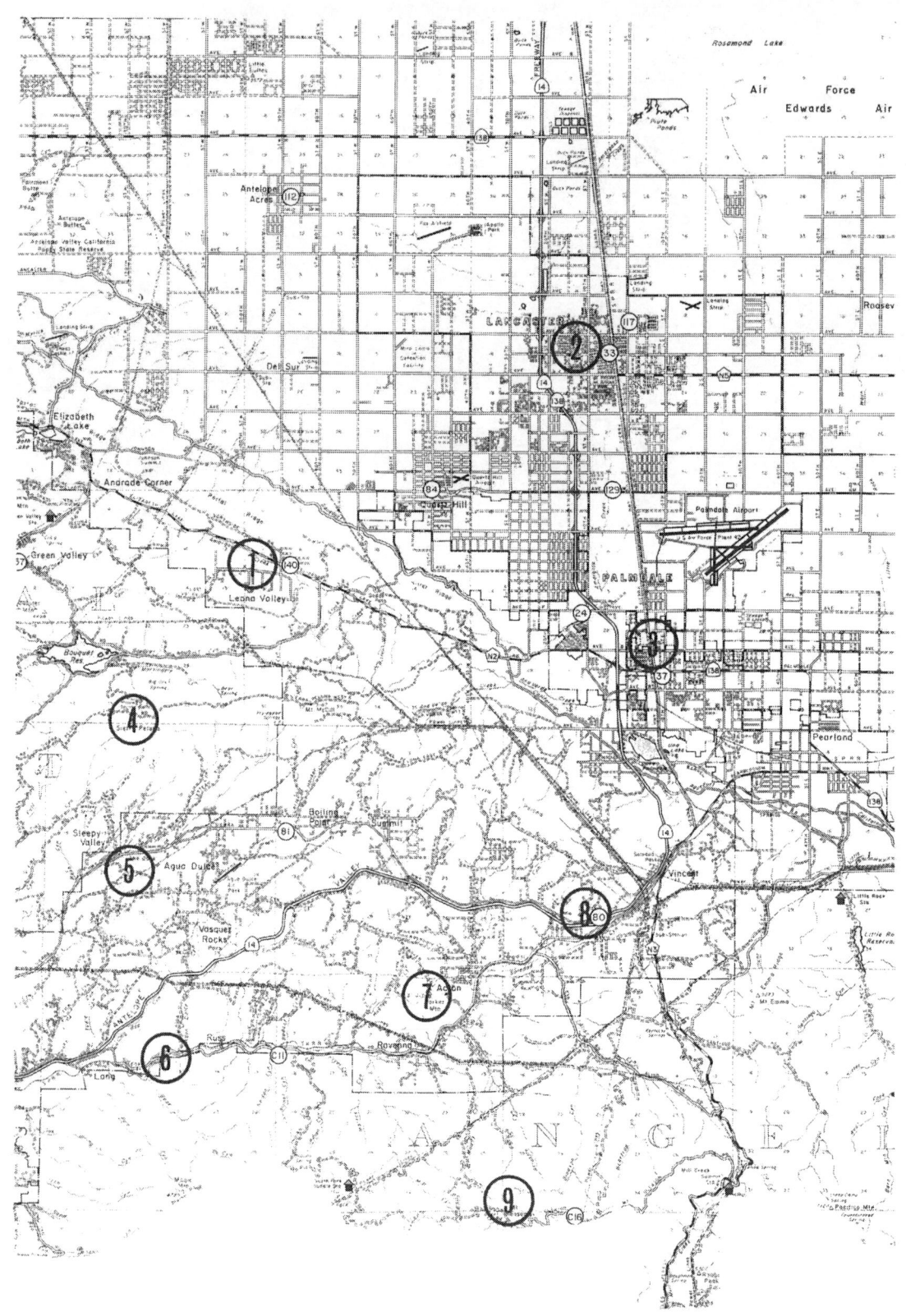

SOLEDAD DIVISION – MAP B

1. LEONA VALLEY
2. LANCASTER
3. PALMDALE
4. SIERRA PELONA LOOKOUT (USFS)
5. MINT CANYON PATROL STATION
6. SOLEDAD CANYON
7. PARKER MOUNTAIN LOOKOUT
8. VINCENT PATROL STATION
9. MT. GLEASON LOOKOUT

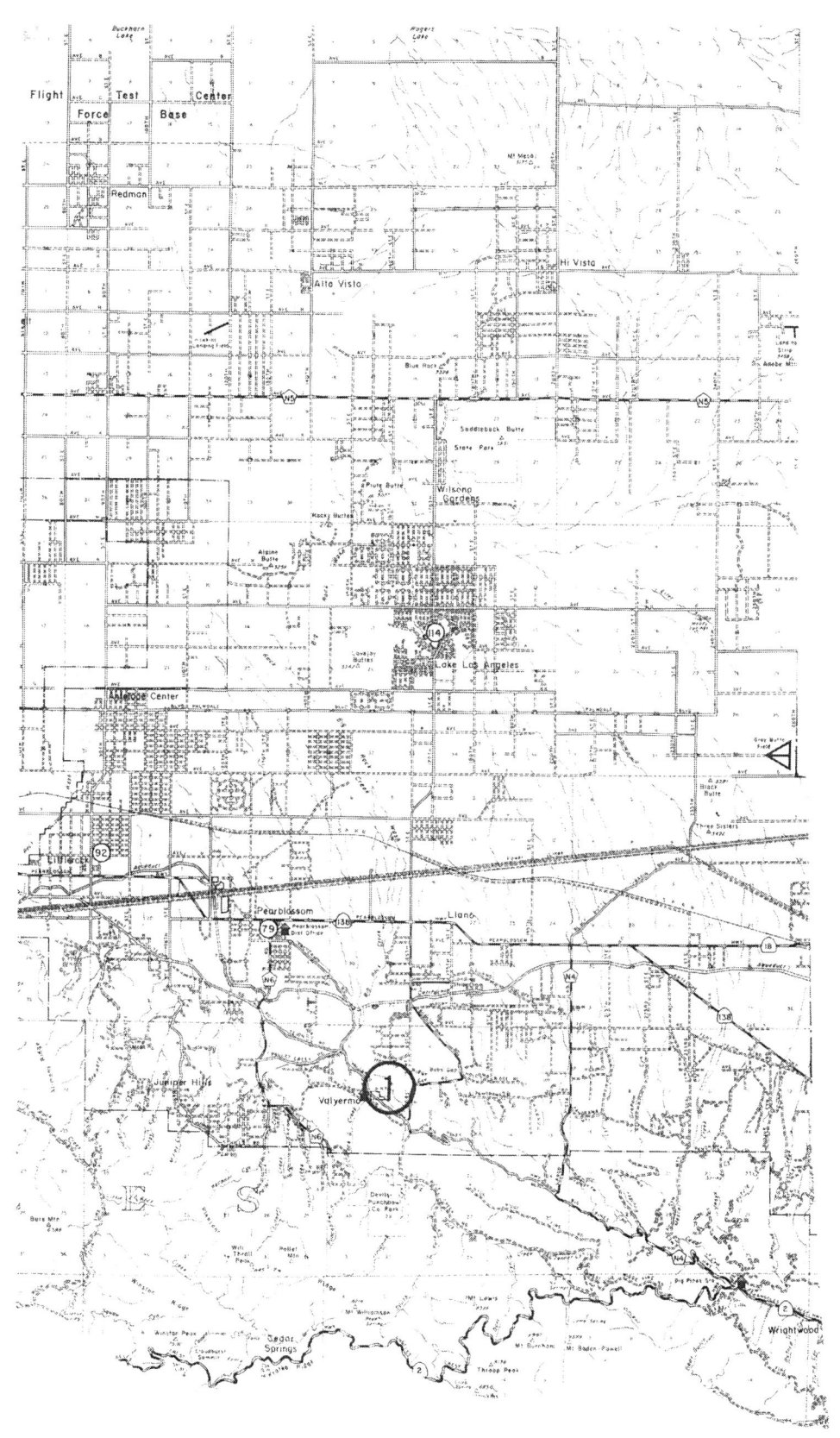

SOLEDAD DIVISION – MAP C
1. BIG ROCK PATROL STATION

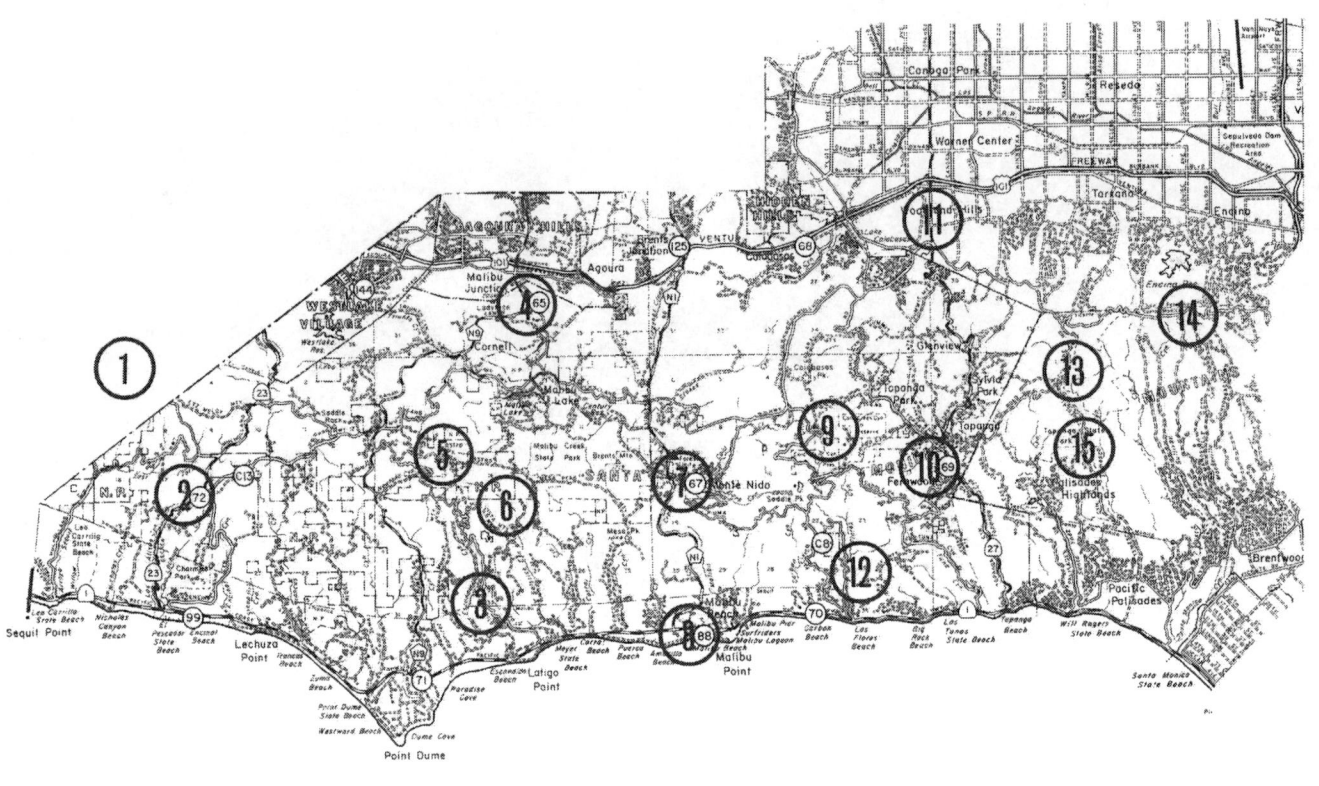

MALIBU DIVISION

1. TRIUMFO LOOKOUT
2. LECHUZA PATROL STATION
3. ESCONDIDO PATROL STATION
4. MALIBU DIVISION HEADQUARTERS
5. CASTRO PEAK LOOKOUT
6. MALIBU MOUNTAINS
7. MONTE NIDO PATROL STATION
8. MALIBU COLONY
9. TOPANGA LOOKOUT
10. TOPANGA PATROL STATION
11. WOODLAND HILLS
12. LAS FLORES PATROL STATION
13. SANTA MONICA MOUNTAINS
14. SAN VINCENTE LOOKOUT (L.A. City)
15. TEMESCAL LOOKOUT (L.A. City Federal Funds)

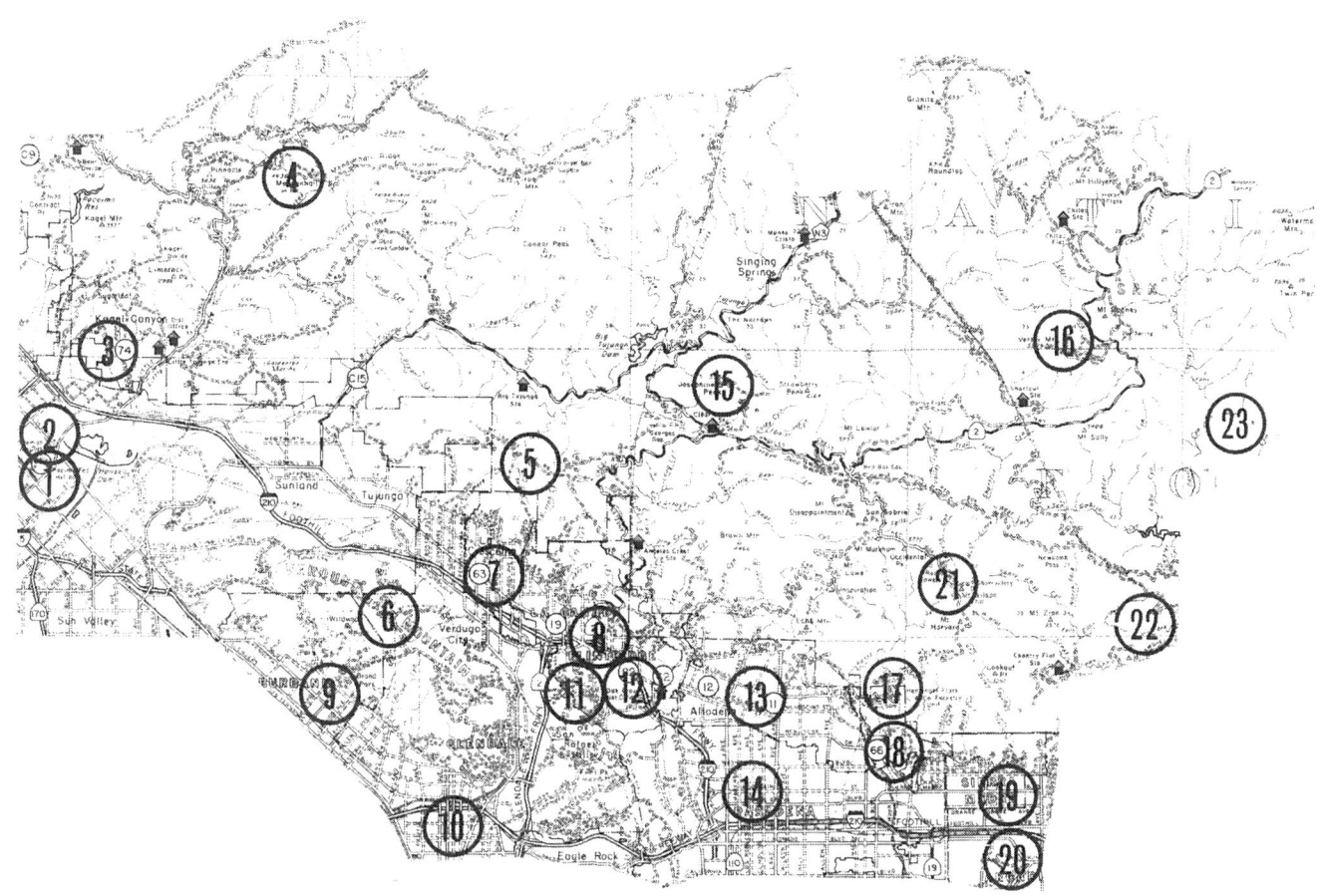

ARROYO SECO DIVISION

1. PACOIMA WAREHOUSE
2. PACOIMA PEAK LOOKOUT
3. KAGEL CANYON PATROL STATION
4. MENDENHALL PEAK LOOKOUT (USFS)
5. MT. LUKENS LOOKOUT (USFS)
6. VERDUGO PEAK LOOKOUT
7. LA CRESCENTA
8. LA CANADA
9. BURBANK
10. GLENDALE
11. SAN RAFAEL LOOKOUT
12. ARROYO SECO DIVISION HEADQUARTERS
13. ALTADENA
14. PASADENA
15. JOSEPHINE PEAK LOOKOUT (USFS)
16. VETTER MOUNTAIN LOOKOUT
17. HENNINGER FLATS
18. EATON CANYON PATROL STATION
19. SIERRA MADRE
20. ARCADIA
21. MT. WILSON
22. MONROVIA PEAK
23. DEVIL'S CANYON-BEAR CANYON WILD AREA

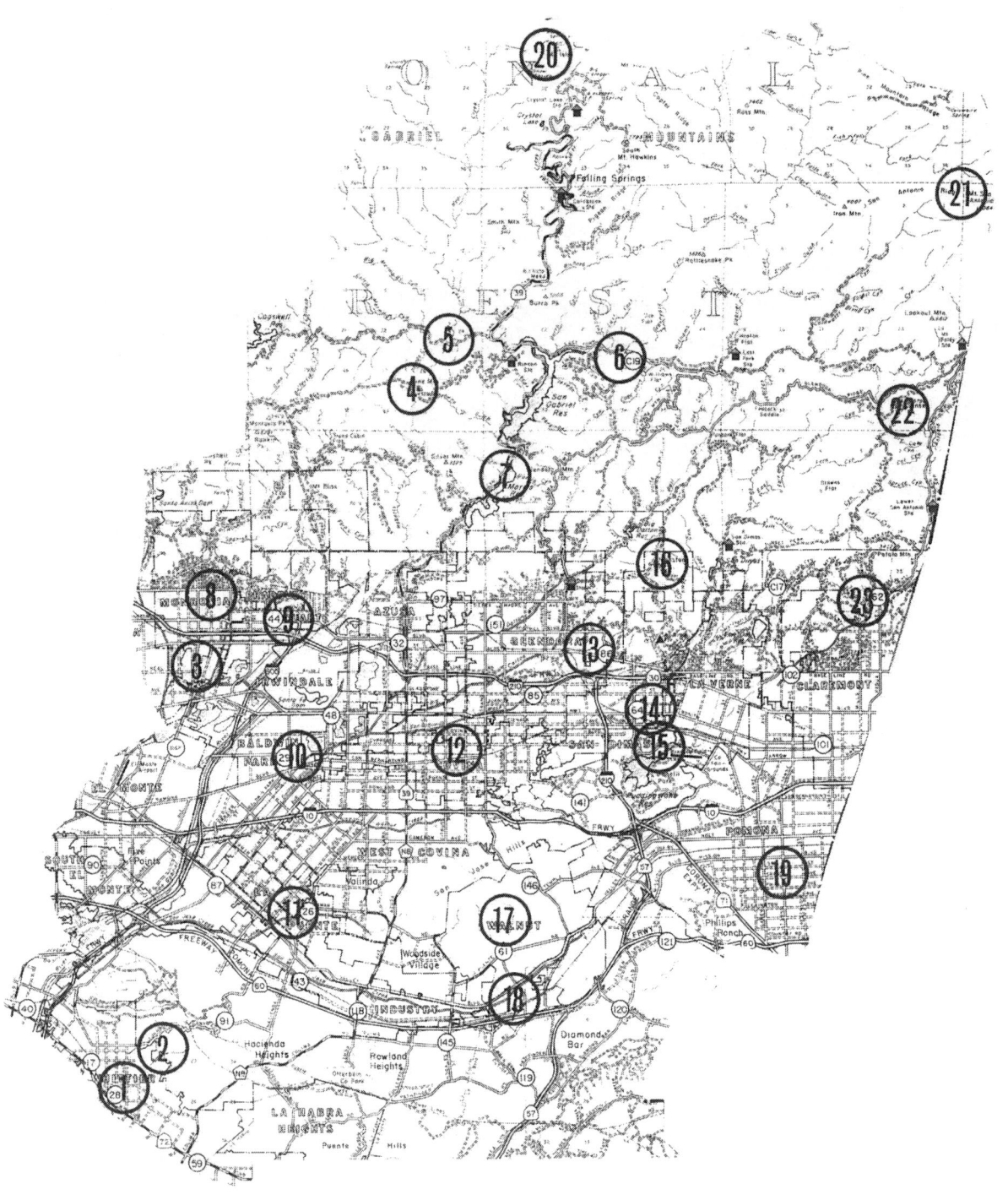

SAN JOSE DIVISION

1. WHITTIER
2. WHITTIER HILLS
3. TEMPLE PATROL STATION & LOOKOUT
4. PINE MOUNTAIN LOOKOUT (USFS)
5. SAN GABRIEL CANYON WEST FORK
6. SAN GABRIEL CANYON EAST FORK
7. SAN GABRIEL CANYON MAIN FORK
8. MONROVIA
9. DUARTE
10. BALDWIN PARK
11. PUENTE
12. COVINA
13. GLENDORA
14. SAN JOSE DIVISION HEADQUARTERS
15. SAN JOSE LOOKOUT (USFS)
16. SAN DIMAS LOOKOUT (USFS)
17. SAN JOSE HILLS
18. SOUTH HILLS PATROL STATION
19. POMONA
20. MT. ISLIP LOOKOUT (USFS)
21. MT. SAN ANTONIO (OLD BALDY)
22. SUNSET PEAK LOOKOUT (USFS)
23. PADUA HILLS PATROL STATION

LOS ANGELES DIVISION

1. SANTA MONICA
2. SHERMAN
3. HOLLYWOOD
4. LOS ANGELES
5. L.A. DIVISION H. Q. & F & FW H. Q.
6. BELVEDERE
7. LENNOX
8. LAWNDALE
9. PALOS VERDES PENINSULA
10. LOMITA
11. FLORENCE
12. WATTS
13. LOS ANGELES RIVER
14. LONG BEACH
15. SIGNAL HILL
16. LAKEWOOD
17. BELLFLOWER
18. NORWALK
19. SANTA FE SPRINGS
20. CERRITOS

COUNTY OF LOS ANGELES
FIRE DEPARTMENT 1989

THE LOS ANGELES COUNTY FIRE DEPARTMENT PROVIDES EMERGENCY SERVICES FOR **2,647,581 RESIDENTS** IN **858,985 HOUSING UNITS**.
48 CITIES IN THE CONSOLIDATED FIRE PROTECTION DISTRICT COVERING **874 SQUARE MILES**
THE UNINCORPORATED AREA OF LOS ANGELES COUNTY COVERING **1,312 SQUARE MILES**
FOR A TOTAL COVERAGE OF **2,186 SQUARE MILES**

FIRE CHIEF P. MICHAEL FREEMAN

DIVISION I
Batt's. 7, 14 (14 Stations)
(8 Cities)
CARSON
LAWNDALE
LOMITA
PALOS VERDES ESTATES
ROLLING HILLS
ROLLING HILLS ESTATES
SIGNAL HILL
RANCHO PALOS VERDES

DIVISION II
Batt's. 2, 12 (21 Stations)
(8 Cities)
AZUSA
CLAREMONT
DIAMOND BAR
GLENDORA
INDUSTRY
LA PUENTE
SAN DIMAS
WALNUT

DIVISION III
Batt's. 6, 11 (23 Stations)
(3 Cities)
LANCASTER
PALMDALE
SANTA CLARITA

DIVISION IV
Batt's. 8, 9 (17 Stations)
(9 Cities)
ARTESIA
BELLFLOWER
CERRITOS
HAWAIIAN GARDENS
LAKEWOOD
LA MIRADA
NORWALK
PARAMOUNT
WHITTIER

DIVISION V
Batt's. 4, 10 (15 Stations)
(8 Cities)
BALDWIN PARK
BRADBURY
DUARTE
IRWINDALE
LA CANADA-FLINTRIDGE
ROSEMEAD
SOUTH EL MONTE
TEMPLE CITY

DIVISION VI
Batt's. 3, 13 (17 Stations)
(8 Cities)
BELL
BELL GARDENS
COMMERCE
CUDAHY
HUNTINGTON PARK
MAYWOOD
PICO RIVERA
SOUTH GATE

DIVISION VII
Batt's. 1, 5 (19 Stations)
(4 Cities)
AGOURA HILLS
HIDDEN HILLS
WEST HOLLYWOOD
WESTLAKE VILLAGE

BATTALION/DIVISION CONFIGURATION

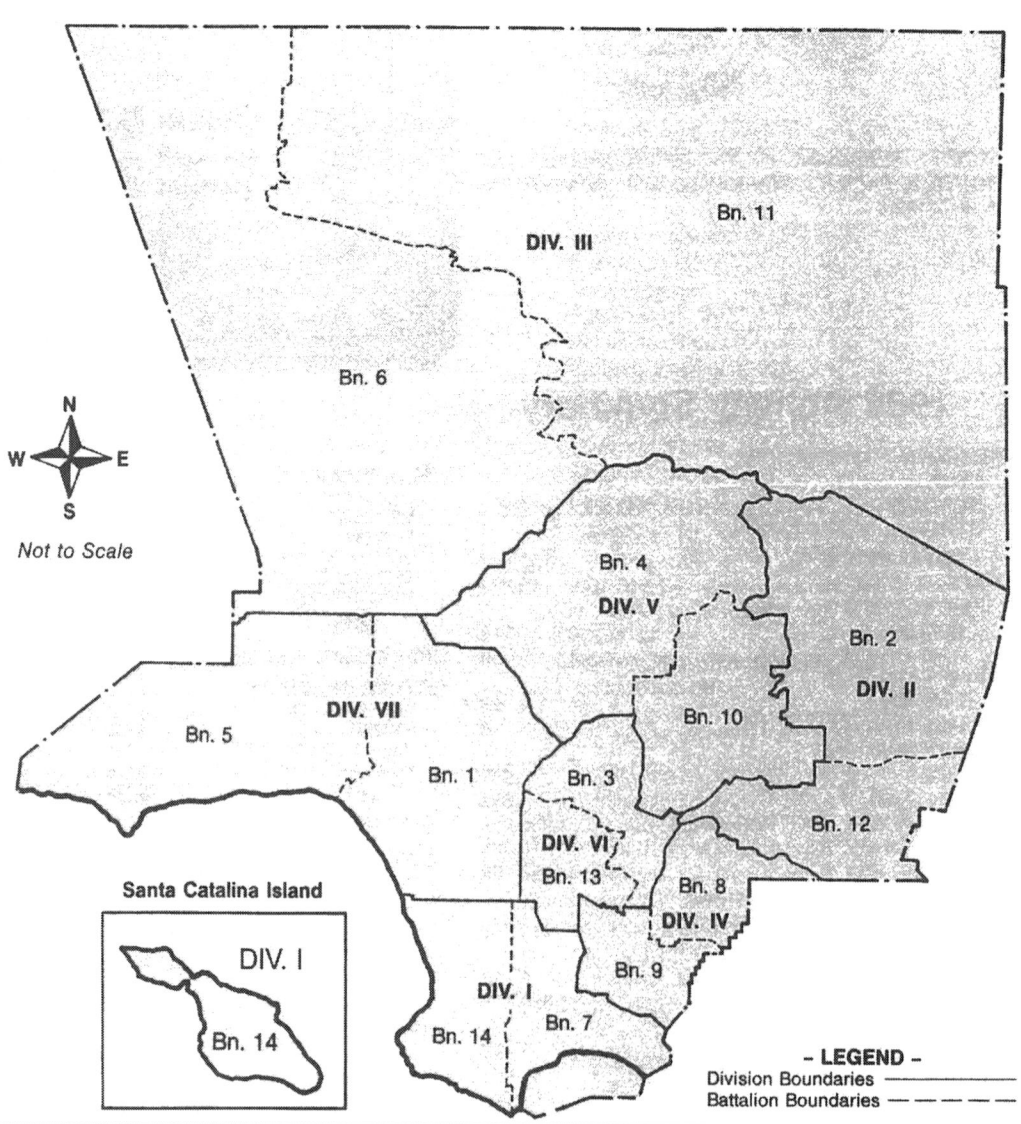

Department Resources

PERSONNEL
UNIFORMED
- CHIEF OFFICERS 75
- CAPTAINS 516
- FF SPECIALISTS 627
- FIRE FIGHTERS 1,021
- (CERTIFIED PARAMEDICS — 672)
- TOTAL 2,239
- FORESTERS 27
- NONUNIFORMED 390

CAMPS
- FIRE SUPPRESSION AIDS ... 131
- (INMATES — 810)

TOTAL PERSONNEL 2,787

FACILITIES
- FIRE STATIONS 127
- FIRE SUPPRESSION CAMPS
  - PAID 3
  - INMATE 8
  - TOTAL 11
- FIRE PREVENTION OFFICES .. 12
- FORESTRY NURSERIES 5

TOTAL FACILITIES 155

EQUIPMENT
AIRCRAFT
- FIXED WING
  - PIPER NAVAJO (4 PASS.) 1
- HELICOPTERS
  - BELL 204 (10 PASS.) 1
  - BELL 205 (14 PASS.) 3
  - BELL 206 (4 PASS.) 1
  - BELL 412 (14 PASS.) 1
  - TOTAL 6
- BUSES 5
- CARGO VEHICLES 10
- COMMAND VAN 1
- COMMUNICATIONS TRAILER 1
- CREW CARRIERS 45
- DELUGE TRUCKS 2
- DOZER TENDERS 8
- DOZERS 6
- DUMP TRUCKS 12
- ENGINE COMPANIES 141
- FIELD KITCHENS 2
- FIRE BOATS 2
- FOAM TRUCKS 2
- FOAM UNITS 2
- FOOD DISPENSERS 6
- FUEL DISPENSERS 2
- GRADERS 3
- HAZARDOUS MATERIAL SQUADS . 3
- HELICOPTER TENDERS 3
- HELIPORT UTILITY TRUCKS ... 2
- HOSE REPAIR TRUCK 1
- HYDROSEEDER 1
- MOBILE AID 2
- MOBILE AIR UTILITY 1
- MOBILE LIGHT UNITS 2
- PARAMEDIC UNITS
  - AIR SQUADS 2
  - ENGINE COMPANIES 3
  - RESCUE SQUADS 40
  - TOTAL 45
- PATROL FIRE TRUCKS 36
- REFRIGERATOR TRUCK 1
- REPAIR TRUCKS 20
- RESERVE EQUIPMENT 41
  - CREW CARRIERS 14
  - ENGINE COMPANIES 40
  - HAZ. MAT. SQUADS 1
  - REPAIR TRUCK 1
  - RESCUE SQUADS 10
  - TRUCK COMPANIES 2
  - TOTAL 68
- SALVAGE TRUCK 1
- STAFF VEHICLES 145
- TRAILERS 7
- TRANSPORTS 7
- TRAXCAVATOR 2
- TRUCK COMPANIES 21
- UTILITY TRUCKS 16
- WATER TENDERS 10
- WATER TOWER (50' SQUIRT) .. 2
- WATERSHED PUMPERS 9

TOTAL EQUIPMENT 703

ARTIST'S RENDERING OF THE NEW COMMAND AND CONTROL FACILITY SCHEDULED FOR COMPLETION IN MAY, 1990.

1988 Activity Summary

EMERGENCY OPERATIONS
- FIRES 11,402
- RESCUES 130,496
- OTHER 20,490
- **TOTAL INCIDENTS** 162,388
- ACRES BURNED 13,283
- FIRE INJURIES
  - CIVILIAN 118
  - FIRE FIGHTERS 59
- FIRE FATALITIES
  - CIVILIAN 28
  - FIRE FIGHTERS 0
- AIR OPERATIONS
  - FIRES 509
  - RESCUES 1,681
  - RETARDANT DROPPED (GALS.) ... 1,395,359
  - PASSENGERS 20,556
  - CARGO (POUNDS) 257,229

NON-EMERGENCY OPERATIONS
- FIRE PREVENTION INSPECTIONS 114,356
- PUBLIC EDUCATION
  - PROGRAMS 5,833
  - ATTENDANCE 1,952,024
- FORESTRY ACTIVITIES
  - TREES AND LOW FUEL PLANTS ... 32,479
  - PROGRAMS AND INSPECTIONS 963
  - PERSONS SERVED 102,141

Five Year Data
1984-1988

FIRE INCIDENTS	1988	1987	1986	1985	1984
STRUCTURES	2,404	2,510	2,702	2,767	2,828
VEHICLES	3,782	3,816	4,068	4,019	3,914
RUBBISH	2,888	2,939	3,029	3,161	3,087
BRUSH/GRASS	2,030	1,821	1,917	2,067	2,390
OUTSIDE STORAGE	24	24	33	35	21
MISC. PROPERTY	274	287	341	358	369
TOTAL	11,402	11,397	12,090	12,407	12,609
PARAMEDIC RESCUES	130,496	125,405	120,361	110,311	100,337
OTHER INCIDENTS					
FALSE ALARMS	4,654	4,137	3,948	3,581	3,358
SMOKE SCARES	4,515	4,952	4,946	4,613	4,375
VEHICLE ACCIDENTS	1,985	1,889	1,916	1,415	1,708
MISC. NON-FIRE INC.	9,336	9,463	8,811	8,706	8,605
TOTAL	20,490	20,441	19,621	18,315	18,406
ALL INCIDENTS	162,388	157,243	152,072	141,033	130,992
LOSS IN DOLLARS					
IMPROVEMENTS	$32,047,000	$32,780,200	$22,324,800	$26,255,200	$18,383,800
CONTENTS	17,823,500	15,009,200	14,396,100	13,838,700	9,430,400
VEHICLE/CONTENTS	17,309,400	8,724,900	8,486,700	7,224,200	14,256,900
MISC. PROPERTY	1,959,000	941,600	14,562,400	1,830,900	2,860,600
TOTAL	$69,138,900	$57,455,900	$59,770,000	$49,149,000	$44,931,700
ACREAGE LOSS	13,283	2,016	6,405	14,317	5,541
INSPECTIONS					
BY STATION	78,292	83,399	73,045	81,278	89,023
BY BUREAU	36,064	32,075	31,908	35,148	38,149
TOTAL	114,356	115,474	104,953	116,426	127,172

County of Los Angeles Fire Department
Fire Chief Daryl L. Osby

2015 STATISTICAL SUMMARY

FIRE DEPARTMENT — Three Year Data 2013 -2015

	2015	2014	2013
Acreage Burned	1,286	2,075	31,625
FIRE INCIDENTS			
Structures	2,272	2,157	2,188
Vehicles	1,853	1,766	1,678
Rubbish	2,527	2,342	2,203
Brush / Grass	578	453	616
Outside Storage	339	370	352
Misc. Property	874	992	871
TOTAL	**8,443**	**8,080**	**7,908**
EMERGENCY MEDICAL SERVICES			
TOTAL	303,151	277,122	245,552
OTHER INCIDENTS			
False Alarms	26,196	24,688	32,372
Mutual Aid Provided	2,983	3,057	2,808
Haz-Mat	770	785	678
Misc. Incidents	47,770	44,503	39,801
TOTAL	**77,719**	**73,033**	**75,659**
TOTAL INCIDENTS	**389,313**	**358,235**	**329,119**

Fire Loss in Dollars 2013 -2015

	2015	2014	2013
Property or Structure	$ 135,265,071	$ 74,956,844	$ 85,066,997
Vehicle Contents	$ 17,518,076	$ 49,591,279	$ 18,141,526
Misc. Property	$ 1,377,011	$ 1,738,412	$ 1,625,245
Total Dollar Loss	**$ 154,161,158**	**$ 126,286,535**	**$ 104,833,768**

LIFEGUARD — Three Year Data 2013 -2015

	2015	2014	2013
Ocean Rescues	15,917	15,851	9,745
Medical Calls	18,610	19,133	16,437
Boat Rescues (Distress)	434	444	382
Missing Persons	1,756	1,673	1,280
Resuscitations	468	559	612
Drownings	5	2	3
Beach Attendance	**72,556,890**	**73,882,107**	**71,367,580**

4,061,584 Residents
1,237,370 Housing Units
58 District Cities and all
Unincorporated Areas
2,305 Square Miles

DIVISION I
Battalions 7, 14 & 18 – 20 Stations, 9 Cities
CARSON — PALOS VERDES ESTATES
GARDENA — RANCHO PALOS VERDES
HAWTHORNE — ROLLING HILLS
LAWNDALE — ROLLING HILLS ESTATES
LOMITA

DIVISION II
Battalions 2 & 16 – 16 Stations, 9 Cities
AZUSA — DUARTE
BALDWIN PARK — GLENDORA
BRADBURY — IRWINDALE
CLAREMONT — SAN DIMAS
COVINA

DIVISION III
Battalions 4, 6 & 22 – 24 Stations, 2 Cities
LA CANADA FLINTRIDGE — SANTA CLARITA

DIVISION IV
Battalions 8, 9 & 21 – 25 Stations, 12 Cities
ARTESIA — LA MIRADA
BELLFLOWER — NORWALK
CERRITOS — PARAMOUNT
HAWAIIAN GARDENS — PICO RIVERA
LA HABRA — SIGNAL HILL
LAKEWOOD — WHITTIER

DIVISION V
Battalions 11 & 17 – 20 Stations, 2 Cities
LANCASTER — PALMDALE

DIVISION VI
Battalions 13 & 20 – 13 Stations, 6 Cities
CUDAHY — LYNWOOD
HUNTINGTON PARK — MAYWOOD
INGLEWOOD — SOUTH GATE

DIVISION VII
Battalions 1 & 5 – 18 Stations, 6 Cities
AGOURA HILLS — MALIBU
CALABASAS — WEST HOLLYWOOD
HIDDEN HILLS — WESTLAKE VILLAGE

DIVISION VIII
Battalions 12, 15 & 19 – 18 Stations, 5 Cities
DIAMOND BAR — POMONA
INDUSTRY — WALNUT
LA PUENTE

DIVISION IX
Battalions 3 & 10 – 16 Stations, 7 Cities
BELL — ROSEMEAD
BELL GARDENS — SOUTH EL MONTE
COMMERCE — TEMPLE CITY
EL MONTE

County of Los Angeles Fire Department
Fire Chief Daryl L. Osby

2015 STATISTICAL SUMMARY

CURRENT PERSONNEL

Chief Officers	122	Administrative Support	787
Captains	646	Lifeguards	161
Firefighter Specialists	747	Seasonal Recurrent	636
Firefighter Paramedics	671	Dispatchers	97
Firefighters	493	Foresters	40
Call Firefighters	57	Haz Mat Specialists	81
Fire Suppression Aides (Paid)	105	**TOTAL PERSONNEL**	**4,654**
Pilots	11		

EMERGENCY OPERATIONS

Battalions	22	Paramedic Units	
Fire Stations	171	Air Squads	3
Engine Companies		Assessment Engines	24
Type 1	163	Assessment Quints	2
Type 3 (Cal EMA)	7	Engines	5
Patrols	34	Squads	68
Reserves	61	Hazardous Materials Squads	4
Truck Companies	32	USAR Squads	2
Light Forces	5	Emergency Support Teams	4
Quints	25	Swift Water Rescue Units	5
Trucks	2	Fire Boats	2
Reserve Trucks/Quints	12	Foam Units	4
		Mobile Air/Light Units	4
		Fuel Tenders	8
		Water Tenders	12

HEALTH HAZ MAT

Emergency Responses	2,071
Response Teams	3

AIR OPERATIONS

Fire Responses	283
EMS Transports	1,072
Facilities	4
Aircraft Mechanics	17
Hoist Rescues	95
Water/Foam Dropped (gallons)	729,760
Helicopters	
Bell 412 (10-Passenger)	5
Firehawk (13-Passenger)	3
Heli-Tenders	9

LIFEGUARD DIVISION

Lifeguard Stations	24
Lifeguard Towers	159
Beach Patrol Vehicles	58
Rescue Boats	8
Paramedic Rescue Boats	2
Baywatch Paramedic Squads	2

FORESTRY

Forest Tree Nurseries	5
Plants Distributed	26,492

WILDLAND DIVISION

Fire Suppression Camps	
Paid	4
Correctional	6
Fire Suppression Crews	
Paid	4
Correctional	24
Dozers	10
Dozer Transport Trucks	10
Equipment	26

250.b

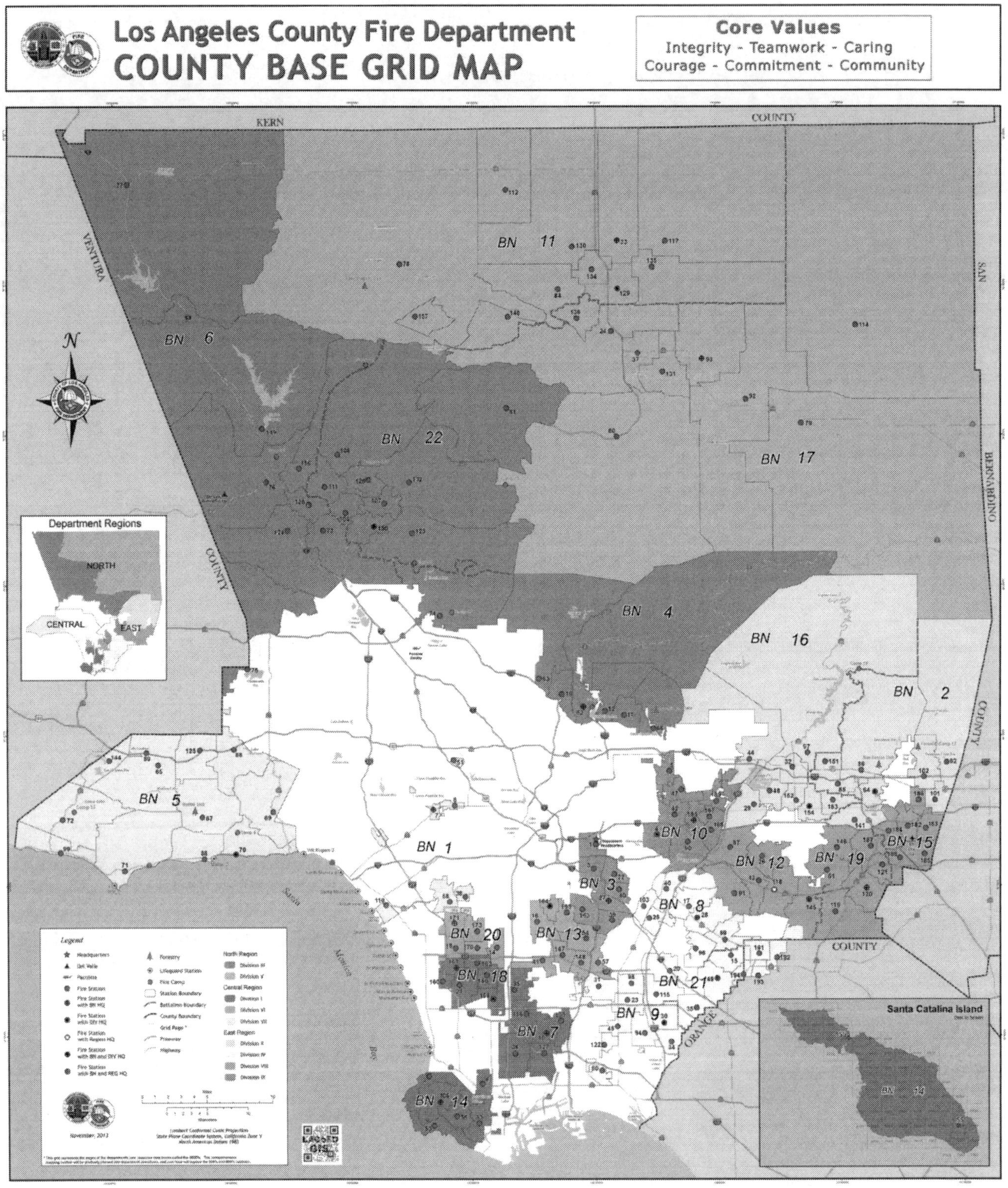
Los Angeles County Fire Department
COUNTY BASE GRID MAP
Core Values
Integrity - Teamwork - Caring
Courage - Commitment - Community
KERN
COUNTY
VENTURA
COUNTY
SAN
BERNARDINO
COUNTY
ORANGE
COUNTY
N
Department Regions
NORTH
CENTRAL
EAST
BN 6
BN 11
BN 22
BN 17
BN 4
BN 16
BN 2
BN 5
BN 1
BN 10
BN 12
BN 19
BN 15
BN 3
BN 8
BN 20
BN 13
BN 18
BN 21
BN 9
BN 7
BN 14
Santa Catalina Island
Legend
North Region
Central Region
East Region
LACoFD GIS

250. c

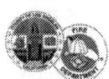

Index

Acton, 228
Agoura Hills, 237
Aikens, Arthur, 69
Aircraft, Blimps, 20
Aircraft, Fixed Wing, 20, 21, 22, 73, 137, 150, 160, 169, 224
Aircraft, Helicopters, 149, 150, 153, 176, 177, 187, 206, 208
Alhambra, 7
Altadena, Foreword IX, 7, 10, 16, 53, 54, 56, 58, 59, 61, 62, 63, 69, 77, 78, 81, 93, 115, 124, 128, 131, 133, 179, 187, 223, 224
Anderson, Harvey T., 48, 74, 95, 96, 120, 121, 129, 146, 156, 168, 169, 194, 201
Andrews, Archie, 56, 61
Angeles Mesa, 78, 81, 104, 120, 221
Angeles National Forest, 4, 11, 16, 19, 63, 88, 107, 123, 129, 218, 219
Antelope Valley, 1, 65
"Aqua Dulce" Fire, 199, 200
Arcadia, 7, 133, 134
Arnold, H.H. "Hap," 20, 22
Arroyo Seco, 3, 13, 35, 39, 41, 72, 73, 77, 82, 84, 88, 93, 98, 99, 103, 104, 108, 112, 158, 179
Artesia, 53, 56, 65, 78, 81, 187
Azusa, 7, 10, 12, 18, 26
Baja California, Foreword IX
Baker, J.R., 30
Baldwin Hills, 86
Baldwin Park, 78, 81, 106, 165, 187, 221, 230
Banbury, Thomas, 2, 5
Barb, Ross, 148, 191
Barlow, Stanley, 209
Barnes, Dan, 39, 75
Bartlett, Jess, 101
Barton, Des, 140, 148, 150, 155
Barton, Roland, 164, 175-177, 187, 189, 206
Bassett, 221
Bell Canyon, 220
Bell, 54-56, 221
Bell, Murray, 101
Bellflower, 30, 53-56, 65, 66, 78, 81, 120, 187, 221
Belliveau, Robert, 202
Belvedere Gardens, 78, 81, 87, 110, 234
Belvedere, 30, 53-56, 59, 68, 78, 81, 87
Bennett, Battalion Chief, 148
Benson, Virgil, 226
Bertz, Gary, 226
Bettner, Jr., James, 4
Beverly Hills, 78, 92, 96
Bicksler, Kenneth, 113
Big Basin, 4
Big Bear Canyon, 3, 27, 28, 158
Big Rock Canyon, 169
Big Tujunga Canyon, Foreword IX, 12, 165
Bishop, Edward T., 29
Bissel, S., 18
Bittle, J.R., 56, 66

Boats, 49, 84, 85, 93, 94, 110
Boers, Lewis, 55, 56
"Bootlegger" Fire, 140
Bradbury, 187, 216, 219
Bragdon, Clyde, 209, 215, 216, 221
"Brea" Fire, 199, 200
Broad Beach, 218
"Bryant" Fire, 212
Buck, Bert, 207
Burbank, 107, 129, 147, 165, 177, 179
Burkhart, Carl, 112
Busch, Joe, 101
Cajon Pass, 4
Calabasas, 168
Campbell, William, 216
"Canyon Inn" Fire, 180
Carroll, J., 54
Carter, Ken, 72, 84, 95
Cates, John L., 56
Cauble, Dale, 191, 202, 204
Cearly, Richard, 209
Cecil R. Gehr Training Center, 145, 152
Cecil, George C., 16
Central Manufacturing District, 57, 78, 81
Cerritos Plane Crash, 224, 225
Cerritos, 187, 221
Chace, Burton W., 144
Charleton, Supervisor, 28
Charleton Flats, 27
Chatsworth Hills, 95, 220
Chatsworth, 106, 110
"Chevy Chase" Fire, 180
Chiquita Canyon, Foreword IX, 12, 165
Christie, Harry, 43
Christie, R.E., 41, 43
Cinader, Robert, 204
"Clampitt" Fire, 199, 200
Claremont, 7, 176
Clark, Bob, 101
Clarke, Congressman John W., 18
Clearwater Hynes, 53-56, 65, 78, 81, 87
Clifton Heights, 78, 81
Cobal Canyon, 72
Coffman, David, 191
Coggins, Ted, 117, 127
Coldwater Canyon, 11
"Colima" Fire, 199, 200
Collison, C.G., 56
Commerce, 164, 187, 219, 221
Compton, 7, 86, 180
Conley, Cecil, 101
Conrad, A.C., 54
Coolidge, President Calvin, 18
Cornell Corners, 77
Costello, L.W., 56, 57
Covina, 7, 18, 76
Crutchfield, Harvey, 132
Cudahy, 187
Cullen, Thomas, 58
Culver City, 86, 147
Cuzan, Judge, 48
D'Andrea, Richard, 226
Darby, Raymond V., 112
Daries, Pierre, 25, 26
David, J.J., 114

Davis, Gary, 202
Davis, Joe, 19, 22, 24, 26, 28, 30, 34, 46, 48, 61, 65, 70, 76, 84, 95
"Dayton" Fire, 220
De Lamere, W.E., 57
De Lapp, Virgil, 145
Decker, Charles, 18
Del Valle, 167, 168
Deleney, Paul, 224
Devil Wind, 168, 172, 180, 238
Devil's Canyon, 27, 28
Diamond Bar, 237
Dickens, Bob, 209
Dickover, Frank L., 158
Disney, Walt, 152
Dittman, Dan, 199
Dobson, S.S., 34, 65
Doke, "Rocky," 202
Dominguez, 165, 187, 223, 235
Dorn, Warren, 158, 167, 168, 184, 190, 195, 201
Dorning, Earl, 101
Douglas, Donald W., 136
Downey, 5, 53-56, 65, 78, 81, 87, 120
Duarte, 10, 82, 126, 187, 216, 219, 221
DuBois, Coert, 20
Dunbar, Robert, 226
Duncan, A.R., 55
Duncan, John, 132, 151
Dunlap, R.L., 30, 34, 46, 48, 76
Dunsmuir Canyon, 88
Eagle Rock, 18, 180
East Montebello, 78, 81
Eastridge, H., 57
Eaton Canyon, 75, 77, 218
Eaton, E.C., 89
Echo Mountain, 3
Eichert, Raymond, 226
Eisenhower, President Dwight D., 158
El Monte, 113, 144, 187, 223
El Porto, 57, 78, 81
Elsey, George C., 55, 66
Encinal Canyon, 191
Engine Co's (Pumpers/Tankers)- Sprite," 183
Engine Co's (Pumpers/Tankers)- American La France, 30, 55-61, 115, 221
Engine Co's (Pumpers/Tankers)- Cadillac, 146
Engine Co's (Pumpers/Tankers)- Coventry, 104
Engine Co's (Pumpers/Tankers)- Crown, 140-143, 166, 169, 184, 186, 190, 205, 233
Engine Co's (Pumpers/Tankers)- F.W.D./Calavar, 42
Engine Co's (Pumpers/Tankers)- Ford, 146
Engine Co's (Pumpers/Tankers)- General Pacific, 159
Engine Co's (Pumpers/Tankers)- GMC Marman-Herrington, 141, 150
Engine Co's (Pumpers/Tankers)- International, 150
Engine Co's (Pumpers/Tankers)- Mack, 102, 108, 115

Engine Co's (Pumpers/Tankers)- Moreland, 35, 98, 99, 184
Engine Co's (Pumpers/Tankers)- REO-Obenchain-Boyer, 30, 53, 55, 56, 59, 60
Engine Co's (Pumpers/Tankers)- Seagrave, 53, 54, 56-58, 102, 115, 179, 224, 229
Engine Co's (Pumpers/Tankers)- Stutz, 30, 53, 55, 57, 58, 67
Englund, John, 168, 200, 215, 218, 224
Escondido, 156
Estes, Loy, 101
Fahrforth, C., 68
Finnerty, John, 226
Fish Canyon, 27, 39, 40
Five Points, 82
Flint, Senator, 18
Flintham, Dorothy, 48
Flintham, Eleanor, 48
Flintham, Stuart, 15, 16, 18, 20, 21, 22, 24, 25, 27, 28, 29, 30, 47, 48, 62
Flintridge, 18, 53, 54, 56, 57, 65, 66, 78, 81, 128, 149
"Flintridge Hills" Fire, 177, 179, 187
Florence, 78, 81, 86, 87, 128, 221
Ford, John Anson, 145, 158
Fowler, A., 168
Fralick, Cindy, 212
Franklin, R., 55
Franklin, Scott, 206, 229
Franklin, W.H., 56
Freeman, P. Michael, 237
French, Ed, 199
Friend, Richard, 204, 205
Frownfelter, Bill, 45, 46, 72, 95
Fry, R., 168
Furber, James, 145
Gardena, 57
Gehr, Cecil R., 95, 96, 117, 127, 128, 129, 130, 132, 144, 145, 212
Gehr, Mrs. Cecil R., 145
Gerhart, S., 57
"Getty Oil" Fire, 64
Gibson, H. Allen, 100
Glendale, 7, 14, 20, 25, 37, 88, 107, 165, 169, 179
Glendora, 2, 26, 91, 113, 119, 193, 221
Goodell, Phil, 226
Gorman, 226
Grace, Harry 133
Grader, William, 158
Grady, Thomas, 226
Graham, 78, 81, 87
Grass Canyon, 72
Graves, Jesse, 25, 34, 39
Greely, William B., 18
Green Meadows, 53-55, 57
Greer, Bob, 188
Greer, Bronelle, 191
Gregory, Dick, 180
Gregory, Jack, 57
Griffith Park, 20
Griggers, Lyndell, 175
Griott, Justin, 191
Griswold, Glen G., 55, 93, 101, 108, 109
Griswold, Mrs. Lucille, 109
Grogan, K.L., 56, 62
Gunsalus, Andy, 26
Hacienda Heights, 223
"Hacienda" Fire, 199, 200
Hahn, Kenneth, 168, 181, 195, 201
Hall, Captain, 113, 114
Hamilton, Larry, 190, 223

Hamp, Frank, 176, 179
Hancock Oil Fire, 160-162
Hancock, J.C., 66
Hartman, Wellesley, 226
Hawaiian Gardens, 187, 221
Hayes, Bill, 101
Heidner, T. William, 158
Heidt, Walter, 106
Heinzeman, A., 30, 58, 65, 93
Hellmers, Theodore, 209
Hennessey, Jack, 177, 187
Henninger Flats, 5, 6, 16, 17, 33-35, 39, 134, 145, 218
Hidden Hills, 187, 226, 237
Hiesel, Jerald, 226
Hill, Chief Raymond, 180
Hinger, Roy, 189, 191
Hodges, Ray, 101
Hogan, S.D., 57
Hollywood, 7, 22, 53, 54, 56, 57, 62, 65, 78, 81, 122, 147, 187
Hooper, "Buck," 188
Horn, Duke, 101
Horne, W.L., 57
Horse Flats, 28
Horses, 41, 72, 95
Houts, Richard H., 158, 197, 204, 208
Howard, 53-57, 65, 78, 81, 87
"Hume" Fire, 157, 158
Hunt, James, 235
Hunt, John, 54, 57
Hunter, Bud, 182
Hunter, Jim, 199
Huntington Park, 7, 78, 221
Huntington, Henry E., 2
Ikeler, Frank, 57
Industry, City of, 186, 187, 221, 230
Irwindale, 187, 228
Jackson, Harold, 112
Jarvi, Sim, 129
Johnson, E., 101
Johnson, Norman C., 20, 24, 29, 53
Jones, D.C., 54
Jones, R.C., 57
Jordan, B.W., 57
Kanallakan, Don, 199
Kanan Fire, 216
Kanoff, Chester, 98
Kearns, Matthew, 223
Kelly, A.J., 56, 58
Kelly, Joseph, 209
Keufer, J.S., 68
Keyes, V.T., 56
King, Toni, 156
Kinneloa Mesa, 4
Kinney, Abbot W., 4
Kleinsmith, Captain Ward, 113, 114
Klinger, Keith E., 101, 104, 110, 125, 129, 130-133, 136, 137, 139, 141, 144, 145, 156, 158, 163, 170, 180, 184, 192, 193, 195, 223, 235
Klinger, W.B., 62, 66, 86, 105, 110
Kneip, E.A., 57
Knight, Goodwin J., 158
Knowles, L., 95
Kuykendall, John, 191
La Canada, 73, 88
La Crescenta Valley, 78, 81, 88
La Crescenta, 1, 18, 25, 30, 35, 40, 53-55, 57, 65, 67, 72, 88, 89, 112, 118, 128, 149, 179, 217
La Crescenta-Montrose Flood, 88, 89
"La Habra" Fire, 147, 148
La Mirada, 187, 221, 230
La Puente, 165, 187, 221
"Latigo" Fire, 91-93

"La Tuna Canyon" Fire, 219
La Verne, 7
Laguna, 53-55, 57, 65, 78, 81, 87, 187
Lake Los Angeles, 223
Lakewood Plan, 146
Lakewood, 82, 128, 145, 187, 221, 228
Lancaster, 57, 65, 78, 81, 144, 165, 167, 187
Lang, L., 40, 50, 84
Lanin, Wayne, 226
Las Flores Canyon, 56, 57, 91, 93, 96, 107, 108, 115
Laski, Frank, 57
Latigo Canyon, 156
Lawndale, 30, 53-55, 57, 65, 78, 81, 128, 187, 221
Leach, Lou, 177
Lee, F.J., 57
Lennox, 53-55, 57, 65, 78, 81, 87, 128, 221
Leona Valley, 237
Lewis, George, 55
Lewis, H.W., 54
"Liberty" Fire, 169
"Liebre" Fire, 192, 199, 200
Lineberry, Gary, 226
Little Bear Canyon, 158
Little Tujunga Canyon, 72, 129, 191
Little, Pete, 158
Lomita, 30, 53-55, 57, 65, 78, 81, 187
Long Beach Earthquake, 85-88
Long Beach, 2, 7, 78, 106, 146, 161, 180, 235
Long, L., 40, 50, 84
Lonsbury, Jim, 178
Lookout Tower- Blue Ridge, 35
Lookout Tower- Bodel Peak, 35
Lookout Tower- Castaic Peak, 207
Lookout Tower- Castro Peak, 35, 36, 140
Lookout Tower- Charlie Point, 209
Lookout Tower- Gilman Peak, 35
Lookout Tower- Grass Mountain, 35
Lookout Tower- Los Penitos, 35
Lookout Tower- Mendenhall, 35, 36
Lookout Tower- Mt. Gleason, 35, 36, 48
Lookout Tower- Mt. Islip, 35, 36, 38
Lookout Tower- Mt. Lukens, 35
Lookout Tower- Oat Mountain, 19, 20, 21, 35, 96, 97, 198, 212
Lookout Tower- Pacoima Peak, 35, 43, 140
Lookout Tower- Parker Mountain, 35
Lookout Tower- San Dimas, 26
Lookout Tower- San Jose, 35, 140
Lookout Tower- San Rafael, 35, 99, 140
Lookout Tower- San Vicente, 35, 36
Lookout Tower- Sawmill, 35
Lookout Tower- Tejon, 35
Lookout Tower- Temple Tower, 140
Lookout Tower- Topanga Canyon, 35, 45
Lookout Tower- Triumfo, 35
Lookout Tower- Zuma, 35
"Loop" Fire, 187
"Lopez Canyon" Fire, 199, 200
Los Alamitos Plane Crash, 160
Los Angeles, 4, 9, 16, 26, 34, 35, 39-41, 57, 58, 59, 60-63, 65, 77, 78, 88, 96, 97, 103, 105, 106, 114, 140, 144, 147
Lowrie, A.L., 56
Lukens, T.P., 5, 7, 8
Lynwood, 180
Mace, James K., 137
Machen, Cliff, 75

MacLeod, Allan, 209
MacMillan, Donald C., 150
Maiben, Gary, 226
Malibu Canyon, 168
Malibu Hills/Mountains, 16, 19, 20, 21, 23, 63, 65, 91, 93, 95, 96, 99, 107, 117, 155, 157, 163, 216, 220, 221, 230
"Malibu" Fire, 19
Malibu, 14, 23, 25, 77, 92, 106, 108, 112, 113, 115, 119, 120, 144, 146, 149, 187, 220
Manchester, Noel, 140, 161
Manhattan Beach, 57
Mansfield, Stubby, 157
Mantooth, Randolph, 204
Mantz, Paul, 139
Marina del Rey, 163, 167, 187, 189, 221, 230
Marty, A.J., 45
Matthews, Ben, 198
May, W.F., 56, 57
McCann, Harold, Foreword IX
McClure, E.L., 59, 66
McCraney, Charles, 188
McFaul, Ed, 206
McIntyre, J.S., 54, 58, 60
McKeeley, J., 68
McNary, Senator Charles, 18
Meagher, Walt, 198
Medaris, Ed, 85
Mendenhall, William V., 20, 123, 133, 136
Meredith, Claire "Spider," 74
Merrill, Harry, 46
Merrill, L.V., 56, 67
Metz, E., 55
Metz, Ray, 48
Meyers, S.O., 55
Michelli, James, 226
Miller, Ezra, 164
Mint Canyon, 69, 71, 126
Miramonte, 78, 81, 87
Mojave Desert, 1
Molotov Cocktails, 180
"Monrovia Peak" Fire, 133, 134
Monrovia, 7, 10, 11, 27, 58, 169
"Monte Cristo" Fire, 226
Monte Nido, 77
Montebello, 57, 65, 78, 224
Montecito, 169
Montrose, 93, 96
Montrose-La Crescenta Flood, 89, 90, 91
Moore, Al, 199
Moore, Walter S., 4
Moreno, Charles, 226
Morgan, W.B., 5, 7
Morin, J.L., 56
Motorcycles, 10, 23, 35, 45, 72, 98
Mt. Baldy, 177
Mt. Gleason, 12, 13, 70, 72
Mt. Lukens, 1, 5, 35, 88, 90
Mt. Pacifico, 27
Mt. Waterman, 27, 28
Mt. Wilson, 25, 133, 134
Mules, 10, 16, 27
Newhall, 18-21, 74, 102, 113, 142, 144, 165, 192, 221, 230
Newport Beach, 2, 86
Nieto, John, 25
Nixon, Richard M., 148
Nolls, Gerald, 202
Nord, Harry J., 54
"Norembega" Fire, 163
Norwalk, 30, 53-55, 57, 78, 81
Norwood, 144

O'Melveny Canyon, 26
O'Ryan, William, 102
Oakdale, 221
Oker, Kenny, 101
Operation Firestop, 147
"Orange County" Fire, 219
Pacoima (City), 23-25, 69, 72, 76
Pacoima Canyon, 4, 187
Padua Hills, 77, 221
Page, James O., 197, 204
Palmdale, 19, 30, 54, 55, 57, 65, 78, 81, 129, 144, 187, 221, 236
"Palos Verdes" Fire, 199, 200
Palos Verdes, 19, 39, 221, 237
Paramount, 187, 230
Pardee, Governor George, 5
Parks, A.J., 65
Pasadena, 2, 3, 5, 7, 10, 11, 13, 35, 88, 106, 124, 133, 149, 160, 180
Patterson, Loren, 209
Paul, Barney H., 74, 84, 95
Peavy, George, 5
Pederson, Orlo, 101, 151, 154
Pemberton, J.E., 84
Percey, L.S., 16, 19, 26, 34, 47, 50, 69, 71, 74, 120
Percey, Roland W., 26, 130, 132, 133, 146, 151
Peterson, E.T., 58
Peterson, J., 15
Phillips, Dave, 202
Pickens Canyon, 88
"Pickens" Fire, 88, 91, 212
Pico Rivera, 187, 221
Pinchot, Gifford, 8
Pine Mountain, 26, 27
"Pinecrest" Fire, 218
Pino, Frank, 209
Pitchess, Peter, 145
Plympton, George, 57
Pomona, 7, 107
Powellson, William E., 65, 93
Priest, Milan, 188
Puente Hills, 76, 78, 81
Puente, 53-55, 60, 65
Quartz Hill, 221
Radenmacher, Clyde, 48
Radio- A.M. Field Transmitter/Receiver, 26, 107
Radio- F.M., 112, 116
Radio- Field Communications Van, 26, 122
Radio- Handi-talkies, 193
Radke, Captain, 134
Randall, Lewis, 147
Redlands, 2
Redondo Beach, 2, 7, 57, 180
Reagan, Ronald, 123
Resuscitators, E and J, 165, 168
Reynolds, Harvey, 24
Rice, Harry, 54
Rippens, Martin, 113, 121
Riverside, 4, 20
Robinson, Byron D., 101
Rockey, Glenn, 147
Rogers, Will, 97
Rolling Hills, 187, 230
Rollinger, Bernie, 176
Roosevelt, President Franklin D., 69, 101, 109
Roosevelt, President Theodore, 4
Rosemead, 82, 128, 150, 187, 221, 224, 229
Rounds, James, 225
Russell, Dean, 188
Saddleback Peak, 25

"Sage" Fire, 212
San Bernardino, 76
San Clemente Islands, 39
San Clemente, 1
San Diego, 20, 156
San Dimas, 2, 11, 19, 26, 30, 54-56, 60, 65, 71, 72, 77, 78, 81, 95, 97, 98, 107, 120, 146, 147, 187, 193, 221, 235
San Fernando Valley, 2, 10, 25, 35, 169, 177, 189
San Francisco Fire, 4
San Gabriel, 104, 224
"San Gabriel Canyon" Fire, 199, 200
San Gabriel Canyon, 12, 26
"San Gabriel" Fire, 26-28, 63
San Gabriel River, 27
San Gabriel Valley, 2, 82, 113, 120, 133, 134, 140, 144, 145, 163, 219, 224
San Jose, 77, 82, 84, 88
San Luis Obispo, 156, 158
Sanchez, James, 209
Santa Ana, 180
Santa Barbara, 169
Santa Catalina Islands, 2, 39, 84
Santa Clarita Valley, 2, 237
Santa Fe Springs, 34, 53, 54, 55, 58, 63-65, 78, 81, 101, 105, 109, 110, 128, 137, 138, 160, 167, 224
Santa Monica Canyon, 4, 24, 30, 54, 55, 58
Santa Monica, 7, 118, 156
Santa, Maria A., 95
Saugus, 20, 165, 192
Schaffer, Bob, 10
Schnabel, Stanley, 226
Schneider, T., 57
Scott, Ralph J., 97
Sepulveda, 24
Sherman, 65, 68, 78, 81
Sherrill, Steve, 224
"Sherwood" Fire, 158
Sherwood, William, 85
Showers, Tom, 138
Sierra Madre, 165
Simons, James W., 117, 118, 119
Singleton, Robert, 129, 148
Sloan, S., 1
Smith, Charles, 54
Smith, Gerald, 191
Smith, Herbie, 54
Smith, L.G., 84, 85, 94
Smith, Marion, 56, 59, 130
Solemint Junction, 165, 166
South Gate, 57, 60, 78, 180, 221
South Hills, 75, 76, 84
Sprague, Homer, 54
Spruill, Edward C., 189
"Stable" Fire, 219
Starr, Don, 132
Stearns, Mike, 206
Stedman, Timothy, 191
Stoker, Mike, 206
Stoneman, Governor, 4
Sunland, 10
Swallow, Hiram, 122, 123
Swanson, A.W., 56
"Switzer" Fire, 149
Sylmar, 10, 60, 149
Sylmar/San Francisco Quake, 205
Taylor, George, 113
Taylor, John, 188
Taylor, Ray, 48
Temple, 53, 54, 56, 177, 187
Thomas, George, 193

253

Thompson, Herb, 129
Thompson, Jim, 132
Thousand Oaks, 157
Thrapp, Clarence, 127
Thurston, O.M., 16, 17, 18, 23, 114
Tighe, Kevin, 204
Tillotson, Charles, 30, 58, 63, 65, 66
Topanga Canyon, 16, 18, 77, 85, 92, 95-98, 117, 118, 120, 126, 129, 169
Torrance, 58
Torres, Salvador, 226
Tractors (Bulldozers/Sprite), 16, 19, 21, 30, 39, 118, 119, 150, 183
"Trippet" Fire, 37, 96, 97
Trippett, Oscar A., 118
Truck Co's (Ladder Trucks/Snorkels), 124, 182, 183, 186, 187, 229, 230
Trucks- American La France Ladder, 53, 54, 144, 222, 229, 230
Trucks- Communications Truck, 39, 122
Trucks- Dodge "Screen," 22, 23, 35
Trucks- Food dispenser, 150
Trucks- Ford Model-T, 5, 29, 44, 54
Trucks- Moreland Squad, 35
Trucks- Patrol, 44
Trucks- REO Speedwagon, 21, 22, 53, 54
Truman, President Harry S., 118
Tuna Canyon, 25, 169
Turner, James, 219

Turner, Spence D., 15, 16, 18, 20, 21, 22, 24, 25, 27, 28, 29, 30, 40, 46, 53, 58, 61, 62, 64, 69, 70, 76, 82, 84, 86, 92, 95, 102, 107, 113, 117, 120, 123, 126, 127, 144
Universal City, 190
"Val Verde" Fire, 199, 200
Valencia, 235
Van Wagner, Ralph, 126, 136, 164, 192
Venice, 7, 118
Ventura, 158
Verdugo Hills/Mountains, 98, 102, 128, 149, 150, 179, 219
Verdugo Peak, 98
Vernon, 7
Vinson, Jan, 209
Walnut Park, 53, 54, 56, 65, 78, 81, 180
Walnut, 18, 187, 221
Warrick, H., 55
Watts Riot, 180, 181
Watts, 180, 181, 221
Webb, Jack, 204
Welk, Lawrence, 127
Welsh, Belford "Dick," 179
Wertz, Heine, 46
West, Randall, 209
Westlake, 237
Whippo, Thad, 149
Whitehead, Alfred K., 132

Whittier Hills, 23, 76, 146, 215
Whittier, 7, 63, 78, 146, 220, 221-224, 225-226
Will, Arthur, J., 146
Williams, Bill, 72
Williams, R.A., 68
Willingham, George, 101
Willowbrook, 221
Wilmington, 7
Wilmore, Red, 184
Wineman, Robert, 218
Winery Canyon, 88
Wood, H.F., 54
"Woodland Hills" Fire, 220
"Woodwardia" Fire, 158, 159, 163, 178, 212
"Wright" Fire, 198, 220
Wright, Wayne, 226
Wrightwood, 237
Wyant, Assistant Chief, 14
Yeager, Roy, 55, 57
Yosemite National Park, 4
Young, C.J., 54
Zabaldano, Joe, 101
Zalaha, Frank, 156, 168
Zeason, William, 224
Zuma, 104, 224

Made in the USA
Columbia, SC
04 January 2018